*Life Histories of
North American Petrels
and Pelicans and Their Allies*

Life Histories of
North American Petrels
and Pelicans and Their Allies

by

Arthur Cleveland Bent

Dover Publications, Inc.
New York

Published in the United Kingdom by Constable
and Company, Limited, 10 Orange Street, London
W.C.2.

This Dover edition, first published in 1964, is an
unabridged and unaltered republication of the
work first published in 1922 by the United States
Government Printing Office, as Smithsonian Institution United States National Museum *Bulletin 121*.

Manufactured in the United States of America

Dover Publications, Inc.
180 Varick Street
New York 14, N.Y.

ADVERTISEMENT.

The scientific publications of the United States National Museum consist of two series, the *Proceedings* and the *Bulletins.*

The *Proceedings*, the first volume of which was issued in 1878, are intended primarily as a medium for the publication of original, and usually brief, papers based on the collections of the National Museum, presenting newly-acquired facts in zoology, geology, and anthropology, including descriptions of new forms of animals, and revisions of limited groups. One or two volumes are issued annually and distributed to libraries and scientific organizations. A limited number of copies of each paper, in pamphlet form, is distributed to specialists and others interested in the different subjects as soon as printed. The date of publication is recorded in the tables of contents of the volumes.

The *Bulletins*, the first of which was issued in 1875, consist of a series of separate publications comprising chiefly monographs of large zoological groups and other general systematic treatises (occasionally in several volumes), faunal works, reports of expeditions, and catalogues of type-specimens, special collections, etc. The majority of the volumes are octavos, but a quarto size has been adopted in a few instances in which large plates were regarded as indispensable.

Since 1902 a series of octavo volumes containing papers relating to the botanical collections of the Museum, and known as the *Contributions from the National Herbarium*, has been published as bulletins.

The present work forms No. 121 of the *Bulletin series.*

WILLIAM deC. RAVENEL,
Administrative Assistant to the Secretary,
In Charge of the United States National Museum.

WASHINGTON, D. C.

INTRODUCTION.

This Bulletin contains a continuation of the work on the life histories of North American birds, begun in Bulletin 107 and continued in Bulletin 113. The same general plan has been followed and the same sources of information have been utilized. Nearly all of those who contributed material for, or helped in preparing, the former volumes have rendered similar service in this case. In addition to those whose contributions have been previously acknowledged, my thanks are due to the following contributors:

Photographs have been contributed, or their use authorized, by A. W. Anthony, D. A. Bannerman, H. H. Bailey, Edwin Beaupre, Biological Survey, W. K. Fisher, Joseph Grinnell, A. O. Gross, J. H. Gurney, Maud D. Haviland, Lynds Jones, F. H. Kennard, R. C. Murphy, E. W. Nelson, and P. B. Philipp.

Notes and data have been contributed by D. E. Brown, T. D. Burleigh, A. J. Campbell, H. F. Lewis, J. T. Nichols, C. W. Richmond, and J. R. Whitaker.

The distributional part of this Bulletin has been done by the author. Messrs. Robert Cushman Murphy and John Treadwell Nichols have examined and revised the distribution of the *Tubinares* and Mr. James H. Fleming has done the same for the *Steganopodes*.

In the two previous Bulletins the author adopted, without any changes, the nomenclature of the 1910 edition of the check list of the American Ornithologists' Union. But, now that a new check list is in preparation, it seems best to adopt the names that will probably appear in the new check list, so far as they are now understood by

THE AUTHOR.

TABLE OF CONTENTS.

LIFE HISTORIES OF NORTH AMERICAN PETRELS, PELICANS, AND THEIR ALLIES, ORDER TUBINARES AND ORDER STEGANOPODES.

By ARTHUR CLEVELAND BENT,

of Taunton, Massachusetts.

Order TUBINARES, Tube-nosed Swimmers.

Family DIOMEDEIDAE, Albatrosses.

PHOEBASTRIA NIGRIPES (Audubon).

BLACK-FOOTED ALBATROSS.

HABITS.

As we steamed out through Dixon Entrance we soon realized that we were actually going to sea, as the good ship *Tahoma* rose and fell on the long ocean swell. The numerous gulls which had been following the ship became fewer and fewer, as the land faded from view, and they were gradually replaced by the pretty little fork-tailed petrels, so common on the north Pacific, and the graceful fulmars which were circling about us. An occasional tufted puffin was seen, a pelagic species during most of the year, but most of the gulls and other migrating waterfowl had been left behind before we began to see the long saber-like wings of the black-footed albatrosses or "goonies," as they are called, skimming low over the heaving billows of the ocean, pelagic wanderers from warmer climes, gleaning a scanty living from the watery wastes. During our four days' trip over the Pacific Ocean to Unimak Pass they were our constant companions. In stormy weather, of which we had plenty, they were more numerous and active, sometimes as many as six being seen about the ship at one time. They will always be associated in my memory with the ocean storms, with the plunging of the ship over mountainous seas and with the whirr of racing propellers over the crests of mighty waves. Amid all the grandeur, excitement, and danger of a storm at sea the albatross glides calmly on, rising easily over the crests of the highest waves and gracefully

1

sailing down into the valleys between them, frequently lost to sight but never troubled or confused, thoroughly at home in its native element. What mariner would not respect the bird that shows such mastery of the sea in all its wildest moods?

Although the black-footed albatross is a bird of the northern hemisphere, living its life on the Pacific Ocean north of the equator, it shares with the antarctic *Tubinares* the habit of breeding during our winter months, resorting to the islands in the Hawaiian group for this purpose early in November. Dr. T. W. Richards (1909) says of its arrival on the Midway Islands, situated in latitude 28° 13″ North and longitude 177° 21′ West:

In 1906 *nigripes* arrived the first week in November, *immutabilis* following a few days later, and by the 20th of the month both species had deposited eggs. Dr. Campbell believes that the birds pair after arrival, but it would seem that some, at least, may have mated previously.

Courtship.—The courtship dance of the Laysan albatross has been fully described by Dr. Walter K. Fisher (1904), and the same curious performance is indulged in by the black-footed species with some variations. Doctor Fisher noted the following differences in the ceremony:

I saw the black-footed albatrosses (*D. nigripes*) rather seldom engaged in the dance, and indeed they impress one as more matter-of-fact creatures. The only difference which was observed in the ceremony as carried out by the two species is that *nigripes* spreads its wings slightly (the metacarpus or " hand " being folded closed) when it lifts its head to utter the nasal song.

Prof. Homer R. Dill (1912) says that it is similar,

but much more elaborate, and they go through the figures slowly and gracefully. Instead of lifting one wing they raise both. They are very neighborly with the other species. We often saw them visiting, and on one to two occasions they were trying to perform with them, but the rapid pace set by the white bird was rather too much for his more deliberate cousin, and the affair ended disastrously.

According to Doctor Fisher (1904a), Dr. Charles H. Gilbert, while cruising about a hundred miles off San Diego, California, on the steamer *Albatross*, saw six black-footed albatrosses pair off and indulge in this peculiar dance. This was during the latter part of March, when the adult birds should have been on their breeding grounds, but these were apparently immature birds.

Nesting.—Doctor Fisher (1906) says of the breeding habits of this species on Laysan Island:

The black-footed albatross is very much less abundant on Laysan than the white species. It colonizes the sandy beaches on the north, east, and south sides, but is not found, except rarely, on the west side. It is likewise common on the sedge-covered slope near the beach, in the same habitat with *Sula cyanops*. On one or two occasions I noted them in the interior with *D. immutabilis*.

The nest is a mere hollow scratched in the bare sand, without even a rim of sand raised around it.

Eggs.—Doctor Richards (1909) describes the eggs as follows:

Each pair of birds—and this applies to both species—rarely lays more than one egg in a season, if undisturbed; and if a second egg should be deposited the first is thrown out, leaving but one to incubate. If, as was formerly the case, the nests are systematically robbed, four eggs are usually supplied by each. In nearly all published descriptions of eggs of the *Diomedeidae* they are referred to in terms somewhat as follows: "White, sometimes speckled or sprinkled on larger end with reddish brown" (Ridgway), giving the impression that they resemble, on a large scale, eggs of the stormy petrel, for example. While this may be true of some species, it would be inappropriate for a great many specimens of *D. nigripes*, though some are faintly speckled or even immaculate. In many instances, however, these eggs are boldly and handsomely splashed with dark brownish red, in some forming a cap or wreath about one end, usually the larger; in others, extending over nearly one-half the shell; in fact there is as much color, relatively, as on an average egg of any of our larger *Buteos*, though it is apt to be more constantly confined to one end. Compared with eggs of *immutabilis* they average more color, but extremes easily overlap and identity can not be determined from the eggs alone.

The measurements of 45 eggs, in various collections, average 108.8 by 70.3 millimeters; the eggs showing the four extremes measure **120.7** by 69.8, 109.5 by **86, 98.1** by 68.4, and 109.3 by **56** millimeters.

Young.—Doctor Richards (1909) says further:

Incubation lasts about six weeks, both birds taking turns on the nest so that the egg is constantly covered. The young are fed, in the well-known manner, by regurgitation from the throat of the parent, remaining about the islands until the following June or July, so that the entire reproductive period occupies about one-half the year.

The young are probably nearly six months old before they are able to fly.

Plumages.—Immature birds, during the first year at least or perhaps longer, are in uniformly dark sooty plumage, a faint suggestion of the white face at the base of the bill and a few white feathers on the upper tail-coverts probably indicate approaching maturity. The dull white face and the pure white rump and under tail-coverts are characteristic of the fully adult plumage which is certainly not acquired until the second year and probably not complete until much later.

Food.—The food of this albatross consists of whatever edible refuse it can pick up from the surface of the sea. It follows vessels persistently for the purpose of picking up bits of garbage thrown overboard, over which it often quarrels with its neighbor. From a slow-moving sailing vessel it can easily be caught with a hook and line, baited with almost any kind of animal food; but we were unable to hook any from our fast-moving revenue cutter, although the birds made repeated attempts to seize the bait. It is said by Baird, Brewer, and Ridgway (1884) to feed largely on " a pelagic crab."

Behavior.—Doctor Fisher (1906) has described the flight of this species so well that I can not do better than quote his remarks as follows:

As is well known, albatrosses are past masters at soaring or sailing. If the wind is favorable they are able to skim over the water for a long time without once flapping their wings. *D. nigripes* is certainly no exception to the general rule, and we had ample opportunity to witness their powers. The long slender wings, with long humeral bones, are eminently fitted for this sort of existence, and their construction renders flapping laborious, for in proportion to its size the albatross is not a very muscular creature and could not fly a great distance if obliged to do so by wing beats. When a stiff breeze is blowing albatrosses can sail only against the wind or with it, and are able to quarter a breeze, or go directly across it only for a short distance and when under great momentum. When we were steaming directly against the wind the albatrosses had no trouble in following us, and they would fly all around the ship without flapping their wings except when the breeze was strong, and then they were obliged to give a few vigorous beats when turning up into the wind. When, however, our course lay at an angle to the wind, they followed us by sailing in a series of ellipses. They would, in this case, sail directly against the wind, approaching us on the starboard quarter, go over the stern a short distance to port, then wheel and scud before the breeze perhaps 100 yards off the starboard quarter, when they turned and approached us as before. Their speed was so superior to ours that they were able to keep up without any trouble, and their frequent trips astern and rapid overhauling again made our cumbersome gait all the more apparent. Of course as they neared the turning point each time they had to quarter the breeze a little and for a moment sail directly across it.

The position in which the wings are held when sailing against or with the wind is quite characteristic in either case. When coming against the breeze the carpal segment and primaries are bent downward, as if to catch the wind, but when the bird turns and goes with the breeze the ends of the wings are bent up. When sailing against the wind they often gradually rise, but they are likewise perfectly capable of descending, and when going swiftly with the wind they not infrequently, in fact usually, make a long swoop downward and skim over the water, rising a little as they turn to come to windward. The position of the wings in the two cases seems to be constant. In the first case they catch more wind, and the fact that the birds generally rise a little shows that the wings act on the same principle as a kite. On the other hand, when sailing with the breeze, the position is such as gives less resistance to the wind.

It was a constant source of delight to watch the graceful evolutions of this albatross, as it followed our ship day after day, rising and falling at will and sailing straight with the wind on rigid wings. The large webbed feet were stretched out beyond the tail, and, with webs extended, served as a rudder in turning. When alighting on the water the feet were spread wide apart, the tail was spread and depressed and the wings were held upwards as it dropped gently down onto the crest of a wave; it deliberately folded its long wings without wetting them. After alighting, it often drifted far astern before rising again. This it could easily do in rough weather by slowly unfolding its wings and launching into the air off the crest of a wave, but in calm weather it was necessary for it to run along the surface to gain a little headway. If the wind was blowing strongly it could easily catch up with the ship without flapping its wings. It sits very high on the water and swims slowly.

Professor Dill (1912) says that the notes uttered during the nuptial dance are softer than those of the Laysan albatross and end "with a sound like the stroke of a bell under water or deep within the bird's stomach." They often give a whirring groan while quarreling over their food, and a similar note is sometimes heard on the wing, though they are usually silent.

The black-footed albatross is usually sociable and gentle with its neighbors on its breeding grounds, where it is more or less intimately associated with other albatrosses, boobies, shearwaters, and terns. It is on particularly intimate terms with the Laysan albatross indulging in the dance with it, but it has a bad habit of abusing its neighbors' young, and Doctor Fisher (1906) says that "the process sometimes finishes the victim, for young which appear to have been misused are frequently seen lying around dead."

Winter.—After the prolonged duties of reproduction are over the birds scatter about for a few months of vacation. Breeding birds may be found on Laysan Island from November to August, but undoubtedly some individuals are earlier breeders than others, and I doubt if the breeding season for each pair of birds is extended over any such long period as ten months; probably it is not much over six months. Certainly, adults are seen at sea, hundreds of miles from their breeding grounds, during at least six months of the year, from May to October.

DISTRIBUTION.

Breeding range.—Central and western Pacific Ocean, north of the Equator (Laysan, Gaspar Rico, Midway, Marshall, Volcano, and Bonin Islands). Formerly on Marcus Island. Breeding grounds protected in Hawaiian Islands reservation.

Range.—North Pacific Ocean, mainly north of the Tropic of Cancer. East to the coast of North America, from the Alaska Peninsula southward to Lower California (San Quentin Bay). South nearly or quite to the Equator. West to Formosa Channel, Japan (Yezzo), and the Kurile Islands. North to the Aleutian Islands and southern Bering Sea (Bristol Bay, Alaska) in summer.

Egg dates.—Bonin Islands: Eight records, September 28 to December 1. Midway Island: Ten records, November 18 to 21. Laysan Island: Six records, November 18 to December 29.

PHOEBASTRIA ALBATRUS (Pallas).

SHORT-TAILED ALBATROSS.

HABITS.

This was one of the species that we expected to find in the vicinity of the Aleutian Islands, but, although we spent the month of June, 1911, in cruising the whole length of the chain as far west as Attu Island and were exploring in the neighborhood of the various islands in Bering Sea all through July, we did not see, well enough to identify it, a single individual, in spite of the fact that we kept a sharp lookout for it and that other observers had found it common there. Possibly some of the dark-colored albatrosses, which we saw on both sides of the Aleutian Islands, and which we supposed were black-footed albatrosses, may have been young birds of this species.

Dr. E. W. Nelson (1887) says that he

found them very common between the islands east of Unalaska. The birds were very conspicuous from their white plumage and great size. During calm days they were most numerous, and ten or fifteen were frequently seen at a time. Unlike the black-footed albatross, these birds do not appear to follow vessels, and, in fact, are so shy that as a rule they give a wide berth to any species of sailing craft.

Yet he says again: "The natives of Alexandroosk sometimes spear them from their kyacks."

Mr. H. W. Elliott (1875), in writing of the birds of the fur seal islands, about 1875, says:

Twenty or thirty years ago, when whaling vessels were reaping their rich harvests in Bering and the Arctic Seas, the albatross was often seen about the islands, feeding upon the whale carrion which might drift on shore. But with the decrease of the whale fishery the birds have almost disappeared. Only a single individual was noted during my two years' residence. This was taken by Dr. Meany on the north shore of Saint George's.

The decline of the whale-fishing industry since that time has probably still further reduced the abundance of this species in those waters.

Mr. Lucien M. Turner (1886) says:

Among the Aleutian Islands they are quite common, but generally far out at sea. They approach the land during dense fogs, and may then be found sitting on a small rock jutting from the water. This species passes the winter in this locality and may be found, during very severe weather, about the western end of Attu Island.

Dr. L. Stejneger (1885) found this species " by no means a rare visitor to the Commander Islands." He differs from Mr. Turner, however, in saying:

They do not remain near the islands during the winter—at least I saw none— but the first ones were observed as early as the middle of March. These were old birds in the white plumage, and on April 14th not less than eight were seen

at one time near the village. During the summer, however, the black young
birds of the foregoing year are more numerous than the adults, of which a few
remain all summer, though without breeding, of course. In the middle of the
immense flocks of *Lunda, Fratercula,* and *Fulmarus,* which in quiet weather
rest on the surface of the sea, covering many acres, can always be seen one
or two of these comparatively gigantic dark birds, which, however, are the
first ones to take the wing at the approach of a boat or a bajdarka. This
species is remarkably shyer than *D. nigripes.*

Nesting.—According to Cassin (1858), Mr. Titian R. Peale found
the short-tailed albatross breeding on Wake Island in the Central
Pacific Ocean, about half-way between the Hawaiian Islands and the
Philippines. He says:

On the 20th of December, we found this bird breeding at Wake's Island.
The single egg of each pair was laid on the ground, in a slight concavity, without any lining material; both sexes take turns in the labor of incubation, and
neither the male nor the female abandoned the nest on our approach, but
walked around us in a very dignified manner, and made but few demonstrations
of defense with their bills when taken up in our arms. The egg is white, of an
oblong figure, with the ends nearly alike, and measures four and two-tenths
inches long, and two and six-tenths inches in diameter.

Eggs.—Seebohm (1890) refers to five eggs, in the Pryer collection
taken by Mr. Holst in the Bonin Islands which vary in length from
4.7 to 4.3, in breadth from 3.0 to 2.9. Twelve eggs, from the same
source, in the British Museum are described by Godman (1907) as
" dull white, and marked on the larger end with a profusion of red
spots and blotches, many of which are confluent and form a distinct
cap. Isolated spots and markings of various sizes are scattered
over the shell." Mr. A. J. Campbell (1901) describes the eggs as
follows:

Lengthened oval or elliptically inclined in shape; texture of shell coarse and
strong; surface rough, with just a perceptible trace of gloss; colour, dirty or
yellowish-white, more or less ingrained or stained with earth, and with a
rusty-colored or rufous-brown cap of freckled or blotchy markings on the
larger end. In addition, some examples have, here and there over the rest
of the shell, dull purplish-brown spots.

The measurements of 43 eggs, in various collections, average 116.1
by 74.2 millimeters; the eggs showing the four extremes measure **125**
by 77, 120 by **79,** and **92** by **64** millimeters.

Plumages.—I can not find any descriptions of the downy young
and doubt if they have ever been collected. The sequence of plumages to maturity seems to require at least three and possibly four
years. Cassin (1858) quotes Peale as giving the following account
of these changes:

The changes are regularly progressive. Until the second year the plumage
remains a dark sooty-brown color; the bird has black feet and a dirty flesh-
colored bill (which becomes black when the skin is dried). In this state they
pair and raise young. After this stage cloudy white spots appear about the

base of the bill and over and under the eyes; their rumps begin to show a conspicuous spot of white; the bill turns yellow, with a tinge of carmine, the tip bluish; the legs are then flesh color; and finally the back, wings, and tail become cinereous-brown; rump, head, and all the under parts pure white; a white margin shows along the back edge of the wing as the bird flies, and a cloudy black spot generally remains in front of the eye. Thus, in some years, the plumage of the body is changed from nearly black to a pure snow-like white.

In his Monograph of the Petrels Godman describes in detail the various plumages of a series of specimens in the British Museum which seem to agree with the above statement by Peale.

Food.—In its feeding habits it does not differ materially from other albatrosses. It occasionally follows vessels for the purpose of picking up what scraps are thrown overboard, though it is shyer than some species and not so constant in its following. It has been caught on a hook and line baited with pork. It evidently feeds largely on squid, and is often attracted by whaling vessels to pick up scraps of blubber and flesh. Where food is so scarce and widely scattered as it is on the ocean, the hungry sea birds can not be too particular about what they eat; but all the albatrosses seem to prefer animal food.

Behavior.—The short-tailed albatross bears a superficial resemblance to the wandering albatross, but it is decidedly smaller and certain details of its color pattern are different. It is said to be less active than some of the other species. In the dark immature plumage it is likely to be confounded with the black-footed albatross, but it is larger and darker, lacks the white face and has a pink bill. Capt. F. W. Hutton's (1903) interesting theory regarding the flight of albatrosses might as well be applied to this species as to any other:

It was pointed out in 1889 by Mr. A. C. Baines that the birds usually rise in a slanting direction against the wind, turn round in a rather large circle, and make a rapid descent down the wind. They subsequently take a longer or shorter flight in various directions, almost touching the water. After that comes another ascent in the same manner, followed by another series of movements. Now, as the velocity of the wind near the surface of the sea is diminished by the friction of the waves, when the bird ascends into the more rapidly moving upper current its *vis inertiae* makes the wind blow past it, and so its stock of energy is increased. When it descends it will be moving faster than the lower stratum of wind and will again develop new energy if its inertia is sufficient to prevent its attaining the new velocity of the wind at once. So that the bird must fly against the wind when ascending and with it when descending. Thus the energy constantly lost by the friction of the air is partially renewed by these maneuvers. This explains why the birds can sail longer in a high wind than in a calm. It is because in a high wind and with a high sea there is much greater difference between the velocities of the wind near the surface and a short distance above it; and this again is an explanation of why an albatross keeps so close to the surface of the sea, only just topping the waves and occasionally rising high in the air.

Cassin (1858) quoting Peale, said of its vocal powers: " Usually birds of this species are silent, but sometimes they quarrel over offal thrown from the ship, then they bray in much the same tone as an ass."

Winter.—At the close of the breeding season in the summer, old and young birds start on their fall wanderings which cover nearly the whole of the Pacific Ocean lying north of the Tropic of Cancer, from Asia to North America. At certain seasons this is evidently a common species on the coast of California, for Mrs. Bailey (1902) says: "At Monterey in stormy winter weather Mr. Loomis has seen some of the birds in the bay. The largest number he recorded from the region were seen off Point Pinos, a dozen being counted in an hour."

DISTRIBUTION.

Breading range.—Western Pacific Ocean, north of the Equator (Wake and Bonin Islands) and perhaps farther north.

Range.—North Pacific Ocean and Bering Sea. East to the coast of North America from Northern Alaska (Norton Sound) southward to southern Lower California (Magdalena Bay). Southern limits not determined; records confused with other species. West to Formosa, China, and Japan seas, Kurile, and Commander Islands and Okhotsk Sea. North throughout Bering Sea to Bering Straits, in summer.

Egg dates.—Bonin Islands: Eighteen records, August 17 to December 3; nine records, October 20 to November 12.

PHOEBASTRIA IMMUTABILIS (Rothschild).

LAYSAN ALBATROSS.

HABITS.

As an introduction to the life history of this species it seems fitting to give a brief description of the wonders of Laysan Island, in our mid-ocean bird reservation, where the specimens were obtained from which the Hon. Walter Rothschild (now Lord Rothschild) first described the Laysan albatross. As I have never visited Laysan Island or seen this albatross in life, I can not do better than to quote from the published account of it by Dr. Walter K. Fisher (1903) to whom we are indebted for most of our knowledge of the breeding habits of this species.

Reaching out toward Japan from the main Hawaiian group is a long chain of volcanic rocks, atolls, sand bars, and sunken reefs, all insignificant in size and widely separated. The last islet is fully two thousand miles from Honolulu and about halfway to Yokohama. Beginning at the east the more important members of this chain are: Bird Island and Necker (tall volcanic rocks), French

Frigate Shoals, Gardner Rock, Laysan, Lisiansky, Midway, Cure, and Morell. Laysan is eight hundred miles northwest-by-west from Honolulu, and is perhaps best known as being the home of countless albatrosses. We sighted the island early one morning in May, lying low on the horizon, with a great cloud of sea birds hovering over it. On all sides the air was lively with terns, albatrosses, and boobies, and we began to gain some notion of what a pandemonium the distant swarm was raising. We landed on the west side, where there is a narrow passage through the breakers, which curl with beautiful hues on the coral reef, and then sweep shoreward with flying foam.

Laysan is a slightly elevated atoll, rudely quadrilateral in contour, and suggests a shallow basin or platter. It is three miles long by one and one-half broad. In the center is a wholly enclosed lagoon, covering perhaps one hundred acres. This is surrounded by a broad, level plain, that part nearest the very saline waters of the lagoon being destitute of any vegetable life. From this plain the land rises as a gentle sandy slope to a low divide or rim (about twenty-five feet above the water) near the sea beach. Not a tree breaks the monotonous expanse, but instead are low bushes (*Chenopodium sandwicheum, Santalum freycinetianum, Scaevola koenigi*) and broad areas of high, tussocky grass. On the narrow seaward slope the turf is short and wiry, and a broad band between the bare shores of the lagoon and the beginning of the bush grass is covered mostly with matted beds of succulent *Portulaca lutea*, and reddish-flowered *Sesuvium portulacastrum*. Beautiful morning glories, yellow *Tribulus* (reminding one of *Potentilla*), showy *Capparis*, and numerous other flowers add a bit of color to the landscape.

Laysan is a bird paradise. Albatrosses (*Diomedea immutabilis* and *P. nigripes*) by the thousands rear their young here each year, free from fear of molestation or injury. More numerous even are the sooty terns (*Sterna fuliginosa*), while the gray-back tern (*S. lunata*), white tern (*Gygis alba kittlitzi*), noio (*Micranous hawaiiensis*), and noddy (*Anous stolidus*) are all abundant. Attractive and interesting birds are the boobies, of which two species, *Sula cyanops* and *Sula piscator*, are on the island in large numbers. The droll frigate bird (*Fregata aquila*) is here in all the glory of his bright red gular " balloon," and the splendid red-tailed tropic bird (*Phaëthon rubricaudus*) in satiny plumage of the palest rose pink, is a familiar member of the community; as he nervously flits by in the tropical sunshine his feathers glisten with the lustre of burnished metal. Among the Procellariidae, the bonin petrels (*Aestrelata hypoleuca*) may be mentioned as exceeding even the Laysan albatross in numbers, but as they live in deep burrows one would hardly think it. Next come the wedge-tailed and Christmas Island shearwaters (*Puffinus cuneatus* and *P. nativitatis*), which are abundant, and the rare sooty petrel (*Oceanodroma fuliginosa*) nests in some numbers during the winter months.

At that time, in 1902, the glories of Laysan Island were in their prime and the number of breeding sea birds was at its maximum. Doctor Fisher agreed with Prof. C. C. Nutting that there were, at least, a million albarosses breeding on the island, in addition to all the hosts of other species. The nests were so close together that the birds were almost touching each other and it was difficult to walk without treading on eggs. But a great change took place during the next ten years, for a party of Japanese feather hunters visited the island and materially reduced its wonderful bird population.

In comparing the conditions, noted by him in 1903 and in 1911, Mr. William Alanson Bryan (1912) says:

The slaughter wrought by the plume hunters is everywhere apparent. One of the work buildings formerly used by the guano company and later as a storehouse by the poachers is still standing. With a side torn out and left open to the weather by the men of the *Thetis*, it is still filled with thousands of pairs of albatross wings. Though weatherbeaten and useless, they show how they were cut from the birds whose half-bleached skeletons lie in thousands of heaps scattered all over the island.

This wholesale killing has had an appalling effect on the colony. No one can estimate the thousands, perhaps hundreds of thousands, of birds that have been wilfully sacrificed on Laysan to the whim of fashion and the lust of gain. It is conservative to say that fully one-half the number of birds of both species of albatross that were so abundant everywhere in 1903 have been killed. The colonies that remain are in a sadly decimated condition. Often a colony of a dozen or more birds will not have a single young. Over a large part of the island, in some sections a hundred acres in a place, that 10 years ago was thickly inhabited by albatrosses, not a single bird remains, while heaps of the slain lie as mute testimony of the awful slaughter of these beautiful, harmless, and without doubt beneficial inhabitants of the high seas.

Fortunately, serious as were the depredations of the poachers, their operations were interrupted before any of the species had been completely exterminated. So far as the birds that secure their food from the sea are concerned, it is reasonable to suppose they will increase in number, and that nature will in time restore the island to its former populous condition if no further slaughter is permitted. Owing to the indiscriminate method of the killing, usually only one or the other of mated pairs was sacrificed. The unmated birds that survive are slow in selecting another mate. As but a single egg is laid by the majority of these birds, it will possibly take 10 years for the sea birds of the colony to regain their former numerical strength.

In his report of the same expedition Prof. Homer R. Dill (1912) estimates the number of Laysan albatrosses on the island in 1911 as 180,000 and the total bird population as over a million, which gives some encouragement that the principal species nesting on the island are in no danger of extermination.

A similar tale of destruction is told by Mr. Bryan (1903) in his account of the Marcus Island colony of Laysan albatrosses which were killed and boiled down to make fertilizer, which was shipped to Japan; the long wing quills were saved and sold, as eagle feathers, to the millinery trade.

Spring.—The Laysan albatrosses begin to arrive on their breeding grounds during the last week in October and in November the nesting season is well under way. Doctor Fisher (1904) says:

The albatrosses live on Laysan nearly ten months of the year. During the last days of October, before the winter storms set in, the first vanguard of the mighty army appears, and for days they continue to flock in from all points of the compass. Dr. H. Schauinsland, who witnessed their advent, says that in exposed places the island becomes literally white with the countless throng, as if great snowflakes had suddenly descended upon the scene.

So vast is the number of birds that many are obliged to be content with rather unsuitable nesting spots, while late comers must leave the overcrowded area. Loving couples defend their rights against the tardy ones, and it is several days before all have settled their respective claims.

Courtship.—On their arrival and all through their breeding season these birds indulge in a very peculiar and interesting dance, which the sailors refer to as a " cake walk." Doctor Fisher (1904) has fully described the performance, as follows:

This game or whatever one may wish to call it, very likely originated in past time during the courting season, but it certainly has long since lost any such significance. At first two birds approach one another, bowing profoundly and stepping heavily. They swagger about each other, nodding and courtesying solemnly, then suddenly begin to fence a little, crossing bills and whetting them together, sometimes with a whistling sound, meanwhile pecking and dropping stiff little bows. All at once one lifts its closed wing and nibbles at the feathers beneath, or rarely, if in a hurry, quickly turns its head. The partner during this short performance, assumes a statuesque pose, and either looks mechanically from side to side, or snaps its bill loudly a few times. Then the first bird bows once, and pointing its head and beak straight upward, rises on its toes, puffs out its breast, and utters a prolonged, nasal, *Ah-h-h-h,* with a rapidly rising inflection, and with a distinctly " anserine " and " bovine " quality, quite difficult to describe. While this " song " is being uttered the companion loudly and rapidly snaps its bill. Often both birds raise their heads in air and either one or both favor the appreciative audience with that ridiculous, and indescribable bovine groan. When they have finished they begin bowing to each other again, rapidly and alternately, and presently repeat the performance, the birds reversing their rôle in the game or not. In the most successful dances the movements are executed in perfect unison, and this fact much enhances the extraordinary effect.

Nesting.—Doctor Fisher (1906) says of the nesting colonies on Laysan Island:

The Laysan albatross or gony is distributed all over the island, with the single exception of the beaches, which on all sides except the west are colonized by the black-footed albatross. The flat plain surrounding the lagoon is their favorite habitat, and we found the young here in far the greatest numbers. This great colony extended all the way around the lagoon, but certain portions were more congested than others. The largest single colony of young is on the south side of the lagoon, where the ground has been leveled off in past years by phosphate-rock diggers. Here from a little eminence one can look off and see many thousands of birds at a glance, but it would be hazardous to guess how many there are on the whole island.

Dr. T. W. Richards (1909) describes the nest as follows:

Regarding the nesting habits, Dr. Campbell noted an interesting point of difference in the two species; both lay in slight hollows scratched in the bare sand, but *immutabilis* usually heaps up this material in a ridge around the " nest." He says " the bird, sitting on the nest and reaching out as far as possible, picks up sand in its bill and deposits same around the edge until it is built up four or five inches. I noticed the difference in contour of nests of the two species, and as a white pair (Laysan) made a nest just beyond my door I was enabled to discover how it was done. The building up of the sides results in making the nest higher and also provides a shallow ditch all around it, which certainly makes it drier when there is rain.

Eggs.—The Laysan albatross lays but one egg which is laid about the middle of November. Mr. Walter Rothschild (1893) has described his series of eggs as follows:

I have received a series of eight eggs of *D. immutabilis*, which vary very much both in shape and coloration. The two extremes are as follows:

1. Very elongate; length, 111.5 mm.; width, 62.5 mm.; ground color, dirty white, marked with numerous large and small blotches of a brownish-maroon color, which are principally massed at the two ends, though there are a few in the central zone.

2. Very thick and short; length, 100 mm.; width, 70 mm.; color, uniform brownish buff without any markings whatever.

The majority of specimens before me are dirty white with irregular patches and spots of brownish-maroon at the larger end.

The measurements of 39 eggs, in various collections, average 109.2 by 69.4 millimeters; the eggs showing the four extremes measure **116** by 72, 109.6 by **75**, and **99** by **62** millimeters.

Young.—Doctor Richards (1909) says:

Incubation lasts about six weeks, both birds taking turns on the nest so that the egg is constantly covered. The young are fed, in the well-known manner, by regurgitation from the throat of the parent, remaining about the islands until the following June or July, so that the entire reproductive period occupies about one-half of the year.

Doctor Fisher (1906) devotes considerable space to the behavior of the young and I quote from his remarks, as follows:

The shallow, basin-shaped hollow in which the egg is deposited, is the young albatross's home, and it usually does not stray far. But as the nestlings grow stronger so that they can walk a little, albeit very awkwardly, they wander sometimes a rod from the home spot and engage in mild squabbles with youthful neighbors. The same feeling of growing strength leads them about this time to slowly fan their wings back and forth from time to time. During a light shower I saw a considerable colony of young birds do this together, after the manner of cormorants drying their wings. When the breeze is rather brisk they usually all face it. Their spare time is taken up with idly dozing in the hot sun, preening their feathers or examining their surroundings. Several times I observed young birds collect dried grass and similar material, which happened to be within reach, and carefully cover the hollow in which they were sitting. Sometimes their spirit of inquiry leads them into trouble. We found a young bird, still lively, buried to its neck in a collapsed petrel burrow. It objected strenuously to being disinterred, but appeared little the worse for its adventure.

These amusing creatures sit on their heels with the whole length of the tarsus on the ground or tilted slightly in the air, as shown in the illustration. Their spare time is spent in gazing stupidly around, but if their reverie is at all disturbed by one passing too near they fly into an apparent rage, lean forward, and snap their beaks viciously, or sway their uncouth bodies from side to side in a frantic attempt to maintain a balance. Sometimes they make a rush, waddling along and darting their heads back and forth to the music of clicking mandibles. But they only occasionally come to the point of biting, and are always amenable to tact and persuasion.

Usually, after the first paroxysm of snapping is over, one can stroke them with little danger of scratched hands. They maintain a small fire of objection, with impotent nips, or try to slide off. But sometimes a youngster is more determined than the rest. It often happens that in an eager rush to scare an intruder the young bird stumbles in a petrel's hole and falls forward with considerable force on its chin. In some way nature never meant an albatross's head to be lower than its stomach, or the concussion affects it unpleasantly for usually it disgorges its breakfast very promptly and energetically, but curiously I never saw them do this without first falling over. After such a performance the young one looks dejected, for it is usually left hungry, and hunger is its chief trouble.

After sunrise the albatrosses begin to feed the young. The old bird, coming in from the sea, alights near her offspring, which immediately takes the initiative by waddling up and pecking or biting gently at her beak. This petitioning always takes place and perhaps acts as some sort of stimulus for in a few moments the mother stands up, and with head lowered and wings held loosely at the side disgorges a mass of squids and oil. Just as she opens her beak the young inserts its own crosswise and skillfully catches every morsel, which it bolts with evident relish. This operation I saw repeated, with short intermissions, ten times. The last two or three ejections of this oily pabulum cost the albatross considerable muscular effort and the last time nothing came up but a little oil, and stomach juices presumably. The young bird is not at all modest in its demands, but keeps asking for more. The old bird now pecks back in an annoyed manner, and if the other still urges, she arises and walks off, usually to some neighboring young one, which she viciously mauls about the neck. This exhibition usually takes place just before she feeds her young and likewise between courses, as it were. Why she does this I am at a loss to suggest, unless it be mere ill will. The old bird does not always confine this ill treatment to one strange young bird, but takes in a circle of those whose parents are absent. The young thus rudely treated sometimes bite back, but usually do not offer resistance, uttering instead a plaintive little squeak. A small mortality is the result of this practice. Dr. Gilbert observed that *Diomedea nigripes* is more savage than the white species. He saw a black-footed albatross thus take in a circle of about twenty young *immutabilis* and "wool" them soundly. Finally, however, the ruffian arrived at a youngster whose parent, being unexpectedly near by, set upon the persecutor, and in the scrimmage *nigripes* was put to rout.

Plumages.—Continuing he says of the development of plumage in the young:

The young are hatched in February, according to Mr. Schlemmer. They then are covered with a grayish-white down which is soon superseded by a plumage of dark-brown down, assumed by a continued growth of the original covering and a wearing off of the gray tips. As the young grow older the white feathers come in on the breast and abdomen first, and the brown down is in direct communication with the terminal barbs of these juvenal feathers, as is, of course, well known. The feathers of the back also come in about the same time, and those of the wings, save the quills. At the time of our visit the young were about two-thirds grown, the white feathers of the breast and abdomen having in most cases the appearance of the adult, but the rest of the body was covered with long brown down, except on the head, where it was short. The beaks of the young are dark dirty gray or brownish gray, while those of the adult are light greenish.

The young of most albatrosses are dark colored in their first plumages, but in this species the young assume a first plumage closely resembling that of the adult, hence the specific name, *immutabilis*.

Food.—Doctor Fisher (1906) says of their food:

Near the forms or nests one not infrequently finds solid pellets—disgorged by the young in all probability, and by old birds too—consisting entirely of squid beaks and opaque lenses of the eyes. These lenses become very brittle and amber-like under the action of stomach juices and show a concentric structure. Candle nuts, the large seed of *Aleurites molluccana*, were found by Mr. Snyder in the interior of the island and were almost undoubtedly ejected by albatrosses. As is well known, albatrosses pick up all sorts of floating material, and candle nuts are frequently seen on the ocean, having been swept seaward by mountain streams.

Elsewhere (1904) he says:

In their hours of toil they hie themselves off to sea and scour the waves for the elusive squid, which is a staple article of diet for the larger members of the vast bird population, the gannets, perhaps, excepted. About sunrise the main body of the white company begins to return, and for several hours they straggle in, tired but full, and seek their sleepy children, who are soon very much awake. Although the Laysan albatrosses undoubtedly do a small part of their fishing during the day, I can not help but feel, from the nocturnal or crepuscular habits of their food—certain cephalopods—and the prevalent feeding hours, that the major portion is done in the very early morning, perhaps from just preceding dawn till light. I noted particularly during the one day I was on the steamer, while she was dredging in the vicinity of Laysan, that very few Laysan gonies were seen at sea after about 9 a. m. That same day we sighted the island about 5 a. m., and when I arrived on deck about 5.30 I distinctly remember seeing many of the white species (*immutabilis*) circling about the vessel. Later in the morning *immutabilis* almost entirely disappeared, but some *nigripes* remained with us all day. On the following morning we landed and I had no further opportunity to observe.

As Prof. C. C. Nutting, one of the naturalists of the expedition, has said, "the most conservative estimate of the necessary food supply yields almost incredible results. Cutting Mr. Schlemmer's estimate (of the total number of albatrosses on the island) in two, there would be 1,000,000 birds, and allowing only half a pound a day for each, surely a minimum for these larger, rapidly growing birds, they would consume no less than 250 tons daily." From rather extended observations on the feeding habits, I would place the quantity fed each young bird every morning at nearer one or one and a half pounds of squid (*Ommastrephes oualaniensis* Less., *O. sloanei* Gray, and *Onychoteuthis banksi* Fér.). I believe Professor Nutting's estimate of a million birds is not too great. Thus, in one day the albatrosses alone would consume nearer 600 tons of squid.

Behavior.—The flight of the Laysan albatross is said to be inferior to that of the black-footed albatross, but, as I have not seen it, I can not say in what way it differs from it. Its vocal powers have been already referred to in connection with the nuptial dance. Doctor Fisher (1906) also refers to the notes of the young as follows:

It is worthy of record that the young often "sing" in a thin, high squeak, which is kept up continuously for periods, and may be of service in guiding the parent, though I could not distinguish the slightest individuality in tone. I do not know whether they do this when the old birds are present, but remember that very many were engaged in the cricket-like song when we visited a populous colony late one moonlight night.

On their breeding gounds the albatrosses live quietly and harmoniously with their neighbors, attending strictly to their own affairs and paying no attention to the populous bird colonies about them, and not minding even the presence of man among them. Doctor Fisher (1906) says:

The old birds do not seem to mind the presence of man. One can walk among them without disturbing their various occupations and amusements in the least. Only when suddenly startled do they exhibit any tendency to snap their bills, and then they are easily calmed. They back away from any proffered familiarity with great rapidity, unless suddenly hindered by a tuft of grass, which event surprises them immoderately. They will not allow themselves to be handled, and make off at a great rate if one offers them this indignity. They have a half-doubting inquisitiveness which leads them sometimes to walk up to the visitor and examine anything conspicuous about his person. One bird became greatly interested in the bright aluminum cap to my tripod and strolled up and examined it with both eye and beak, appearing somewhat astonished when the cap tinkled.

Winter.—During July and August the young albatrosses learn to fly and to follow their parents out to sea in search of food, after which both young and old birds begin to desert the breeding islands and to wander over the Pacific Ocean for two or three months before the beginning of another breeding season, hardly more than a short vacation.

DISTRIBUTION.

Breeding range.—Islands northwest of Hawaiian group, in mid-Pacific Ocean. (Laysan, Midway, French Frigate, Necker, Bird, and Lisiansky Islands.) Formerly in Marcus Island. Breeding grounds protected in Hawaiian Islands reservation.

Range.—Central Pacific Ocean. East to the coast of Lower California (between Guadalupe Island and coast of Lower California). North to about 40° north. West to the Bonin Islands. Southern limits not well defined.

Egg dates.—Laysan and Midway Islands: Twenty records, November 15 to December 29; ten records, November 19 to December 26.

THALASSOGERON CHRYSOSTOMUS CULMINATUS (Gould).

YELLOW-NOSED ALBATROSS.

HABITS.

This species has but slight claims to a place on the list of North American birds, and it can not be regarded as anything but a rare straggler off our coasts. Considerable confusion seems to exist among writers as to the status of the two species, *Thalassogeron culminatus* and *T. chlororhynchus*, which are evidently closely related, and the identity of American specimens does not seem to be well established. Godman (1907) says of *T. culminatus:* "The species is widely distributed in southern waters, especially in the Australasian seas, whence it ranges throughout the Pacific to South America, extending north to the coast of Oregon; it is also found in the South Atlantic and Indian Oceans;" and that "*T. chlororhynchus* is an inhabitant of the South Atlantic, the South Indian, and the Australian Oceans." Both species have been called yellow-nosed albatross, and many observers have probably not detected the slight differences on which the species have been separated, so that it becomes a difficult, if not impossible, task to properly separate the references between the two species, and I shall not attempt to do so.

Audubon (1840) referred to a specimen of yellow-nosed albatross, said to have been taken by Doctor Townsend off the mouth of the Columbia River; Audubon called this bird *Diomedea chlororhynchos*, but Professor Baird afterwards identified it as *Thalassogeron culminatus*. Doctor Cooper saw a skull, which "was taken by Dr. W. O. Ayres from a dead specimen found on the outer beach near the Golden Gate," according to Baird, Brewer, and Ridgway (1884), and which he identified as belonging to this species. In Nuttall's Manual, by Chamberlain (1891), the following statement occurs:

The claim of this species to recognition here is based upon the capture of an immature bird near the mouth of river St. Lawrence in 1885. I examined the skin, which is preserved in the Museum of Laval University, at Quebec, and was told by the curator, Mr. C. E. Dionne, that he purchased it from the fisherman who shot the bird. The claim is slight, but there is no reason why it should be ignored.

Nesting.—Very little is known about the breeding habits of the yellow-nosed albatross. Mr. Robert Hall (1900), in his notes on the birds of Kerguelen Island, says:

Of the yellow-nosed albatross I saw no nests, but birds were observed near the entrance to the harbor of our last anchorage (Fuller's). Suitable lofty islets were near this coast, and the birds in adult plumage would probably be breeding there or on the cliffs to the southward of Christmas Harbor. This species makes an addition to the list of Kerguelen birds.

Mr. W. Otto Emerson (1886) has published the following notes on an egg of this species which he obtained:

It was collected January 12, 1880, by Captain Thos. Lynch, at Diegos, Kavnen's Rocks, S. by E., fifty-two miles from Cape Horn. The nest was composed on the outside of tussocks of grass and mud, inside of fine grass and feathers. The diameter outside at the top was twelve inches, and at the base eighteen. Inside it was ten inches, and the depth inside was five inches. It was situated on the top of the rocks, on a loamy plain. The incubation was fresh. The following notes by J. W. Detmiller, M. D., were on the back of the data: " The nests are very nicely and solidly built, lasting two or three seasons, even in that fearful climate. They are built very closely together, and are probably often mistaken by one and another of the birds, after the fashion of many sea birds. The nests are high, to enable the long-winged creatures to rise easily to wing, which they can not do on a level. The birds are very tame, allowing themselves to be handled while sitting."

Eggs.—The egg now before me measures 4 6–8 by 2 6–8 inches [120.6 by 69.8 mm.], is of an oblong form, smaller at one end than at the other. Both ends are quite blunt. The surface of the shell is in character like a common hen's egg. The color inclines to a light creamy white, with a ring of seemingly fine spattered burnt sienna specks or spots, like those made by drawing a brush of color across a stick, as a painter does to get the effect of granite. They form a ring around the larger end, being about two inches across from one side of the ring to the other. The center of the ring runs together in the fine markings, making the color almost solid, and fades away from the outer edge of the egg, almost to needles points.

There are numerous eggs in various collections labeled yellow-nosed albatross; but, as I have been unable to definitely determine which are *culminatus* and which are *chlororhynchus*, I shall not attempt to describe or give the measurements of either species.

Plumages.—I can not find any description of the downy young or immature plumages, but Gould (1865) says that young birds "may be easily distinguished from the adults, especially while flying, by the darker coloring of their wings, back, and tail, and by the culmen of the bill being less distinctly marked with yellow."

Behavior.—Mr. John Treadwell Nichols has contributed the following notes on the behavior of this species:

The yellow-nosed albatross is a common south temperate species coming about ships at sea for the scraps from the galley. It can be easily caught with fish-hook and salt pork. The tip of the hook catches under its upper mandible, and if the line be held taut the bird may be hauled on deck along the surface of the water, or through the air like a kite. Except rarely when it catches in the soft parts of the mouth, the hook does not penetrate anything and if the line be slackened drops out by itself; but as a rule the bird foolishly braces back, sticking its feet out in front of it, or setting its wings, and is readily drawn inboard. On deck it is stupid, helpless, unable to rise, and after a few minutes seems to become dizzy from the vessel's motion. Its legs fail it so that it will often squat instead of trying to stand, and with every appearance of seasickness it regurgitates oily matter. Though generally silent, when being hauled aboard I have heard it give a goose-like honking or grunting note. It rises from the water with much awkward flapping, kicking, and splashing, especially in light breezes, and when fairly launched sails on stiff, motionless wings, occasionally giving them a few flaps, less frequently as the wind increases in force. In moderate breezes the wings are held quite widely extended; in high winds they are somewhat folded, exposing less surface. It sails straight away, swinging into the air and then down close to the water, leaning to one side or the other as it curves its course. Its flight is never high above the water, but about the ship it rises somewhat higher than the smaller birds. Attracted by food in the wake, it alights to seize it, but the wings are at such times often held half raised over the back. Though adults are readily distinguishable, young of this species and of the spectacled albatross, the other common small albatross of the south, can be differentiated with difficulty in life. The offshore habits of the two seem identical.

Winter.—Between breeding seasons this species, like others of its tribe, is given to wandering though it rarely crosses the tropics into the northern hemisphere. In addition to our North American records there is another North Atlantic record mentioned in Godman's Monograph (1907) as follows:

Dr. Knud Andersen, of Darlmenats, says a specimen was obtained on the ice in the North Atlantic in April, 1834, at Fiskumvand, Eker, Norway, about 59° 50′ N. Lat., and was sent by Professor W. Boeck to the Christiania Museum, and determined by Professor Collett. It had previously been wrongly identified with *T. chlororhynchus.*

DISTRIBUTION.

Breeding range.—The records of *T. culminatus* and *T. chlororhynchus* are hopelessly confused, but apparently the former breeds in the South Atlantic Ocean (probably South Georgia), in the South Pacific Ocean (Campbell Island), in the South Indian Ocean (Kerguelen and the Crozet Islands) and on islands near Cape Horn (Diego Rameres).

Range.—Southern portions of the Atlantic, Pacific, and Indian Oceans, mainly between 30° and 60° South.

Casual records.—Has wandered northward in the Atlantic Ocean to Quebec (mouth of Moisie River, August 20, 1885) and Norway (Fiskumvand, Eker, April, 1834); and in the Pacific Ocean to Panama, California, and Oregon.

Egg dates.—Cape Horn: Four records, January 8 to February 8. South Georgia Island, January 22. Campbell Island, October 10.

THALASSOGERON CHLORORHYNCHUS (Gmelin).

PINK-FOOTED ALBATROSS.

HABITS.

Dr. Leonard C. Sanford has recently added to his magnificent collection of *Tubinares* a specimen of this species taken on August 1, 1913, off Machias Seal Island, Maine, near the entrance to the Bay of Fundy. This record adds a new species to the North American list.

As stated in the life history of the preceding species, the two yellow-nosed albatrosses, *Thalassogeron culminatus* and *T. chlororhynchus,* are so much alike that their status and distribution are hopelessly confused. It is almost impossible to separate the references to these two species; therefore, my attempt to write a separate life history and give a separate distribution for each has not been very satisfactory and I have no confidence in the correctness of either;

however, they will have to stand until further investigation throws more light on the subject.

Mr. G. E. Verrill (1895) has described the yellow-nosed albatross which breeds on Gough Island, in the South Atlantic Ocean, as a new species under the name *Thalassogeron eximius*, which he says most closely resembles *T. chlororhynchus.* Other authorities differ as to whether this bird is nearer to *chlororhynchus* or to *culminatus.* Apparently it is very close to both and perhaps all three may eventually prove to be identical, as the slightly differentiated characters may prove to be age, seasonal, or individual variations. There are also several other species of *Thalassogeron*, which seem to have a more or less doubtful status and which may eventually be lumped together, when this group is better understood.

Nesting.—Assuming that the Gough Island bird may be this species, I quote what Mr. Verrill (1895) has to say about it:

Concerning the "molly mokes" Mr. Comer has the following notes: "There is but one kind, which are known as blueheads, on Gough Island. Back and heads light blue, top of wings dark, white breasts, top of beak yellow, while the lower part is black, feet white. On this island they lay separately, keeping well apart and scattered about the island, among tussocks and brakes, more like the albatross (*D. exulans*) but at South Georgia and most of the islands they build close to each other in rookeries. At Gough Island they commence laying the 20th of September. They lay but one egg. If robbed they do not lay again, but leave the nest and do not return until another season. Nests are built the same as the albatross (*D. exulans*), only smaller." In his journal at Gough Island, on September 7, Mr. Comer notes that "the molly mokes have commenced to make their nests." Again, on September 27, that he "got a few molly moke eggs," and from then on he frequently speaks of taking their eggs.

Eggs.—Of the eggs he says:

The shape of the 75 eggs is comparatively pretty uniform, as a rule more elongate and nearer elliptical than the following species, most of them approaching an elliptical ovoid. Several are nearly perfect ellipsoids. The texture and surface of the shell is much like that of *D. exulans*, but finer and smoother in proportion to their smaller size. The ground color is white, generally with a very slight grayish or dusky and sometimes reddish tinge, and the whole egg is covered with minute specks of a reddish brown, darker than in *D. exulans;* in some they are even dark brown. These specks vary in number and are, for the most part, in the small pits and depressions on the surface of the shell. About one-third of the eggs are otherwise unmarked, so that at a little distance they simply have a dusky appearance. In the other two-thirds the specks become larger and thicker toward the larger end, often forming a more or less perfect zone about it, in other cases they run together and form a blotch which is, in some, quite heavy and conspicuous. As in *D. exulans*, the color is very superficial and many have larger spots or small blotches, unevenly distributed, that scale off when very dry, and like the eggs of the large albatross, most of them, when held to the light, show spots and blotches of color in the shell. Three are quite different from the rest in markings, two being heavily streaked over the whole egg with reddish brown, thickest at the large end. The other is streaked, not quite so heavily, with pale lilac, which is not so superficial.

Until more satisfactorily indentified eggs are available, I shall not attempt to give any measurements.

Behavior.—Godman (1907) publishes the following scanty information about this species:

T. *chlororhynchus* is an inhabitant of the South Atlantic, the South Indian, and the Australian Oceans. Gould relates that the species came under his observation for the first time on the 24th of July, 1838, in lat. 30° 38' S., long. 20° 43' W., from which period till the ship reached New South Wales scarcely a day passed without its being seen. Upon some occasions it appeared in considerable numbers, many of the birds being apparently one or two years old, and these were easily distinguished from the adults, especially when flying, by their dark-colored wings, back, and tail, and by the culmen of the bill being less distinctly marked with yellow.

Dr. E. A. Wilson, the naturalist on board the *Discovery*, says that the species was first encountered in the South Indian Ocean on September 22, 1901, in lat. 35° S., long. 14° W., and remained with the ship till the 30th of that month; it reappeared quite close to shore off False Bay on the coast of South Africa, as well as in the neighborhood of the Agulhas Sandbank, but eastward of this in the southern ocean its place was taken by T. *culminatus*, which had not previously been observed. T. *chlororhynchus* appears to frequent different localities varying with the season of the year.

Mr. Robert Hall mentions T. *chlororhynchus* as frequenting the entrance of Christmas Harbor in Kerguelen Island, but he did not find it breeding. Dr. Filhol says that the species breeds on Campbell Island, but there is some doubt whether he identified the bird accurately (Ibis, 1903, p. 266). Mr. Nicol, however, believed, that at the time of the " Valhalla's " visit to Tristan da Cunha, the " Yellow-nosed albatross " was nesting on the top of the crater, but the weather was too unfavorable to allow of his reaching its haunts.

Gould (1865) says of it:

The yellow-nosed albatross is plentiful off the Cape of Good Hope, and in all the intermediate seas between that point and Tasmania ; I also observed it off Capes Howe and Northumberland on the southern coast of Australia, and Gilbert states that he saw it flying about Rottnest Island on the western coast.

In its flight and general economy it greatly resembles the next species (*Diomedea melanophrys*) with which it is often in company.

DISTRIBUTION.

Breeding range.—Not well defined, and confused with that of *T. culminatus.* Said to breed on Falkland Islands and probably on other islands in the South Atlantic (Tristan da Cunha and Gough Islands) and in the Indian Ocean.

Range.—South Atlantic and South Indian Oceans and Australian seas, ranging farther north than *culminatus.*

Casual record.—One taken near the Bay of Fundy, New Brunswick (off Machias Seal Island, August 1, 1913) and one near Kongsberg, Norway (April, 1837).

Egg dates.—Falkland Islands: Six records, October 8 to 23. Gough Island: Two records, September 1 to 3.

PHOEBETRIA PALPEBRATA AUDUBONI Nichols and Murphy.

AUDUBON SOOTY ALBATROSS.

HABITS.

This is another species of ocean wanderer which has but a slight claim to a place on our list. It is a common species of wide distribution in southern and antarctic oceans; but its wanderings seldom bring it to our coasts, where it is very rare and of doubtful occurrence at the present day. Audubon (1840) first introduced it to our fauna and described it under the name of *Diomedea fusca*, from a specimen procured by Doctor Townsend off the coast of Oregon; so far as I know, no other specimen has ever been taken in American waters.

Nesting.—Sir Walter Buller (1888) says:

This species is more wary in its breeding habits than any other species of albatross. It breeds both in the Auckland and Campbell Islands. But it usually selects, as a nesting place, a ledge of rock high up on the face of the cliff, and quite inaccessible either from above or below.

Not far from Tristan da Cunha, in the South Atlantic Ocean, lies a beautiful and picturesque island, on the rocky cliffs of which the sooty abatross finds a congenial breeding place. Mr. W. Eagle Clarke (1905) has given us the following description of this ocean gem:

Gough Island rises on every side abruptly from the ocean in sheer precipices several hundred feet high. The general aspect of the island, as seen from shipboard, is very beautiful, with its green slopes and moss and lichen-covered cliffs, over which numbers of rushing waterfalls shoot out into the sea with a drop of several hundred feet. The only apparent landing place is on the eastern side, where the party from the *Scotia* landed. Here a ravine runs down from the interior to the coast and along it flows a small stream. Near the seaward end of this ravine are a few acres of level ground covered with grass or, in the moister parts with ferns and rankly growing celery and docks. Here, too, is a narrow beach, perhaps a hundred yards long, strewn with many large boulders and numerous fern rhizomes of considerable size. At the southwest end of the island there appears to be a plateau of about half a square mile in extent at an elevation of some 300 feet, but everywhere else the island rises into steep ridges separated by narrow valleys, which must render its exploration a matter of extreme difficulty. On the lower ground and up to a height of over 1,000 feet the island is thickly covered with tussock grass (*Spartina arundinacea*) and bucking trees (*Phylica nitida*); the former spread profusely over the steeper slopes, and the latter gnarled and stunted, yet growing vigorously even on the most exposed ridges. These trees appear hardly to rise beyond twenty feet in height and generally bear a thick growth of lichens on their stems. Under the waterfalls and along the sheltered banks of the streams ferns and mosses grow in luxuriance. More than the general aspect of the vegetation on the higher ground could not be determined, but the very summit of the island seemed by its green appearance to be clothed with mosses and lichens.

He also says of the albatross that breeds there:

Mr. Comer describes the species breeding at Gough Island as having the beak dark with "a yellow stripe on each side." It is common, but does not breed in "rookeries;" it places its nests separately on cliffs or projecting rocks, where it is most difficult to get at them. The bird commences to lay by the middle of September, and while sitting, keeps up a continual cry similar to that of a young goat.

Mr. Robert Hall (1900) found the sooty albatross breeding on Kerguelen Island, in the South Indian Ocean, and gives the following account of its nesting habits:

A trumpet-like screech and cat-like noise seem to be the vocabulary of this bird, as it wends its curving flight along the face of the cliffs, in the lower parts of which it places its nests. January 5th saw me investigating three nests on Murray Island in Royal Sound. Two were within three feet of each other, while the third was several hundred yards away, but all were placed under the ledges of rocks some 300 feet high and facing the sea. The first nest contained an egg which was undoubtedly addled, as I became aware when blowing it, and so were the other persons in the cabin; yet upon this egg the bird still sat. Two nests placed together contained, respectively, a young bird a few days old, and an egg with an almost matured embryo. This egg I took, and five days later I annexed the young of the other nest. All this time the egg-nest was still being sat upon by the sooty albatross. The young one, when left by its parent, stood up to assert its rights, and snapped its bill in the manner of the adult, but feebly. A cormorant's fresh egg, partly broken, was near, so the little gallant lived well in the start of its career, and disgorged enough food in a mass to give a meal to half a dozen ordinary birds. The general hue of the nestling was slate-color; the bill slate-black; legs bluish; iris faint hazel, and pupil blue. The ring of white had begun to show round the eye. The nests were neat, saucer-like, and of fine fibrous loam, caked. The dimensions were: Breadth 17 inches, diameter of cavity 12 inches, depth of cavity 3 inches, depth of structure about 4 inches.

Dr. J. H. Kidder (1875) spent four months, September to January, on this island, and I quote the following from his report:

October 24 two of the dusky albatrosses had made a nest upon a shelf formed by a considerable tuft of cabbage and azorella, at the entrance of a small cavity in the perpendicular face of a lofty rock, near the top of a hill some two miles away. Here the birds could be both seen and heard. Their scream is very loud, and not unlike one of the calls of a cat. At a distance, it has often been mistaken for the hail of a man. The name "pee-arr" has been given as descriptive of this call, which is, I believe, peculiar to the breeding season. Another pair was seen same day circling around the same hill top. No eggs. November 2, secured one egg and both birds. The nest is a conical mound, seven or eight inches high, hollowed into a cup at the top, and lined rudely with grass. The male was sitting when captured; the female standing on another old nest, not far away, but higher up the face of the rock. There was no evidence of an intention to rebuild the old nest. Both birds, but particularly the male, showed fight when approached, clattering their large bills with an odd noise, and biting viciously when they got a chance. The male is perceptibly the larger bird of the two. The oviduct of the female was distended, and no other egg seemed to be on its way from the ovary, making it probably that she had just laid the single large egg found; but, of course, the evidence is not absolute that *these* two birds had paired, although found so near together.

He also says of the egg:

Egg is single, broadly ovoidal, generally white, marked by a collection of specks about the larger end, somewhat like the adventitious stains on the eggs of *D. exulans*, but, as well as we can judge, less superficial. The shell is compact in structure, rather thin for its size, and superficially smooth to the touch. Under the lens, it is seen to be marked by minute pits and linear depressions, being thus decidedly different, both to the eye and to the touch, from those of *D. exulans*.

Eggs.—An egg of the sooty albatross, obtained by Captain Armuson in the Crozette Islands, has been described by Baird, Brewer, and Ridgway (1884) as follows:

It measured 4.20 inches by 2.60 [106.68 mm. by 66.04 mm.] and resembled generally the egg of *D. exulans*, being chalky white, coarse to the touch, and of squarely truncated form. It was also minutely pitted with reddish dots in an indistinct band at the obtuse end."

Sir Walter Buller (1888) describes the egg as follows:

An egg of this species examined by me is of a narrow elliptical form, measuring 4.2 inches [106.68 mm.] in length by 2.7 [68.59 mm.] in breadth; of a dingy brownish white, splashed, dotted, and marked all over its larger pole with dull blackish brown. Another of the same length, but somewhat narrower, is of a clear greyish white, minutely and indistinctly spotted, and presenting a pretty regular zone of sepia-brown near its larger end.

Young.—Sir Walter Buller (1888) has also described the downy young as follows:

Covered with very long and thick down of a pale sooty color; on the forepart and sides of the head feather-like and several shades darker in tint. A band of feather-like down encircles the eyes, and extends forward to the base of the bill; having very much the appearance of a pair of spectacles. Bill black, legs brownish-grey, claws lighter.

Behavior.—Mr. John Treadwell Nichols writes to me:

The wedge-tailed sooty albatross comes frequently about vessels and does not differ markedly in habits from the yellow-nosed species. Its flight is similar but more graceful. Its wings not held so stiffly, are occasionally moved slightly, a tremor which it would be difficult to call either a flap or an adjustment to the wind. It sometimes sails for long periods and circuitous distances on set wings, even when the wind is but moderate. I have sometimes seen it fly higher than the other southern tubinares commonly do, higher than the masts, passing directly over the ship. In my experience it is rather wary of a baited hook. I have never seen it caught.

Gould (1865) says of the flight of the sooty albatross:

The cuneated form of the tail, which is peculiar to this species, together with its slight and small legs and more delicate structure, clearly indicate that it is the most aerial species of the genus; and accordingly we find that in its actions and mode of flight it differs very considerably from all the other species of albatross, its aerial evolutions being far more easy, its flight much higher, and its stoops more rapid; it is moreover the only species that passes directly over the ship, which it frequently does in blowing weather, often poising itself over the masthead, as if inquisitively viewing the scene below; at this moment it offers so inviting a mark for the gunner, that it often forfeits its life.

The sooty albatross is known by the sailors as the "cape hen" or "blue bird"; it is also called "peearr" or "peeu" from its note. It seem to be universally recognized as distinct from other dark colored albatrosses and all writers agree that it is in a class by itself in appearance and flight.   Dr. Edward A. Wilson (1907) has thus characterized it:

The sooty albatross is perhaps the most striking bird of all in the Southern Oceans, as it is the most sinister in expression and the best adapted by its dusky plumage, and its interested manner, to form the basis of sailors' legends and superstitions.

There is no bird in the south with which it is possible to confuse these birds. The only other abundant large dark bird is *Ossifraga*, which, with its ungainly body and its enormous and pale yellow bill, in no way resembles the dark-billed, close-feathered *Phoebetria*. The latter, moreover, has an easy sailing flight, which is perhaps more perfect than that of any other albatross, and many of us considered it the most fascinating to watch of all the ocean birds on this account.

Since the above was written Messrs. Nichols and Murphy (1914) have published a review of the genus *Phoebetria*, in which they have shown that the American specimen of the sooty albatross belongs to a new subspecies which they have named *Phoebetria palpebrata auduboni*. As the earlier writers, from whom most of the above quotations were taken, did not distinguish the two subspecies of *P. fusca* and the three subspecies of *P. palpebrata*, it is practically impossible to separate the references; it therefore seems best to let the life history stand as first written.

DISTRIBUTION.

Breeding range.—For the subspecies which belongs on the North American List, *Phoebetria palpebrata auduboni*, the breeding range seems to be unknown. Other subspecies of *palpebrata* breed on various islands in the South Atlantic (South Georgia), South Pacific (near New Zealand), and South Indian Oceans (Kerguelen Island).

Range.—Southern portions of the Atlantic, Pacific, and Indian Oceans, Weddell Sea, Australian and New Zealand seas. Ranges of the subspecies of *palpebrata* and of *fusca* are much confused, but the former ranges farther south. The latter is probably the breeding bird about Australia and on Tristan da Cunha.

Casual record.—One taken off the coast of Oregon (Audubon's record).

Egg dates.—South Georgia Island: Six records, October 8 and 10, December and January. Kerguelen Island: Three records, October 1 and December. Cape Horn: Three records, November.

Family HYDROBATIDAE, Fulmars, Shearwaters, and Petrels.

MACRONECTES GIGANTEUS (Gmelin).

GIANT FULMAR.

HABITS.

This great fulmar or overgrown petrel, as large as the smaller albatrosses, is one of the best known birds of southern oceans and antarctic seas, for which the sailors have a variety of names, such as " Nellie," " cape hen," " Mother Carey's goose," " bonebreaker," or " stinker." Almost every writer on antarctic birds has added something to our knowledge of this " vulture of the seas " and almost every southern navigator is more or less familiar with it.

Nesting.—Mr. W. Eagle Clarke (1906) gives an interesting account of his experiences with this bird on its breeding grounds on the South Orkney Islands; he says:

The giant petrel was present at the station all the year around, but was very much less numerous during the winter months. There was a decided falling off in May, but the lowest ebb was reached in June and continued until September, when the summer birds of this species commenced to arrive. During the nesting season it was estimated that about 5,000 were on Laurie I. alone, and when one remembers the savage nature and almost insatiable appetite of these giants, it is easy to realize what a terrible scourge they must have been to the penguins, upon which and their eggs and young it was their one aim to gorge themselves to repletion.

They were to be seen everywhere in the summer time, but their rookeries were confined to the north and east coasts. Three of these rookeries were visited, two of which, namely, those on the Watson Peninsula, contained two hundred nests each, while the third at Cape Geddes comprised only about one hundred. One of the larger colonies was situated on bare rocky ground from 300 to 400 feet above sea level, and the other on a moraine at an elevation of from 250 to 300 feet. The nests consisted of great piles of small angular stones, and were about two feet in diameter. The third and smaller rookery was on a low strip of ground between a cliff and the shore, and was close to the sea; the nests were similar to the others. Although these contained no eggs on November 3d, yet the birds allowed a close approach, one of the parents sitting on the nest, the other usually standing close alongside.

The first eggs were laid on November 4th, but four only were found on that date. On the 19th, however, eighty were obtained, all single specimens, except in two instances where two were found, probably laid by as many females. The birds had to be pushed off the nest ere the eggs could be taken, for very few flew away of their own accord. They showed no fight when evicted, and usually sat down a yard or two away; nor did they shoot oil from their nostrils, but they vomited contents of their stomachs, not as a mode of defense, but to get rid of ballast in order to take wing. They resorted to the same lightening process when chased. Unfortunately, the weather conditions and those of the ice did not permit of these rookeries being again visited, so that the period of incubation could not be ascertained nor the capture of young be effected.

Mr. G. E. Verrill (1895) says that, on Gough Island:

They lay separately, in open land or knolls. The nests are low, and built of grass and moss. Commence laying the middle of September. They lay one egg, which is usually quite rough; but, if robbed, will lay a second and a third time. These birds leave their nests when you approach them, while the other birds do not.

Eggs.—The eggs of the giant fulmar have been described by various writers as ovoid-conical, ovoid, or elliptical in shape. The shell is exceedingly coarse and granulated, rough and glossless, frequently with limy nodules. The color is dull dirty white and often much nest stained, owing to the filthy habits of the birds. Clarke (1906) gives the average length of 80 eggs as 103.8 and the average breadth as 65.7 millimeters.

The measurements of 35 eggs in various collections average 103 by 66.4 millimeters; the eggs showing the four extremes measure 115 by 65, 108.5 by 70, 93.6 by 65, and 102 by 61.4 millimeters.

Young.—Capt. F. W. Hutton (1865) says that:

The young are at first covered with a beautiful long, light-gray down; when fledged they are dark brown, mottled with white. When a person approaches the nest the old bird keeps a short distance away, while the young ones squirt a horridly smelling oil out of their mouths to a distance of six or eight feet.

Mr. Robert Hall (1900) gives us a good description of a colony on Kerguelen Island containing young; he writes:

Having ascended the short eastern summit, I noticed near the bottom of a wind-sheltered slope a fine colony. To commence with, I surprised two just below the crest, and they started running with wings outstretched but not flapping, and continued, with short stoppages, several hundred yards to the beach, keeping just ahead of me. Of the colony, some birds were sitting and others standing, a few with expanded wings, and others essaying jumps on to Azorella clumps 2 feet in height. Several pairs, with stretched necks, appeared to be engaged in controversy, and occasionally a low squeaking noise was uttered. On the first sight of me they moved toward the edge of the cliff; but when I sat down within 100 yards of them they became more confiding, and many gradually approached me, not flying, and without noise. Both young and old seemed to be inquisitive, but a gunshot half a mile away would cause them to look shy for a minute. After a rest, which they often took by sitting down, they would fly over with a prolonged guttural croak. There were from 50 to 70 of them, and by appearances many young birds were already abroad at this date (January 7th). As I drove them to the beach I stumbled upon quite a strange sight; it was their rookery, and some twenty-one grey fledglings, as large as full-grown geese, were nestling among the scattered tussocks of Azorella. The nests were made by tearing away the soft stems of this plant and then sitting upon them.

On approaching a bird, which was always a few yards apart from its fellows, it would utter a low grunt, bite, and stand upon the defensive, ejecting a quantity of oily matter that would ruin almost any suit of clothes. The adults preferred to run along the cliff top rather than fly, and I drove them like any other fowls. They have no confidence in taking wing from the land, but do so at once on reaching the water. This rookery faces the entrance to Royal Sound and is about 200 feet above sea level. The birds possibly lay in September. The nests, some 3 feet in diameter, are merely hollows among the broken stems of Azorella and in the sand, and in the former the young are partially hidden and sheltered. The rookery extended for some 200 yards.

I found several young birds which had just lost their grey down and had assumed a shining black plumage, a phase on which I know of no observations. I do not see why this coat should be exchanged later on for what is a very poor one in comparison. I also saw this black phase 800 miles east of Kerguelen, on the return to home (February 22d). Near Accessible Bay, on February 8th, I observed many young birds nearly ready to fly. In their stomachs I found the tongues of prions and penguins.

Plumages.—The plumage changes of the giant petrel are not very well understood, but evidently the first plumage assumed by young birds is the shining black plumage referred to above. Mr. Clarke (1906) noted that:

The color of the birds ranged from very dark brown through all shades of chocolate, and from gray through light gray and mottled white to white. Some of these facts indicate interbreeding between the two forms and, perhaps, between their offspring and typically colored birds of others. Dr. Pirie thinks that they interbreed, because he has no recollection of seeing two white birds together on the nesting grounds.

He also stated that: " The proportion of birds in pure white plumage in the rookeries was not more, perhaps less, than 2 per cent." Some writers seem to think that the dark colored birds are the young birds and that, as they grow older, they become lighter gray, then mottled with white, and finally pure white. Others suggest that there may be two color phases and that the mottled birds are the results of interbreeding. There is not much positive evidence in support of either of these theories, and very little is known about any definite sequence of molts to produce the various plumages.

Food.—The giant fulmar has been well named the " vulture of the sea," as the following accounts of its gluttonous habits will show. Dr. E. A. Wilson (1907), the antarctic explorer, writes:

Ossifraga feeds mainly upon carrion, though its character is not above suspicion in the matter of attacking living animals. In one case, at any rate, the evidence of its having attacked man in the water is hardly open to doubt; I quote Mr. Howard Saunders, who writes: " Mr. Arthur G. Guillemard states that a sailor who was picked up had his arms badly lacerated in defending his head from the attacks of an ' albatross,' which may well have been this giant petrel."

We constantly saw it feeding upon seals' blubber, dead penguins, and any other animal refuse that happened to lie in its way; and although we ourselves never saw any living animal attacked; and although Mr. Eagle Clarke (1906) mentions " abundant remains of recently killed young penguins " in their rookeries in the South Orkneys, he says nothing in this case to prevent one from believing that the birds merely picked up the remains of what the skuas had killed, or of birds that had succumbed to climatic causes.

The habit that this bird has, in common with most of the petrels, of disgorging semidigested food when disturbed or annoyed is very commonly seen in putting it to flight after feeding. It is interesting to notice how small an amount of such ballast removed by vomiting seems to turn the scale, for it is quite insignificant when compared with what the stomach actually contains; yet the bird seems so utterly unable to run or to rise from the ice until relieved, that, no matter how closely it is pressed, it will come to a dead stop in order to disencumber itself by a number of voluntary efforts before making a serious effort to rise.

The giant petrel lives on any carrion that it is able to discover, and it can never be at a loss during the Antarctic summer for a plentiful supply of dead seals and penguins. I know not whether in the Macquarie and Auckland Islands and elsewhere it is also mainly a carrion feeder, but I can answer for this in the Antarctic. One has but to kill a seal on the shore in summer and visit the blubber refuse day by day to realize how quickly such food attracts the birds who are looking for it. None but the carrion feeders come to it; one sees no albatross, no snow, antarctic, or wilson's petrel, though all must often scent it; but the giant petrel and the skuas come in constantly increasing numbers.

Dr. J. H. Kidder (1875) draws a realistic, though not an attractive, picture of these gluttonous birds in the following words:

I found the adult birds in considerable numbers feeding on the carcass of the sea elephant, December 14. With their huge whitish beaks, lighter-colored heads (then covered with clotted blood), and disordered dun plumage, they reminded me strongly of vultures. Like vultures, also, they had so crammed themselves that they were unable to rise from the ground, although it was sufficiently rocky and irregular for them to do so with ease under ordinary circumstances. They waddled and stumbled to the sea, swam away, and did not rise into the air until half an hour or more of digestion, and perhaps of vomiting, had made it possible. I shot two on this occasion; but one succeeded in getting into the water with a broken wing. The individual secured vomited copiously, as soon as wounded, an immense mass of undigested blood, fat, and intestines.

Buller (1888) says of a captive bird:

Its capacity for swallowing was surprising, and it gorged its crop with fresh meat until it could hold no more; then it stretched its neck on the ground and worked it violently in its efforts to accommodate another piece. Curiously enough, it would not touch fish of any kind. Although, by way of experiment, starved for several days, it still obstinately declined the fish offered it. When, however, its mate died and had been skinned, the survivor regaled itself freely on the carcass till it became decomposed.

Behavior.—Buller (1888) gives the best account of the flight of this fulmar, which I quote in full:

Their power of wing is something marvelous. For hours together they keep up their rapid sailing movement without ever resting or descending to the water for a moment. It is very interesting to watch them in this tireless flight and to observe how completely they have their wings under control. They approach the steamer at a swift rate with a slow flapping movement of the wings, and then make a wide circuit, keeping them perfectly rigid, but shifting the balance of the body in such a way as to make alternately one wing and then the other incline upwards or downwards, thus altering the plane without the slightest visible alular movement. The manner in which the bird steers itself through the air, first ascending far above the masthead, then sweeping downwards, with the point of the wing at its lowest inclination just skimming but never actually touching the water, even in a turbulent and broken sea, is really wonderful, and would seem to indicate very perfect organs of vision as a means of measuring distance. Now and then it alters its mode of flight and sails or glides over the surface of the sea with its wings formed into a bow shape, and with an occasional flap to give it fresh impetus.

Like the albatross, it descends into the water in a very ungainly, straddling way, and, if in a hurry, with an awkward splash; keeps its wings uplifted till the body is steady, then deliberately folds them up and settles down to dinner or floats lazily on the surface, with upstretched neck and eyes ever on the alert. When garbage or food of any kind is thrown overboard, they all descend together and congregate around it, uttering low guttural notes as if disputing for its possession; but they never seem to quarrel or fight over it, and when disposed of they generally break up into pairs and float about in friendly company till, actuated by some common impulse, they mount again in the air and come sweeping up astern. On the wing the tail is usually spread and has a broad cuneiform appearance.

It is capable, too, of very rapid movements. On one occasion I was attentively watching six or seven of them, sailing about in circuits that ever crossed but never clashed, and had turned to my notebook for a few seconds to refer to something. On looking up again they had all disappeared as if by magic; and then I descried them in the water more than a mile astern, with their heads together, discussing some object that had been thrown overboard and had excited their notice. They are untiring, too, in their pursuit, for I have noticed that at sundown, when the albatrosses have drawn off from the steamer and disappeared one by one, the giant petrel (or "stink-pot," as the sailors sometimes call it) had remained, still crossing and recrossing the wake of the ship in undiminished numbers and unaffected by the deepening gloom.

As might be expected of such big, strong, ravenous birds, the giant fulmars are arrant bullies and are justly dreaded by the other sea birds among which they live. They undoubtedly work great havoc among the young penguins and other sea birds which nest on or near their breeding grounds. Clarke (1906) writes:

The heavy toll ruthlessly demanded from the penguins was very manifest on visiting their rookeries. Here abundant remains of recently killed young penguins in the shape of clean-picked skins and bones were lying all around, while the gorged feathered giants were either waddling about or sleeping off the effects of their orgies on the neighboring snow-slopes.

Again he (1905) says:

The giant petrel breeds at Gough Island, where Mr. Comer says that it is not numerous, and commences to lay at the middle of September. He tells us that it enters the penguin "rookeries" and carries off the young to eat and also pulls birds (petrels) out of holes in the ground.

Buller (1888) "observed at a distance one of these giant petrels pursue and capture a small bird (apparently *Prion turtur*), and then, holding it by the wing, batter it against the water till it was killed." Darwin (1889) says that:

It was observed by some of the officers at Port St. Antonio chasing a diver, which tried to escape by diving and flying, but was continually struck down and at last killed by a blow on its head. At Port St. Julian these great petrels were seen killing and devouring young gulls.

Winter.—Mr. W. Eagle Clarke (1907) says:

That at the close of the southern summer numbers of giant petrels (*Ossifraga gigantea*) cross the Antarctic Circle and sojourn among the polar ice ere they retreat northwards to pass the winter in more genial oceanic resorts. It is possible, however, that some of these visitors to the far south are non-breeding birds, and, if so, they may have spent the entire summer there. The *Tubinares* are, as is well known, great wanderers, but these very remarkable southern incursions are, perhaps, to be explained by the extraordinary abundance of food to be found in the waters of the far south in the summer and autumn, which allures some of the birds farther and farther toward the pole, until the ice barrier which almost girdles the Antarctic Continent, arrests further progress, since at its base the food supply entirely ceases.

DISTRIBUTION.

Breeding range.—South Atlantic Ocean (South Orkney, South Shetland, South Georgia, Falkland, and Gough Islands) ; South Pacific Ocean (Macquarie, Campbell, Graham, Antipodes, Chatham, and Snares Islands) ; South Indian Ocean (Kerguelen and Crozet Islands) ; and on the Antarctic continent.

Range.—Southern portions of Atlantic, Pacific and Indian Oceans. North in the Atlantic Ocean to 31° South; and probably farther north in the Pacific. South to the Antarctic continent or the edge of the Antarctic ice, at least as far south as 78°.

Casual record.—Once taken off the coast of Oregon (Audubon's record).

Egg dates.—South Georgia Island: Thirteen records, December 1 to January 13; seven records, December. Falkland Islands: Two records, October 19 and November 8.

FULMARUS GLACIALIS GLACIALIS (Linnaeus).

FULMAR.

HABITS.

The fulmar is a distinctly pelagic species of arctic seas, where it is ever associated with drifting icebergs and floating pack ice. Like the albatross it spends much of its time on the wing and is particularly active in rough and stormy weather. It is the constant companion of the arctic whalers and is well known to the hardy explorers who risk their lives in dangerous northern seas, where it follows the ships to gorge itself on what scraps it can pick up, rests to digest its unsavory food on some rugged block of ice and retires to some lonely crag to rear its young. There is little that is attractive in its surroundings at any time, in the forbidding climate of the rugged, frozen north, but there it seems to live and flourish, rising successful and triumphant over adverse conditions.

Spring.—On the north coast of Labrador late in the spring, and even early in the summer, fulmars are often seen and are sometimes quite abundant from the Straits of Belle Isle northward to Cape Chidley. Mr. Lucien M. Turner, in his unpublished notes, writes:

When the fog lifted great streams of this species could be seen moving either southward or northward. Huge icebergs had their tops fairly alive with these birds, riding slowly to the southward, to which direction they advanced until far enough, and then returning to repeat the trip if opportunity occurred.

These were probably migrating birds, for no breeding grounds have yet been discovered on the Labrador coast, and Turner found them very scarce after entering Hudson Straits. Audubon (1840) mentions a migratory flight on the coast of Greenland, quoting the remarks of Captain Sabine, as follows:

Whilst the ships were detained by the ice in Jacobs Bay, in latitude 71° from the 24th of June to the 3d of July, fulmars were passing in a continued stream to the northward, in numbers inferior only to the flight of the passenger pigeon in America.

Nesting.—Probably the southernmost breeding colonies on the western side of the Atlantic are those mentioned by Kumlien (1879), as follows:

I also procured a few that were ashy; these I presumed were young birds; but in July, 1878, I found a few of these dark colored ones, darker than any I ever saw in fall, breeding near Quickstep Harbor, in Cumberland, on some small, rocky islands. When fresh these dark-colored birds have a bright olive-green gloss, especially apparent on the neck and back. The bill is shorter, stouter, and thicker, dusky brown instead of yellow. On Blue Mountain, Ovifak, Greenland, these birds breed by myriads to the very summit of the mountain, about 2,000 feet. Here I could see but few dark birds; even the full-fledged nestlings were white.

In Exeter Sound and to the northward along the west shores of Davis Straits and Baffin's Bay, the dark variety seems to predominate. Near Cape Searle they are extraordinarily abundant, breeding by thousands on the Padlie Island, and they are so tame about their nesting places that they can be killed with a stick. The eggs, even after being blown, for many months still retain the musky odor peculiar to the birds. Perfectly fresh eggs are quite good eating but if a couple of days old the musky odor has so permeated them, even the albumen, that they are a little too much for a civilized palate.

Nelson (1883) writes that:

It breeds abundantly on Bear Island (near Spitzbergen) on some of the sloping cliffs not difficult of access. One case is mentioned where on May 26, 1876, the eggs were seen deposited directly upon the bare ice which covered the rocks at the time. In one place a bird was found frozen fast by one leg as it sat upon the eggs, in August, 1596, as recorded by one of the old Dutch expeditions which touched that coast. On the northern half of Nova Zemla,

Barents found some fulmars nesting upon a piece of ice covered with a little earth. In both of these cases the underpart of the egg during hatching could not be warmed above the freezing point.

Macgillivray (1852) gives a very good account of the breeding habits of this species at St. Kilda, quoting from the notes of his son, who visited the locality in 1840; he writes:

St. Kilda has long been noted as the only breeding place in Britain of the fulmar petrel, *Procellaria glacialis* (An Fulmar, or Fulimar). This bird exists there in almost incredible numbers, and to the natives it is by far the most important of the productions of the island. It forms one of the principal means of support to the inhabitants, who daily risk their lives in its pursuit. The fulmar breeds on the face of the highest precipices, and only on such as are furnished with small grassy shelves, every spot on which above a few inches in extent is occupied with one or more of its nests. The nest is formed of herbage, seldom bulky, generally a mere shallow excavation in the turf, lined with dried grass and withered tufts of the sea pink, in which the bird deposits a single egg of a pure white color when clean, which is seldom the case, and varying in size from 2 inches 7 lines to 3 inches 1 line in length, and 1 inch 11 lines to 2 inches in breadth. On the 30th of June, having partially descended a nearly perpendicular precipice 600 feet in height, the whole face of which was covered with the nests of the fulmar, I enjoyed an opportunity of observ ing the habits of this bird, which has fallen to the lot of few of those who have described them, as if from personal observation. The nests had all been robbed about a month before by the natives, who esteem the eggs of this species above all others; those of the auk, guillemot, kittiwake, and puffin ranking next, and the gannet, scart, and cormorant last of all. Many of the nests contained each a young bird a day or two old at furthest, thickly covered with long white down. Such of the eggs as I examined *in situ* had a small aperture at the broad end, at which the bill of the chick was visible, sometimes protruding a little way. Several addled eggs also occurred. The young birds were very clamorous on being handled and vomited a quantity of clear oil, with which I sometimes observed the parent birds feeding them by disgorging it. The fulmar is stated in most works on ornithology to possess the power of ejecting oil with much force through its tubular nostrils, using this as a mode of defense, but, although I surprised several upon the nest, I never observed them attempt this. On being seized they instantly vomit a quantity of clear amber-colored oil, which imparts to the whole bird, its nest and young, and even the very rock which it frequents, a peculiar and very disagreeable odor.

A slightly different account of this breeding place is given by Baird, Brewer, and Ridgway (1884), based on the observations of Captain Elmes (written Elwes by Godman), as follows:

Soon after landing he started with some of the best cragsmen for the cliffs at the north side of the island. On reaching the summit of Conachan, the highest point, he came suddenly on a precipice not less than 1,220 feet in height. The whole of this immense face of rock was so crowded with birds that the water was seen far below as if through a heavy snow storm, and the birds, which were flying in front of the cliff, almost obscured the view. All the ledges near the top were covered with short turf, full of holes, in which the fulmars were sitting on their eggs, with their heads and part of their bodies exposed outside. In some cases they were quite concealed, but generally the soil was too thin for them to make more than a slight excavation. Thousands of fulmars were flying backward and forward with a quiet, owl-like flight, and, although the air was full of them, hardly one ever came over the top of the cliff.

Eggs.—The fulmar lays but one egg, which is elliptical ovate or elliptical oval in shape. The shell is rather rough or granulated and quite lustreless. The color is dull, dirty white, usually immaculate, but often much nest-stained and sometimes partially or wholly covered with very fine dots or sprinklings of reddish brown. These dots look more like particles of soil or dirt lodged in the pitted surface than actual color markings. The surface of the egg is often more or less covered with little nodules or small excrescences, but in many cases it is quite smooth.

The measurements of 77 eggs, in various collections, average 74 by 51 millimeters; the eggs showing the four extremes measure **81.5** by 50.5, 72.5 by **54.1**, **69** by 49.1, and 74.1 by **43.2** millimeters.

Young.—The period of incubation, which is performed by both sexes, is said to be from 50 to 60 days. The young fulmar is carefully guarded by its parents and is fed on regurgitated food, consisting of an amber-colored, oily fluid. The young bird is at first covered with a thick coat of long, soft, white down, which is worn until the bird is nearly fully grown. The first plumage, which is fully acquired before the young bird leaves the nest, is similar to that of the adult, in the white phase at least.

Plumages.—Morris (1903) describes the immature plumage, presumably of the dark phase, as follows:

The young in the second year have the tip of the bill yellowish, the remainder greyish; iris, pale dusky; there is a dark spot before it. Head, crown, neck, and nape, greyish brown, the edges of the feather paler; chin, throat, and breast, pale greyish brown, the edges of the feathers lighter coloured; back, darker greyish brown, the edges of the feathers paler. Primaries, secondaries, and tertiaries, greyish brown. Tail, greyish brown, the edges of the feathers paler. Legs and toes, pale brownish or greyish yellow; webs, pale brown.

Mr. W. Eagle Clarke gives some interesting notes (1912) on the juvenile plumage of *Fulmarus g. glacialis* from specimens obtained at St. Kilda. He states that the upper parts of the juvenile are of a decidedly paler gray than in the adult and more uniform in tint, while the head, neck and underparts of the juvenile are pure white and silky in appearance, whereas in the adult these parts have a yellowish hue. Mr. Clarke also mentions that in the adults some feathers of the mantle and scapulars are edged with ashy brown, as also are some of the wing coverts on their outer webs. A full description of the coloration of the bill and a few remarks on the pale and dark forms are added.

Food.—Much has been written about the feeding habits of the fulmar, which are interesting though not attractive. The following quotations will show that it is a greedy and voracious feeder on a varied diet. The best account seems to have been given by Macgillivray (1852) as follows:

From the various statements made by observers, it appears that the fulmar feeds on fishes, cephalopodous mollusca, cirripedia, most other kinds of animal substance, especially such as are oily or fatty. The Rev. Mr. Scoresby, in his "Arctic Regions," states that it is the constant companion of the whalefisher, joining his ship immediately on passing the Shetland Islands, and accompanying him to the highest accessible latitudes, keeping an eager watch for anything thrown overboard. Fulmars are extremely greedy of the fat of the whale. Though few should be seen when a whale is about being captured, yet, as soon as the fleshing process commences, they rush in from all quarters and frequently accumulate to many thousands in number. They then occupy the greasy track of the ship; and, being audaciously greedy, fearlessly advance within a few yards of the men employed in cutting up the whale. If, indeed, the fragments of fat do not float sufficiently away, they approach so near the scene of operations that they are knocked down with boat hooks in great numbers, and sometimes taken up by the hand. The sea immediately about the ship's stern is sometimes so completely covered with them that a stone can scarcely be thrown overboard without striking one of them. When anything is thus cast among them those nearest the spot where it falls take the alarm, and these exciting some fear in others more remote sometimes put a thousand of them in motion; but, as in rising into the air, they assist their wings for the first few yards by striking the water with their feet, there is produced by such a number of them a loud and most singular splashing. It is highly amusing to observe the voracity with which they seize the pieces of fat that fall in their way; the size and quantity of the pieces they take at a meal; the curious chuckling noise which, in their anxiety for dispatch, they always make; and the jealousy with which they view and the boldness with which they attack any of their species that are engaged in devouring the finest morsels. They frequently glut themselves so completely that they are unable to fly; in which case, when they are not relieved by a quantity being disgorged, they endeavor to get on the nearest piece of ice, where they rest until the advancement of digestion restores their wonted powers. Then, if opportunity admit, they return with the same gust to the banquet as before; and though numbers of the species may be killed, and allowed to float about among them, they appear unconscious of danger to themselves. When carrion is scarce the fulmars follow the living whale, and sometimes by their peculiar motions, when hovering at the surface of the water, point out to the fisher the position of the animal of which he is in pursuit. They can not make much impression on the dead whale until some more powerful animal tears away the skin; the epidermis and rete mucosum they entirely remove, but true skin is too tough for them to make way through it.

Captain Collins (1899), writing of its habits on the Newfoundland Banks, says:

The fulmar subsists chiefly on small fishes, and, doubtless, participates with the hagdon in the pursuit of the squid; but I have no recollection of noticing in its stomach, as I have in that of the hag, the presence of pieces of squid or the beaks of that animal. I have, however, frequently observed that the contents of the stomachs of many of this species consisted almost entirely of small fish. Like *Puffinus*, it is very fond of oily food, which it swallows with

astonishing greediness. It devours large quantities of codfish liver in a ravenous manner that would astound one unacquainted with its habits, and it certainly would tax their credulity to believe statements that might be made
bearing on this subject.

Behavior.—The flight of the fulmar is a much more graceful performance than one would expect from such a short, heavily built
bird and it is a pleasure to watch this miniature albatross, which
to my mind it closely resembles, as it circles about in the wake of
the ship, quartering the ground in search of what morsels it may
pick up, with frequent periods of rapid wing beats alternating with
longer periods of sailing on stiff pinions. Macgillivray (1852) says:

The fulmar flies with great buoyancy and considerable rapidity, and when
at sea is generally seen skimming along the surface of the wave at a slight
elevation, though I never observed one to alight or pick up anything from the
water. At its breeding places, the fulmar is always in motion, comparatively
few being to be seen upon the rocks, the great mass being engaged flying in
circles along the face of the precipice, and always in the same direction, none
crossing, probably on account of the confusion this would cause among such
an immense multitude.

Mr. John Treadwell Nichols writes to me, regarding the appearance of this species in flight as follows:

On the wing the fulmar is a stocky appearing bird, its dark-primaried, gull-
like plumage, relieved by an obscure pale spot back of the tip of the wing,
suggesting the better marked, diagnostic, pale area in the wing of *Priocella*.
They flap their wings a great deal, interspersing frequent short sails, and their
flight has the stiff character usually characteristic of the *Tubinares*, as op-
posed to the buoyant flight of the *Longipennes*.

The fulmar is usually a silent bird, but, when feeding, Morris
(1903) says:

The noise that a large flock make is described as almost deafening, something
between the cackle of a hen and the quack of a duck.

Captain Collins (1899) refers to its note as " a sort of chuckling
sound somewhat resembling a low grunt."

The St. Kildians consider the fulmars of great importance in the
economy of their lives, for both old and young birds, as well as the
eggs, are largely used for food. They regularly risk their lives
in going over the cliffs on long ropes and are quite expert in catching the old birds and gathering the eggs and young. Macgillivray
(1852) gives a good account of their methods and says:

Fulmar oil is among the most valuable productions of St. Kilda, and is
procured of two kinds by different processes. The best is obtained from the
old bird by surprising it at night upon the rock, and tightly closing the bill
until the fowler has secured the bird between his knees, with its head downwards. By opening the bill the fulmar is allowed to disgorge about a table-
spoonful, or rather more, of oil into the dried gullet and stomach of a solan
goose, used as a reservoir for that purpose. These, when filled, are secured

with a string, and hung on cords across the interior of the huts until required for use. The oil thus procured and preserved, besides supplying their lamps, is used by the inhabitants as a medicine, being sometimes of considerable efficacy in chronic rheumatism, and acting as a cathartic; while, from its nauseous taste and smell, it would doubtless prove an effectual emetic also to any but a St. Kildian. In the beginning of August the natives descend the rocks for the young fulmars, which are then nearly fledged; and by boiling with water, in proper vessels, are made to furnish a large quantity of fat, which is skimmed off, and preserved in casks in the solid form.

Winter.—The principal winter resorts of the fulmar on the American side of the Atlantic Ocean are in the vicinity of the Grand Bank, off Newfoundland, and Georges Bank, off Massachusetts, where it is usually common and often abundant. It is known to the cod fishermen on the banks as the "noddy," "marbleheader," "oil bird," or "stinker." Captain Collins (1899) says:

The fulmars are probably more abundant on the Grand Bank than on any other of the fishing grounds commonly resorted to by American vessels, with the exception, perhaps, of the halibut grounds in Davis Straits, or the Flemish Cap to the eastward of Grand Bank, which are not visited by many fishing schooners.

The marbleheader is quite as greedy as the hagdon, and quite as bold when in pursuit of food; but, unlike the latter, which is always quarrelsome and noisy, the fulmar confines itself to a sort of chuckling sound, somewhat resembling a low grunt. It will swallow a piece of cod liver with even as great voracity as the hag, but it rarely, if ever, seems to exercise the cunning or caution of the latter in trying to avoid the hook, and, as a consequence, it is more easily captured. It is caught in the same manner as the hag, but owing to its comparatively small numbers on the fishing grounds, the fishermen do not depend upon it so much as a source of bait supply as upon *Puffinus major*, since one would be likely to catch twenty, or perhaps many more, of the latter to one noddy.

DISTRIBUTION.

Breeding range.—North Atlantic and Arctic regions. East to Spitzbergen and Franz Josef Land. South to the British Isles, where its range is extending to the mainland of Scotland (Sutherland and Caithness) and Ireland (Mayo and Ulster); Iceland; southern Greenland (69° north); and eastern Baffin Land (Cumberland Sound). West to Melville Island. North to Northern Greenland (about 76° North on the west coast and about 81° north on the east coast). Ranges north in summer to 85°.

Winter range.—North Atlantic Ocean. South on the American side to the fishing banks off Massachusetts regularly and farther south occasionally. South in the Atlantic Ocean at least to 43° north. North to the limit of open water.

Spring migration.—Early dates of arrival: Davis Straits, April 19; northeastern Greenland, 79° north, middle of April; Jones Sound, May 1; Wellington Channel, May 23; Spitzbergen, April 7; Franz

Josef Land, April 24. Leaves Georges Bank, Massachusetts, about middle of March.

Fall migration.—Early dates of arrival: Labrador, Cape Harrison, July 19, and Ragged Islands, August 9. Late dates of departure: Wellington Channel, September 2; Hudson Straits, September 15; Cumberland Sound, middle of October; Franz Josef Land, October 28; Spitzbergen, October 6. Arrives on Georges Bank, Massachusetts, in October or earlier.

Casual records.—Massachusetts (Chatham, September 23, 1912). Connecticut (Stony Creek, October 10, 1907). New Jersey (Ridgewood, December, 1891). Accidental in Madeira.

Egg dates..—St. Kilda Island: Twenty-eight records, May 6 to June 15; fourteen records, May 22 to June 5. Iceland: Nine records, May 14 to July 1; five records, May 30 to June 15. Greenland: One record, July 2.

FULMARUS GLACIALIS GLUPISCHA Stejneger.

PACIFIC FULMAR.

HABITS.

The relationships of the three fulmars found in the northern parts of the Atlantic and Pacific Oceans are none too well understood, and I very much doubt if their relationships are correctly designated in our present classification of the three forms.

The Pacific fulmar, with its light and its dark phases, is now regarded as a subspecies of the Atlantic fulmar, with its two similar phases, and the Rodgers fulmar, with no dark phase, is recognized as a distinct species. For reasons which I have briefly stated, under that species, I doubt if the Rodgers fulmar will eventually prove to be even subspecifically distinct from the Pacific fulmar, as the characters on which the former species is based can be accounted for by age, seasonal or individual variations. This fact is beautifully illustrated in the magnificent series of fulmars which Mr. Loomis has ,accumulated in the collection of the California Academy of Sciences.

The Pacific fulmar may be correctly regarded as a subspecies of the Atlantic bird, although one of the principal characters which separates the two birds, the color of the bill, is very variable. Although I have never seen the theory advanced, there are several good reasons for regarding the dusky birds, of both oceans, as a distinct species, rather than regarding them as dark phases. The color-phase theory has always been a convenient method for disposing of a problem which we could not otherwise solve, but I believe that it should be used only when definitely proven. In this case we have some good evidence to the contrary. Stejneger (1885) suggests that:

There seems to be a decided difference in the geographical range of the two phases in both oceans. It appears that the dark phase in both instances is a particularly western bird, while the light-colored ones seem to have a more eastern distribution.

If the dark form had occurred breeding in Iceland, where Faber found the white one exceedingly numerous, he could scarcely have escaped mentioning it. Nor does it seem to have been found in Saint Kilda by John Macgillivray, and the form at present breeding on the Faer Islands seems also to be the unmixed light phase. In the Pacific a similar distribution obtains, the dark form being comparatively scarce on the American side, while it is by far the predominating form on the Asiatic shore, at least as far south as Kamtschatka.

The dark phase has not been recorded from any of the breeding places in Bering Sea, which is the basis for the belief that the so-called Rodgers fulmar has no dark phase. If the dusky birds represent only a dark phase, it seems strange that they should have such a different breeding range, which is not usually the case in well-known color phases in other species. Furthermore, where the breeding ranges of the two phases overlap, they do not intermingle and have never been seen mated together. Stejneger (1885) says:

The dark phase was found by me on the Commander Islands in countless numbers. In the colonies breeding on Bering Island not a single light bird was to be seen, and the same was the case at the rookeries on the northern part of Copper Island—for example, that close to the village. At Glinka, near the southern extremity of the latter island, were found a few small white colonies, but the percentage of the light-colored birds was quite trifling, as I estimated it to be between 1 and 5 per cent.

In the light of what evidence we have, it seems to me more logical to recognize a light and a dark species, each perhaps with Atlantic and Pacific subspecies, and to eliminate *rodgersi* as not separable from the light bird of the Pacific Ocean.

Nesting.—Very little has been published about the breeding habits of the Pacific fulmar. It is supposed to breed on some of the western Aleutian Islands, but although we cruised as far west as Attu Island we did not even see any of the birds. We were unable to visit Semichi Island where it is said to breed. Stejneger (1885) found it breeding abundantly in the Commander Islands and has given us the following account of it:

The fulmar is the first one of the nonresident water birds to arrive at the rookeries in early spring, usually in March, the order of arrival being *Fulmarus*, *Uria arra*, *Lunda cirrhata*, *Fratercula corniculata*. One specimen of the white form was obtained on Bering Island, February 7, which would indicate that the advance guard had already reached the islands by that time, or else, what I am rather inclined to believe, that many of the birds pass the winter on the open ocean not so very far from the shores they inhabit in summer.

The " glupisch " is one of the commonest summer visitors to the islands, and breeds in enormous numbers in suitable places, that is to say, in high and steep rocky bluffs and promontories boldly rising out of the sea 300 to 800 feet high, and I have spent hours under their rookeries listening to their whinnying voice and watching their high and elegant flight in sailing out and in and around the cracked rocks like bees at an immense beehive. I have mentioned above that nearly all the birds belonged to the dark phase, and that only a very small percentage of white birds breed, apart from the dark ones, on Copper Island.

Eggs.—I can not find anything distinctive in the eggs of this subspecies, which are in every particular indistinguishable from those of the Atlantic fulmar.

The measurements of 19 eggs, in various collections, average 72.7 by 50 millimeters; the eggs showing the four extremes measure **77.5** by 49.5, 72 by **52, 68** by 51.5, and 77.5 by **48** millimeters.

Plumages.—I have never seen the downy young of this fulmar and can not find any description of it in print, but probably it is similar to that of the Atlantic subspecies. The sequence of plumages to maturity and the seasonal molts are also probably the same.

Food.—Mr. A. W. Anthony (1895) gives a very good account of the feeding habits of the fulmars on the California coast, which I quote as follows:

Although mention has been made of their following fishing sloops, fish form a very small part of their diet while on this coast. In fact, it is the exception, I have never found small fish in the stomachs of those I have taken, nor have I seen them catch fish for themselves, though I have no doubt regarding their ability to do so should they fall in with a school of small herring or anchovies, and from their associating with the flocks of shearwaters I infer that they derive a part of their food from such schools of small fry when they are common. There is, however, a large jelly fish (*Medusa?*) that is usually abundant along this coast during the time of the fulmars' sojourn, and these are never disregarded by the ever hungry birds. I have often seen a fulmar sitting on the water by the side of a jelly fish, part of which it had eaten, so filled that it would scarcely move out of the way of the boat. Specimens shot while these *Medusae* are common I have always found with the stomach filled with these alone, and half a pint of the slimy mass will often run from their mouths when lifted from the water by their feet.

I think the fulmars enjoy a monopoly of this diet, for I have never seen other species eating it, nor will gulls, nor any of the sea birds that I have observed, pay any attention to a fulmar that is eating a jelly fish though they all claim their share if the food is of a kind that they care for.

The abundance of the fulmars off this coast would seem to have some relation to the abundance of the *Medusae*, since the winter of 1893–94 was noted for the almost if not entire absence of fulmars as well as jelly fish until some time in late February or March, when both jelly fish and fulmars appeared in small numbers.

I have occasionally seen fulmars busily engaged in picking small crustacea (?) from the kelp, but as a rule they prefer to obtain their food in open water where they are much oftener seen than along the immense beds of kelp (*Macrocystis pyrifera*) and "bull kelp" (*Nerecystis lutkena*) that fringe the shores for miles along the southern coast. These kelp beds, however, acting as barriers to drifting *Medusae*, often entangle a quantity of them, and for the time being fulmars are common near shore. They will also follow the shearwaters which at times drive schools of small fish into the kelp beds. In diving for fish in competition with shearwaters they are badly handicapped; their plumage being much less compact makes it not only more difficult for them to get under the water but they can not dive so far nor swim so fast below the surface as can the shearwaters.

Mr. C. B. Linton (1908*a*) publishes the following short note on the subject:

During February, 1908, I observed several Pacific fulmars (*Fulmarus glacialis glupischa*), both light and dark phases, about the pleasure wharf at Long Beach, California. These birds were exceedingly tame, swimming about within a few inches of the numerous fish lines and often making a dash for the baited hooks as the fishermen cast them. Upon tossing a handful of fish scraps overboard I was surprised to see the fulmars dive for the sinking pieces, sometimes going two or three feet under water and bouncing almost clear of the suface upon returning. They were also somewhat quarrelsome, fighting fiercely over a fish, uttering a harsh rasping note the while.

Behavior.—What has been said about the flight and behavior of other fulmars would apply equally well to this subspecies. Cassin (1858), in quoting from Doctor Pickering's journal, says:

In alighting in the water, these birds take the same care in folding and adjusting their wings, without wetting them, as the albatrosses. One was observed to seize a *Thalassidroma* violently, and to hold it under water as if for the purpose of drowning it, but whether the attempt succeeded or not was not noticed. On the other hand, the small petrels do not appear to be afraid of this species.

Mr. Anthony (1895) adds the following notes on the habits of this fulmar off the California coast in winter:

There are often large schools of small fish on the surface, which attract large numbers of sea birds, including the fulmars, and it is along this bank that fulmars are to be found if anywhere near shore. They are hardly what one would call gregarious, although several are often seen in company flying along in a loose, straggling flock. More often they are seen in flocks of *Puffinus gavia*, one or two in a flock of 50 shearwaters.

Unlike the shearwaters, however, they seldom pass a craft without turning aside to at least make a circuit about it before flying on. If the vessel is a fishing sloop sounding on the banks the chances are in favor of the shearwaters being forgotten and allowed to disappear in the distance while the fulmar settles lightly down on the water within a few yards of the fisherman. The next fulmar that passes will, after having made the regulation circuit, join the first until within a few minutes a flock of six or eight of these most graceful and handsome petrels have collected, dancing about on the waves as light and buoyant as corks. As the lines are hauled up after a successful sound, the long string of often twenty to thirty golden-red fish are seen through the limpid water while still several fathoms in depth, and great excitement prevails. Any fulmars that have grown uneasy and have started out on the periodical circuit of the craft immediately alight a few yards to the windward. Those that are on the water and have drifted away hasten to the spot with wings outspread and feet pattering along on the water.

It is more than likely that in hauling up the net one or more fish become detached from the hooks; such fish, if loosened after having been raised twenty fathoms, are sure to rise to the surface a few feet to the windward of the boat. The pressure of the water being suddenly removed, the internal pressure becomes so great that the fish is greatly distended and rises helpless to the surface.

With a hoarse croak and wings outspread the nearest fulmar pounces upon the unfortunate cod, keeping all others at bay with threatening beak. A few hasty snaps at the eyes or air bladder protruding from the mouth convinces him that codfish are tough, and the first floater, if a large one, is abandoned for the moment, for the second, should there be more than one, or for a snap at the bait on the hooks.

Their excitement by this time has attracted the attention of several Western and American herring gulls, which hover screaming over the sloop, too shy to attempt to touch the fish while it is so near. Another ocean wanderer meantime has arrived; a short-tailed albatross, sweeping along, has noticed the commotion among his lesser brethren, and with a groaning note settles down by the floating fish, keeping all trespassers away by a loud clattering of mandibles; though not infrequently a fulmar will dispute possession for some time with an albatross before leaving a fish he has torn open, and I think a fulmar will usually rout a Western gull entirely.

In attacking a fish under the above conditions the eyes and air bladder are first eaten, after which the abdomen is torn open, if possible, and the entire contents of the skin torn out piecemeal. I have, however, seen birds seated on the water by the side of fish from which they had eaten the eyes, but were unable to tear open the tough skin.

The bait on fish hooks left hanging over the sides of the boat is often taken within a few feet of the fisherman, and birds are not infrequently hooked, much to the disgust of both the fisherman and the bird. Their confidence in mankind is at all times very great. I have several times seen them killed by Portuguese fishermen who had but to drop a small piece of fish overboard and hit the bird with a club when it swam up to get it.

DISTRIBUTION.

Breeding range.—Coasts and islands of northeastern Asia. From the Kurile and Commander Islands northward along the Kamchatka coast to East Cape, Siberia. The breeding range of *rodgersi* might be added to this, as the two are probably the same species.

Winter range.—Northern portions of Pacific Ocean. South on the American side to Lower California (San Geronimo Island), in the Pacific Ocean to about 30° North and on the Asiatic side to Japan (Yokohama). North to the Aleutian Islands and southern Bering Sea, as far as open water extends.

Spring migration.—Leaves southern California in April: Point Pinos, April 15; San Diego, April 26.

Fall migration.—Early dates of arrival: Alaska, Baranof Island, September 6; British Columbia, Ilwaco, October 30 to November 10; California, Monterey, October 13 (July and August records are for summer loiterers).   Late dates of departure: Alaska, Point Barrow, September 19; Herald Island, September 26.

Egg dates.—Kamtschatka: Four records, June 4 to 20.   Semidi Islands, Alaska: Two records, June 30 and July 1.   Copper Island: Two records, May 14.

FULMARUS RODGERSI Cassin.

RODGERS FULMAR.

HABITS.

A southwest gale in Bering Sea drove us to shelter under the lofty, red granitic cliffs of Hall Island, the summer home of this boreal fulmar.   The sea was lashed to foam by the gale which cut off the tops of the waves and sent them scudding along before it in a foamy spray; off shore was a heavy bank of fog or dusky clouds, against which was clearly outlined a beautiful aurora borealis, a complete semicircle above the sea, a broad band of light showing all the colors of the spectrum; the sky above was clear blue; and over the frowning, rocky cliffs of the island rolled heavy clouds of fog, shrouding them in misty haze and chilling us with the cold dampness of the snow-drifts on the hills.   The swift-winged murres and puffins, returning to their nests, were flying high and made but slow progress against the gale, but the fulmars gloried in its fury and sailed at ease against it under perfect control and with perfect mastery of its forces.   The fiercest storms at sea have no terrors for these birds; the treacherous "woolies," terrific wind squalls, which sweep down without warning over those forbidding cliffs, can not drive them from their homes. There they sit upon their eggs and rear their young on narrow shelves of rock, hundreds of feet perhaps, above the rough and stormy Arctic sea.

Nesting.—On July 9, 1911, we examined another large colony of Rodgers fulmars at the north end of St. Matthew Island where they were breeding in company with large numbers of Pallas murres and a few California murres on the precipitous rocky cliffs which towered for 200 or 300 feet above the sea.   The murres were mostly on the lower ledges but the fulmars were scattered all over the higher ledges in inaccessible places on the perpendicular or over-hanging cliffs.   In a sheltered cove we found a landing place and climbed up a steep slope in the valley of a little brook which had cut its way under the snow banks to the sea.   The hard snow banks were preferable to the soft, muddy, and stony hillsides above, where our toilsome ascent was gladdened by the sight of the pure white Mackay snowflakes flitting about among the rocks and by the pro-fusion of beautiful flowers in bloom on the grassy slopes.   The sudden transition from snowdrifts to flowers is one of the charms or an arctic summer. On the crest of the cliffs it was blowing so hard that it seemed dangerous to venture too near the edge, but I crawled down into a sheltered gully where I could watch the graceful fulmars sailing in and out below me, to and from their nesting ledges, or see them bedded in a large flock offshore. Besides the murres below, they had other neighbors; little groups of horned puffins, pigeon guillemots and paroquet auklets were sitting on the ledges all about me or flying to and from their nests in the crevices in the rocks. As the fulmars flew below me I could plainly see the mottled back, supposed to be the character of *rodgersi;* there were also many plain light birds and a great variety of color patterns, which raised the question in my mind whether the so-called characters of this species represent anything more than individual variations in *Fulmarus glacialis glupischa.*

The fulmars were sitting on their nests, or rather on their single eggs, for they build no nests. The eggs were laid on the bare rock, wherever suitable ledges or little shelves were available, but they were widely scattered. Many incubating birds were in sight at various points, but none of the eggs were accessible or even approachable. I had to be content with distant views. Once I saw what I thought was a courtship performance; a bird, presumably a female, was sitting on a ledge when a male flew up and alighted beside her; with his beak wide open and his head thrown back until it pointed straight upwards, he slowly waved his head from side to side uttering a soft, guttural, croaking note; after this short ceremony the pair sat quietly together on the ledge for some time.

For nearly all of our knowledge regarding the nesting habits of the Rodgers fulmar we are indebted to Mr. Henry W. Elliott (1880); the following extract from his notes has been often quoted:

This is the only representative of the *Procellarinae* I have seen on or about the Pribylov Islands. It repairs to the cliffs, especially on the south and east shores of St. George; comes very early in the season, and selects some rocky shelf, secure from all enemies save man, where, making no nest whatever, but squatting on the rock itself, it lays a single, large, white, oblong-oval egg, and immediately commences the duty and the labor of incubation. It is of all the water-fowl the most devoted to its charge, for it will not be scared from the egg by any demonstration that may be made in the way of throwing rocks or yelling, and it will even die as it sits rather than take flight, as I have frequently witnessed. The fulmar lays about the 1st to the 5th of June. The egg is very palatable, fully equal to that of our domestic duck; indeed, it is somewhat like it. The natives prize them highly, and hence they undertake at St. George to gather their eggs by a method and a suspension supremely hazardous, as they lower themselves over cliffs five to seven hundred feet above the water. The sensation experienced by myself, when dangled over these precipices attached to a slight thong of raw-hide, with the surf boiling and churning three or four hundred feet below, and loose rocks rattling down from above, any one of which was sufficient to destroy life should it have struck me, is not a sensation to be expressed adequately by language; and, after having passed through the ordeal, I came to the surface perfectly satisfied with what I had called the improvidence of the Aleuts. They have quite sufficient excuse in my mind to be content with as few fulmar eggs as possible. The lupus, laying so early as the 1st of June, is the only rival that the cormorant has with reference to early incubation.

Eggs.—Like other fulmars this species lays but one egg, which is said to be more elongated than those of other species and somewhat rougher. I can not find any constant difference between the eggs of this so-called species and those of the Pacific fulmar, though the eggs of both seem to average smaller than those of the Atlantic bird.

The measurements of 16 eggs, supposed to be *rodgérsi*, average 72.8 by 49 millimeters; the eggs showing the four extremes measure **77.2** by 50, 75.2 by **51, 68** by 47.2, and 70.2 by **45** millimeters.

Plumages—Mr. Elliott (1880) says:

The chick comes out a perfect puffball of white down, and gains its first plumage in about six weeks. It is dull, gray-black at first, but by the end of the season it becomes like the parents in coloration, only much darker on the back and scapularies.

This statement is somewhat at variance with my experience, for specimens of young fulmars, collected by our expedition on St. Matthew Island on September 15, 1911, show the molt from the white natal down directly into a light-colored plumage resembling the adult. Dr. E. W. Nelson (1887) mentions seeing young birds in both light and dark stages of plumages in September and October, but I am inclined to think that these represented light and dark phases, in spite of the fact that this species is said to have no dark phase. There is much yet to be learned about the molts and plumages of the fulmars, and large series of birds have yet to be collected and studied before these can be understood and before the validity of this and other forms can be definitely established. I very much doubt if *Fulmarus rodgersi* will finally prove to be, even subspecifically, distinct from *Fulmarus glacialis*.

Food.—The food of this and other fulmars consists of whatever fragments of animal food can be picked up on the surface of the sea; it shows a decided preference for oily substances.

Doctor Nelson (1887) says:

They gather about a whale carcass and drink the large globules of oil which cover the sea, sometimes for miles, about a decaying cetacean. In Plover Bay, Siberia, on one occasion, we noticed the oil thus floating about in the morning, and in the afternoon a fulmar was shot from which ran a considerable quantity of putrid oil when the bird was taken up by the feet.

Wherever a walrus or other sea animal is killed the fulmars will congregate and gather up blood, grease, and floating fragments of soft flesh. They also follow ships to some extent to pick up bits of offal thrown overboard.

Behavior.—My first view of a fulmar in flight was a pleasing surprise, for I never imagined that so short and heavy a bird, as it appears in a dry skin, could be so light and graceful on the wing. Its long, slender, pointed wings, give it the appearance of a small albatross, but its characteristic flight is shown in the frequent periods of rapid wing strokes, almost as rapid as those of a duck, with which it rises or turns into the wind, followed by a long scaling flight slightly downward on outstretched wings. Its short, thickset body and its peculiar flight are quite distinctive. Fulmars rest lightly on the water, swimming easily and buoyantly; they can ordinarily rise readily from the surface, but in calm weather they experience some difficulty. They are great wanderers, of restless habits, and are seldom seen near land except in the vicinity of their breeding grounds.

Fulmars are usually silent; the only sounds I ever heard from them were the soft, gutteral croaking love notes, on their breeding grounds. Mr. Elliott (1880) says:

I have never heard it utter a sound, save a low, droning croak when disgorging food for its young.

Winter.—During the southward movement in the early fall the fulmars often gather in large numbers, associating with the shearwaters and other ocean birds, in localities where whales are abundant, particularly in the passes among the Aleutian Islands, after which they scatter for the winter over the broad expanse of the north Pacific Ocean.

DISTRIBUTION.

Breeding range.—The breeding range of this supposed species includes the islands in northern Bering Sea (the Pribilof, St. Matthew, Hall, and St. Lawrence Islands) and in the Arctic Ocean (Wrangel and Herald Islands). In the author's opinion this is part of the range of the Pacific fulmar, from which this species should not be separated. The winter ranges and migrations of the two seem to be identical. Breeding grounds protected in Bering Sea and Pribilof reservations.

Egg dates.—Pribilof Islands: Two records, May 28 and June 28. Saint Matthew Island: One record, July 9.

PRIOCELLA ANTARCTICA (Stephens).
SLENDER-BILLED FULMAR.
HABITS.

This fulmar was described by Audubon (1840) from a specimen taken by Doctor Townsend, "within a day's sail from the mouth of the Columbia River.   Its habits are very similar to those of *Procellaria capensis*, keeping constantly around the vessel, and frequently alighting in her wake for the purpose of feeding.   They are easily taken with a hook baited with pork, and at times, particularly during a gale, they are so tame as almost to allow themselves to be taken with the hand.   The stomachs of most of those that I captured were found to contain a species of sepia and grease." Audubon referred to it as " common," but no other living specimens have ever been recorded from our coasts and subsequent developments have shown that it is an antarctic species and that Doctor Townsend's specimens were rare stragglers from southern oceans.

The silvery-gray fulmar or " cape dove," as it has been called, is now well known as a species of wide distribution in Antarctic seas, where it replaces to a certain extent our common fulmar of the north Atlantic Ocean.   Godman (1907) gives a long list of localities where it has been seen or taken and then says:

It will be seen from the above list of localities that the species is found in the neighbourhood of the Antarctic pack ice from August to March, and I am of Dr. Wilson's opinion that it is a migratory bird, as it has been observed in the southern seas during the summer months, December, January, and February, while its farthest northern records occur during the southern winter, when it retires to the open sea.   It will therefore be noticed that *P. glacialoides* does not habitually frequent the ice, but keeps almost entirely to the open ocean.

Nesting.—Our knowledge of its breeding habits is exceedingly fragmentary and quite unsatisfactory.   Perhaps its principal breeding grounds have never been found.   Dr. E. A. Wilson (1907) says:

Kerguelen Island is supposed to be a breeding place.   Nothing appears to be known of its breeding habits; the Scottish expedition were unable to find it nesting, though they strongly suspected that it bred on the north side of Laurie Island; nor were we in the *Discovery* any more successful.   I can only suggest the Balleny Islands as a possible nesting place, but if the bird breeds upon Kerguelen Islands it is much more likely that the more northern sub-Antarctic islands will prove eventually to harbour them.

Gould (1841) writes:

I am informed that it arrives in Georgia in September for the purpose of breeding, and that it lays its eggs in holes in the precipices overhanging the sea.   On the approach of winter it is said to retire from that island.

More recent explorations in Antarctic lands by Sir Douglas Mawson (1914) and by various members of his party have discovered what are probably the main breeding grounds of this species.   Their accounts are decidedly fragmentary, but they demonstrate beyond doubt that the " silver-grey petrel," or " southern fulmar," as they call it, breeds at extreme southern latitudes, on the very edge of the Antarctic ice and snow.   At Penguin Point, on Adelie Land, they found these birds nesting in hundreds on December 31, 1912.   Here the coast, even in summer, is almost concealed in perpetual ice and snow; only occasional outcroppings of rocky ledges protrude through the heavy banks of snow or glaciers on the land; and only here and there the summits of rocky islets appear above the sea ice. The larger islands off this coast, which are surrounded by water in summer, furnish suitable breeding grounds for large colonies of this and other species, such as Antarctic petrels, Wilson petrels, pintado petrels, McCormick skuas, and various penguins. One of the most populous colonies was on Haswell Island, where, during the first three days in December, " the silver-grey or southern fulmar petrels were present in large numbers, especially about the steep northeastern side of the island. Though they were mated, laying had scarcely commenced, as we found only two eggs. They made small grottoes in the snowdrifts, and many pairs were seen billing and cooing in such shelters."

Stillwell Island, a large, high, rocky island, a few miles off the coast of Adelie Land, was visited on December 30, 1913. During the previous summer, two of the eastern sledging parties had for the first time observed the breeding habits of these birds among isolated rocks outcropping on the edge of the coast. But here there was a stronghold of hundreds of petrels, sitting on their eggs in niches among the boulders or ensconced in bowers excavated beneath the snow, which lay deep over some parts of the island.

Food.—Godman (1907) says:

It feeds on dead animal matter, when it can be procured, and Dr. Townsend found in the stomach of a bird that he examined some oil and the remains of a cuttle fish.

Behavior.—Regarding its flight and behavior, Gould (1841) observes:

It is a tame, sociable, and silent bird, and often settles on the water. When thus resting it might from a distance be mistaken, owing to the general color of its plumage, for a gull.

Godman (1907) says:

It is said to fly higher above the water and to rest more frequently than the smaller species.

And Mr. John Treadwell Nichols writes me as follows:

The cape dove, or slender-billed fulmar, is much rarer on the South Seas than the cape pigeon, with which it is practically identical in flight and habits, being equally fearless, eager for scraps, and easily caught with hook and line. A light mark near the end of its wing, conspicuous in flight, suggest the stronger, not dissimilarly placed white mark of the more boldly colored cape pigeon.

DISTRIBUTION.

Breeding range.—Reported as breeding on Louis Philippe Land (Cape Roquemaurel) and known to breed abundantly on Adelie

Land and on islands near it (Stillwell and Haswell Islands). Breeding records for islands off the coasts of Chile and Patagonia are probably erroneous.

Range.—Southern oceans and Antarctic seas, mainly between 30° and 70° south, and circumpolar. Ranging north in the Atlantic Ocean to Saint Helena Island and in the Pacific Ocean as far north as Peru (Mazorca Island). South in Weddell Sea to 71° 22′ South; also to the edge of the pack ice on the Antarctic lands.

Casual records.—Accidental off the west coast of Mexico (Mazatlan) and off the coast of Oregon (Audubon's record).

Egg dates.—Adelie Land: December 1 to 31.

DAPTION CAPENSE (Linnaeus).

PINTADO PETREL.

HABITS.

The pintado petrel or cape pigeon, as it is called by the sailors, is a familiar bird to everyone who has navigated the southern oceans, where it is one of the most widely distributed and most abundant species of all the *Tubinares*. Both of its names are appropriate, pintado because of the striking color pattern with which it is painted and pigeon because of its resemblance in appearance and behavior to our familiar domestic fowl. Sir Walter Buller (1888) gives us the following vivid picture of this bird on the wing:

I do not know any more pretty sight than to watch the cape pigeons on the wing. They move about with such absolute command of wing, presenting to the observer alternately their snow-white breast and then their prettily marked upper surface, the whole set off by their sooty black head and neck, that they look like large painted moths hovering in the air. The eye never tires of following them and noting their ever-varying evolutions, all performed with the utmost ease and gracefulness. Unlike the albatrosses and other sea birds which exhibit a considerable amount of individual variation, one is struck with the wonderful uniformity in the plumage of these birds. All have the same freckled and spotted back and rump, and the same broad splash of white on the upper surface of each wing. There is no transition plumage from the young to the adult states, and no difference observable between the sexes.

Nesting.—Mr. W. Eagle Clarke (1906) seems to have given us the best account of the breeding habits of this species, as follows:

Although the cape petrel or "cape pigeon" is one of the most familiar birds to voyagers in the southern oceans, and one, too, that has been known since the days of Dampier (that is to say, since the closing years of the 17th century), yet the eggs remained entirely unknown until December 2, 1903, when Dr. Pirie took the first specimens at the South Orkneys.

The three nests from which eggs were then obtained were placed on open exposed ledges of cliffs on the west side of Uruguay Cove, Laurie I., at heights of from twenty to a hundred feet above sea level. The nests were composed of a few small angular fragments of rock and a little earth, and contained single eggs which were quite fresh. When approached, the sitting birds ejected an evil-smelling reddish fluid composed of the semidigested remains of crustaceans of the genus *Euphausia*. It was extremely disagreeable to the collector to receive it in his face when peering over a ledge, and the odor of it was found to cling to clothes for a very long time. The birds can squirt this fluid with great precision for a distance of six or eight feet. They did not leave their nests readily, and even allowed themselves to be captured while sitting. The pure white eggs seemed very large for the size of the bird.

On December 3 three more eggs were obtained. There were six nests on the ledge where they were found, but three of them were empty. On the following day about two dozen eggs were taken on the cliffs under Mount Ramsay, and on the 5th some fifty eggs were found on the cliffs on the east side of Uruguay Cover. The birds seemed to be of a sociable nature, for several were frequently found nesting near to each other on the same ledge, but isolated nests were not uncommon.

The work of collecting the eggs of this species proved to be such an unpleasant business, owing to its nasty methods of defense already alluded to, that a long ski pole was used. With this the birds were pushed off their nests and the eggs secured without the captor being defiled. When thus removed they took short flights and then alighted near the nest. Both birds were often found sitting side by side (one on the nest and the mate close alongside) and cooing and clucking to each other, though not to the same extent as during the month previous, when courtship was in full swing.

On December 12th more eggs were procured from the locality in which they were obtained on the 5th, and the nests robbed on that day, though still empty, were covered by sitting birds. On January 13th, 1904, a fresh egg marked on December 2d was found chipped, so that the period of incubation was not less than forty-two days. On January 18th a chick five days old was taken for a skin, and young birds were still in down on February 5th, after which date the state of the ice did not permit of further observations being made ere the expedition left for the far south.

It was noted that before laying its eggs this petrel sits close on the nest for about a month, and it was also observed that it entirely disappeared from its nesting haunts for some ten days before the first eggs were laid.

The eggs vary from oval to elongate-ovate in form. Taking two extreme forms, I find their dimensions to work out as follows: Oval type, 56.5x43 mm.; elongate-ovate type, 67.2x43.3 mm. The average of a large number of specimens is 62.35x43.11 mm. The length varies from 56.5 to 67.2 mm. and in breadth from 46.5 to 40.5 mm.

The numerous nests found were placed either on ledges of cliffs, or, though these were few, in hollows in the earth and among small stones on steep scree-slopes, and all were quite open. These are noteworthy facts, for the nests (containing young) found previous to the discoveries of the Scottish expedition were obtained in burrows and grottoes on the Island of Kerguelen. There is little doubt that the cape petrel breeds at South Georgia, and Mr. Mossman tells me that he saw it in numbers off Deception I., one of the South Shetlands, in the height of the nesting season.

About 20,000 resort to Laurie I. for nesting purposes, and they are found in hundreds all round the coast. In Uruguay Cove alone there were over one hundred accessible nests, and many others were out of reach. They also nest on Saddle I., where both young and old were obtained on February 4th, 1903, and are doubtless abundant throughout the other islands of the Archipelago, which may be regarded as a metropolis of the species.

Mr. Robert Hall (1900), who found the pintado petrel breeding on Kerguelen Island, says:

At Accessible Bay (Betsy Cove) on February 7th I observed four nests, each one with one young partially covered with down. The nests were in the cavities of a rough cliff and were simply hollows, without any attempt to place weeds in them. I saw adults sitting in a sheltered nook, without egg or young; and one of these birds was placing little stones, one by one, around it with the bill, as if to make the nesting place comfortable. The instinct of the bird evidently is to collect something to make a nest, but it is almost lost, and the few stones in all the nests were of no use, so far as I could see. These cavities or grottoes (approximately 6x3x3 feet) were about 50 feet above the sea level, and by stooping I could get inside them, except in one case. A little climb brought me to an old bird, which clucked and made its trill; and I surprised another on its nest, but it did not fly, though it vigorously defended its young, and jumped backward and forward. I kept a respectful distance from the young one, as it had an unknown supply of oily matter. In each of these nests was a young bird, partially in down, about as large as the parents, and in the day time each of them was attended by one parent. The young may be described thus:—Length 12.75 inches; down, generally grayish above, grayish white below; bill black.

Plumages.—Mr. Clarke (1906) adds the following notes on the development of the plumage:

The chick in down, five days old, taken on January 18th, 1904, is slate-grey above, and paler and sooty on the under surface.

A young bird obtained at Saddle I. on February 4th, 1903, has the head and body clad in down, with feathers developing on the wings and scapulars. The down on the upper surface is sooty (darker on the head and cheeks) and paler and greyish on the under parts. The wing-quills, the largest of which are 2 inches in length, are black, some of them with the inner webs white towards the base. The feathers of the scapulars are black and white. There are no signs of tail feathers. Wing 8 inches.

The mature birds from the South Orkneys and the Weddell Sea present two types of plumage. The first of these, which perhaps represents old birds in weathered dress, were captured towards the end of summer (in February); and in them the dark portions of the plumage are blackish with a brown cast, the head alone being black; the feathers of the mantle have whitish bases; and the marginal and lesser coverts show less white than in the next form. In the second type the dark portion of the plumage is slate-black, and the bases of the feathers of the mantle are dusky. Specimens in this phase were obtained early in the autumn (late in March), and are either in new or first plumage. A male captured on the nesting ledges on December 3rd, 1903, is intermediate in plumage between these two forms.

Food.—Mr. John Treadwell Nichols writes to me that:

This species is preeminent among the southern birds for the eagerness with which it picks up scraps from the galley, and its readiness to take a hook baited with the standard salt pork. After being on deck a few minutes it regurgitates a rank oil. Like its relatives it usually comes about a ship most fearlessly in heavy weather. As the wind moderates, I have seen a little flock of them lose their appetite, settle on the water and busy themselves preening their feathers, only rising from time to time to catch up with the ship. Some bathed more or less after the manner of land birds.

Though generally silent when offshore, when squabbling for food the Cape Pigeon at times gives a grating chatter. It occasionally will plunge almost or quite under water after some tit-bit, but usually sits on or flutters eagerly along the surface when feeding.

Dr. E. A. Wilson (1907) says:

No other petrel is so common in the Southern Oceans, and probably no other is so easily taken by thread entanglements. It feeds upon minute crustaceans, most of which appear to be coloured with the bright orange pigment that is so marked a feature in those animals. They are freely ejected in a mucoid orange-coloured mess when the bird is caught and handled, and the same objectionable habit is said to be indulged in when the birds are disturbed upon their nests, six or even eight feet being given as the distance to which it can be ejected, and with great precision.

Mr. Hall (1900) says of its feeding habits:

The cape pigeon is a fearless bird. In Greenland Harbor I observed them in flocks of from 20 to 30, and at Accessible Bay found their nests. When the seal-skins were being towed by the small boat, a flock of 17 would sit on the water around the floating skins and vigorously peck at their edges to get as much fat as possible, using all their energy in the work, and " clucking " rapidly and tremulously.

Behavior.—Referring to the behavior of the pintado petrel, Gould (1865) says:

This martin among the petrels is extremely tame, passing immediately under the stern and settling down close to the sides of the ship, if fat of any kind or other oily substance be thrown overboard. Swims lightly, but rarely exercises its natatorial powers except to procure food, in pursuit of which it occasionally dives for a moment or two. Nothing can be more graceful than its motions while on the wing, with the neck shortened, and the legs entirely hidden among the feathers of the under tail coverts.

Earlier he wrote (1841):

Their flight is not rapid, but elegant; and as these prettily mottled birds skim the surface of the water in graceful curves, constantly following the vessel as she drives onward in her course, they afford a spectacle which is beheld by everyone with interest. Although often spending the whole day on the wing, yet on a fine moonlight night, I have repeatedly seen these birds following the wake of a vessel, with their usual graceful evolutions.

Mr. J. T. Nichols has sent me the following notes on this petrel:

The strongly marked, usually omnipresent cape pigeon is the most conspicuous and best known pelagic bird of the southern temperate oceans. A sailing ship in these regions is commonly attended by about half a dozen of them, crossing her wake, hanging above and to one side of her high stern deck, circling about her. One swings out until almost lost to view in the ocean distances, to come circling back about the ship again.

Rounding the Horn in a merchant sailing ship on one occasion when they were seen daily almost without exception from the time when the region of westerly winds was entered from the north in the Atlantic until it was left behind going north in the Pacific, I have seen nothing to lead me to suppose that the same individuals of this or other species stayed with the ship for many days in succession. My observations rather foster the belief that the personnel is constantly changing. The number of birds varies from day to day, and on several occasions when birds with some peculiar mark, which would not be readily duplicated, have been noted, they have not been seen again. Furthermore, I have so frequently had intelligent persons (obviously in error, or quite unjustified in their convictions) point out sea birds as having followed a ship for long periods, that I have become very sceptical of such assertions.

The cape pigeon has something the build of the domestic bird, the name of which it bears, being stockier than the shearwaters. Its flight is more truly sailing than that of any northern bird known to me, and typical of the southern sailing *Tubinares*. It flaps its wings much less frequently than the shearwaters, though at times with a good breeze these also scud over and among the waves for considerable periods on stiff, motionless wings. In the high winds which predominate on the seas it inhabits, one may watch an individual cape pigeon in the air for a long time without seeing a flap of the wings. In more moderate breezes it not infrequently gives them a few flaps. Like other sailing petrels, it often leans to one side as it goes, usually turning toward the down wing.

Relating to what Mr. Nichols says about certain individual birds following a ship, Captain Hutton (1865) was "informed by Lieutenant Weld, R. N., that a cape pigeon, with a piece of red ribbon round its neck, once followed the ship he was in for 1,500 miles."

Mr. Robert C. Murphy (1914) made the following observations on this species:

They ran like albatrosses—that is, foot after foot—along the surface when launching into flight. They followed a trailing bait by setting their wings as gliders, keeping the breast just an inch or so above the sea, and propelling themselves with rapid, alternating strokes of their feet. In this manner they sometimes covered long distances without an apparent beat of the wings.

The birds rarely, if ever, flew directly before the wind, but either took it "on the quarter" or else headed into it, raised the body axis, and allowed themselves to be carried backward like a kite. The last method was regularly adopted by *Petrella capensis*, flocks of these birds covering considerable distances tail foremost.

Godman (1907) refers to the notes of this species as follows:

The cape pigeon, unlike most of its allies, utters a distinct cry, strong and raucous—cac-cac, cac-cac, cac—increasing in rapidity, but during the period of courtship the birds coo and cluck, and continue, Dr. Pirie says, their love-note, though to a less degree, throughout the period of incubation. They make a great noise when attacking a dead seal, the fat of which they are very fond.

Winter.—At the close of the breeding season in May these petrels migrate northward or move away from their breeding places, to which they do not return again until about the first of October. In the meantime they wander widely over the southern oceans, but seldom venture as far north as the Equator. What few specimens have been taken in Europe and North America were either rare stragglers from southern seas or were perhaps brought north by sailors as pets and released.

Breeding range.—Antarctic seas. Breeds in the South Orkney, South Shetland, South Georgia, and Kerguelen Islands; also on islands of Adelie Land; probably also on Snares and Antipodes Islands and on Victoria Land.

Range.—Widely extended throughout southern oceans around the world. North in the Atlantic Ocean to the Tropic of Capricorn (Sao Paulo, Brazil); in the Pacific Ocean to about 5° South (Payta, Peru), and occasionally farther north (16° North, Acapulco); and in the Indian Ocean to the vicinity of Ceylon. South in Antarctic seas to about 76° South.

Casual records.—Accidental in Maine (Harpswell, Casco Bay, September, 1876), off the California coast (opposite Monterey), in Great Britain (Dublin, October 30, 1881, Bournemouth, 1894, and Cardigan, Wales, October, 1879), and in France (Bercy). There are some other European records.

Egg dates.—South Orkney Islands: Three records, December 4 and 5; one record each, April 12 and May 12. South Shetland Islands: One record, December 14. Adelie Land: One record, December 2.

CALONECTRIS KUHLII BOREALIS Cory.

CORY SHEARWATER.

HABITS.

The Chatham bars, dangerous, shifting sand shoals, guard the entrance to a broad and placid bay at the elbow of Cape Cod which is separated from the ocean by a narrow strip of beach many miles long, known as Nauset Beach and made famous by Thoreau. Exposed to the unbroken swell of the Atlantic Ocean these bars are nearly always white with combing breakers and during easterly storms are seething masses of foam and flying spray, beautiful to look upon, but much dreaded by sailors, as they have proved to be the graveyard of many a good ship. Only during the smoothest weather do the fishermen dare to venture out across the bars to their fishing grounds offshore. Many a time have I joined them on their trips in their staunch catboats, picking our way safely among the bars, leaving the gulls and terns behind us as the land faded in the distance. When safely over the bars we could feel the gentle ground swell of the ocean and begin to look for the gliding forms of the shearwaters, the slender winged ocean wanderers. We were seldom disappointed, for this is a famous summer resort for *Tubinares* and the birthplace of the, so called, species *Puffinus borealis.* Here on October 11, 1880, Mr. Charles B. Cory (1881) obtained the type specimen from which he described the species.

Although the Cory shearwater has stood, unchallenged as a distinct species, for all these years, it is now generally recognized as a subspecies of the Mediterranean shearwater, *Calonectris kuhlii*. There are now three recognized subspecies of this species, *C. kuhli kuhlii* in the Mediterranean, *C. kuhlii edwardsi* breeding in the Cape Verde Islands and *C. kuhlii flavirostris*, or *C. kuhlii borealis*, as it should be called, breeding in the Canary Islands and the Azores and migrating to the North American coast. As the latter is the bird which belongs on the American list, I shall quote freely from what has been published about its habits.

Nesting.—Mr. W. R. Ogilvie-Grant (1905) gives the following account of the breeding habits of this species in the Azores, under the name, *Puffinus kuhlii flavirostris* (Gould) :

This shearwater is very common throughout the seas of the Azores, and during our journeys between the different islands we steamed through large flocks either resting on the water, or skimming over the waves, in their characteristic manner. The greatest number were to be seen about the central group of islands, especially round Graciosa, San Jorge, Pico, and Fayal. We saw none in the neighborhood of Corvo, and though we sent men in the middle of April to several places on Flores where these shearwaters were known to breed, we were unable to procure specimens. Toward the end of May, during our stay at San Roque, on the north coast of Pico, numbers of " cagarros " had arrived at their breeding-places in the rocks below the village and flew over our house at night uttering their weird cry.

When we visited Santa Maria early in March we procured a few specimens captured in the holes in the rocks on Villa Islet, but at that season only a small number were to be found in their breeding haunts. On our return, however, to that island on June 1st we found a large colony had arrived, and nearly all the nesting holes contained a bird sitting on its single white egg, which was either fresh or only slightly incubated. On the Cabras or Goat Islets, off the south of Terceira, which we visited on May 30th, about a dozen birds were found sitting, but many nesting places were still empty, and the fishermen who accompanied us said that a little later the " cagarros " swarm on these rocks. Another large breeding station is on the small island of Praya, off Graciosa, but owing to the impossibility of landing in a heavy sea we were unable to visit the spot in person, though we subsequently secured a number of birds caught by some fishermen sent for the purpose.

Mr. David A. Bannerman (1914) has given us a very full and interesting account of the distribution and habits of this shearwater in the Canary Islands, from which I quote, as follows:

A little to the east of Mount Amarilla, just above high watermark, lies a mass of huge boulders piled up one upon another, over the top of which loose sand has drifted, the whole being closely overgrown with a scrubby plant. Small gaps are left between the boulders, and through one of these we managed to squeeze; once inside, our electric torches revealed low caves, into which we had to crawl on hands and knees, and from which a network of subterranean passages led in all directions. In these dark recesses, abounding in nooks and crannies, the large shearwaters were sitting. The glare of the torches dazzled their eyes as they shuffled into crevices and behind loose rocks in their vain endeavor to escape from the brilliant light. No nest of any description was attempted by the birds in these caves.

Another colony had chosen a very different situation on the plain east of Mount Amarilla, about a quarter of a mile from the sea. Here the birds were nesting in burrows in the earth, which was so hard that it absolutely resisted our attempts to dig out the occupants with a sharp-pointed spade. I imagine the shearwaters had excavated these burrows themselves, as there are no rabbits on Graciosa whose holes they could make use of. I only found one other small colony on Graciosa, where the birds nested in burrows which likewise were too difficult to excavate.

Not content with nesting round the coasts, these birds had resorted in numbers to two of the volcanoes. A few nests were found amongst the lumps of loose lava on the summit of Montana Bermeja (550 feet), but a considerably larger colony was discovered on the eastern slopes of the big central volcano (Montana de las Agujas). Here, at an altitude of 300 to 600 feet the face of the crater was honeycombed with caves, in almost all of which birds were nesting. As this was the most interesting of all the various sites chosen, I will give a short description of my visit on June the 1st. Two fisher lads acted as guides, and after a weary climb up 600 feet of loose crumbling lava, we gained the entrance to the largest cave, which measured 6 by 3 feet. At one end of this outer cave a narrow tunnel ran into the heart of the mountain, through which, by lying full length, it was just possible to squeeze; after being pulled in front and pushed behind for some fifteen yards, I at last found myself in another small cave, with yet another tunnel leading out of it at right angles to the last. This second tunnel was a little wider, but twisted and turned in the most bewildering manner, gradually opening out into a good-sized cavern which must have been quite twenty yards from the entrance. All the large holes and crevices in the walls of this cave had been utilized by the shearwaters. A very large number must resort to this particular spot. At this distance from the fresh air an indescribable smell of petrel greeted our nostrils. The floors of both caves and passages, which were composed of crushed lava, were thickly strewn with the feathers of the birds, and I was unlucky in finding all the occupants out at sea. They had not yet commenced to lay, at any rate in this cave, but we had obtained a fair number of eggs from other parts of the island.

Eggs.—The eggs of the Cory shearwater vary considerably in size and shape but are indistinguishable from those of the closely related Mediterranean birds. The shape varies from ovate or even pointed ovate to elliptical ovate. The color is pure white. The shell is smooth, though slightly pitted, and without luster.

The measurements of 70 eggs, from the Canaries and the Desertas, collected for me by Rev. F C. R. Jourdain, average 75.30 by 50.3 millimeters; the eggs showing the four extremes measure **83** by 48, 79 by **55, 66** by 47, and 73.5 by **45** millimeters

Behavior.—Mr. Ogilvie-Grant (1896) writes of the habits of this species on the Salvages:

Our arrival on Great Salvage apparently caused great excitement among the bird inhabitants, our tent being a special object of wonder, the pardelas, or Mediterranean shearwaters, being especially bold and noisy in their greeting. The high volcanic rocks surrounding the south bay are full of miniature caves, in most of which a pair of the pardelas had their home, and toward sunset the whole population turned out, wheeling and screaming around our encampment and offering the most tempting rocketing shots as they swept over the high rocks above us.

The male, in a harsh guttural voice, cried *"ia-gow-a-gow-a-gow,"* and the female chimes in *"ia-ia-ia,"* and it may be imagined that with thousands of these miscreants circling close round our tent during the entire night, tired as we were, sleep was almost impossible on the first evening of our stay. During the whole of our visit we used every night to be mobbed by these noisy birds. The " march past," as we called it, generally commenced about six and continued with unabated zest till we turned in about 10.30 and heard no more. In spite of the tempting shots they offered, we killed very few of these birds, only such as we required for specimens; but our men were not so sparing, for they used every day to catch numbers for food (they skinned and boiled them!) and took back sackfuls to Las Palmas, where, when salted, they are much esteemed by the Spanish fishermen.

The pardela breeds late, and though during the daytime we found most of the birds in pairs in their rocky nesting chambers, we never procured a single egg. Enormous numbers of the young are collected by the Portuguese fishermen every autumn, being valued for their oil and downy feathers. The oil is of poor quality, and, as we were informed, is chiefly used for dressing coal sacks. The happy couples greatly resent being disturbed in their nesting cavities, and unless extracted without hesitation retaliate by biting with great vigor, their curved bills, with their sharp, cutting edges, being apt to leave an ugly wound on those unskilled in the mode of handling them.

Though the majority pass the day in the holes in the rocks, many also rest at sea and may be seen in flocks floating quietly on the surface at most hours of the day. On our return journey the *Pedro* ran right over one of these shearwaters sleeping peacefully with its head under its wing, but beyond a rough awakening it flew off apparently none the worse. On several occasions, when sitting in our camp by lantern light, skinning the birds collected during the day, we were startled by one of these great shearwaters dashing into our midst like some great white moth dazzled by the light. Fortunately none of them ever struck us or we might have had the worst of the encounter. These birds are evidently the cormorants alluded to by Mr. Knight in his " Cruise of the *Alerte*" (p. 85). He writes: " The cormorants dwelt with their families in fine stone houses which they had constructed with great ingenuity. Some of the stones were large and heavy. It would be interesting to observe how the birds set to work to move them and how they put the roof on. I have been told that they rake up a mound of stones with their powerful wings in such a way that by removing some of those underneath they leave the roof above them." This is, of course, obviously impossible, some of the stones being of great weight. The fact is that these little stone huts are put up all over the top of the island by the Portuguese fishermen for the birds to nest in, so that the young may be the more easily obtained when they visit the place in autumn. This is commonly done also in the Canaries.

When pulled out of their stone houses during the daytime these birds present a very ludicrous spectacle as they stalk slowly off with a bewildered air, not unmixed with reproach. After a time they get on the wing and make off, their eyes having, I suppose, got accustomed to the light; but if taken from their nesting chambers and thrown up into the air they drop to the ground like stones, without making any attempt to save themselves with their wings. Bulwer's petrel acts in exactly the same way.

Food.—Audubon's (1840) description and plate both evidently refer to this species, under the name *Puffinus cinereus*, in which he evidently was more nearly correct than some later writers in identifying this with the Mediterranean species. He says of its food: "In the stomach of those which I opened I found fishes, portions of crabs, seaweeds, and oily substances." All of the shearwaters are, to a certain extent, scavengers of the seas and probably feed on whatever scraps of animal food they can pick up. They follow the whales and schools of large predaceous fishes to pick up bits of their food left on the surface and frequent the vicinity of fishing vessels to gorge themselves on the offal thrown overboard while cleaning fish. They are particularly fond of cod livers and other oily portions, with which they can be readily tolled up to the boat or caught on baited hooks.

Behavior.—The flight of this species is much like that of the other large shearwaters, swift, strong, and graceful. It glides along smoothly on its long, stiff, pointed wings, rising easily over the crests of the waves and coasting down into the valleys between them. It usually flies very close to the surface, even in the roughest weather, and I have often admired the skill and confidence with which it rises and skims over the tops of the largest waves in which it seems as if it must be engulfed. Audubon (1840) says that "like the small petrels, it frequently uses its feet to support itself on the surface without actually alighting." I have never seen it do this. It swims lightly and rapidly and frequently dives beneath the surface in pursuit of its food. In calm weather it experiences a little difficulty in rising from the surface, but in rough weather it glides off the top₁ of a wave with the utmost ease. It is easily distinguished, on the wing, from the greater shearwater by its larger size, its lighter color, its big yellow bill, and by the lack of any distinctly dark cap so conspicuous in the other.

Its behavior toward other species is not above suspicion. Mr. B. H. Dutcher (1889), who saw some of these shearwater near Little Gull Island, New York, stated that they "seemed always to keep in company with the jaegers, and to be engaged in the same occupation, that of robbing the terns." Mr. Ogilvie-Grant (1896) adds the following evidence of misconduct:

It has already been remarked that we were inclined to suspect the pardelas of stealing the young of the yellow-footed herring gull, but it must be admitted that there was no direct evidence against them, beyond the fact that they quartered the ground every evening, apparently in search of food, in the immediate neighborhood of the gulls' nests, and were armed with strong hooked bills, which looked capable of making short work of downy young, and caused their owners to be regarded as suspicious characters.

Mr. William C. Tait (1887) says:

The shearwaters are very useful to the Portuguese fishermen, as they indicate by their presence the neighborhood of the sardine shoals, and also contribute to the general stewpot. They are caught by trailing after the boat, along the surface of the sea, a line baited with a sardine. It is usual to skin these birds before adding them to the pot, and the fishermen say they are fat, and consider them a great delicacy. *P. major* is said to be better eating than *P. kuhli*, as it is fatter and tenderer. They generally keep well out to sea, and approach nearer the coast during rainy weather with southerly winds.

Fall.—The sojourn of this shearwater on our coasts is what we might expect of a species which breeds in the northern hemisphere and helps to indicate that our birds are identical with those of the Azores and the Canary Islands. I can not find that there are any spring or early summer records, as there are for both the greater and the sooty shearwaters. They seem to arrive on our coasts early in August and spend the next three months with us, mainly between Cape Cod and Long Island Sound. Most of them disappear about the end of October. While here they associate freely with the other two species, named above, but are never so abundant. They usually stay well offshore, but on one occasion, September 5, 1909, I saw several and shot two, in company with a large flock of sooty shearwaters, well inside the harbor at Chatham, Massachusetts.

DISTRIBUTION.

Breeding range.—The American subspecies, *borealis*, breeds in the Azores, Madeira, Salvage, and Canary Islands. Other subspecies of *Calonectris kuhlii* breed in the Mediterranean Sea and the Cape Verde Islands.

Range.—Atlantic Ocean. South to at least 36° south. West to the coast of Brazil (off Bahia) and North America (from Newfoundland to North Carolina).

Migrations.—Arrives on its breeding grounds late in February or early in March and leaves them late in October or early in November. Dates of occurrence on American coast: Massachusetts, Cape Cod, August 2 to November 1; Rhode Island, August 15 to October 26; New York, Long Island, August 6 to November 29; North Carolina, September 3 to December.

Casual records.—Accidental in England (Sussex, March 14, 1914).

Egg dates.—Azores, Canary, and Madeira Islands. Sixty-six records, May 28 to June 23.

Since the above was written Mr. Robert Cushman Murphy (1922) has shown that the Mediterranean shearwater, *Calonectris kuklii kuhlii*, should be added to our list, as he has examined a number of specimens of this form taken off our coasts. Probably the Mediterranean form is much commoner here than is generally supposed, as all the specimens examined were labeled "Cory's shearwater" and were mistaken for that form.

ARDENNA CARNEIPES (Gould).

PALE-FOOTED SHEARWATER.

HABITS.

This large dusky shearwater resembles the sooty shearwater and might easily be mistaken for it in life, but it is distinguished from it by having a light-colored bill and flesh-colored feet and by the absence of any whitish or ashy gray on the under wing coverts. Owing to its resemblance to the commoner species it may have been often overlooked and perhaps has visited our Pacific coast much oftener than is supposed. It has only recently been added to our list. Mr. Rollo H. Beck (1910) has reported the capture of 10 specimens of this shearwater, taken at various seasons of the year in the vicinity of Point Pinos, California.

The following quotations from Godman (1907) will give a fair idea of what we know of its life history:

Mr. A. J. Campbell gives the habitat as the "seas of Western Australia, and probably other parts of the southern coasts, including Tasmania." Mr. Ernest Saunders procured specimens on Norfolk Island and Lord Howe Island.

Dr. E. P. Ramsay, who has written an account of *P. carneipes*, says that it represents *P. tenuirostris* on the coasts of New South Wales and South Australia, where it is as numerous as that species in certain places. He further states that these shearwaters frequent the Solitary Islands in great numbers during the breeding season, which extends from September till December.

Sir Walter Buller relates that *P. carneipes* breeds in large colonies on some of the small islands, and is comparatively common off the coast of New Zealand—Captain Fairchild procured two living birds for him, which he found nesting on White Island in the beginning of November. After the breeding season in Australia *P. carneipes* passes north to the seas of Japan, but has not yet been found in the intervening area, nor is it known to nest in its northern habitat. Mr. Seebohm, who records its occurrence in Japanese waters, observes that it is probably a nonbreeding summer visitor in the North Pacific, and supposing this to be correct, we may regard *P. carneipes* as a petrel which, like *Oceanites oceanica*, breeds in the southern hemisphere during our winter, and visits the northern hemisphere during our summer, but in the latter instance without breeding.

Nesting.—The nesting habits resemble those of other species of the genus. Doctor Ramsay, in acknowledging the receipt by the Australian Museum of a fine series of birds and eggs from the Solitary Islands, gives the following notes, derived from his correspondence: The birds arrived early in September, and at once began excavating their nesting holes, which consisted of short burrows about 6 inches in diameter and from 12 to 20 inches in length. The eggs were laid at night, but in no instance was more than one obtained in a burrow. Although both sexes assisted in the incubation, out of five specimens taken from the burrows four proved to be females. The birds arrived in countless thousands in the evening, and most of them—the males probably, or those not engaged in hatching—returned to sea at daybreak.

Eggs.—There are four eggs of the pale-footed shearwater in Col. John E. Thayer's collection, taken by Mr. Thomas Carter on Breaksea Island, West Australia, on November 23, 1910, and October 16, 1911. There were "many hundred" nests in the colony, according to the data given, each nest containing a single egg in a burrow. These eggs are elliptical ovate or elongate ovate in shape; they are pure white, smooth in texture, and somewhat glossy, rather different from the eggs of other shearwaters that I have seen. These four eggs measure 67 by 38, 66 by 39, 61 by 38, and 60 by 38 millimeters.

Winter.—The following quotation from Prof. Leverett M. Loomis (1918) tells us about all we know of the pale-footed shearwater as a North American bird.

So far as I am aware, this Southern Hemisphere shearwater has been reported for the eastern side of the Pacific only from the vicinity of Point Pinos, California, where Mr. R. H. Beck has secured during his various expeditions ten specimens for the Academy and four for the University of California. Mr. Beck's notes concerning them are as follows:

During my eleven months' stay in 1907 I saw nine flesh-footed shearwaters. They were then perhaps more plentiful than in other seasons, though the close watch I kept on shearwaters that year and the abundance of sooty shearwaters partly account for so many being seen. On February 27, while I was out six miles northwest of the buoy amongst a large flock of fishing birds, I noticed a flesh-footed shearwater flying past. A long shot caused him to circle off and drop, but in the choppy sea I would have lost him had not a Cooper's shearwater circled about and showed me the dead bird's position. On April 29, about six miles northwest of the buoy, I scared up a small bunch of sooty shearwaters, and a flesh-footed swung up and was shot. June 25 was foggy, with shearwaters abundant from Moss Beach to Seal Rocks. A mile or so off Seal Rocks a flesh-footed shearwater, two hundred yards away, was seen flying along toward Point Pinos. A dead sooty shearwater thrown into the air called him over and he was secured. He flew with slower wing beats and was more deliberate in flight than the sooty shearwater. On July 22, while I was trying to get early southbound Sabine's gulls that were resting in company with sooty shearwaters some distance off Point Cypress, a flesh-footed shearwater flew up. A hasty shot, with but one barrel loaded, sent him off wounded, but I could not find him on the rippling water. August 27 I was out about four miles northwest of Point Pinos amongst thousands of sooty shearwaters. As one of the constantly passing throng flew by me, I noticed the light-colored bill and shot the bird, securing thus another flesh-footed shearwater. September 2, while in the same vicinity, one of the shearwaters that flew over my head from behind had a light-colored bill. Hastily dropping the oars and grabbing my gun, I shot the bird, and, as anticipated, it proved to be a flesh-footed shearwater. October 28 I was out about six miles northeast of the buoy and noticed a flesh-footed flying south with a single sooty shearwater. A long shot at seventy-five yards distance failed to stop him. November 4 I got out about eight miles north of Point Pinos and in a large flock of about twenty thousand sooty shear-waters secured two flesh-footed that flew up to me. No others were seen, though possibly present in other portions of the scattered flock. Two Buller's shearwaters were taken here and also a slender-billed shearwater and several Cooper's shearwaters.

Judging from the manner of their occurrence, it seems evident that the flesh-footed shearwaters frequenting the ocean in the vicinity of Point Pinos, California, are regular but not common visitors from the antipodes, and that they followed in their exodus and return migrations the American coast route of the sooty shearwaters.

DISTRIBUTION.

Breeding range.—Australian and New Zealand seas. Known to breed on Breaksea, North, White, and Solitary Islands, and perhaps others in that region.

Range.—Migrates northward in the Pacific Ocean, between breeding seasons, to Japan (Hakodate) and California (off Monterey), probably regularly but sparingly. California dates fall in February and April and in every month from June to November.

Egg dates.—Breaksea Island: Three records, September 11, October 16, and November 23.

ARDENNA CREATOPUS (Coues).

PINK-FOOTED SHEARWATER.

HABITS.

This large shearwater is referred to by Godman (1907) as " the Pacific representative of *Puffinus kuhli*," to which it bears a certain amount of superficial resemblance. It is distinguished from that species, however, " by the black tip to the bill and the general sooty color of the axillaries and under tail coverts. The species was first described by the late Dr. Elliott Coues from a specimen procured by Dr. Cooper on San Nicholas Island, off California."

Nesting.—Nothing was known about the nesting habits of this species until Mr. Rollo H. Beck, of the Brewster-Sanford expedition to South America, found them breeding on islands in the Juan Fernandez group, off the coast of Chile. He has kindly sent me the following notes:

On December 12, 1913, I started out from the settlement on Masatierra Island, of the Juan Fernandez group (which lies about 400 miles to the westward of Valparaiso, Chile), to find the nests of the pink-footed shearwater. About four miles from the village many holes were found, but nearly all were too deep and long to be opened without pick or shovel. One hole 6 feet long was opened and a pair of birds was found at the end. Burrows were found from near shore up into the ferns at 1,500 feet elevation. On the 15th I went again to the colony with a man to dig for me. One burrow was followed for 10 feet. It then branched for the third time and went too deep to follow. Nearly all the burrows were 6 feet or more in length; sometimes a little grass was found in the nest, but usually only bare earth in the enlarged end of the burrow. Three eggs only were taken, although a number of holes were opened. On the 31st of January we tried the colony again and found a few birds on eggs nearly ready to hatch. In two holes examined cold eggs were found containing young birds alive, though barely able to move. One young bird 3 days old was found in another burrow. Several single adult birds of both sexes were taken from holes and these on dissection showed small sexual organs. Some holes that showed fresh soil about them were opened, but no birds were found in them. On February 7th several rotten and a couple of fresh eggs were found where they had been scratched out of holes, and many holes showed signs of digging.

On the 19th of January, 1914, I visited Santa Clara Island 10 miles off Masatierra and found colonies of birds nesting in the soft ground on top of the island. Some of the burrows here were just below the grass roots and easily opened while others ran deep down. Nearly all the nests were nicely lined with foxtail straws and an occasional burrow also had a lining. Most of the eggs were well advanced in incubation and in one nest I found a bird setting on two eggs. One of these proved however to be rotten and was probably a last year's egg. The pink-footed shearwater when disturbed on its egg becomes decidedly pugnacious picking wildly at any object and frequently at a single blow will break its egg before it can be removed from the nest. The birds about the island in the daytime spend most of their time sitting on the water in flocks differing in this respect from their neighbors, the neglected petrels which nest along the cliffs, and spend their daylight hours in swinging singly about over the ocean.

Eggs.—The eggs of the pink-footed shearwater vary greatly in size and shape. They are usually " elongate ovate," sometimes nearly " cylindrical ovate," and occasionally " ovate." The shell is smooth, finely grained, and without lustre. The color is white, which is often more or less stained, sometimes with a pinkish tinge. The measurements of 11 eggs, collected by Mr. Beck, average 71.7 by 46.2 millimeters; the eggs showing the four extremes measure **79** by 47, 76.2 by **48.8,** and **53.5** by **42.2** millimeters.

Eggs in American collections, supposed to be of this species, collected on Breaksea Island, western Australia, are probably eggs of *Ardenna carneipes*, which has also been called the pink-footed shearwater. The eggs described above, collected by Mr. Beck, are, I believe, the only eggs of *Ardenna creatopus* in existence.

Young.—There are three specimens of the downy young of the pink-footed shearwater in the Brewster-Sanford collection, which are probably the only specimens in existence. They were also collected by Mr. Beck, on Masatierra Island, on January 31, 1914. They are thickly covered with long fluffy down, which varies on the upper parts, from " drab " to " cinnamon drab," the exact color depending on how the light strikes it; the color fades off to " drab-gray " on the sides, to " pale drab-gray " on the throat and to pure white on the chin, breast, and belly. There are no specimens showing the subsequent changes into the adult plumage.

Plumages.—Mr. Leverett M. Loomis (1900) says regarding plumages:

Several specimens (apparently adult) have the white of the under parts immaculate anterior to the lower abdomen. Others (apparently immature) have the white more or less variegated with gray, the chin and throat being densely mottled, sparsely mottled, or faintly streaked, and the breast and abdomen, in extreme examples, transversely marked. The majority of forty-seven specimens have whitish mixed with the dark of the lower tail-coverts.

Behavior.—We saw a few pink-footed shearwaters, one of which was shot, while cruising off the coast of southern California, between Santa Cruz Island and Santa Barbara, on June 4, 5, and 6, 1914. They were associated with large numbers of sooty shearwaters, circling about over the roughest parts of the channel, and, as they did not appear to be migrating, were probably summer sojourners. In general appearance and behavior they closely resembled our familiar Cory shearwater of the Atlantic coast.

Baird, Brewer, and Ridgway (1884) publish a brief account of the habits of this species, based on Doctor Cooper's observations, as follows:

They are generally seen in flocks several miles off the shore, flying like the albatross, by rapid flappings, alternating with sailings. They congregate quickly around shoals of fish, and dive to a short distance beneath the water in pursuit of them. They often rest on the water, swimming very lightly, but not rapidly, and appear to be the most active when the wind roughens the surface of the water, enabling them to scoop up small fish from the agitated tops of the waves. Dr. Cooper further states that he found this species most abundant and most approachable about San Nicholas Island, where the water is shoal and small fish are numerous. The birds were molting about the first of July.

Mr. Rollo H. Beck (1910) says of the occurrence of this species near Point Pinos, California:

These shearwaters are common sojourners in this vicinity after their breeding season in the South Temperate Zone. Eight individuals seen February 27, 1907, probably belonged to the vanguard of that year. Before the end of November the majority take their departure, only stragglers remaining.

Mr. Leverett M. Loomis (1895), who has made exhaustive studies of the *Tubinares* in the vicinity of Monterey, California, says that:

The flight of these shearwaters when migrating is not as direct as that of the black-vented and dark-bodied. They circle frequently and cross their track, much as swallows are wont to do when migrating singly or in small companies.

Again he says (1900):

Previous to May 27 comparatively few pink-footed shearwaters were observed. In June they became quite abundant. Males greatly outnumbered the females, which was also the case in the autumn of 1896. Individuals frequently came close to the boat, seemingly prompted by curiosity.

Breeding range.—Known to breed only on Juan Fernandez and Santa Clara Islands, off the coast of Chile.

Range.—Eastern portions of Pacific Ocean. North to southern Alaska (Forrester Island) and south to southern Chile (San Carlos).

Migrations.—Not well marked. Seems to be present on California coast nearly every month in the year, but main northward flight seems to be in summer and fall.

Egg dates.—Juan Fernandez Islands: Four records, December 12 and 15 and January 19 and 31.

ARDENNA GRAVIS (O'Reilly).

GREATER SHEARWATER.

HABITS.

Contributed by Charles Wendell Townsend.

To the bird student who rarely ventures from the beaches or sheltered bays out onto the unprotected ocean a glimpse of a shearwater—the hag, hagdon, or hagdown of sailors—is most unusual. In easterly storms, however, these birds may sometimes be seen close to our Atlantic shore and I have seen them fly within a stone's throw of Ipswich beach. Under ordinary conditions, however, they are not often found less than 5 miles from land. Graceful birds they are and well do they deserve their name, for on nimble wing they are ever on the alert to cut or *shear* the water in their search for food.

The largest number I ever saw was on a July day on the Labrador coast between Battle and Spear Harbors. The wind was strong on shore, bringing in wisps and clouds of fog from the numerous icebergs which beset the coast. At first our steamer disturbed from the water groups of fifty to a hundred shearwaters, but, as we pushed north, larger and larger flocks arose and flew outside until we had seen at least ten thousand of these splendid birds. The great flock extended for several miles along the rugged coast and with the exception of three sooty shearwaters all were the greater species.

Nesting.—As there are no authentic records of the breeding of this abundant bird in the northern hemisphere, as specimens taken here in the summer show no evidence of breeding, and as it has been found in southern seas, there is reason to believe that, like the Wilson petrel, it breeds in the Antarctic summer, our winter, and comes north during our summer, the antipodal winter. As yet, however, its breeding place has not been found.

[AUTHOR'S NOTE.—Since Doctor Townsend wrote this life history, Rev. F. C. R. Jourdain has sent me the following notes, which contain practically all that is known at present of the breeding habits and eggs of this species.

Nothing was definitely known of the breeding of this species till 1908, although erroneous reports of nesting have been received from time to time. At one time it was believed to breed somewhere in the north Atlantic, owing to the fact that large numbers may be seen there in summer. In collections eggs of *Puffinus kuhlii* from the Mediterranean and the Atlantic isles have done duty for it. The supposed eggs in Herr Nehrkorn's collection are said to have come from Greenland, but their origin is stated to be doubtful, and Reinhardt's statement that it breeds there is now generally discredited. Hewitson figured an egg attributed to this species from the Desertas near Madeira, but this is now known to be that of *P. kuhlii borealis* Cory (*fortunatus* Bannerman). Gradually the idea gained ground that the true breeding haunts must be looked for in the south Atlantic. Here another source of confusion arose, for eggs of *Puffinus griseus*, the "great" shearwater of the Chatham Islands and the New Zealand seas, were in several cases sold as those of this species. In 1906 the S. Y. *Valhalla* lay to for four days off Tristan d'Acunha in January, but owing to rough weather landing proved impracticable. Numbers of *P. gravis* were seen in pairs, and when about 140 miles east of the island large numbers were again observed. It was evident that they must be breeding somewhere in the vicinity, but no further investigation took place till Mr. P. C. Keytel visited the group in 1908. On that occasion he made an expedition to Inaccessible Island, and obtained at least four or five eggs of this species, together with skins, and on his return presented two of the eggs as well as skins to the South African Museum. Another egg was given by Dr. L. Péringuey to Dr. P. L. Sclater, who on his return from the cape to England, presented it to the British Museum. A fourth egg was purchased by me from Mr. Keytel and is in my own collection. Unfortunately I have been unable up to the present to obtain any notes from Mr. Keytel on the nesting habits and haunts of these birds.

Eggs.—The measurements of these four eggs are as follows:

1. 81 by 49.1 mm. British Museum. Presented by Dr. P. L. Sclater.
2. 79.5 by 50 mm. South African Museum, Cape Town.
3. 78.5 by 51 mm. Presented by Mr. P. C. Keytel.
4. 71.6 by 44.3 mm. Rev. F. C. R. Jourdain's collection.

All the eggs are white with no traces of markings, though slightly stained by the soil. The shape is a pointed oval, and they are entirely devoid of gloss. The surface is tolerably smooth, but under the microscope appears quite different in texture to that of *P. kuhlii*, being covered closely with minute granulations instead of a few scattered deep pittings. The shell of No. 4 is extremely thick and heavy, but this may be partly due to the fact that it is a somewhat undersized egg.

Mr. Jourdain has recently discovered another egg of this species in the collection of Mr. J. G. Gordon in Scotland. It came from Tristan da Cunha, was taken on May 29, 1917, and measures 70.30 by 46.9 millimeters.]

On the American side it ranges north along the Labrador Coast and off the southern part of Greenland. Captain Collins (1884), records that it arrived at latitude 43° 10′, longitude 62° 23′, on May 26, 1879, that it was most abundant near Le Have Bank to and including the Grand Bank, and that it departs for the south about the middle or last of October, and occasionally later. He says that for a few days after the arrival of the shearwaters in the spring, the birds do not seem to be on the lookout for food, but pass the time in resting in large flocks on the water, and that the same is their custom for a few days before their departure in the fall.

Food.—Off Chatham on Cape Cod or off the end of Cape Ann one may study the feeding habits of these birds to good advantage from a fishing boat, where fish cleaning is going on and the entrails and heads thrown overboard. One may go provided with fish livers and other choice titbits and from a clear sky attract these birds. From all sides they come skimming over the waves, alight softly on the water, and with head and breast held high and wings curved up and partly spread, they advance by rapid foot strokes to their feast. Greedily they seize the food with head and necks stretched along the surface of the water and they pay but little heed to the men in the boat.

As petrels and shearwaters suddenly appear even in a thick fog whenever oily fish gurry is thrown on the water, sailors believe that the birds are attracted by scent. But the organs of smell are very imperfectly developed in this family and it therefore seems much more likely that in their wide wanderings some birds chance upon the food, and that the cries of the fortunate ones soon attract others. Indeed fishermen sometimes immitate their cries in order to attract them. The following graphic account of the greater shearwaters on the fishing banks is contributed by Mr. Walter H. Rich:

The discovery of a morsel of food adrift means that every hag within reach will come charging down at full speed and plump headforemost into the midst of a plunging, striking mass of birds upon the water. Presently one will get a good hold upon the prize and strive to bear it away. Instantly he is mobbed, and a mix-up as desperate as any college football game can show is in progress at once. Here and there a bird slips quietly out of the mass and hurriedly gulps down the bit he has managed to secure, gasps a couple of times, sounds his squealing war cry, and runs upon the water with rapidly moving feet, his half-opened wings fanning the surface, his body held almost erect upon his tail, and plunges again head long into the mêlée. Here and there the curving fin or the waving fluke of the big blue shark shows above the water where he sculls lazily through the seas, rolling clumsily to snap at floating fish or waste and missing as often as he wins, for the hags take desperate chances with him, scuttling clear only at the last instant. Perhaps they are not always fortunate, for birds minus a foot or otherwise maimed are not lacking in the flocks. I saw one whose upper mandible was missing from the nostrils out. The bird seemed in pretty good condition, too, for food was plentiful and easily secured.

The meal finished they rest upon the water, if the weather is fine, bathing and dipping like sparrows in a puddle, with much shaking of wings, wagging of tails, and dipping of heads and beaks, rising on their tails to splash, dive, and splutter. This over, they settle down upon the sea to drift at ease, only rising to fly lazily to a position slightly in advance of the steamer, thus paralleling her course and making sure that they are properly placed at the next signal for hauling the net.

Besides refuse matter, shearwaters feed upon all sorts of surface swimming life, such as small fish and squids. I have found as many as 24 of the horny beaks of squids in the stomach of one shearwater. Mr. Rich adds:

Apart from that furnished by the fishing industry, the food of the hag consists of surface-swimming young fish of various species, a large amount of squid, and the "sand eels," the later, no doubt, furnishing a considerable portion in the menu. At the turn of the tide when the water is slack there is great activity among the hags, the birds flying about constantly at a considerable height—for them—sometimes fifty yards in the air, apparently searching for these fish, the lancelets, which are said to school at the surface in vast numbers at this time. I have seen vast schools of these "sand eels" with thousands of hags, an occasional shark, and even whales pursuing them.

Behavior.—The flight of the greater shearwater is extremely graceful and very characteristic. With long sharply pointed, slightly decurved wings they scale along close to the waves, sailing into the teeth of the wind by skillfully taking advantage of the air currents deflected upward from the surges. Now they turn on their side with one wing just grazing the water, the other high in the air. Again they take a few quick wing strokes and launch themselves just above a breaker, but so close that one expects to see them overwhelmed in the foam. One can not help noticing the shape of their bodies, cylindrical and tapering posteriorly, a cigar shape well adapted for rapid passage through the air without "dragging."

Owing to the great length of their wings shearwaters need a strong wind to rise from the surface of the water, and even then they often make the surface foam as they climb up the waves paddling vigorously with alternate feet. In perfect calms the advent of a swift-moving steamer in the midst of a flock becomes for these birds a matter of serious concern. They flap along the surface heavily, using both feet and wings, and as they struggle they "lighten ship" by vomiting up the contents of their crops and stomachs. Some, unable to rise above the water, endeavor to hide themselves below the surface by vigorous action of both wings and feet, but in this, as in the case of the proverbial ostrich in the sand, they are only partially successful. Like petrels the shearwaters occasionally skip along the surface of the water on their feet, using their wings to balance and support them.

The greater shearwater is on occasions an active diver, and is able to swim well under water. It dives from the surface of the water on which it first alights. Captain Collins (1884) says: "It is a common occurrence for a number of these birds to chase a boat for half an hour or more at a time, diving like a flash, every few minutes, after the bubbles made by the oars, which these winged rangers seem to imagine some kind of food beneath the surface of the water. They will also persistently follow a dory from which a trawl is being set, and diving in the wake of the boat, after the sinking gear, make desperate endeavors to tear the bait from the hooks." He states in a note that his brother in hauling trawls had found shearwaters caught by the hooks in their endeavors to steal the bait.

Audubon (1840) tells us that:

Two that had been caught with hooks, walked as well as ducks, and made no pretence of sitting on their rumps, as some writers have said they do. On being approached, they opened their bills, raised their feathers, and squirted an oily substance through their nostrils, which they continued to do when held in the hand, at the same time scratching with their sharp claws and bills. They refused all sorts of food; and as they were unpleasant as pets, they were set at liberty. To my great surprise, instead of flying directly off, as I expected, they launched toward the water, dived several yards obliquely, and on coming to the surface splashed and washed themselves for several minutes before they took to wing, when they flew away with their usual ease and grace.

The vocal performances of the greater shearwater are limited to harsh cries and screams which they emit when eager for food. Whether they have a nuptial song or not is unknown.

The eagerness of these birds for food is so great that they seem to be devoid of all fear of man and recklessly approach close to the boat from which the food supply comes. At such times they fight with other birds of their own or different species with great vigor. This pugnacity has led in times past to a cruel sport by fishermen which is thus described by Captain Collins (1884):

Perhaps a dozen or more hags may be caught, and having been put in a hogshead, tub, or in a "gurry pan," on the deck of the vessel, the fishermen bring about an internecine war by stirring them up with a stick. At such times the birds evidently imagine that their comrades are avowed enemies, and, pitching into their nearest neighbors, a general fight and terrible commotion ensues, while the feathers fly in all directions, much to the amusement of the men. The fishermen also sometimes tie two hags by the legs, using a string about one foot in length, which enables the birds to swim, but keeps them in unpleasant contact, the consequence being that they fight until one or both succumb.

Although shearwaters are exceptionally adapted to breast the storm, even they at times succumb. In the cyclone of August 26 to 27, 1894, which visited the southern coasts of the United States, Wayne (1894) found at Long Island, South Carolina, "countless numbers of *Puffinus major* dead upon the beach."

Prior to 1875 sea birds notably the greater and sooty shearwaters, were extensively used for bait on the Grand Banks, and the fishermen who used them were called "shack fishermen." Since that date the birds have been used less or not at all, for it has been more profitable to use other sources of supply. The methods used by shack fishermen have been described by Capt. J. W. Collins (1884). He says that two men in a dory provide themselves with lines five or six fathoms long, and mackerel hooks baited with large pieces of cod liver which float on the surface of the water.

Should there be a large number of hags, and more especially if they have been without food for a short time, they display an almost indescribable voracity. In their eagerness to obtain the large pieces of liver, which they swallow at a gulp, as they fight among themselves, they do not seem to care whether a hook is concealed within the bait or not. At such times the birds may be easily caught, and are rapidly pulled in by the fishermen, who usually derive much gratification from the sport, not only from the excitement which it affords, but also on account of the prospective profits which may result in obtaining a good supply of birds for bait. When a victim has been hooked, and is being pulled toward the boat, it struggles most energetically to make its escape by vainly endeavoring to rise in the air, or by spreading out its feet to hold itself back as much as possible as it is dragged unceremoniously over the water, while its vociferous companions follow after it, attempting to snatch away the piece of liver with which it has been decoyed. At times a bird may succeed in disengaging the hook from its beak, but usually the barbed point is well fastened and the hag is landed in the boat. A fisherman then places it under his left arm to prevent its struggles and grasping the head of the unfortunate bird with his right hand he crushes its skull with his teeth. Or he may try to deprive his victim of life by wringing its neck, striking it on the head with a " gob stick," etc. This may continue until one hundred or perhaps two hundred birds are captured, but usually not so many.

A comparatively short time passes before some of the birds become gorged with the pieces of liver which they have obtained, and then they exhibit the greatest cunning in eluding capture. They seem to be fully conscious of the fact that within the liver there is concealed something which for their own good they should avoid. With wonderful instinct that almost approaches reason, they cautiously approach and take hold of the bait with the tips of their bills, and, by flapping their wings, endeavor to tear it to pieces. In this maneuver the birds are often successful, and as a reward for their enterprise they secure a good lunch, which they hasten to devour as the disappointed and disgruntled fisherman rebaits his hook with the hope of decoying some less wary individuals.

Captain Collins says the shearwaters were formerly important items in the bill of fare of a Grand Bank fisherman, and that the men were sometimes very fond of this food. I have eaten both the greater and sooty shearwater and have found them not unpalatable, in fact rather good. In preparing sea birds much of the extreme fishy taste can be avoided by first removing the skin and underlying fat and replacing it by a thin covering of crumbs and small pieces of pork or lard. The birds should be roasted only slightly so that " the blood follows the knife."

The cylindrical tapering body, the long-curved and pointed wings and graceful flight make the recognition of the shearwater an easy one. The black bill, white breast and belly, the grayish-brown back, and dark head, the white patch at the base of the tail, and the dark bars on the sides and flanks are all points to be noted in the recognition of the greater shearwater.

Breeding range.—Known to breed only on Inaccessible Island in the Tristan da Cunha group in the middle of the South Atlantic Ocean.

Range.—The entire Atlantic Ocean, from northern Europe (Heligoland) to southern Africa (Cape of Good Hope) on the eastern side; and from the Arctic Circle in Greenland to southern South America (Tierra del Fuego) on the western side.

Spring migration.—Early dates of arrival: Atlantic Ocean, 43° 10′ north, May 26; Bermuda, June 2; Rhode Island, off Seaconnet Point, June 2; Massachusetts, Cape Cod, May 26; Nova Scotia, June 19; southern Greenland, Cape Farewell, June 7.

Fall migration.—Late dates of departure: Greenland, Cape Farewell, September; Nova Scotia, Sable Island, September 3; New York, Long Island, October 2; Massachusetts, November (latest December 31).

PUFFINUS PUFFINUS PUFFINUS (Brünnich).

MANX SHEARWATER.

HABITS.

Contributed by Charles Wendell Townsend.

The Manx shearwater, so called because it formerly bred in great numbers on the Isle of Man, is mainly a bird of the British Islands. As it is the familiar shearwater of Great Britain and bears a general resemblance to the greater shearwater, it is probable that some of the early records of this bird for America should be referred to the latter species. Audubon (1840) says, " I have procured this species to the westward of the banks of Newfoundland, or between their soundings and the American coast." Baird, Brewer, and Ridgway (1884) say:

Mr. Boardman informs me that a single individual of this species has from time to time been met with at sea off the coasts of Maine and Nova Scotia, but he regards such an occurrence as something extremely uncommon and as purely accidental. This bird is also mentioned as being only an accidental and very rare visitor on the coast of Long Island.

Putnam (1856) included it in the avifauna of Essex County, Massachusetts, from a skull in the Essex Institute, of a bird said to have been killed in Salem Harbor, August 13, 1855. The skull has since disappeared and there is no other record or remembrance of it. Reid

(1884) has this to say of the Manx shearwater in his Birds of Bermuda:

A specimen in Mr. Bartram's collection was captured while sitting on its solitary egg in a rocky hole on a small island in Castle Harbor, in April, 1864. The egg was unfortunately broken. There is no record of the birds' breeding on any other occasion, nor of any other specimen being obtained.

The Manx shearwater is generally said to be of accidental occurrence in Greenland, usually on the authority of Professor Reinhardt (1824). Captain Collins, who has had many opportunities to study the petrels and shearwaters on the Grand Banks and other American fishing grounds, has never seen it. Saunders (1889) says: "I saw two examples outside the Straits of Belle Isle on August 13–14, 1884, looking very black as compared with the great shearwater."

Nesting.—The Manx shearwater breeds in colonies on high cliffs, turfy slopes, and rocky islands. A single smooth white egg of fine texture is laid at the end of a burrow or in a crevice or under a fragment of rock, either on the bare rock or soil, or in a nest loosely constructed of dry grass or leaves. Turle (1891) says of its nesting habits on the Skellig Rocks:

There are plenty of shearwaters on the Little Skellig, but their great breeding grounds are on Puffin Island, between the Little Skellig and the mainland. This island ought to be called Shearwater Island rather than Puffin Island. I was astonished at the enormous number we found nesting; they seem completely to have taken possession of the island, and far predominate over the puffins; indeed, the whole of both sides of the island was inhabited by them. They lay only one egg, some considerable distance down their burrows; several which I dug out were four feet from the entrance. They make no nest, but lay their egg on the bare ground. In every case where I took an egg the old bird allowed itself to be lifted off the egg upon which it was sitting. These birds are never seen at their breeding grounds in the day time.

Eggs.—The measurements of 45 eggs, made by Rev. F. C. R. Jourdain, average 60.64 by 42.58 millimeters; the largest eggs measure **66.5** by 42 and 63.7 by **45.1**; the smallest eggs measure **56** by 42.5 and 58.5 by **39** millimeters.

Plumages.—The nestlings are covered with sooty-brown down with the exception of a white stripe along the center of the belly. The adult is about 15 inches long, a little larger than the Audubon shearwater, which it resembles in general coloration, and about 3 inches shorter than the greater shearwater. The bill is blackish-brown, the legs and feet yellowish flesh color. The plumage of the upper parts is sooty-black, of the lower parts, white. It would be well to bear these field marks in mind for a critical examination of the large flocks of shearwaters seen on the Labrador coast, for example, together with the judicious use of the gun, which might serve to give this species a more secure standing than it now holds in the American avifauna.

Food.—The Manx shearwater has feeding habits similar to those of other shearwaters. It is practically never seen by day about its breeding grounds, but appears as soon as the sun goes down. Its food consists of small fish, crustacea, squids, and surface-floating offal. When caught it emits a greenish oily fluid which leaves a yellow stain. Wright (1864) says that at the island of Filfola near Malta "both young and old feed on *Inula crithmoides,* one of the few plants that grow on that desolate rock." This habit, he says, accounts for the green color of the ejected fluid.

Behavior.—The flight is rapid and skimming, and the birds not infrequently settle on the water and dive freely; they remain under water but a short time. According to Saunders (1889) its "note is a *cuck-cuck-oo,* generally repeated three times." From its gutteral notes it obtains several local names. Thus in the Scilly Islands it is known as crew and cockathodon, and skidden; in Wales it is called cuckle. Yarrell (1871) speaks of "the gutteral melodies they pour forth as the spade approaches the end in which the egg is deposited. I once caught a pair in one burrow who were crooning a duet of this kind before we commenced operations. I presume they were in the honeymoon, as there was no egg."

Bewick (1847) quotes Willughby to the effect that at the Isle of Man the young of this species "become extremely fat, and are taken and salted down for keeping, and that the Romish Church permitted them to be eaten in Lent. * * * They usually sell them for about ninepence the dozen, a very cheap rate." It hardly seems necessary to invoke the agency of rats as a cause of the extermination of this bird in the Isle of Man.

DISTRIBUTION.

Breeding range.—On Iceland and the Faroe Islands; on the coasts of Wales and Ireland; on the Shetland, Orkney, and Scilly Islands; on the Inner and Outer Hebrides; and on the Azores, Salvages, and Madeira Islands. Formerly on the Isle of Man. The bird found breeding in Bermuda has been described as a distinct subspecies.

Range.—Northeastern Atlantic Ocean, chiefly in the vicinity of Great Britain. North to the coast of Norway and south to the Canary Islands. Westward rarely to Greenland and North America and perhaps regularly to South America.

Migrations.—Arrives on its breeding grounds in February and March; and leaves them in October and November.

Casual records.—Has been taken in Greenland (Umanak, 1872), Brazil (Iguape, September 21, 1901), and Argentina (Mar del Plata, October 4 to 9, 1914, 4 taken). The latter may be a regular winter resort. One found dead on Long Island, New York (Fire Island Beach, August 30, 1917).

Egg dates.—British Isles: Thirty-four records, March 14 to June 23; seventeen records, May 17 to June 1. Iceland: Three records, June 6, 10, and 15.

PUFFINUS LHERMINIERI LHERMINIERI Lesson.

AUDUBON SHEARWATER.

HABITS.

Contributed by Charles Wendell Townsend.

Audubon in The Birds of America begins his account of this species by the following sentence:

On the 26th of June, 1826, while becalmed on the Gulf of Mexico, off the western shores of Florida, I observed that the birds of this species, of which some had been seen daily since we left the mouth of the Mississippi, had become very numerous. The mate of the vessel killed four at one shot, and, at my request, brought them on board. From one of them I drew the figure which has been engraved. The notes made at the time are now before me and afford me the means of presenting you with a short account of the habits of this bird.

The great Audubon not only procured specimens, but he sketched them in the flesh, and recorded his notes on the spot, and with such care and detail that in many cases one can find nowhere else such a complete description of habits. Audubon considered this bird to be *P. obscurus.* Godman (1907), the latest authority on this group of birds, says that the Audubon shearwater " so much resembles *P. obscurus* that some of the American specimens are scarcely to be distinguished from it, and I separate the two with great hesitation."

Nesting.—The Audubon shearwater arrives on the breeding grounds early in the season. Bryant (1861) found that incubation had already begun in the Bahamas by March 24, Lowe (1911) found it with eggs at the Bermudas on May 12, and reports that Colonel Feilden obtained eggs of this bird in Barbados in March. Bonhote (1903) found in the Bahamas that the young were in most cases just hatched at the beginning of May, although several fresh eggs were procured. At the present day the bird is known in the Bahamas as the " pimlico " or " pemblyco."

Social in its disposition, this bird breeds in communities in holes, or crevices of the rocks, but seldom more than a foot from the surface. The single egg is laid on the rock or in a loosely constructed nest of twigs or dried grass. The egg is white, fragile, and not highly polished. The measurements of 39 eggs, in various collections, average 52.5 by 36.2 millimeters; the eggs showing the four extremes measure **57.3** by **40.8, 49.2** by 35.2, and 50 by **34** millimeters.

Young.—Incubation is carried on by both parents, and before the egg is laid both occupy the hole together. Bonhote (1903) says "the parent apparently does not brood the young, but merely sits beside it during the first day or two of its existence, after which it is left alone during the daytime."

Plumages.—The downy young is of a dusky gray color, whitish on the abdomen. The adult is only 12 inches in length while the greater shearwater is 20 inches. The upper parts including the wings and tail are a dark, sooty, brownish black; the under parts white; the sides of the breast grayish white. The bill is black. Godman (1907) gives the following critical analysis of the differences between this form and *P. obscurus:*

> The measurement of these two forms afford no characters for specific separation though *P. auduboni* would appear to have a slightly larger tarsus than *P. obscurus.* I find that the chief difference between the eastern and western birds lie in the browner color of *P. auduboni,* which is never so black as *P. obscurus.* The patch above the thighs is brown in the former bird, not black, and the band round the edge of the wing below is browner, and less distinct than *P. obscurus.*

Behavior.—About the breeding ground, the birds are seen and heard only at night, when they appear to be very active. The daytime is spent by those who are not on the eggs at a distance on the sea generally out of sight of land, where they rest on the water in large flocks. At times they are very shy, but in the Martinique Channel the birds are said to be so bold as to attempt to rob the fishermen of their fish in the canoes. Audubon (1840) says they skim low over the water near bunches of gulf weeds.

> Flap their wings six or seven times in succession and then sail for three or four seconds with great ease, having their tail much spread and their long wings extended at right angles with the body. On approaching a mass of weeds, they raise their wings obliquely, drop their legs and feet, run as it were on the water, and at length alight in the sea, where they swim with as much ease as ducks, and dive freely, at times passing several feet under the surface in pursuit of fishes, which, on perceiving their enemy, swim off but are frequently seized with great agility. Four or five, sometimes fifteen or twenty, of these birds will thus alight, and, during their stay about the weeds, dive, flutter, and swim with all the gaiety of a flock of ducks, newly alighted in a pond. * * * At times, as if by way of resting themselves, they alighted, swam lightly, and dipped their bills frequently in the water, in the manner of mergansers.

At the breeding grounds, according to Bryant (1861), " all night long their mournful cries can be heard." Bonhote (1903) says that he never saw the birds outside their holes, " nor could I distinguish their cries at night from those of the sooties." Wells says, in his notes sent to Mr. George N. Lawrence (1889), that they have a "peculiar cry resembling a cat howl." He also says (1902) : " They make a most unearthly noise when leaving and returning to their nest, hence the name given them by the fishermen [diablotin], which literally means ' little devil.' " Feilden (1889) says: " The young shearwaters uttered a plaintive, liquid-sounding note, something like *whitter, whitter, whit, whit, wit.*" Reid (1884) speaks of a young bird that " had become remarkably tame, following me about the house and garden, waddling along awkwardly enough on his tarsi, and uttering a musical ' chirrup ' the while."

Even this bird of the ocean is not proof against storms, for Wayne (1894) found a specimen of the Audubon shearwater washed up dead on the coast of South Carolina after the great cyclone of August 26–27, 1894, that destroyed countless numbers of the greater shearwater.

Reference has already been made to the use by the early colonists of this species as food. The recent history of this use is thus described by Wells (1902) : " When the young arrive at a certain stage they become simply a ball of fat inclosed in down; it is then that the fishermen take them in large numbers, and, after salting and drying them, they are taken to the different markets in Grenada, where they are readily bought and appear to be relished by certain people." Feilden (1889) quotes a letter from Rev. G. Duncan Gittens, who says " the birds, if very young, are a mass of gluten, and although very strong-tasted, when properly purified by lime juice and salt are by some considered a delicacy."

DISTRIBUTION.

Breeding range.—Bermuda, Santo Domingo, the Lesser Antilles (St. Thomas, Dominica, Barbados, Carriacou, Grenada, etc.), and the Bahama Islands (Andros and the Ragged Islands, Green, Washerwoman, and Ship Channel Keys, etc.). A subspecies breeds in the Cape Verde Islands.

Range.—The warmer portions of the western North Atlantic Ocean. West, more or less regularly, to Cuba, the Gulf of Mexico, and the coast of Florida. North to about 37° north, off Chesapeake Bay.

Casual records.—South Carolina (Sullivan Island, August 10, 1911), North Carolina (Beaufort, July 28, 1910), Virginia (Cobb Island, September 1, 1893), and New York (Bellport, Long Island, August 1, 1897).

Egg dates.—Bahama Islands: Thirty-five records, April 4 to 20; eighteen records, April 12 to 14.

HABITS.

The above name represents our present knowledge of this group of small shearwaters, about which there has been much misunderstanding and confusion. A specimen was taken on Sable Island, Nova Scotia, on September 1, 1896, and sent to Dr. Jonathan Dwight, who identified it as this species, which at that time was known to inhabit Australian and New Zealand seas and the Atlantic Ocean, as far north as the Madeira Islands. Since that time, however, European writers have recognized the birds of the North Atlantic as at least subspecifically distinct. Godman (1907) called it *Puffinus bailloni*, evidently considering it a distinct species, and gave quite a full account of its status. A still later account by Dr. E. Hartert [1] goes into the matter still further, using the name *Puffinus assimilis godmani*. Rather than discuss the matter here, I would refer the reader to these two publications. In compiling the life history it seems best to add to what has been published about the Maderian bird, which, of course, is the one that belongs in the American list, anything published about the bird of the southern hemisphere which will make the life history more complete. It is scanty enough at best.

Nesting.—Mr. David A. Bannerman (1914), under the name *Puffinus assimilis baroli*, says of its breeding habits in the Canary Islands:

The little dusky shearwater, concerning which so much discussion has recently taken place, was found breeding on Montana Clara. I had certainly not expected to meet with this usually very early breeder in any of the islands so late as June the 7th. The fact that I actually took eggs as well as the young in all stages, shows that there is great variation in the time of breeding of this species in the different islands of the group. It will be recollected that if the fishermen are to be believed, and I have often proved their statements to be correct, *P. a. baroli* had already bred and left the island of Graciosa by the 27th of May. Mr. Meade-Waldo took the young of this species in Teneriffe on April the 26th, and an adult on March the 16th with the bare hatching spot on its breast.

Shortly before our arrival a party from Haria had specially made the journey to Montana Clara to collect "tahoces," as *P. a. baroli* are locally called. Whether these individuals had succeeded in making a good haul I did not learn, but the only breeding-station which existed contained a very small number of birds. To reach this colony it was necessary first to ascend the mountain and having crossed the plateau, which lies at the summit, to descend the almost perpendicular inner wall of the crater of the floor beneath. In this basin, one side of which lies open to the sea, the little dusky shearwaters were

---

[1] British Birds, vol. 8, 1915, pp. 282–283.

breeding under the huge rocks which had fallen from above. It being impossible to reach this spot after dark, I was unable to obtain, as I had hoped, a series of adult birds, although several had practically attained mature plumage and could only be distinguished by one or two downy filaments still adhering to the feathers on the flanks. Only two eggs were obtained and a few nestlings in down.

Under the name of *Puffinus assimilis*, Mr. Ogilvie-Grant (1896) gives the following account of the breeding habits of the Madeiran bird:

Gould's little shearwater, so far as we ascertained, was the only other bird of the genus that visits Great Salvage. At Porto Santo we had already found it breeding plentifully on the Lime Island, and satisfied ourselves that it is this species—and not *P. obscurus*—that occurs there. The young birds do not show the white inner webs to the quills clearly, and hence Mr. Salvin and I were both led to believe that the specimens brought back in 1890 were the young of *P. obscurus*. I recently examined more than a dozen of old birds in Padre Schmitz's collection at Madeira, which had been obtained at Porto Santo, and these were, without exception, typical *P. assimilis*. At Great Salvage we procured downy young in various stages, and one late egg, almost fresh; this is large for the size of the bird, and the shell is pure white and perfectly oval in shape, the two poles being equally rounded. We never saw much of these birds. During the daytime there were generally some to be seen at sea, often in company with the Mediterranean shearwater, and one night an old female flew into our camp attracted by the powerful lantern. Every night our men used to sally forth in pairs to search for this and other species of petrels in their nesting cavities on the sides of the cliffs—bad enough walking, even in daylight, but no harm came of it. One man carried the lamp (a tin coffee pot it looked like, filled with kerosene oil, and with a coarse cotton wick protruding from the spout), which gave out a brilliant light, while his companion searched the numerous miniature caves and crevices till he had filled his own and the lamp bearer's shirts with birds of various kinds. In this way we got several nice adults of this species, which were never to be found with their young during the day. The note of these birds we never ascertained, and when seen on the wing they were always perfectly silent so far as we noticed.

Eggs.—The single egg of this species is nearly oval in shape, pure white in color, smooth, and without luster. The measurements of 43 eggs, in various collections, mainly furnished by Rev. F. C. R. Jourdain, average 50 by 35 millimeters; the eggs showing the four extremes measure **54.2** by 35.5, 50.5 by **37.5, 45** by 34, and 51 by **32.5** millimeters.

Plumages.—Buller (1888) describes the nestling as " covered with very thick slate-colored down on the upper and white on the under surface " and says: " A fledgling which I received from Sunday Island (one of the Kermadecs) is a very pretty object. The plumage is as in the adult, except that the longer wing-coverts and inner secondaries are minutely tipped with white; but the long, fluffy, dark-grey down still adheres to the sides of the body, and as the bird squats it looks as if reposing in a luxurious nest of down, which projects an inch or more from the body, and has a charming effect."

Behavior.—The same writer describes the flight of the allied shearwater, in which it seems to differ from the larger species of *Puffinus*, as follows:

They congregate in flocks, often of considerable size, and fly in a compact body, generally in a zigzag course, with a very rapid movement of the wings and not far above the water. Their flight is peculiar, too, in this respect, that they appear all to turn at the same moment, like a company of soldiers, showing first the dark plumage of the upper surface and then the white underparts as they simultaneously dip toward the water.

Their habits are sociable, and flocks may often be seen in the daytime disporting themselves in the sea, making short flight just above the surface, and then flopping into the water, splashing and chasing one another in their playful gambols, and when tired of their fun rising in a body and rapidly disappearing from view.

They seem to scatter at night, for as darkness approached I have noticed numerous single examples, as if the flocks of the daytime were dispersing over the surface of the ocean in quest of their food. They fly low but swiftly, and utter a note resembling the native name by which the bird is called, but somewhat prolonged, *paka-ha-a--paka-ha-a*.

Occasionally, perhaps once in several years, they appear in prodigious flocks and seem to cover the sea for miles around; but they soon scatter again over "ocean's boundless bosom," and are then not more plentiful than the other petrels.

DISTRIBUTION.

Breeding range.—The form which belongs on the American list, *Puffinus assimilis godmani*, breeds in the Azores, the Canary Islands, and the Madeira group. Represented by other allied forms in other parts of the world. Much confusion exists as to the relationships, nomenclature, and distribution of *Puffinus assimilis*, *Puffinus obscurus*, and their subspecies.

Range.—North Atlantic Ocean, mainly on the eastern side. Probably south to the Equator.

Casual records.—Accidental off Nova Scotia (Sable Island, September 1, 1896). Six records for Great Britain, most if not all of which are for this subspecies.

Egg dates.—Madeira and Canary Islands: Nineteen records, January 2 to July 2; 10 records, February 2 to 22.

PUFFINUS OPISTHOMELAS Coues.

BLACK-VENTED SHEARWATER.

HABITS.

Although this is one of the most abundant of the shearwaters on the Pacific coast, it is only within recent years that we have learned very much about its habits. Prof. Leverett M. Loomis has given us, in his various papers, much information regarding its migratory flights along the California coast, but we are indebted to Mr. A. W. Anthony for practically all we know of its life history.

Spring.—The migration is difficult to trace or define, owing to the wandering habits of this species, which seems to drift up and down the coast in search of a food supply. A general northward or southward movement is further obscured by the habit, common to this and other shearwaters, of flying in large circles or long loops. Mr. Anthony (1896*b*) noted that during February and March " 98 per cent of the black-vented shearwaters observed off San Diego were flying northward, and the reproductive organs of those taken late in February indicated that the nesting season was very near at hand. They would have bred within two or three weeks, I think." These birds were doubtless moving toward their breeding grounds at that time, where they probably arrive and begin preparations for nesting before the end of March.

Nesting.—Mr. Anthony (1896*b*) first found the black-vented shearwater breeding on Guadalupe Island, " which lies about 220 miles south of San Diego and about 65 miles from the nearest mainland, Punta Baja, on the peninsula." He visited the island on May 15, 1892, and writes:

The island is entirely of volcanic matter, huge cliffs of lava rising often 3,000 feet from the sea. These are honeycombed by thousands of holes and miniature caves, offering unexcelled nesting sites for Cassin's auklet, Xantus's murrelet, and other burrowing species, including the black-vented shearwater.

The cliffs about the North Head are all inaccessible, rising directly from the water, from a few hundred to nearly or quite three thousand feet, so that nothing could be learned of their nesting at that point. Three days later, however, we dropped anchor in Wheeler's Bay, at the southern end of the island, where the land is somewhat lower, and here a colony was found near the water. The burrows were in every instance either under a huge block of lava or in a crevice, where they were as much out of our reach as they were in the cliffs. A few of the burrows might have been opened, possibly, had we been provided with crowbars and suitable tools for wedging apart the blocks of lava, but after several ineffectual attempts with the tools nature provided we gave up and set a few steel traps at the mouths of some of the burrows in order to establish beyond dispute the identity of the species.

Again he writes (1900) of other breeding grounds farther south:

On the San Benito Islands, lying between Guadaloupe and Cerros Islands, I have also found a few *P. opisthomelas* nesting. So far as I have been able to discover, there are no burrows on these islands, all the nests being in small caves, which are nearly filled with deposits of guano left by untold generations of *Puffinus*. The caves are all small and the nests inaccessible, but I think that each cave was inhabited by several pairs of birds, judging by the outcry and warning hisses that greeted my approach to the entrance.

About thirty-five miles south of San Benito Islands lies Natividad Island, a lower and more sandy island than those previously mentioned—a condition which seems to suit the requirements of the black-vented shearwaters to a nicety, for here are found thousands of them, nesting the full length of the island, some three miles in extent. With the exception of a few rocky slopes and ridges, the entire island may be said to be one almost continuous colony. This island I first visited in August, 1896. The size of the burrows at once attracted my attention, and a closer examination revealed the unmistakable tracks of a *Puffinus*. Though the footprints were abundant and fresh, proving that the burrows were still visited at night, all of those examined were unoccupied. I again called at Natividad April 10, 1897, and found the breeding season at its height, each burrow containing either a pair of shearwaters or one shearwater and a fresh egg. In no case, I think, did I find an egg in a burrow with two birds. The burrows were usually about ten feet in length, seldom if ever straight, but with one or two sudden turns to the right or left, the nest sometimes being but two feet from the entrance, though at the end of a ten-foot burrow. Few of the nests were over eighteen inches below the surface, the burrows being for the most part nearly horizontal, and the loose nature of the soil made walking anything but a pleasure, as one constantly broke through into tunnels the exact location of which it was impossible to determine.

The tracks in the fresh soil about the entrance to the burrows showed the imprint of the tarsus for its full length, showing that the birds rest their weight on the tarsus as much as on the toes.

There was little attempt at nest-building, the eggs for the most part being laid in a depression in the sand at the end of the burrow. In a few cases a number of small twigs and sticks had been placed in the hollow, forming a very crude nest. Before the egg is deposited the burrow is occupied by both birds, and I have found them on the nest at least a month before any eggs were laid. Just how early they take to the burrows I am unable to say, not having visited the nesting colony earlier than the first week in March, when all the burrows were occupied.

Eggs.—The single egg of the black-vented shearwater is not very different from the eggs of other species of the genus *Puffinus*. In shape it is elliptical ovate or elliptical oval. The shell is somewhat pitted but fairly smooth and not glossy. The color is pure dead white. The measurements of 38 eggs, in various collections, average 60.9 by 41.2 millimeters; the eggs showing the four extremes measure **69** by 40, 60.5 by **43.5, 56.6** by 41.4, and 62.8 by **38.6** millimeters.

Plumages.—The young bird remains in the nesting burrow until it is fully fledged, which is not until it is fully grown also. It is covered for the first few weeks with long soft down, varying in color from "light drab" to "pale smoke gray" below. The first plumage begins to appear late in June or early in July. Mr. Anthony (1900) says of this plumage:

On July 1, I found the burrows on Natividad occupied entirely by young birds that were nearly or quite as large as the adults, but still clothed in down, through which were growing a few feathers. They were sooty black above and lighter below. When brought to the light they gave vent to their feelings in the characteristic notes of the adults.

The first plumage of the young bird is apparently similar to that of the adult and probably the seasonal changes do not produce any distinctive plumages. Mr. Leverett M. Loomis (1900), however, says:

In certain black-vented shearwaters (apparently immature birds) the white of the lower parts is also invaded by gray, the jugulum and throat being mottled, and in some cases the chin and fore breast. An extreme specimen is sparsely spotted on the abdomen and posterior portion of the breast. Some specimens display considerable white on the lower tail coverts."

Mr. Anthony (1896*b*) says that:

A complete molt of all the feathers occurs in July and August in this species and a more or less complete molt of the feathers of the head and body takes place in January and February.

Food.—The principal food of the black-vented shearwater seems to be small fish. Mr. John Treadwell Nichols writes me that he has "found a mass of partially digested, fine-boned fish in their stomachs." Mr. Anthony (1896*b*) writes:

The presence of this species along the coast of Southern and Lower California seems to be governed very largely by the food supply. They are common at any time, less so during the breeding season, when many are in the burrows during the day, and vastly more abundant in late July, August, and September, when they follow the large schools of herring and other small fish that come inshore at that season.

They are often seen in flocks of several thousands where fish are plenty. On one occasion I met with a flock on the coast of Lower California that I estimated contained not less than 50,000 shearwaters. Many were so gorged with herring that they could not rise from the water, but flapped along the surface in advance of the steamer until nearly overtaken, when they would dive. They would usually come up near enough to the vessel to be, if anything, more frightened than before, but could not take wing until they had disgorged a quantity of half-digested fish, after which they flew off with apparent ease.

On January 23 I was drifting in a skiff off Point Loma, watching the black-vented shearwaters, which were flying south along the western edge of an extensive bed of kelp. A garbage scow had sailed out through the kelp an hour before, leaving a broad oily "slick" a hundred yards in width, extending 2 or 3 miles westward, at right angles to the course taken by the shearwaters, which were passing in small flocks of four or five to a dozen every ten or fifteen minutes. Each flock turned sharply about when at a distance of a hundred yards from the oily water, and keeping at about that distance and to the windward, hurried on toward the west. *Not one bird* did I see cross contaminated water. I could detect no odor from the oil nor could the birds, had any existed, for they were flying down the wind.

I have never seen black-vented shearwaters pay any attention to bait or refuse thrown from the ship's galley, though dark-bodied, pink-footed, and slender-billed shearwaters will light to pick up floating garbage.

Though all of our shearwaters prefer to keep rather well offshore, they will at times follow schools of small fish into shoal water. I once saw a flock of one or two hundred black-vented shearwaters feeding in the surf at Cape Colnett. Hovering over the advancing breaker, they followed it to the beach, returning to meet the next, plunging repeatedly into its foamy crest for some species of small fish. They evidently did not feel at home so near land, for after a few minutes fishing they hurried out to sea again.

Behavior.—In the same paper Mr. Anthony makes the following observations on the flight of this species:

It is only during very calm weather that this species is seen resting on the water. At such times they collect in very compact flocks, covering the water till there is but little room left within the circle that they almost invariably form. The first gentle breeze will start them on their journey again, and I have learned to have confidence in a breeze that starts them flying, for as far as my observations go, they only rise if the wind is to be continuous, and will pay no attention to a gentle puff that will die out in a few minutes.

None of our Pacific coast sea birds adhere so closely to established fly lines as do the three species of *Puffinus;* even when flying fifty miles or more from land the first flock that passes will, with almost absolute certainty, mark the line which the next will follow, even though they be an hour behind. And I have long since discovered that in order to secure specimens of these shy species the boat must be placed in their fly lines. A flock will, on encountering a skiff directly in their path, either divide and pass on either side or all swerve slightly to one side, immediately resuming their line of travel in either case. At times, however, they are easily turned from their course.

The flight of the black-vented shearwater is more erratic, with more constant flapping, than that of other species. Mr. A. B. Howell writes me that he has seen them "progress by a series of ellipses when feeding, one side of which is within a foot of the water and the other eight or ten feet above."

Mr. Anthony (1896b) describes the notes of this species, as he heard them about Guadalupe Island, as follows:

It would be impossible to describe accurately these notes. They were a series of gasping, wheezy cries, resembling somewhat the escape of steam through a partly clogged pipe, uttered in a slightly varied key and repeated from four or five to ten times. During calm weather in January, February, and March flocks of a dozen to several hundred of these shearwaters often collect on the water well offshore, and at such times I have heard the same notes from two or more birds as they chased each other, half running, half flying, over the water. From the notes that came from the cliffs, I thought that the birds were chasing one another, and a little later many of them came down to the water and were occasionally seen as they flashed by within the circle cast by our anchor light. After an hour or so the outcry somewhat subsided, and I think most of the birds went offshore to feed, returning before daylight, for during nearly two weeks spent in cruising about the island only one flock of shearwaters was seen in the daytime.

Winter.—At the close of the breeding season these shearwaters wander from their breeding grounds northward, and perhaps southward as well. They are frequently seen along the California coast in the fall and winter, as far north as the Columbia River. These wanderings could, perhaps, hardly be considered a migration, as they are in the opposite direction to that usually taken by birds that breed in the Northern Hemisphere; but many of them certainly spend their season of leisure far north of their breeding grounds, to which they return during the latter part of winter or early spring.

DISTRIBUTION.

Breeding range.—Islands off the west coast of Lower California, Mexico (San Benito, Natividad, and Guadalupe Islands).

Range.—Abundant off the California coast except during the breeding season. Ranging northward more rarely to Washington and British Columbia (off Albert Head, October 24, 1891).

Migrations.—The main flight northward occurs in August and September and the return flight in February, March and April.

Egg dates.—Natividad Island: Twenty records, April 10.

PUFFINUS AURICULARIS C. H. Townsend.

TOWNSEND SHEARWATER.

HABITS.

This small shearwater, which resembles the black-vented shearwater in general appearance, was discovered and described by Mr. Charles H. Townsend (1890), who found it to be "a common species about the islands of the Revillagigedo group," during the visit of the United States Bureau of Fisheries' steamer *Albatross* to that remote region in 1888 and 1889. These islands lie way off in the Pacific Ocean, several hundred miles southwest of Cape San Lucas. To Mr. A. W. Anthony (1898) belongs the honor of having added this species to the North American list, as he found it "fairly common April 23, and again in early June" about Cape San Lucas, which brings it within the limits of our check list.

We are also indebted to Mr. Anthony (1898a) for practically all we know about the life history of this obscure species. He found it breeding abundantly on San Benedicte Island (also spelled Benedicto or Benedictu), in the Revillagigedo group. He says of this island:

The islands are all volcanic in origin and, in general, extremely rough and broken. On San Benedicte is found a heavy growth of coarse grass, wherever there is sufficient soil. But little other vegetation is found on the island. This grass, growing to the height of a man's head, made travel extremely disagreeable, as the barbed seeds penetrated our clothing by thousands and caused us much more trouble than the cactus thickets which we encountered on Clarion later. San Benedicte is a small island about three miles in length with an average width of half a mile.

Nesting.—Of the breeding habits of the Townsend shearwater, Mr. Anthony (1900) writes:

On San Benedicto Island I found a few nesting the last week in May. At this date most of the young were but a few days old, covered with sooty down above, and paler-grayish below. With the smaller young I often found one of the parents, but they were as frequently alone. The burrows were all confined to the higher parts of the island about 500 feet above the sea, where they were dug among the bunches of thick, tangled grass, and were well scattered, a dozen or so being a large colony. The burrows were not so deep or long as were those of *P. opisthomelas* of Natividad, averaging about 5 feet in length. On Clarion Island this species was again found in a similar location, all of the burrows being confined to a thick growth of grass, on the high parts of the island.

The Clarion colonies were more extensive, each suitable patch of grass being well populated. Few birds were seen at sea during the daytime and at night, those that visited the nest must have been much more silent than is the black-vented shearwater, in the vicinity of its colonies, for I do not remember hearing any notes that I could attribute to *P. auricularis* though one or two of those that were dragged from their nests gave vent to their displeasure in notes similar to those of *P. opisthomelas*.

Eggs.—Of the eggs, Mr. Anthony (1898a) says:

A single egg was found addled, and is now in the U. S. National Museum. It is pure white like the eggs of the other species of the genus that I have seen.

The egg referred to above was collected on San Benedicto Island, on April 30, 1897, and is, so far as I know, the only egg in existence. It is ovate in shape, slightly elongated, and is pure white in color. The shell is smooth and only slightly glossy. It measures 57.3 by 40.4 millimeters.

Young.—I have examined a specimen of the downy young, taken on San Benedicto Island on May 1, 1897, now in the collection of the Carnegie Museum (No. 21943); it is covered with long, soft, silky down on the upper parts, varying in color from "light drab" to "ecru drab," and with shorter, white down on the belly.

DISTRIBUTION.

Breeding range.—Known to breed only on the Revillagigedo Islands (Clarion and San Benedicto Islands) off the west coast of Mexico.

Range.—Does not wander far from its breeding grounds. North to Cape San Lucas and south to Clipperton Island.

Egg dates.—San Benedicto Island: One record, April 30.

PUFFINUS GRISEUS (Gmelin).

SOOTY SHEARWATER.

HABITS.

The ocean wanderers from Antarctic seas that spend their winters during our summer months off our coasts are better known to fishermen than to ornithologists, who have long remained in ignorance of the habits of the living birds. Their breeding habits have been a mystery and for many years they were supposed to breed far north and to be found off our coasts only in winter. Mr. Leverett M. Loomis, who has made extensive studies of the migrating water birds off the coast of California, has made some valuable additions to our knowledge of these birds and their movements. The results of his observations as applied to the sooty shearwater are summed up in the following well-chosen words of Mrs. Florence Merriam Bailey (1902):

The shearwaters taken at Monterey in May were in worn, molting plumage, common with birds just after the breeding season; while their sexual organs showed none of the functional development of birds about to breed. The migratory movements of these birds increased from May until September, when there was an abrupt decrease in their numbers, only stragglers being seen afterwards. Not only were the September and October birds in fresh plumage, but those secured had their sexual organs enlarged as in birds in the flush of the breeding season. As the shearwaters are known to breed from October to March on oceanic islands in the south temperate zone, the case seems to be a simple one.

The southward movement of this species, which is really its spring migration, begins in September and the bulk of the flight is over before the end of that month, though it is still to be found here in diminishing numbers during October and November on both our Atlantic and Pacific coasts. Mr. Loomis (1900) says: " These shearwaters *in transitu*, were exceedingly abundant on the 23d and 24th of September. Afterwards the species rapidly declined in the scale of abundance, in October and November only stragglers appearing."

Nesting.—Mr. F. Ducane Godman (1907) gives the following account of the nesting habits of this species:

It breeds in great numbers on some of the small islands off the coast of New Zealand, the nesting places being much harried by the natives, who esteem these shearwaters as an article of food. The burrows on the Chatham Islands are usually formed in peaty soil, running horizontally for three or four feet and then turning. The nest, a rude structure composed of sticks and dead leaves, is placed at the end of the hole. A single egg is laid, both sexes assisting in the work of incubation, and when the parents return to roost on shore in countless thousands, the noise they make is deafening. If removed from their burrows they flutter about on the ground for some time in a confused way, but eventually make for the sea.

Sir Walter Buller (1888) says of its breeding habits:

On the Island of Karewa and on the Rurima Rocks large numbers annually breed, sharing their burrows with the tuatara lizard, and submitting, season after season, to have their nests plundered by the Maoris, who systematically visit the breeding ground when the young birds are sufficiently plump and fat for the calabash.

Eggs.—He also describes an egg as follows: " An egg, supposed to belong to this species, is ovoide elliptical in form, measuring 3.1 inches in length by 1.95 in breadth; it is white, with a smooth surface, but much discolored by soiling." Mr. A. J. Campbell (1901) describes the single egg as " round oval in shape, texture of shell somewhat coarse, surface minutely pitted and slightly glossy, colour, pure white, but frequently more or less stained with dirt."

The measurements of 34 eggs, collected from various sources, average 74 by 48 millimeters; the eggs showing the four extremes measure **81.7** by 49.2, 79 by **53.4, 58.5** by 42.5, and 60.5 by **42** millimeters.

Young.—Sir Walter Buller (1888) in referring to the young says:

Mr. Marchant informs me that he found this species breeding in burrows near the summit of the Island of Kapita about the end of February. The excavations were in peaty ground over which a fire had passed, destroying all surface vegetation. The young at this time were half-grown, covered with light grey down, and extremely fat. On being held up by the feet, oily matter ran freely from their throats. The old birds, on being taken hold of, fought fiercely with their bills.

There are some nesting grounds of this species on Whale Island on the Bay of Plenty. I visited these breeding places about the middle of January and found the nestlings still occupying their deep burrows, but they were well grown, with black quills and tail feathers sprouting vigorously through their thick downy mantle of slate grey.

Probably, as is the case with nearly all of this genus, the young bird passes from the downy stage directly into a plumage resembling the adult. Apparently there is only one complete annual molt long after the close of the breeding season or during our summer.

Food.—Capt. J. W. Collins (1884) says in regard to their food:

From my observations I am of the opinion that the hag subsists chiefly on squid, which, of course, it catches at or near the surface of the water. I have opened many hundreds of them and have never, to my recollection, failed to find in their stomachs either portions of the squid, or, at least, squid's bills. It may be interesting also to mention the fact that in the fall of 1875, when the giant *Cephalopods*, or "big squid," were found on the eastern part of the Grand Bank between the parallels 44° and 45° north latitude, and the meridians of 49° 30′ and 50° 30′ west longitude, flocks of hagdons were invariably found feeding on the dead "devil fish" which were floating on the water. In nearly all cases these "big squid" were found in a mutilated condition, usually with their tentacles eaten off almost to their heads, and the fishermen soon learned to detect their presence by the large flocks of birds collected about them. The small species of fish which frequent the waters of the eastern fishing banks, such as the lant, capelin, etc., also furnish *Puffinus* with a portion of its food. But birds of this species, as well as most all others found at sea, are excessively fond of oily food, and especially the livers of the Gadidae, cod, hake, etc., and this extreme fondness for codfish livers, which they swallow with great avidity, renders their capture possible by the fishermen with hook and line.

Behavior.—The flight of the sooty shearwater is swift, graceful, and strong; like other species of *Puffinus*, it can sail for long distances on its long, stiff wings without even a tremor, except to adjust them slightly to the wind, rising at will over the crests of the waves or gliding down into the valleys between them and turning as the albatrosses do by lowering the wing on the inner side of the curve and raising the wing on the outer side, both being held in a straight line, the angle of incline depending on the sharpness of the curve. It frequently flaps its wings, however, when occasion requires it and uses them freely in its squabbles for food. It sometimes experiences a little difficulty in rising from the water in calm weather, but ordinarily it does so very readily. It swims lightly and swiftly on the surface and dives below it occasionally in pursuit of food, using its wings freely under water. It has frequently been caught on the trawl hooks of the cod fishermen.

While with us this shearwater is usually silent except when squabbling for food, but on its breeding grounds it is evidently quite noisy. Sir Walter Buller (1888) says: "These birds are at all times more nocturnal than diurnal, and when hovering overhead at night utter a frequent call note, like *tee-tee-tee*, from which the Maori name is derived." Mr. Walter H. Rich writes to me that when on Georges Bank he "did not hear the nasal, squealing battle cry from a black hag," and the only sound which he "could with certainty trace to this species was a low, gutteral '*wok-wok-wok*' when much excited."

Although usually to be found only far offshore, shearwaters are occasionally driven in near the land in stormy weather, particularly when gathering into flocks or migrating. Mr. Loomis (1900) says: "During a dense fog on the morning of June 2, and again on the morning of the 3d, many in going down the coast passed within a few hundred yards of the Monterey Wharf, illustrating the deflecting influence of low fogs upon movements." Only once have I known them to come inside the harbor at Chatham, Massachusetts, which the fishermen said they had never known them to do. On September 5, 1909, the weather was very thick and stormy outside, and there was a strong flood tide, on which a large flock of shearwaters had apparently drifted in over the bars. We were anchored, fishing, near the entrance of the harbor as they drifted past us, sitting on the water in a large scattered flock and facing the strong northeast wind. I counted about 275 of them; there were about a dozen of the Cory shearwaters, and all the rest were sooty shearwaters. When disturbed by a passing boat they all rose and flew past us out toward the bars, only to drift in again with the tide and repeat the operation.

Winter.—On their return to northern waters these shearwaters may be looked for in May and they become very abundant at times during the summer, but in order to find them one must look well offshore as a rule. I have frequently seen them in large numbers about 10 miles out at sea, off Chatham, Massachusetts, near the elbow of Cape Cod. Here we used to go out with the fishing fleet to the cod banks, when the sea was smooth enough to allow them to navigate among the dangerous sand bars that guarded the entrance to the harbor. It seemed as if we were really at sea when the boat began to rise and fall on the long ocean swell, gliding down into the valleys and over the crests of mountainous seas; here the little Wilson petrels flitted past us, pattering over the waves, and these real pelagic wanderers, the shearwaters, were first seen gliding along close to the water on long pointed rigid wings, like miniature albatrosses. There were three species—the greater, the sooty, and the Cory shearwaters; the first species far outnumbered all the others and the last was much the rarest of the three. The dark bodied and still darker winged sooty shearwater could be easily recognized at any distance. We experienced no difficulty in tolling them up to the boat, where we could study them at close range, by throwing overboard the oily livers of what fish we had caught or any other greasy offal. It was remarkable to see how quickly they would gather; even when none were in sight for miles around us, they seemed to scent the presence of food and would come from far and wide to gorge themselves on the feast we had provided. Even in foggy weather they seemed to have some means of locating us and would suddenly appear, as if by intuition, when they could hardly have been guided by sight. They must have some means of communicating with each other or indicating by their movements where food is to be found. When a morsel of food is discovered the bird plunges awkwardly down onto the water, striking on its breast with a great splash and gulping down the savory morsel with eager haste.

Occasionally it plunges beneath the surface to catch a sinking bit of flesh and often great squabbles take place between several birds, struggling to secure the same pieces and making the water fly in their greedy eagerness. It is not difficult to get them near enough to photograph them and it is not necessary to shoot any for specimens for they can be easily caught on baited hooks. They are hard to kill, however, as they are very tenacious of life. They eject from their mouths and nostrils, when caught, a great profusion of bad smelling oily fluid, which soils the plumage and is very difficult to remove.

The sooty shearwater is known to the fishermen as the "black hagdon," "hag," or "haglet." On the fishing grounds about the Grand Bank off Newfoundland the shearwaters are very abundant and were formerly caught, with hook and line, in enormous numbers to use for bait. According to Capt. J. W. Collins, the sooty shearwater is much less abundant on the fishing banks than the greater shearwater, which outnumbers it about 100 to 1. Capt. Collins (1884) published, in the tenth annual report of the United States Fish Commissioner, an exhaustive and very interesting account of the habits of the shearwaters and fulmar, part of which was reprinted in *The Osprey* and is well worth reading. He gives a full account of the method of catching codfish, known as "shack-fishing," in which the "hagdons" were largely used as bait prior to 1875, and says that since that time "it has generally been found more profitable to depend on other sources for a bait supply;" he also describes the methods used in catching the shearwaters and preparing them for bait. Referring to the social habits of these birds he says:

When the birds reach their destination in the spring, for a few days after their arrival, they do not seem to make any special effort for the purpose of securing food, but pass most of their time sitting in large numbers on the water, and at this period it is somewhat difficult to catch them on hook and line. Occasionally a flock will make a short flight and again settle down, but there appears to be a strong inclination, at that time, to huddle together and keep up the organization which has probably existed during their migration from distant regions. The same thing in regard to going in flocks is noticeable in the fall when they collect for their autumnal migration from the fishing-banks.

DISTRIBUTION.

Breeding range.—Islands in New Zealand seas. On New Zealand (Otaya, Kaimanawa Ranges, and near Wellington), on Norfolk, Stewarts, Kapiti, Snares, St. Stephens, Auckland, and Chatham Islands, and probably many others. Also breeds on islands near Cape Horn.

Range.—Widely distributed over both great oceans. North in the Atlantic Ocean in summer, to Labrador, southern Greenland, the Faroe and the Orkney Islands; and in the Pacific Ocean to the Kurile and Aleutian Islands. South in the southern oceans, probably to about 60° south.

Spring migration.—Appears on the Atlantic coast of North America in May; North Carolina, Fort Macon, May 21; New Jersey, Sea Isle City, May 25; Rhode Island, off Seaconnet Point, June 2; Massachusetts, Pigeon Cove, May 29; southern Greenland, off Cape Farewell, June 22. On the Pacific coast the main flight arrives off California in May, but the species has been recorded in every month in the year.

Fall migration.—Disappears from the north Atlantic in September and October; most of the British records are in these two months. Main flight leaves the California coast at about the same time.

Casual records.—A straggler was taken in Rhode Island (off Point Judith, March 28, 1902).

Egg dates.—Islands near New Zealand: Nineteen records, November 16 to April 28; ten records, November 19 to 26. Cape Horn: Two records, December 23 and January 1.

PUFFINUS TENUIROSTRIS (Temminck).

SLENDER-BILLED SHEARWATER.

HABITS.

Among the vast flocks of dark colored shearwaters which we saw as we passed through Unimak Pass and entered Bering Sea, on June 4, 1911, we were confident that this species was represented. Unfortunately, we were unable to collect any specimens for identification and we shall therefore never know whether these immense gatherings of sea birds were made up of sooty or slender-billed shearwaters or both. Mr. Rollo H. Beck and I thought we recognized both species, as they flapped away almost under our bow, but I have since decided that any such identification would be worthless, as it is difficult to distinguish the two species even in the hand. Whatever the species may have been, its numbers were beyond estimate, the smooth surface of the sea was covered with them for miles and miles, a vast multitude, far greater than I had ever seen, or ever conceived, and as we passed through this great sea of birds they merely parted under our bow sufficiently to let us pass. After seeing such a spectacle, I can more easily believe the accounts I have read of the astonishing abundance of the "mutton bird," as this shearwater is called, on its breeding grounds about New Zealand, Australia, and Tasmania.

The following remarkable statement by Flinders, quoted by A. J. Campbell (1901), seems almost incredible:

A large flock of gannets was observed at daylight, and they were followed by such a number of sooty petrels as we had never seen equaled. There was a stream of from 50 to 80 yards in depth and 300 yards or more in breadth. The birds were not scattered, but were flying as compactly as a free movement of their wings seemed to allow, and during a full hour and a half this stream of petrels continued to pass without interruption, at a rate little inferior to the swiftness of the pigeon. On the lowest computation, I think the number could not have been less than a hundred millions. Taking the stream to have been fifty yards deep by three hundred in width, and that it moved at the rate of thirty miles an hour, and allowing nine cubic yards of space to each bird, the numbers would amount to 151,500,000; the burrows required to lodge this quantity would be 75,750,000; and allowing a square yard to each burrow, they would cover something more than 18½ geographical square miles of ground.

Nesting.—Of the several accounts that have been published I have selected the following, by the Rt. Rev. H. H. Montgomery, D. D., bishop of Tasmania (1898), which describes most fully and graphically the nesting habits of the slender-billed shearwater in the neighborhood of Bass Strait, Australia:

For many years, as episcopal duties have called me to the Furneaux Islands in Bass Strait, I have given attention to the habits of what is locally called the "mutton-bird." This petrel is now adequately protected by an act of the Tasmanian Parliament; and although some 400,000 young birds are salted down for consumption in a good year, chiefly by half-castes, yet there is no chance of the extinction of this species under present conditions. The day may come, indeed, when the population of these islands shall have increased so much that fresh legislation may have to be initiated, but that day has not yet arrived. There are also numerous islands near the Victorian coast, at present absolutely unvisited, swarming with these birds. The absence of boat harbors, and as well as of fresh water and wood, protect these summer visitors from depredators. The following facts may be taken as accurate; there is certainly no difference of opinion about them among the people who have spent their lives in these islands: The mutton-bird (*Puffinus tenuirostris*) appears with the greatest regularity about September 17th in these waters, having come apparently from the direction of the South Pole; for, after inquiry of the captains of ships, I can discover no one who has met with them between May and September, although their numbers at other times can be computed only by millions. The obvious difficulty is that the season when they disappear is midwinter. It is also noteworthy that the whole period from September 17th till the beginning of May is taken up with the rearing of their young. When they appear in September they are believed to have paired already, and they commence at once to scratch out their holes, the process lasting, with intervals, for six weeks. One bird is seen to be at work at a time, and always in the night. In the daytime they depart seaward. Indeed, so persistent is their desertion of the breeding-places by day that it would be quite possible for unobservant persons to live on these islands and to be unaware that the petrels breed there at all, except perhaps at the season when the young birds take to the water. It is almost true to say that I never saw a petrel in the daytime near their rookeries during the eight years that I have been visiting them. The universal belief is that these birds dare not alight on the ground in daylight because of the gulls and crows, for the length of their wings make them unable to fly off flat ground. The petrels depart about November 1st, and are only seen occasionally till November 20th, when they return in tens of thousands to lay their eggs, one for each pair, and they are laid almost on the same night in each locality. Islands differ, some being earlier than others, but I have heard of no egg being taken before November 18th. If the egg is taken, there is good reason to believe that no other is laid; but the birds, being very gregarious, return to sleep on the rookery, although they may have no young to tend. The Government permits consumption of the eggs on the island, but none are to be exported. As a matter of fact, the eggs are not fit to take after they have been laid three days. During the period of incubation the parents take it in turns to sit, exchanging positions after about a week. The young birds appear about January 15th, and for a fortnight or so they are in danger of snakes, which swarm on some islands, such as Chappell Island and Babel, and are entirely absent from others, such as Little Dog Island. The eggs, however, are safe, for the old birds can easily defend themselves when sitting. "Birders" say that birds and snakes are not found in the same hole; but if a man seizes a snake in place of a bird he must pull it out, for to relax his grip is to court danger. There are always signs if there is a bird in a hole, for the parents carefully clean out the passage before they depart for the day and stuff the entrance with dry rookery grass. In March the feathers of the young begin to grow; before this they are fat, downy creatures. By act of Parliament "birding" commences in Tasmanian lands on March 20th and continues till the surviving birds fly away about the beginning of May. When the young petrels are fully feathered the parent birds desert them altogether and depart seaward, the result being that the new generation is driven from the holes by hunger, and, without assistance from the old ones, they have to find their way to the water and to learn to fly and feed. All their traveling is done by night, for fear of their enemies (the large gulls); but even so, a great many are killed upon the water or upon the shore when too weak or inexperienced to escape. Still, in spite of the efforts of man and of winged bipeds, the sea is black with young birds in May, and fully one-third of the young petrels survive.

Let us now imagine ourselves standing on a rookery in the evening awaiting the arrival of the old birds as the sun approaches the horizon. The islands where the petrels breed are as a rule devoid of trees. They are sandy knolls covered with long grass, and seem useless, except to feed a few sheep. Chappell

Island has an area of 1,200 acres, Little Dog Island about 120 acres. These are fair specimens of the rookeries, and I have calculated that 40,000 holes per acre is not an exaggerated estimate. All day long the young birds are absolutely silent. The uninitiated might imagine that nothing edible existed underfoot, and that they stood upon a deserted rabbit-warren. Gazing out to sea on all sides, the watcher will not yet detect a single petrel; not till the sun has set and the darkness is increasing is there any sign of the wonderful rush of birds, which, to a naturalist, is so fascinating a sight. The following figures, noted in the month of February, may be of interest: 6.36 p. m., not a petrel in sight; 6.40, the first bird visible out at sea; 6.43, the sun disappeared; 6.48, sunset from the top of the lighthouse (Goose Island) and the light flashed out; 6.53, the first petrel flew rapidly over the island without settling; 6.56, the numbers so great that I ceased counting; 6.58, the numbers become bewildering; 7.06, the numbers at their maximum—tens of thousands whirling, wheeling, flashing up from all sides, are whistling like bullets past one's head, till it seemed almost dangerous to stand up; 7.30, nearly all the birds had arrived. Then, and not till then, do the noises commence. The flight inward of the parent birds is conducted in absolute silence. Nothing, indeed, can be more weird than this rush of dumb creatures, so perfect in flight, but uttering no sound. As soon as the majority have arrived the ground emits the most extraordinary sounds—gurglings, groaning, and hoarse laughter. It must be confessed that there is no music in the note. On Chappell Island some 300,000 young birds would at this moment be receiving· oil into their throats, poured into them by the parents, who thus give them the one meal the fledglings receive in the 24 hours.

I now proceed to give the results of a whole night spent on a large rookery on Big Dog Island, under a full moon, a roaring westerly gale blowing over the island. It was March 1, 1896. With watch and pocketbook I lay among the birds or walked silently about noting what I now set down: Up to 10 p. m. the underground noises continue, then silence falls on the rookery. The young birds are digesting; the parents are resting; but the latter are not by any means all in the holes for some of them come out almost immediately and walk about among the long grass, and many of them sleep in the open air. I stepped silently about among them as they crouched on the ground; in no case did they put their heads under their wings, as many birds do. Often one of them walked up to my foot, and the slightest movement on my part sent him scurrying away like a rabbit quite unable to fly off the ground. The moon was so bright that the rookery was almost as light as day. All night long a few score of birds flitted noiselessly over the rookery, just skimming the tops of the low bushes and passing within a foot of my face as I lay concealed. Hour after hour this graceful quadrille proceeded almost without sound of wings and as from creatures absolutely incapable of speech. At about 2.30 a. m. the rookery awoke. Noises came from all sides; a larger number of birds flashed silently over the ground. I walked toward a sandy ridge some thirty yards from the shore. Scores of birds walked up to the edge, then they raised their wings right over their backs till they nearly met at full stretch. They stood thus quivering in the wind for a few seconds, and then launched themselves into the air and were at once in flight. Close by a bird underground was sending a fountain of sand into the air as he cleaned out the hole preparatory to departure. At 3.15 a. m. the rookery was fully awake; hundreds of birds were leaving. I passed on and laid myself down within eight paces of a large rock with sloping sides and watched the birds as they clambered up it, and, extending their wings in the manner I have described, launched themselves into the air. In every case, they faced the wind to perform this operation. At times, indeed, they were so numerous that they were jostling each other, but in perfect harmony. At 4.43 I counted a score on the rock together, and they were all silent; at the approach of daylight, 4.53, quite a rush of birds anxious to depart; 5.05, a few still left; 5.15, the last bird flew away from the rock I was observing. All around hardly a petrel was visible; just a few were wheeling in mid-air. At 5.19 the last of these birds disappeared and the rookery seemed to be absolutely devoid of life. At 5.23, just four minutes after the last petrel had flown away, I heard the wailing of a Pacific gull, and its form was visible in the distance. In a few minutes more a squadron of twenty of these creatures, accompanied by as many crows, came sailing over my head, croaking and calling, and quartering the ground to see whether any belated bird could be discovered. At 5.41 the sun rose. I advance my theory, which is borne out by the experience of all the half-castes and white men who have spent their lives in these regions, that the sooty petrels come to feed their young only and in complete silence, and leave again before the other birds are awake, because only by this means are they safe from enemies in whose presence they are helpless when on the land. In the air, of course, they fear no such foes.

Buller (1888) makes the following statements regarding the nesting habits of *Puffinus tenuirostris* in New Zealand:

This species of petrel is very abundant on our coasts, and retires inland, sometimes to a distance of fifty miles, to breed. It nests in underground burrows, forming often large colonies, and resorting to the same breeding place year after year.

It is very plentiful in the Hauraki Gulf, and is diurnal in its habits. It associates on the water in large communities, has a vigorous flight; and utters a peculiar cry represented by the syllables *na-kwa-kwa,* from which it takes its native name. It breeds on all the islands in the gulf, not, however, in colonies, but each pair selecting its own locality and excavating a burrow, sometimes five feet in extent, with a rounded chamber at the farther end where a single egg is deposited about the end of September. A specimen in my son's collection, from Lord Howe's Island, is of a rather elliptical or slightly pyriform shape, measures 2.75 inches in length by 1.6 in breadth, and is perfectly white.

Young.—Mr. A. J. Campbell (1904) describes the early life history of the young bird as follows:

After the pure white egg is deposited by the female, she goes to sea for a week to recruit and grow fat and saucy, while her lord takes his domestic turn and sits steadfastly on the egg. He goes out the following week, and they proceed, turn after turn about, for eight weeks, till the precious chick is hatched. The young are fed in the burrows for about three months, till about the middle of April. Just fancy what a strange existence for the happy, or unhappy, chick to be reared in a sandy burrow for three long months, and to be alone every day from dawn till dark. The young are curious-looking objects, clothed in long, dark down, with black bill and eyes and feet to match. At a certain stage a young bird will weigh about 3¼ pounds, and be heavier than either of its parents, who at this stage desert it and proceed to sea for good. The youngsters will then thrive on their own fatty nature for a week or so; quills and feathers sprout, and the birds becoming hungry, and, having learnt to stretch their own wings, proceed to follow their parents. Quitting Bass

Strait, all will disperse for the winter over the milder waters of the Pacific, some of the birds wandering even up to Japanese waters before returning in crowds to Phillip Island again the following nesting season. How marvelous, without a chart or compass, to roam the western Pacific from north to south, and without calendar to return to land again almost to a day to lay.

Eggs.—Mr. Campbell (1901) describes the egg as follows: " Clutch, one; inclined to oval shape, occasionally more elliptical; texture of shell somewhat coarse; surface minutely pitted, slight trace of gloss on some examples; color, pure white."

The measurements of 40 eggs, in various collections, average 71 by 47 millimeters; the eggs showing the four extremes measure **77.2** by 40.5, 73 by **51.5, 63.5** by 44, and 65.2 by **41** millimeters. The period of incubation is said to be 56 days.

Food.—Capt. William Walter (1902), of the steamship *Westralia*, gives us the following account of its food habits:

When coming out of Otago Harbor on Sunday, the 26th of November, some of these petrels, in immense numbers, were settled on the water and feeding on what is locally known as " whale feed "—small shrimplike creatures about an inch long, and which at times are so numerous as to color the water for acres brick-red. It was almost calm, and as we drew up to the birds a passage was opened up through them as we passed. It was amusing to watch their efforts to escape—many of them were so filled as to be unable to fly, and attempted to escape by diving and paddling frantically away from the vessel. It was noticed that many, in their efforts to escape, ejected the reddish substance they had been feeding upon. They appeared to extend several miles north and south of Otago Heads.

The birds which we saw in Unimak Pass were probably feeding on similar food, for we were told that their presence in large numbers was always dependent on the abundance of whales. Small whales were certainly plentiful at that time and the birds were probably feeding on the refuse left by the whales or were chasing the same kind of small marine animals.

Behavior.—Mr. R. H. Davies (1843) describes the following method of capturing these birds for their feathers in their breeding grounds in Tasmania:

The birds can not rise from the ground, but must first go into the water, in effecting which they have made a great many tracks to the beach similar to those of a kangaroo; these are stopped before morning, with the exception of one leading over a shelving bank, at the bottom of which is dug a pit in the sand. The birds finding all avenues closed but this follow each other in such number that as they fall into the pit they are immediately smothered by those succeeding them. It takes the feathers of forty birds to weight one pound; consequently sixteen hundred of these birds must be sacrificed to make a feather bed of forty pounds weight. The feathers, as Tasmanian travelers well can tell, have a strong, disagreeable scent.

Mr. Davies says further:

The young birds leave the rookeries about the latter end of April or form one scattered flock in Bass's Straits. I have actually sailed through them from

Flinders Island to the heads of the Tamar, a distance of eighty miles. They shortly afterwards separate into dense flocks, and finally leave the coast. The old birds are very oily, but the young are literally one mass of fat, which has a tallowy appearance, and hence I presume the name of "mutton bird." To this I may add that the young birds are very good when fresh, and the old birds after being skinned and preserved in brine are excellent eating.'

Winter.—After the breeding season is over, in April, the slender-billed shearwaters apparently migrate into the Northern Hemisphere in the north Pacific Ocean. The northward migration route seems to be mainly on the Asiatic side, probably to the vicinity of the Commander and Aleutian Islands; Doctor Stejneger (1885) suggested that a few of these shearwaters might breed in that region, but it now seems to be well established that the species is merely a summer sojourner in northern seas between its breeding seasons in Australian waters. Mr. Leverett M. Loomis tells me that this species is seen on the California coast only late in the fall on the return migration to its breeding grounds. The large numbers seen off Monterey between the 14th and 20th of December, in 1895, by Mr. Joseph Mailliard were probably belated migrants.

The large series of slender-billed shearwaters in the collection of the California Academy of Sciences is conclusive evidence of the abundance of this species on the coast during the southward migration in the fall.

DISTRIBUTION.

Breeding range.—Southern Australian and New Zealand seas. Mainly in Bass Straits and vicinity (Flinders, Phillip, Big Dog, Kings, and Green Islands, etc.). Also on Lord Howe Island and on New Zealand (Kaimanawa Ranges).

Range.—Migrates northward throughout the north Pacific Ocean to the Okhotsk and Bering Seas and eastward, mainly on the return migration, to the coast of North America.

Migrations.—Northward in the western Pacific Ocean and southward in the eastern. Dates: Commander Islands, Copper Island, May 29, and Bering Island, August 22; Aleutian Islands, Unimak Pass, July 29, and Unalaska, August 31; Alaska, Ugashik, September 15; British Columbia, Victoria, October 24; Washington, August to November; California, Point Pinos, October 13 to January 30. Main flight passes California in November and December.

Casual records.—Northernmost record is one taken in northern Alaska (Kotzebue Sound, July 4, 1899). Latest winter record is for British Columbia (one taken February 23, 1904).

Egg dates.—Islands in Australian and New Zealand seas: Twenty-three records, November 11 to March 3; twelve records, December 1 to 17.

THYELLODROMA PACIFICA (Gmelin).

WEDGE-TAILED SHEARWATER.

HABITS.

This species seems to range entirely across the Pacific Ocean from Volcano Island, south of Japan, to the islands off the west coast of Mexico, including the Marshall Islands, from which it was described by Salvin, and the Hawaiian Islands. Mr. A. W. Anthony (1898) was the first to record it as a North American bird, finding it about Cape San Lucas associated with the Townsend shearwaters in " April 23 and again in early June."

Nesting.—Mr. Anthony (1900) found the wedge-tailed shearwater breeding abundantly on San Benedicto Island, concerning which he writes:

About Cape St. Lucas, and between that point and the Revillagigedo Islands, the wedge-tailed shearwater (*Puffinus cuneatus*) is found in abundance in May and June. It probably may occur at other seasons, but as I have not visited the region of the Cape during other seasons I can give no assurance of its doing so. This species is of exceptional interest, as it belongs to a group of shearwaters new to the North American fauna, and of which little is known. I was so fortunate as to discover a large colony nesting on San Benedicto Island, from which was obtained a fine series of skins with all of the intergrades between the white-bellied phase of *cuneatus* and the dusky form described by L. Stejneger from the Sandwich Islands as *knudseni*.

On first landing on San Benedicto, the 1st of May, I heard a low murmuring noise which seemed to come from the opposite side of the island. Thinking it might come from a rookery of seals, I started out to investigate, but soon found that I was getting no nearer the source of the noise, which possessed a ventriloquial power difficult to locate. I soon, however, found myself surrounded by large burrows which fairly honeycombed the entire south end of the island, which was so completely undermined that one constantly broke through into burrows, frequently sinking to the hips in ground that had every appearance of being solid.

From many of the holes came moans and sobs in soft, low tones, inexpressively sad and weird—the love notes of *Puffinus cuneatus*.

A number of the burrows were opened, and from each were taken two birds, which fought and bit most savagely on being dragged to the light. By far the greater number were in dark plumage, but many showed lighter underparts, and in some cases a perfectly typical " *cuneatus*," with pure white underparts, was found in the same burrow with a dark " *knudseni*."

At this date the burrows were about four to five feet in length, most of them running in a nearly horizontal direction along the sides of the steep narrow ravines that everywhere cut this end of the island.

The soil is chiefly of fine pumice, in some places soft and easily excavated, but in others so hard as to require the use of a pick in opening the burrows. In most of the excavations was a rude attempt at nest building, consisting of a few sprigs of green grass and other vegetation which grew about the colony, and on this meager platform were both birds, but no eggs. Nor did the condition of the birds indicate that the actual nesting season was at hand.

Thinking I would find eggs, I returned to San Benedicto from Socorro Island two weeks later, but was disappointed. Many of the burrows were empty, and all had been extended two feet or more in length, and the nest of green plants moved back to the end. As before, when birds were found there were usually two.

The two following weeks were spent at Clarion, between two and three hundred miles west of San Benedicto. At Clarion *P. cuneatus* was rare and only seen at sea. Neither here nor at Socorro were there any signs of nesting colonies. San Benedicto was reached again May 31, and though dozens of burrows were opened, scarcely any birds were found. The tunnels had now a length of from eight to ten feet, having been extended another two feet or more, and as before, the nesting material moved to the end. The few birds found were generally in the shorter burrows, which were perhaps incomplete. Only one egg was found with the parent, a white-bellied bird.

Toward evening a greater percentage of birds began to appear from seaward, but at no time before dark did the numbers congregated about the island equal those seen a month earlier.

From the data obtained I would place the nesting season of *P. cuneatus* at least three months later than that of either *opisthomelas* or *auricularis*, which both deposit their eggs at about the same time, in early March.

Maj. G. Ralph Meyer writes to me that:

This bird breeds quite abundantly on Rabbitt Island, a small volcanic island off the east shore of Oahu (in the Hawaiian Islands). They occupy deserted rabbit burrows, going in a short distance. In each case I could see the old bird sitting on the egg. I captured one of the old birds and finally killed it. It was very vicious and its sharp bill and claws drew blood from my hands in several places. The birds would not leave the nests even after I had taken the eggs and tried to drive them out. The only bird in sight was the one on the egg in each case. It is probable that only one bird remains in the vicinity of the nest at a time.

Dr. Walter K. Fisher (1906) gives a very good account of the burrowing habits of the wedge-tailed shearwater on Laysan Island, from which I quote as follows:

The uau kane is an abundant bird on Laysan, and far and away the form most familiar to persons cruising in Hawaiian waters. Although so common on Laysan, Mr. Schlemmer estimates that in point of numbers it is second to *Aestrelata hypoleuca*. The greater number are congregated in a zone perhaps 50 yards wide around the lagoon, some distance seaward from the bare flood plain mentioned in the narrative. It is surprising how consistently they keep to this locality, as they are rare elsewhere on the island. This area is shared with albatrosses, rails, and in places with *Sterna lunata*, and overlaps the wide *Aestrelata* colonies. The burrows are among tall bushy grass as well as in the open among matted juncus and succulent portulaca.

While we were on the island the birds sat in pairs all day near the entrance to their homes, or if the sun grew too warm retired a short way into the tunnel, where they kept up an almost constant cooing.

Not infrequently one will observe the shearwaters cleaning out old burrows or in the act of lengthening them. I saw but one tunnel newly started, so that the number of yearly visitants seems to keep fairly constant. In digging, the birds scratch with bill and feet, and with the same implements shove the loose sand and soil under their bodies, when they kick it in little jets far out behind.

As they remove the sand they lie first on one side and work a foot and then shift to the other. One is sometimes startled, while standing quietly among the bushes, by being suddenly beset with little showers of sand, which on closer inspection are found to originate with some shearwater toiling into the earth. In their search for nesting sites they do not hesitate to wedge themselves into all sorts of places, apparently without thought of escape, but we never found any birds actually trapped. The burrows enter the ground at a slant and then become horizontal. They are at least 3 feet long and often very much deeper. Rarely they are only about 2 feet, and these are new, while the longer ones are the older, having been dug out by successive tenants from year to year. The birds had not yet begun to lay, and do not till early in June, according to the testimony of Mr. Schlemmer.

Eggs.—The single egg of the wedge-tailed shearwater is elongate ovate in shape and pure white in color; the shell is smooth, but not glossy. The measurements of 25 eggs, in various collections, average 63 by 41.5 millimeters; the eggs showing the four extremes measure **68.5** by 43.5, 66 by **44.5, 58.4** by 41.5, and 59.4 by **38.5** millimeters.

Plumages.—Major Meyer describes the downy young as " covered with a soft whitish down." Professor Loomis (1918) quotes Mr. W. A. Bryan as calling it " a smoky lilac-gray over the back and top of the head, and very light pearl gray on the under parts, darkest on the abdomen."

I doubt if any specimens of this species in later immature plumages have ever been collected. There are, apparently, two widely different color phases of this species, with a puzzling series of intergrades, which have led to some confusion in nomenclature. The dark phase, which is wholly dark sooty brown, has been described as a distinct species, *Puffinus knudseni;* it also closely resembles another so-called species, *Puffinus chlororhynchus*, but there does not seem to be any well established evidence of intergradation with the latter. Mr. Godman (1907) has given a very clear statement of the relationship and status of the two species, and I would refer the reader to what he has to say about both *cuneatus* and *chlororhynchus*. Mr. Anthony says that, about San Benedicto Island, " both phases were seen, the sooty plumage outnumbering the light-bellied form about two to one. In a series of about 75 specimens all manner of intergrades can be found, from those with pure ·white lower parts, including under wing-coverts, to those having gray and sooty brown plumage. In the upper surface there is very little variation."

Food.—Doctor Fisher (1906) states that the " stomachs of these birds contained the hard parts of small cephalopods (squid, octopus, and the like)." This is all we know about its food.

Behavior.—Referring to the flight of the wedge-tailed shearwater, Mr. Anthony (1900), writes:

About sunset the birds from the island began to seek the water, meeting a similar tide moving in from the sea. They mostly centered about the south end of the island, which soon presented the appearance of a vast beehive. Thousands upon thousands of shearwaters were circling about with easy flight, much more airy and graceful than that of shearwaters with which I am familiar; especially was the difference accentuated when an occasional *auricularis* with typical shearwater flight, skimmed through the throng. The greater part of those birds which came from the higher parts of the island descended at an angle of about 45°, with wings set until near the water, when they sailed off over the waves until lost to view, while others descending in a spiral course joined their fellows in circling about the water at the foot of the cliffs. There was little, if any, outcry, though the sobbing notes were often heard from the birds on shore. One bird—doubtless an albino—had a pure white head and dusky body, strongly suggestive of a Heermann's gull. It circled several times about our skiff, which was an object of great interest to the busy throng.

Doctor Fisher (1906) says:

A comparatively few at this season fly abroad during the day, but after dark they begin to move about more, and one moonlight night we found them very active and owl-like in their flight. At sea they are expert fliers, sailing with immovable wings rapidly and ·readily close over the waves, as well against as with the wind, and they can go across the breeze much more easily than can the albatross.

Regarding their vocal powers the same writer observes:

Their note varies. When undisturbed they utter a dove-like *khoo-whó*, which changes to a loud *khoo-ów* as they grow excited, and finally at the height of their enthusiasm one hears only a *yow-ów* or *oo-ów*, quite like the nocturnal serenade of cats. It seems to be a courting song, but is decidedly unmusical.

Mr. Homer R. Dill (1912) says, of the behavior of this species on Laysan Island:

It does not fly about much during the day, but sits in the mouth of its burrow and dozes in the sun. At times a dozen or more of these birds congregate, apparently for the purpose of quarreling. Their cat-like squalls will soon make the listener wish to move out of hearing. The young were nearly fledged. Apparently these birds were not killed to any extent by the poachers and they number about 100,000.

Dr. E. W. Nelson (1899) noted this species near the Tres Marias Islands in April and May; he writes:

During our trip to and from the islands we saw 100 or 200 wedge-tailed shearwaters. They were usually seen singly skimming along over the sea, at an elevation of a few yards, making widely sweeping circuits and pausing occasionally to pick up bits of food. When about midway between Isabel Island and the Tres Marias we encountered several schools of small porpoises of 150 or more individuals, which traveled in close array, frequently gamboling about and playfully leaping high in the air. A swarm of sooty terns followed the porpoises, and twice when they passed near us I saw considerable numbers of these shearwaters among the terns. Judging from the numbers, they must be rather common in these waters, but none were seen near the islands.

DISTRIBUTION.

Breeding range.—Warmer portions of Pacific and Indian Oceans. In the western Indian Ocean (Seychelle and Mascarene Islands) ; in Australian seas (Lord Howe, Norfolk, Kermadec and Surprise Islands, etc.) ; in the North Pacific Ocean (Bonin, Volcano, Marshall, Marcus, Laysan, and Hawaiian Islands) ; and off the west coast of Mexico, in the Revillagigedo Islands (San Benedicto Island). Some of these have been split into subspecies of doubtful standing. Breeding grounds protected in Hawaiian Islands reservation.

Range.—Does not extend far beyond the vicinity of the breeding range, but includes a wide belt across the Central Pacific and Indian Oceans from Central America to Asia, Australia, and Africa.

Egg dates.—Islands in Australian seas: Six records, November 20 to December 12. Bonin Islands: Five records, June 8 to August. San Benedicto Island: Two records, May 31 and July 26. Hawaiian Islands: One record, July 15.

THYELLODROMA BULLERI (Salvin).

NEW ZEALAND SHEARWATER.

HABITS.

This little known species is one of the rarest of the shearwaters. In 1907 Godman (1907) wrote that only " six examples are now known, viz., the type in the British Museum, two in the Rothschild Museum, one in the Buller Collection (now in the Carnegie Museum at Pittsburgh, U. S. A.), one in the Colonial Museum at Wellington, and one recorded by Mr. L. M. Loomis (1900).

Mr. A. W. Anthony (1898) saw a bird off the coast of Lower California, which he thought might be this species, but he did not secure it. To Mr. Leverett M. Loomis (1900) belongs the honor of definitely adding this species to the North American list by actually taking a specimen; he describes the event as follows:

On the 6th of November, about six miles west of Point Pinos, two white-breasted shearwaters dashed up to the boat—one a pink-footed, the other a slender bird without conspicuous mottling on the sides of the head. The first glance revealed that the bird was a stranger. It was only a few yards away and I had to wait a moment for it to pass astern and get within proper range. A successful shot brought it down in perfect condition for a specimen. Dissection proved that it was a female, perhaps a young one, for the ova were indistinct as in a bird that had never bred.

Upon consulting the literature it was found that the specimen agreed with the descriptions of Buller's shearwater, and was the fourth one known to science. The bird had been secured in a region far remote from the supposed habitat of the species, the types and third specimen having come from New Zealand seas. It may confidently be expected that persistent observation off Monterey will add to the list of pelagic wanderers from austral regions.

Since the above statements were made Mr. Rollo H. Beck has taken 15 specimens of this rare bird off Point Pinos. Mr. Loomis (1918) quotes from his notes, as follows:

1907. In February I returned to Point Pinos to spend a year endeavoring to replace in some degree the academy's water bird collection destroyed in the great fire of 1906, giving especial attention to the Tubinares. Not till September 2 did I see a Bullers' shearwater. On that day I went out on Monterey Bay three or more miles to the northeast of Point Pinos and found a large number of black vented and sooty shearwaters fishing. The weather was propitious, there being only a light breeze. As I rowed along from one flock to another, a flesh-footed shearwater flew over my head from behind and was shot. A few minutes afterward, as I proceeded leisurely, being then about four miles north of Point Pinos, I saw a lone Buller's shearwater fishing with a few Spanish mackerel. As the fish went down the shearwater lit one hundred and fifty yards away from the boat. I rowed with all my might but the bird arose out of range. As it circled, seventy yards distant, I fired, but merely caused it to settle for a few moments, only a single shot probably hitting it. As the bird shook its wings and rose I fired both barrels and stopped it again. When I came up within long range it started off once more, but this time I secured it.

On November 4 I went out seven or eight miles north of Point Pinos and finally reached the gathering of shearwaters I was looking for. There were about twenty thousand sooty, two hundred or more black-vented, and about thirty Cooper's shearwaters. They were scattered about over considerable water, and as I approached one of the larger bunches I saw two Buller's shearwaters fly around it and enter the bay. Farther on I discovered one on the water apart from a flock of sooty shearwaters, and I secured it. Another was seen sitting in the midst of a flock of sooty shearwaters. Another still was sitting close to two of these shearwaters. It decoyed to a dead bird thrown into the air, but unfortunately was missed with my first barrel and escaped, my other barrel being out of commission. Later in the day I secured a second specimen of Buller's shearwater from the concourse of shearwaters. I also obtained from it two flesh-footed and a slender-billed, the only ones noted.

On November 8 about four miles north of Point Pinos a single Buller's shearwater, in worn plumage, was seen flying about in search of food, but too far away to be secured.

1909. I spent the last four months of 1909 in collecting on the bay and ocean adjacent to Point Pinos. On October 9 I got out about four miles northeast of Point Pinos and found a few sooty and Cooper's shearwaters in bunches on the water. The first flock of these shearwaters I neared rose out of gunshot range, and with them a Buller's shearwater. They all flew north and appeared to settle in the far distance. I rowed in their direction and presently a Cooper's shearwater flew past me, and shortly after a Buller's, which I shot. An hour later I approached a flock of shearwaters on the water, but they rose when 100 yards distant and flew to the northward. With them were two Buller's shearwaters. As the weather was not settled and as I was alone as usual in a rowboat I followed no farther.

On the 13th of October when I was out about four miles north of Point Pinos a Buller's shearwater came along, going south. It swung up 20 yards astern of the boat, and I shot it. October 15 there was a low fog all day, and part of the time a drizzle. I went out about five miles northeast of Point Pinos and found a few Cooper's shearwaters fishing about, and working out to sea. One Buller's shearwater was seen flying with a couple of Cooper's shearwaters, a few hundred yards outside the boat. Presently another Buller's came along and I winged it. Another one appeared and started after the wounded bird, which was swimming rapidly away. I tossed up a dead Bonaparte's gull and then a Western gull and the flying bird swung back toward me and I shot it. Later, two other Buller's shearwaters came my way and were secured. The flight of all these birds, in the light wind, was similar to the albatross flight, there being no flapping of wings as in Cooper's shearwater, except when rising over the crest of a wave. Three of the four specimens taken had the generative organs slightly enlarged.

Eggs.—I have been able to locate only one egg of this rare shearwater. It is in the collection of Col. John E. Thayer and was collected by William Bartlett on Mokohinu Island, New Zealand, on October 20, 1900. It is ovate in shape, dull, dirty white in color, and the shell is smooth but not glossy. It measures 45.5 by 32 millimeters.

DISTRIBUTION.

Breeding range.—New Zealand seas. The only recorded breeding place is on Mokohinu Island, New Zealand.

Range.—Extends across the South Pacific Ocean to the coast of Chile (Valparaiso) and north in the North Pacific Ocean to the coast of California (Point Pinos).

Migrations.—Dates: Chile, Valparaiso, February 24 to March 9; California, Point Pinos, September 2 to November 4.

Egg dates.—Mokohinu Island: One record, October 20.

PRIOFINUS CINEREUS (Gmelin).

BLACK-TAILED SHEARWATER.

HABITS.

This large grey shearwater is a bird of the southern oceans and owes its place on our list to one accidental record many years ago on the coast of California. Mr. George N. Lawrence (1853) added this species to the North American Fauna, when he recorded a specimen, " from the collection of N. Pike, Esq., killed off the coast of California near Monterey." So far as I know, no further specimens have ever been taken or recorded in North America.

Dr. Edward A. Wilson (1907), naturalist of the National Antarctic Expedition, relates his experience with this species as follows:

Priofinus cinereus, the great grey shearwater, is a very characteristic bird of the southern oceans, considerably larger than the cape pigeon, grey or bluish grey all over the upper parts, and white beneath; it may be seen occasionally in the ship's wake without drawing the attention of the casual observer. But one morning he will go on deck to find the ship followed by the bird, perhaps in hundreds. Very hungry or very greedy, they then afford much amusement as they drop suddenly beneath the surface of the water with their wings spread to seize some scrap of food. They unhesitatingly go completely under and reappear again with their wings still spread. We were visited by such a flock on November 1, 1901, in the Southern Indian Ocean. Having first seen it on September 25, 1901, we had never had more than two or three with us until this flock arrived. Many of them were evidently molting, as several of the smaller primaries were missing on either side. This exposed the paler part of the primaries still present, and gave the appearance of a white patch and a piece cut out from the center of the wing. They may be caught and landed with stout thread entanglements, but ordinary thread should not be used, as it is apt to entangle the bird and break, leaving it disabled in the water. This large flock remained with us for about a week, when it began to dwindle, and on November 12, on our turning to go south, the birds left us altogether.

Nesting.—Capt. F. W. Hutton (1865) gives us the following brief account of its breeding habits:

It is very common at sea from May to August; but retires to Kerguelen's Land and other places in September or October, to breed. Each pair burrows horizontally into wet, peaty earth from 2 to 18 feet. At the end of the hole they form a large chamber, and construct in the center of it a nest similar, except in size, to that of the albatross (*D. exulans*), in the hollowed top of which the female lays one white egg. They seldom leave their burrows in the daytime, and when one happens to do so it is at once hunted by a "Nelly," although no such jealousy exists at sea. From this habit of flying only by night it is called "Nighthawk" by the sealers.

Mr. Harris's party, when wrecked on Kerguelen's Land, used to dig these birds out of their burrows, and eat them; and in order to save useless digging, for their spades were only made from the staves of old casks, they would hold one to the mouth of a hole, and make it cry out, when, if another was inside, it would answer.

If the black-tailed shearwater breeds regularly on Kerguelen Island, it seems strange that it was not noted by Doctor Kidder (1875) during his protracted visit on this island in 1874 and 1875.

Eggs.—Mr. A. J. Campbell (1901) describes the single egg as:

Roundish or broad oval in shape; texture of shell close but somewhat coarse; surface very slightly glossy; color, pure white when first laid, but soon becomes soiled with brownish earthy stains.

The eggs above described were collected on Macquarie Island the latter part of November, 1896, by Mr. Joseph Burton, per favor of Mr. Joseph Hatch, the lessee of the island. The eggs were accompanied by a skin of the bird. Macquarie Island is an exceedingly rough and rugged place, almost devoid of vegetation, situated 860 miles southeast by south from Hobart. It is about 20 miles long by about 7 miles broad, its greatest height being 1,300 feet above sea level.

During an interesting conversation with Mr. Burton, after his return from Macquarie Island, where he remained 3½ years, he informed me that brown petrels generally appear in numbers after the middle or towards the end of August (he noted one bird as early as the 12th of that month), and depart about the end of May. Fresh eggs may be collected the end of November or beginning of December, but, strange to say, in March and April (1900) some fresh eggs were observed in the burrows.

The burrows are in great numbers on the hillsides from sea level up to about 400 or 500 feet, and extend on an average four or five feet in the soft soil the nesting chamber being sparingly lined with portions of tussock grass. The burrow apparently always extends a little beyond the nesting chamber, because, if a sitting bird were disturbed, it usually got out of reach by moving further in. If a burrow be in use, a few blades of tussock grass will be noticed in the entrance.

The birds generally go to sea at daylight, which, on account of the latitude, occurs there about 2 o'clock in midsummer, returning about dusk (10 p. m.); but, just before laying season, usually two birds (presumably a mated pair) were found in the burrows during the day.

The call of the brown petrel, when flying, is a single whistle-like cry. In the burrows they coo like prions, only of course, louder.

The measurements of 7 eggs, furnished by Mr. Campbell, average 70.6 by 50.9 millimeters; the eggs showing the four extremes measure **71.5** by 51.4, 71.1 by **51.8, 69.1** by 51.2 and 69.2 by **49.8** millimeters.

Behavior.—Darwin (1889) relating his experience with this shear-water on the cruise of the *Beagle*, writes:

I do not think I ever saw so many birds of any sort together, as I once saw of these petrels behind the island of Chiloe. Hundreds of thousands flew in an irregular line for several hours in one direction. When part of the flock settled on the water, the surface was blackened; and a cackling noise proceeded from them as of human beings talking in the distance. At this time the water was in parts colored by clouds of small crustacea. * * * At Port Famine, every morning and evening, a long band of these birds continued to fly with extreme rapidity up and down the central parts of the channel, close to the surface of the water. Their flight was direct and vigorous, and they seldom glided with extended wings in graceful curves, like most other members of this family. Occasionally they settled for a short time on the water; and they thus remained at rest during nearly the whole of the middle of the day. When flying backwards and forwards at a distance from the shore, they evidently were fishing, but it was rare to see them seize any prey. They were very wary, and seldom approached within gun shot of a boat or of a ship, a disposition strikingly different from that of most of the other species. The stomach of one, killed near Port Famine, contained seven prawn-like crabs, and a small fish. In another, killed off of the Plata, there was the beak of a small cuttlefish. I observed that these birds, when only slightly winged, were incapable of diving.

Captain Hutton (1865) says of its diving habits:

This bird is by far the best diver of all the sea-going petrels. It seems even fond of it, and often remains under water for several minutes, when it comes up again shaking the water off its feathers like a dog. Sometimes I have seen it, as it flies past, poise itself for a moment in the air (and hence perhaps its name) at a height of about twenty or twenty-five feet above the sea, and, shutting its wings, take a header into the water. It dives with its wings open, and uses them under water much in the same manner as when flying.

Captain Hutton (1865) observes that "its cry is something like the bleating of a lamb." He writes that "the young bird has been figured and described by Dr. Andrew Smith in his Illustrations of South African Zoology."

Mr. Robert C. Murphy noted and collected this species on his cruise to the island of South Georgia; his notes state that on November 14, 1912, in latitude 42° 24' south and longitude 42° 28' west, many black-tailed shearwaters followed the ship "all day long, flying low over the water, gliding a good part of the time. When they beat their wings it was with a more rapid motion than the other petrels; the flight was, indeed, somewhat ducklike. Toward night we passed great bands of *Priofinus* sitting on the water."

DISTRIBUTION.

Breeding range.—Known to breed only on Kerguelen Island, in the southern Indian Ocean, and on Macquarie Island, south of New Zealand.

Range.—Southern oceans. North in the South Atlantic Ocean to about 25° South; in the South Pacific Ocean, perhaps regularly, to Peru; and in the Indian Ocean to about 35° south.

Casual records.—Accidental on the coast of California (off Monterey).

PTERODROMA HASITATA (Kuhl).

BLACK-CAPPED PETREL.

HABITS.

In the latest edition of our check list this species is entered as "probably now extinct." This statement was probably premature, but doubtless it was somewhat warranted by the increasing rarity of the species, which is perhaps on the verge of extinction. It is a bird of the tropical waters of the Atlantic Ocean, and once bred abundantly on several islands of the West Indies. Mr. George N. Lawrence (1878) referred to this species under the local vernacular name of "diablotin," not knowing at that time just what species it was. Quoting from Mr. Frederick A. Ober's notes, who was collecting birds for the Smithsonian on the island of Dominica, he says:

Twenty years ago it was abundant. Said to have come in from the sea in October and November and to burrow in the tops of the highest mountains for a nest. In those months it incubated. It goes and comes, doubtless, mostly, if not altogether, at night. If the burrows made by it could be found when the birds are incubating, probably they could be unearthed in the daytime, and thus be secured.

Mr. Lawrence (1891) published another note on the subject from Doctor Colardeau, whom he had requested to look for the species on Guadeloupe. Doctor Colardeau writes:

I do not believe the diablotin is extinct in our island; only we have no more the old sportsmen who used to go after them out of pure frolic, with plenty of dogs and black servants, when I was a child some fifty years ago. The diablotin is not pure black; that I feel certain from distinct recollection, and you may consider the specimens sent by the old Dr. L'Herminier as correct, as he was one of those old sportsmen I have just spoken of, who, in company with my great uncles, grandfather, and other relatives and friends, used to go after them amongst the rocks and mountains surrounding the Soufrière. A few years ago, even as low as Camp Jacob, there was a diablotin caught by a dog in a hole in the bank of a mountain stream. The master of the dog was satisfied to eat the bird, and I only knew of it when it was too late. The bird was black above and white below, crooked beak, and webbed feet.

The name "diablotin" has also been applied to Audubon's shearwater, but in this case he probably referred to the black-capped petrel, for Mr. Lawrence (1891) finally concluded that, "from the description given by Doctor Colardeau of the specimen obtained in Guadeloupe lately, it was probably *Aestrelata haesitata*, which species Prof. Alfred Newton determined the specimens sent by L'Herminier to Lafresnaye to be."

Godman (1907) gives the following fragments of the life history of this little-known species:

Ae. haesitata is described as a very rare bird, nocturnal in its habits, and frequenting rabbit-like burrows, in which the eggs are laid. The old birds, when leaving the nest at night, utter a mournful cry as they go out to sea. The flesh was much prized as an article of food, and the native hunters have been known to return with a dozen or more birds hung round their necks.

In 1696 Pere Labat landed in Guadeloupe, and shortly after his arrival he accompanied four black hunters to the breeding-places of the "diablotin," which he also mentions as occurring in Dominica. The "diable" arrived in the month of September in Guadeloupe, where the birds occupied their burrows in pairs till the end of November, when they all disappeared and were not seen again until about the middle of January. Only a single male or female remained in the holes till the month of March, when the female was found with "two" nestlings, covered with a thick yellow down and resembling little balls of fat. The young birds are able to fly at the end of May, when they disappear, and are not seen again till September, at which season they return with great regularity.

In 1791 Mr. Thomas Atwood wrote a history of the island of Dominica and compared the "diablotin" to an owl from its nocturnal habits and its owl-like cry. Mr. F. A. Ober, an enthusiastic American naturalist, made a special expedition to the highlands of that island to search for the nesting places, but was unsuccessful. The next attempt was made by Colonel Feilden himself, with Admiral Markham and other friends, and accompanied by some Negroes who had actually taken the birds in former years. They ascended the Morne au Diable in Dominica, but, though the burrows under the roots of trees still remained, no traces of the bird could be found.

M. Jean Baptiste Labat (1722) gives the most detailed account of these birds; he says:

We were at that time, [March 14, 1696] in the season for hunting certain birds which are called "devils," or "little devils" [diablotins]. I do not know if they are met with elsewhere than in Guadeloupe and Dominica, whither they come at certain seasons of the year to mate, to lay their eggs, and to raise their young.

This bird is almost the size of a "poule à fleur"; that is what in the islands we call the young chickens which have not yet laid but which are in condition to lay very soon. Its plumage is black; its wings long and strong; its legs rather short; its feet like those of ducks, but furnished with strong and long claws; its beak is a good inch and a half long, pointed and extremely hard and strong; it has large eyes on a level with its crown which serve it admirably well at night, but which are so useless in the daytime that it can not endure the light nor distinguish objects, so that when it is surprised outside of its retreat it hurls itself against everything it meets and finally falls to earth.

These birds live on fish which they go to sea at night to catch. After their fishing is finished they return to the mountain where they withdraw into burrows like rabbits, and they do not leave these burrows to return to the sea until night has come again. They cry on the wing as if they called or replied to each other. They begin to appear toward the end of the month of September. They are then found in pairs in each burrow. They live in this way until the end of November, after which they disappear and not a single one is seen or heard until the middle or thereabouts of the month of January, when they again appear. At this time there is never found more than one, male or female, in each burrow until the month of March, when the mother is found with her two young. When the little diablotins are taken at this time they are covered with down, thick and yellow like the down of goslings; they are like balls of fat; they are called "couttous." They are ready to fly at the end of May; at this time they leave and are neither seen nor heard again until the month of September. All that I have just said regarding the diablotins' visits to and residence in Guadeloupe and Dominica recurs regularly and without ever having failed during all the years. The flesh of this bird is blackish and tastes a little of fish; otherwise it is good and very nutritious. The "couttous" are regarded as being more delicate, and this is true; but they are too fat, so that they give off grease as if they were full of oil.

The manner of cooking them when they are fully grown is to boil them in water with salt and fine herbs until they are half done, when they are taken out and allowed to drain; this partial cooking removes the fat and takes away the flavor of fish. The process is finished by making them into a stew, a "ragout," or otherwise, with orange peel and leaves of "bois d' Inde."

The little diablotins, or "couttous," are better roasted on a spit, or on a gridiron, sprinkled with salt, pepper, and the seeds of "bois d' Inde" mixed together.

It may be said that these birds are a manna which God sends every year for the negroes and for the lowly inhabitants, who do not live on anything else during the season.

The difficulty of hunting these birds preserves the species, which would have been entirely exterminated years ago, according to the bad custom of the French, did they not retire to localities which are not accessible to everyone.

In spite of the dangers and inconveniences inseparable from hunting them, my curiosity led me to accompany four of our negroes who left one Sunday afternoon and who did not have to return until the next evening; for that length of time was necessary to reach the locality, to seek the game, and to return. Besides my negro I took with me a young creole who was apprenticed to us to refine sugar, and whose name was Albert de Launay. We walked along the bed of our river until we found a place less steep than elsewhere where we ascended, one after the other, helping each other, or rather mounting on the shoulders of those who remained below, whom we then drew up to us with lianas, as well as our dogs. I thought that after passing this difficult place our troubles would be over, but these bad spots occurred each time it was necessary to pass streams or rivers, which happened seven or eight times before we arrived at the top of the birds' mountain, which is at the side of the Soufrière. It was almost 6 o'clock when we arrived at the place where our hunters had planned to make their cabin. We set ourselves to work on our lodging, some cutting poles, others gathering ferns, while the two hunters went to look for some birds for supper. I had taken the precaution of bringing with me my cloak, a good bottle of Madeira, and some bread, with some brandy and farina for our negroes. Our cabin was very soon built; we covered it with " cachibou " leaves which we had cut on the road as we knew well that we would not find them in the place where we were going. We made a good litter of ferns to sleep upon, and built a large fire to cook the game which the hunters had gone to get for supper as well as to warm us during the night, which is always very cold in these elevated places.

Our two hunters were successful; they returned fairly soon with fifteen or sixteen diablotins. Each set to work plucking them. As for me I made the spits upon which to roast them. After they were plucked and singed they were opened along the back; the entrails, together with the feet, the heads, and the bases of the wings, served for supper for the dogs. The body is spitted diagonally—that is to say, the spit is passed from one thigh to the opposite shoulder. It is then planted in the ground before the fire and turned from time to time to cook the meat on both sides, and when it is almost cooked, salt is thrown upon it; a " cachibou " or " balisier " leaf serves as a plate. It must be confessed that a diablotin eaten from the spit is a delicious morsel. I thought that I would be satisfied with one diablotin, but because either the cold air of the mountain or the fatigue of the journey had increased my appetite, or because the diablotins of this region are more delicate and more easy of digestion than others, it was necessary to do as my companions did and to eat a second. The night was fine and without rain, and we slept well, although the diablotins kept up a great noise in leaving their homes to go out to sea and in returning to them.

The next day at daybreak we started out to hunt them. Each hunter is armed with a long pole an inch thick and seven or eight feet long, rather supple, and with a hook at the end. The dogs which we had brought along searched for and ferreted out all the burrows. When they perceived that there was a diablotin in a burrow (for this mountain is perforated like a warren) they yelped and began to scratch; but the hunter takes care to prevent them from spoiling the entrances, for then the diablotins would not reenter them another year. The pole is thrust immediately into the burrow until it reaches the bird, which when it feels it seizes it with its beak and holds it fast and allows itself to be drawn outside rather than let go. When it reaches the mouth of the burrow the light blinds it, it is dazzled, and wishes to retreat into its burrow; but the hunter closes this with his foot. Then the bird turns on its back to defend itself with its beak and claws. It is then seized by the head, its neck is wrung, and the hunter attaches it to a cord or liana which he wears about his body after the fashion of a belt. It sometimes happens that the bird does not wish to bite the pole; then the latter is poked about in the burrow from side to side until it becomes caught in the bend of the wing which, being very large, the bird can not extend sufficiently to free itself, and it is thus drawn out from its home. The chase is ordinarily continued all the morning, which can not be done without traveling far from the cabin and ascending and descending very difficult places. I sent the negroes to the distant localities and kept the creole with me to hunt in the neighborhood of the hut. He knew the business perfectly well, and he had a very good dog. After two or three hours of hunting I returned with my negro to rest and to cook some birds for dinner. I began finally to hunt alone. We reassembled at midday. The four negroes had 138 diablotins, Albert had 43, and I 17. Each of us ate two, and we left carrying the rest of our game.

On Sunday, April 8, 1696, M. Labat started out to make an ascent of the Soufrière. That night, at a camp much farther on than the previous one, half the party erected a hut, while the other half hunted diablotins, for supper and for food on the following day.

Those who read these memoirs will doubtless be surprised that we should eat birds in Lent; but the missionaries who are in these islands, and who in many matters exercise the power of bishops, after serious deliberation and a consultation of medical men, have declared that lizards and diablotins are vegetable food, and that consequently they may be eaten at all times.

I am including the above account at the suggestion of certain friends of mine in Washington in spite of some doubt in my mind as to whether it refers to this species or not. Inasmuch as Pere Labat describes the "diablotin" as black, his account may refer to *Pterodroma caribbea*, the Jamaican petrel. But, as both species may have formerly bred on these islands, as Pere Labat's observations have always been associated with *Pterodroma hasitata* and as it is an interesting account historically, it seems best to include it.

The Reverend Father Jean Baptiste du Tertre (1654) says:

The "devil" is a nocturnal bird, so named by the inhabitants of the Indies on account of its ugliness. It is so rare that I have never been able to see a single one except at night and on the wing. All that I have been able to learn of it from hunters is that its form closely approaches that of a duck; that it has a hideous voice and mixed white and black plumage; that it lives on the highest mountains; that it breeds like the rabbit in burrows which it makes in the ground in which it lays its eggs, incubates them, and raises its young; I have not been able to learn with what food it nourishes them. When it appears in the daytime it rushes forth so unexpectedly that it frightens those who see it. It never comes down from the mountain except by night, and on the wing it gives forth a very lugubrious and hideous cry. Its flesh is so delicate that no hunter ever returns from the mountain who does not ardently desire to have a dozen of these "devils" hanging from his neck.

The latest information we have, on the disappearance of this species, is contained in the following quotation from Mr. G. K. Noble (1916):

One of the chief reasons of my visit to Guadeloupe was to obtain information about the black-capped petrels. A few days after landing I had the good fortune to meet Monsieur C. Thionville, president of the Club des Montagnards. The name diablotin was associated in his mind with the past history and early colonization of the French in Guadeloupe. He immediately began to make inquiries about Basse Terre but without much success. Finally we made a trip together high up into the hills of Matouba to visit an old Negro called Père Lownisky living on the slopes of the Soufrière. This old man in his early youth had often hunted Diablotins and had joined several of the large parties which had camped on the Nez Cassé to dig out the diablotins from their burrows. Since Pere Lownisky had spent his entire life in Matouba he knew all the old breeding grounds of the black-capped petrels. He told us that the diablotins formerly bred on the north and northeast slope of the Nez Cassé. The birds arrived in late September and the period of incubation for the colony as a whole extended through November and December. The young birds remained in the nest until March. He asserted positively, however, that no diablotins had been heard or seen since the great earthquake of 1847. The old Negro remembered that earthquake for during it the whole side of Nez Cassé, on which the petrels bred, had collapsed and fallen into the valley. Pere Lownisky ended his exposition by dramatically raising his withered hand, exclaiming again in his " créole " French that the diablotins had not been heard of for nearly seventy years, " Jamais! Jamais ! "

Undoubtedly the volcanic disturbances in these islands have done much toward reducing the numbers of these petrels and the introduction of the mongoose has carried the work of destruction still further. Perhaps it is doomed to extinction within a few years, but I doubt if this has yet been accomplished. Mr. John T. Nichols (1913) reported seeing a specimen in the vicinity of the West Indies as recently as January 25, 1913; I quote from his notes, as follows:

On January 25, 31° 48' North 75° 58' West (250 miles east of Savannah), on blue water, alternating sunny and showery with a little lightning, the steamer butting into a brisk southwesterly breeze, a sharp lookout was kept for *Puffinidae*, as they had been seen near this latitude the year before. Once or twice thin vanishing vertical shadows against the myriad horizontal wave shadows of the distance led me to believe there were some of these birds about, and as I stood by the port side, forward, looking toward the bow, a black-capped petrel (*Aestrelata hasitata*) darted away to the eastward above the waves, and I had a splendid view of its long, narrow, stiff wings, blackish cap and back, black tail, white side of neck, underparts, lining of wings and upper tail coverts. First one, then the other wing uppermost, it was shooting across the wind with almost unbelievable speed and soon out of sight among the distant seas. An Audubon's shearwater, which appeared in the trough of a sea near the vessel almost immediately, was noticeably smaller than the first bird. Two or three other birds, obviously *Puffinidae*, were seen later in the day, but these were the only ones which came within fair binocular range. The flight and appearance of the black-capped petrel were very much like those of the greater shearwater. The distinguishing large amount of white over the tail was conspicuous.

The black-capped petrel has a well established claim to a place on the North American list, for it has repeatedly been taken, as a straggler, on our continent and often well inland, at various times during the summer, fall, and winter months. Dr. J. A. Allen (1904) has tabulated ten such records which are substantiated by eleven specimens.

Breeding range.—Bred formerly in the Lesser Antilles (Guadeloupe and Dominica).

Range.—Warmer parts of the North Atlantic Ocean.

Casual records.—Ten records for eastern North America. South to Florida (Indian River, winter, 1846). West to Kentucky (Augusta, October 4, 1898,) and Ohio (Cincinnati, October 5, 1898). North to Ontario (Toronto, October 30, 1893,) and New Hampshire (Pittsfield, August 30, 1893). Other records are for intermediate localities. Accidental in England (Norfolk, March or April, 1850).

PTERODROMA CAHOW (Nichols and Mowbray).

CAHOW.

HABITS.

The earlier writers on Bermuda birds had much to say about a mysterious bird, now supposed to be extinct, which was very abundant at one time and very well known by the earliest inhabitants as the " cahow," " cowhow," or " cowkoe." Much confusion has existed as to what bird these names were applied. For example Capt. Savile G. Reid (1884) writes, under the name *Puffinus obscurus:*

Since Mr. Hurdis, in 1849, identified the " cahow " or " cowhow " of the historians of Bermuda with this interesting species, very few observations have been made on the few pairs still frequenting the islands. That the poor " cahow " has almost ceased to breed there is a melancholy fact. Formerly it was plentiful, and even within the last fifteen years, Mr. Bartram informs me, there were many nests in the isolated rocks, both on the north and south shores. On the north side the bird was formerly called " pemblyco " or " pimlico," probably from its call note, while on the southern shores the name " cahow " or " cowhow " was applied to it. I found two nests in 1874, each containing a single young bird, one of which I kept alive for about six weeks, intending to send him to the Zoological Society's Gardens in London; but before I got an opportunity of doing so the unfortunate bird died. An egg of this species, kindly presented to me by Mr. Bartram, is, of course, pure white; it has a considerable polish and is about the size of a bantam's, but less elongated in form. Mr. Bartram was good enough also to present me with two skins of the adult bird. He tells me that the statement made by the old historians of Bermuda as to the capture of the " cahow " at night is no exaggeration, for on visiting an island one night where there were several pairs breeding he quickly caught half a dozen of them, the stupid things settling on his body as he lay on the ground and allowing themselves to be taken in his hand. I know of only one instance of a " cahow " being seen on the wing in the daytime in Bermudian waters; this was in August, 1874, when one was shot crossing Castle Harbor by Lieutenant Hopegood, 97th Regiment, but I believe they are occasionally observed by fishermen on the south side.

With reference to local names " cahow " or " cowhow," and " pemblyco " or " pimlico," Mr. Bartram writes to me on the 19th July, 1878: "About twelve months ago I came across an old book called A Complete System of Geography, printed under the name of Herman Moll, etc., September 21, 1747, and the greater part of it professedly taken from a much older work called Britannick in America. After describing Bermuda and its animal, insect, and vegetable productions, it gives the following account of the birds that were found on the islands at that time (say, between 200 and 300 years ago) : " There was a great variety of fowl, both wild and tame, such as hawks of all sorts, storks, herons, bitterns, ospreys, cormorants, baldcoots, moor-hens, swans, teal, snipes, ducks, widgeons, sparrows, woodpeckers, and a vast multitude and variety of the smaller kinds, besides owls, bats, and other nocturnal birds. Here was likewise formerly a kind of waterfowl, peculiar to those islands, which used to come to land and hatch its young in holes and burrows of the rocks, like rabbits. They were in great plenty, and were called cowkoes. They were easily caught, and good to eat, the size of a sea-mew. Our English made such havoc among them they are become scarce. Here is likewise found the tropic bird and the " pemlico." The last is seldom seen in the daytime, and, when it is, it is looked upon as the unwelcome harbinger of a storm."

Now, my belief is that the cowkoes of old are lost and gone long ago, and that the cahow of the present day is neither more nor less than the old and ancient pemlico. For, in the first place, the cahow of this day is not nearly so big as the sea-mew ; secondly, the pemlico has never been lost sight of by the Bermudians, the name having been handed down from father to son from the earliest times to the present day ; and, thirdly, the habits of the old pemlico and the cahow of to-day correspond to a T—that is, they are seldom seen flying in the daytime, only at night.

Mr. Bartram goes on to say that on making inquiries of the people of Tucker's Town, St. David's, and Bailey's Bay, they knew nothing of the cahow, but all could tell him of the pemlico. From the above interesting account and from strong evidence adduced by Mr. Bartram, I am inclined (with all due deference to Mr. Hurdis) to share his opinion as to the proper local name for *P. obscurus* being pemblyco or pemlico, and further to believe that the cowkoes or cahows of old were of a larger species, probably manx shearwaters (*P. anglorum*). This, after all, is pure conjecture and of doubtful interest to any but Bermudians themselves ; still I venture to mention the facts in the hope that some more conclusive historical evidence may be forthcoming.

On the strength of evidence recently brought to light, it now seems to be well established that the name " pimlico " or " pemblyco " was applied to a shearwater, probably *Puffinus puffinus bermudae*, Nichols and Mowbray, a local race of manx shearwater, and that the name " cahow " or " cowhow " was applied to a petrel, probably *Pterodroma cahow* (Nichols and Mowbray).

Mr. Thomas S. Bradlee (1906) published the following note :

On February 22, 1906, Mr. Louis L. Mowbray took a Peale's petrel (*Aestrelata gularis*) in a hole of the rock overlooking the sea and washed by the spray. The bird was taken after a southwest gale. Peale's petrel is not included in the A. O. U. Check-List, but I am sure of the identification of the bird, and am glad to be able to put on record the first instance of Peale's petrel being taken in the Northern Hemisphere. The bird is now in the collection of the Bermuda Natural History Society.

It was afterwards discovered by Messrs. John T. Nichols and Louis L. Mowbray (1916) that this bird is not Peale's petrel, but a new and undescribed species to which they gave the name *Aestrelata cahow*. In their description they state that the "upper surfaces" are "dark sooty, darkest on the primaries, grayish on the back and nape;" and that the "forehead, lores, and underparts" are "white." They also say:

The name "cahow" was used by early settlers in Bermuda for an *Aestrelata* abundant at Cooper's Island, a mile at the most from where the type was taken and presumably of the same species. Numerous partially fossil bones (including skulls) which, after comparison, we believe to belong to the form here described, have been found by Mr. Mowbray in various caves in the eastern end of the Bermudas, some about a half mile from where the bird was taken.

A few months later Dr. R. W. Shufeldt (1916) appears in print with the description of a new species under the name *Aestrelata vociferans*, which is apparently the same bird. His description is based on the study of a large collection of bones, collected by Mr. Edward McGall and Mr. Louis L. Mowbray in the bird caves of the Bermudas. In this interesting paper he gives us some information about the former abundance and the habits of the "cahow." He says:

These Bermudan caves are very recent in their formation; they certainly are not, at the very limit, more than five centuries old, and maybe a century or so less. My particular interest centered about the unraveling of the history of the famous bird long known by the name of "cahow" and by several other names, which are not necessary to enumerate here. At one time the "cahow" was extremely abundant on these Bermuda Islands, and bred there in untold millions at the time of the early settlers, some three centuries ago. It was a nocturnal species, possessing discordant notes; and so fearless of man were these birds that they would alight on the head, shoulders, and arms of any person visiting their breeding grounds. This unusual fearlessness resulted in the final extermination of the species; for the first inhabitants of the islands, and those that followed them in a comparatively short period, utterly destroyed the birds for food, notwithstanding their enormous numbers. All this has now become a matter of history, and one of the most extensive contributors to it is Prof. Addison E. Verrill, of the present faculty of Yale University. There are a great many writers on the subject, and most of them firmly believe that the cahow was a shearwater of the genus *Puffinus;* in other words, that it was a bird still to be found on the Atlantic Coast, and known as Audubon's shearwater (*P. lherminieri*). Others, however, doubted this, and believed the bird to be an extinct petrel; and there were other opinions in regard to the matter, all of which have been fully set forth in my memoir on the subject, which will presently be published by the American Museum of Natural History.

In one of the three stalactites collected by Mr. Mowbray in Crystal Cave he discovered three feathers embedded about an eighth of an inch in the calcite, one of which was brown and the other two white. With respect to these Mr. Mowbray wrote me on the 10th of February, 1916: "The finding of these feathers, agreeing in color with the description of the early writers that the cahou was russet and white, and the skull differing from those of the shearwater, convinced me that the find was a good one and without question the long-looked for cahou."

When my above-mentioned work on the cahow appears there will be found in it a full discussion of these "russet feathers" and of the hazy idea the early writers had of that color. Then, too, the fossil bird bones from Bermuda turned over to me for description go to prove that the extinct cahow was a petrel and *not* a shearwater at all.

Doctor Shufeldt has also very kindly sent me the original manuscript of his exhaustive memoir, as yet unpublished, entitled: "Comparative Study of Some Subfossil Remains of Birds from Bermuda, including the Cahow," which he read long ago at a regular meeting of the New York Zoological Society. This excellent paper is far too technical and goes into the matter too much in detail to warrant quoting from it extensively, but the following short quotations will cover the most important points in his conclusions regarding the status of the species. He says:

It has long been a question among ornithologists as to whether the famous "cahow" was a shearwater (*Puffinus obscurus?*) or a petrel (*Æstrelata*). In so far as my observation carries me, there is at least one character in the skeleton by means of which we can with certainty distinguish from each other these two different kinds of birds. This character is seen in the form of the *cnemial process of the tibiotarsus.* In the genus *Puffinus*—and possibly in some of its near allies—the cnemial process of the tibiotarsus is conspicuously elongate, as we see it in the grebes and loons, while in the petrels it is notably shorter, with rounded superior margin. Judging from this character alone there is no question but that the "cahow" of the Bermuda Islands was an *Æstrelata* and not a *Puffinus*. This fact is sustained by other osteological as well as external characters found in the representatives of the two genera in question. For example, both the horny sheaths to the mandible, as well as those parts in the dried skulls when deprived of the sheaths, are positively diagnostic with respect to these two groups of tubinarine birds.

Prof. Addison E. Verrill (1902) has given us the following interesting account of the early history of the cahow:

The most interesting as well as most important native bird, when the islands were first settled, was called the cahow, from its note. It bred in almost incredible numbers on some of the smaller islands near St. Georges and Castle Harbor, especially on Coopers Island. It was nocturnal in its habits and was readily called by making loud vocal sounds, and then easily captured by hand, at night. Its flesh was described as of good flavor and its eggs were highly prized as food. As it came to land and bred in the early part of the winter, when no other birds or eggs were available, it was quickly exterminated for food by the reckless colonists.

It laid a single large white egg, described as like a hen's egg in size, color, and flavor. The nest, according to the earliest writers, was a burrow in the sand like a coney's, and *not* in crevices of the rocks, like that of the shearwaters, with which many writers have tried to identify it. Governor Butler, in his "Historye of the Bermudaes," alone stated that its eggs and young were found in crevices of the ledges, but he evidently did not have the advantage of personal experience, for at that time the bird was probably extinct or very nearly so.

The time of laying its eggs is a very remarkable point, in which it differed from all other birds of northern latitudes. . The early contemporary writers all agree that it laid its egg " in December or January " or " in the coldest and darkest months of the year." The shearwaters, even in the West Indies, lay their eggs in spring—March and April—and their eggs are so musky that they are not edible; certainly no one would compare them to a hen's egg. Their flesh also has so strong a flavor of bad fish oil and musk that no one would eat it unless on the verge of starvation, though the newly hatched young are sometimes eaten by sailors for lack of anything better.

The bird itself was variously described as of the size of a pigeon, green plover, or sea mew; its bill was hooked and strong, and it could bite viciously; its back was " russet brown " and there were russet and white quill feathers in its wings; its belly was white. It arrived in October and remained until the first of June.

There is no known living bird that agrees with it in these several characters. Most certainly it could not have been a shearwater, as Hurdis and others have supposed, nor any known member of the petrel family, all of which have such a disagreeable flavor that neither their flesh nor eggs are used as food unless in cases of starvation.

The following graphic account of the bird and its habits was written by Mr. W. Strachy, one of the party wrecked with Sir George Somers in the *Sea Venture*, July, 1609:

" A kind of webbe-footed Fowle there is, of the bigness of an English greene Plover, or Sea-Meawe, which all the Summer we saw not, and in the darkest nights of November and December (for in the night they onely feed) they would come forth, but not flye farre from home, and hovering in the ayre, and over the Sea, made a strange hollow and harsh howling. They call it of the cry which it maketh, a cohow. Their colour is inclining to russet, with white bellies, as are likewise the long feathers of their wings, russet and white, these gather themselves together and breed in those lands which are high, and so farre alone into the Sea that the Wilde Hogges cannot swimme over them, and there in the ground they have their Burrowes, like Conyes in a Warren, and so brought in the loose Mould, though not so deepe; which Birds with a light bough in a darke night (as in our Lowbelling) wee caught, I have beene at the taking of three hundred in an houre, and wee might have laden our Boates. Our men found a prettie way to take them, which was by standing on the Rockes or Sands by the Sea-side, and hollowing, laughing, and making the strangest outcry that possibly they could; with the noyse whereof the Birds would come flocking to that place, and settle upon the very armes and head of him that so cried, and still creepe neerer and neerer, answering the noyse themselves; by which our men would weigh them with their hand, and which weighed heaviest they took for the best and let the others alone, and so our men would take twentie dozen in two hours of the chiefest of them; and they were a good and well relished Fowle, fat and full as a partridge. In January wee had great store of their Egges, which are as great as an Hennes Egge, and so fashioned and white shelled and have no difference in yolke nor white from an Hennes Egge. There are thousands of these Birds, and two or three Islands full of their Burrows, whether at any time (in two houres warning) we could send our Cockboat and bring home as many as would serve the whole Company: which Birds for their Blindnesse (for they see weakly in the day) and for their cry and whooting, wee called the Sea Owle; they will bite cruelly with their crooked Bills."

The " cahow " is generally supposed to be extinct, but if the birds described by Messrs. Nichols and Mowbray and by Doctor Shufeldt are really one and the same bird, as they seem to be, the capture of a living bird so recently as 1906 raises the question as to whether there may not be a few specimens still living.

PTERODROMA INEXPECTATA (Forster).

PEALE PETREL.

HABITS.

The above name should replace on our check list the names of the two supposed species known as *Aestrelata scalaris* Brewster, scaled petrel, and *Aestrelata fisheri* Ridgway, Fisher petrel, for both of these are represented by unique types only and are undoubtedly only age, seasonal, or individual variants of *Pterodroma gularis* (Peale), Peale petrel. Mr. Leverett M. Loomis (1918) evidently agrees with me, for he says, referring to *P. inexpectata* which he regards as the same bird as *P. gularis:*

Besides the type of *Procellaria gularis*, I have examined the type of *Œstrelata fisheri* Ridgway (No. 89431 U. S. Nat. Mus.) and that of *Æstrelata scalaris* Brewster (No. 5224 Coll. W. Brewster). The type of *Œstrelata fisheri* is a worn, faded, and rather weak-billed example of *Pterodroma inexpectata*. The white-headed aspect is caused chiefly by wear and accidental loss of feathers, exposing the white bases. The feathers of the upper parts of the body are much worn, accounting for the absence of the whitish margins characteristic of the fresh plumage of *Pterodroma inexpectata*. The weak appearance of the bill is largely due to mutilation, the basal portion of the unguis having been torn off and the nasal tubes flattened. The color above is darker than in No. 1134 and lighter than in No. 1139 of the Expedition collection. The markings of the pileum and nape and the extension of the white of the rectrices, greater wing-coverts, and secondaries break down through an intermediate New Zealand specimen (No. 24345 Carnegie Mus.). The type of *Æstrelata scalaris* is merely a bird in fresher plumage than the other types. The supposed differences in the nasal tubes do not exceed the normal variation occurring in *Pterodroma inexpectata*.

The only known specimen of *Pterodroma scalaris* is the type, in the collection of Mr. William Brewster (1886) from which he described the species in 1886. Mr. Brewster (1881) published the following account of the capture of the specimen which he obtained from Mr. E. H. Woodman, for whom the bird was mounted:

The bird had been sent him by a client, Mr. Nathan F. Smith, who conducts a large farm at Mount Morris, Livingston County, New York. One of the laborers while ploughing an old cornfield, noticed it running in a freshly-turned furrow and despatched it with a stick. It was apparently exhausted, for it made no attempt to escape. This was early in April, 1880, probably not far from the fifth of the month, as I find its reception recorded on Mr. Knowlton's books as April 10. A letter afterwards received from Mr. Smith confirms all of these facts, but adds nothing of interest, save that the farm comprises what are known as flats, lying along the Genesee River, about forty miles south of Lake Ontario.

At the time Mr. Brewster obtained this specimen he recorded it as a specimen of Peale petrel, *Pterodroma inexpectata*, after comparing it with Peale's type of that species in the United States National Museum collection. It was not until five years afterwards, when he had again compared it with the type of *inexpectata*, as well as with the type of *fisheri*, that he came to the conclusion that the three species were distinct and described his bird under the name, scaled petrel, *Aestrelata scalaris*.

Pterodroma fisheri, Fisher petrel, is supposed to be a bird of the Pacific Ocean. There are only two specimens in existence, the type in the United States National Museum, collected by Mr. William J. Fisher at Kodiak Island, Alaska, on June 11, 1882, and a mounted specimen in the University of Washington collection in Seattle, taken at Sitka, Alaska. The latter specimen, which I examined on my return from Alaska in 1911, is, as I remember it, the same as the bird we collected in the Aleutian Islands that summer. As it appears in my published note (1918) on the subject, Dr. H. C. Oberholser agrees with me in referring this and the specimen collected by Dr. Alexander Wetmore on the Alaska Peninsular, August 6, 1911, to *Pterodroma inexpectata* (-*gularis*). This leaves only the unique type to represent *Pterodroma fisheri*, which I believe will prove to have no standing.

Nesting.—Although the Peale petrel seems to be a fairly common species in the North Pacific Ocean in summer, very little seems to be known about its ranges and nesting habits. Mr. S. Percy Seymour found a breeding colony of these petrels on Preservation Inlet, New Zealand, which he evidently visited several times for he collected a series of the birds, as well as their eggs and young, which have found their way into American collections through the late Manly Hardy and his family. I have recently examined 18 of these birds, now in the Thayer Museum, and should judge from copies of correspondence, shown to me by Colonel Thayer, that Mr. Brewster pronounced them, while still in the Hardy collection, as identical with his type of *Pterodroma scalaris;* and that since then Doctor Oberholser has compared them with Peale's type of *Pterodroma gularis* and pronounced them identical with that species. These are significant facts and, when taken in connection with the fact that Godman (1907) evidently regarded Mr. Seymour's birds as *gularis*, tend to prove that the two species are identical. There is considerable individual variation in this series of birds of which Mr. Brewster's type of *scalaris* represents one extreme and Peale's type of *gularis* another.

Eggs.—There are also in the Thayer collection three eggs, collected by Mr. Seymour, on Preservation Inlet, on December 12, 1899, and January 7, 1900. The parent birds were collected with the single eggs in each case. The nests are described as made of "small sticks, ferns, etc., in a burrow." The eggs are oval or elliptical oval in shape; the surface of the shell is smooth but lustreless and the color is dirty white.

The measurements of eight eggs, in various collections, average 60.4 by 43.8 millimeters; the eggs showing the four extremes measure **63** by **45.5, 56** by 43, and 57.5 by **41.5** millimeters.

Young.—The nestling is described by Godman (1907) as "covered with sooty-grey down, not perceptibly whiter below." The Park Museum, in Providence, Rhode Island, kindly loaned me for study a mounted specimen of the downy young of this species which came to them in the Hardy collection. It was collected on Preservation Inlet, presumably by the same Mr. Seymour, on March 14, 1898. It is practically fully grown and seems to be much bulkier than the adult; the wing-coverts are fully feathered with "slate colored" feathers and the scapulars show large tracts of "plumbeous" feathers; the face and cheeks are feathered and mottled with black and white; and under the down on the breast and belly many white feathers, broadly tipped with "plumbeous," may be seen; otherwise the entire body, including the crown of the head, is covered with long, soft, fluffy down, "ecru-drab" or "drab-gray" in color, which is fairly uniform and only slightly paler below. This specimen would seem to indicate that the first plumage assumed by the young bird is similar to that of the adult, as is the case with most of the petrels, but Buller (1888) says:

The bird of the first year differs from the adult in being generally darker in plumage. The whole of the upper surface, the sides of the breast, the sides of the body, flanks and abdomen, dark slaty-grey, the feathers very minutely margined with paler. Chin pure white; lores, lower side of face, fore-neck, breast, and under tail-coverts white, varied with slaty-grey, in freckled wavy lines on the breast. All the medium wing-coverts are stained with brown; the inner webs of all the quills pure white, as also are the larger under wing-coverts.

The above statement that the feathers are "very minutely margined with paler" is further evidence that Mr. Brewster's *scalaris* is merely an immature specimen of *inexpectata*.

Behavior.—Very little is known about the habits of *inexpectata*, but Godman (1907) gives us the following scanty facts in regard to it:

Peale says this fulmar was found among icebergs buffeting the storms and fogs of the Antarctic regions. He saw but few examples, and only obtained a single specimen, on March 21st, while the ship *Peacock* was enveloped in a fog, in lat. 68° S., long. 95° W. It occurs in the New Zealand seas, and Buller mentions many places whence he had received specimens; among these are the Spencer Mountains in the Province of Canterbury. Mr. Percy Seymour discovered a nesting colony at Preservation Inlet, and, according to Buller, the species has also been found on the Auckland Islands.

During our cruise across the north Pacific Ocean, when 200 miles or more from the nearest land and long before we reached the vicinity of the Aleutian chain, we frequently saw day after day a number of large light colored petrels, which we were firmly convinced were of this species, for which we had been cautioned to be on the lookout. They did not, as a rule, come very near the ship, but, on June 2 and 3, 1911, in rough and stormy weather, they were fairly common and several times came within gunshot range, near enough for us to identify them as *Pterodroma*. Mr. Beck and I tried to persuade the captain to lower a boat and let us try to collect some, but perhaps he was wise in refusing to do so for the sea was too rough for a small boat; we might have shot some from the ship but we could not have secured them. I should not have felt so confident of the correctness of our identification, except for an incident which followed. We subsequently saw a few specimens of apparently the same species in the vicinity of the Aleutian Islands, and on June 17, 1911, Mr. Rollo H. Beck and I settled to our own satisfaction the identity of the *Pterodroma* we had been seeing. We were out near the entrance to Kiska Harbor in a small boat collecting auklets; the sea was smooth but there was a dense fog and birds of various kinds were very tame; I saw a large bird, dimly outlined in the fog, flying by Mr. Beck's end of the boat and told him to shoot it; we were both surprised on picking it up to see that it was evidently a Peale petrel. If I had realized what it was I might have kept still and shot it myself, in which case it would now be in the United States National Museum collection or my own, instead of Dr. Leonard C. Sanford's, where it is at present.

DISTRIBUTION.

Breeding range.—New Zealand seas. Known to breed only at Preservation Inlet, New Zealand.

Range.—Widely extended over the Pacific Ocean, from the Antarctic regions to the Aleutian Islands (Kiska Island) and Alaska (Kodiak Island and Sitka).

Casual record.—Accidental in New York (Mount Morris, April, 1880).

Egg dates.—Preservation Inlet: Five records, December 24 to January 7.

BULWERIA BULWERI (Jardine and Selby).

BULWER PETREL.

HABITS.

This large dusky petrel enjoys a wide distribution in both hemispheres, for it ranges over the north temperate zones of the Atlantic and Pacific Oceans with breeding stations in both oceans. It was originally described in 1828 from a specimen taken near .Madeira and sent to Sir W. Jardine by Doctor Bulwer, for whom it was named. Our claim to it as a North American bird is based on its supposed accidental occurrence in Greenland; Mr. Howard Saunders (1889) says: "An example in the Leiden Museum is said to have come from Greenland, but Reinhardt informed Mr. P. E. Freke that he thought it might be from one of the Moravian settlements in Labrador."

Nesting.—Godman (1907) says:

Bulwer's fulmar breeds, according to Doctor Heineken, in the Madeira and Canary groups of islands; the birds arrive in March and begin to lay early in June. The young are hatched in July, and after September but few are seen till the following spring. These birds are purely nocturnal in habits and although very rarely found in flocks like shearwaters, remain almost constantly at sea, except during the breeding season; they may then be found in considerable numbers on the Desertas, whence many eggs, now in the British Museum, were procured by Padre Schmitz.

He had previously written elsewhere (1872):

I found Bulwer petrel breeding in considerable numbers on the small Deserta. It appears so nocturnal in its habits that I never once saw it flying about in the daytime, though there were plenty of another, smaller species. The nests I found were for the most part low down at the foot of the cliffs under the fallen rocks, where the birds were easily caught with the hand while sitting on their eggs.

Mr. David A. Bannerman (1914) writes of the nesting habits of this petrel on Montaña Clara Island in the Canaries:

This was the only small island on which we found Bulwer's petrel breeding. Here, however, they were quite common, although their numbers seemed scant in comparison with those of the large shearwaters. By far the most attractive in appearance of all the petrels, these somber-colored little birds were breeding all round the island under the large boulders which had fallen from the cliffs. They were most common in the actual neighborhood of my camp, where many of their nesting sites were under rocks only just beyond the reach of the waves. Holes were sometimes utilized, and we found two close together about 40 feet up the side of the cliff, each containing a bird. We dug these holes out and found the birds sitting about 2 feet from the entrance. In no case was there any attempt at a nest, the single egg being deposited on the bare stone. At the time of my visit all the birds had laid. In one case a fisherman brought in two eggs, which he assured me he had found in the same "nest" lying side by side, doubtless the product of two females. All the eggs were freshly laid, and I gathered from the fishermen that the birds had not long come to land.

Bulwer's petrel is almost entirely nocturnal in its habits, and we never saw any flying in the neighborhood of the island during the day. If pulled out of their holes these birds seemed very dazed, but invariably attempted to escape by crawling under stones. In one case, however, a bird which we had placed on a rock in the brilliant sunlight waddled to the edge and immediately flew out to sea.

The Bulwer petrel breeds abundantly on several of the islands in the Hawaiian group. Dr. Walter K. Fisher (1906) writes:

We found the Bulwer petrel breeding on Necker Island in considerable numbers. Here the birds nest in rather deep, bubblelike holes in the rocks, as far from the light as possible. We found the first bird by discovering a white egg under a loose, flat rock back in a cavity. When the stone was lifted the petrel was under the far side. The favorite site, however, is a hole about 2 feet deep, with a narrow entrance, and wider cavity at the rear. These are probably bubbles in the lava. The nest, scarcely worthy of the name, consists of a few old tern feathers gathered rudely around the egg, as if merely to hold it in place. Sometimes there is no trace of a nest, and again I found a few wing bones of a tern, as though these had been used in place of sticks. We found many nests, each with one egg, or occasionally the birds had not yet begun to lay. Once we found a set of two eggs. They are a glossless pure white and differ much in shape, no two in the collection of nine being alike. Ovate is the most prevalent type, more or less acute, varying to elliptical ovate and short ovate. One egg is nearly elliptical. An ovate specimen measures 44 by 30 millimeters, another 41 by 31. An almost elliptical egg is 45 by 30.

Eggs.—Rev. F. C. R. Jourdain has sent me the measurements of 66 eggs from Madeira and the Desertas, which average 42.95 by 31.21 millimeters; the largest eggs measure **47** by 30 and 42 by **33,** and the smallest eggs measure **39.6** by 30.4 and 44.6 by **29.6** millimeters.

Young.—Yarrell (1871) says: " The nestling is said to be covered with a sooty-brown down." Probably, as in other closely allied petrels, the first plumage assumed is similar to that of the adult.

Food.—Doctor Fisher (1906) says that birds which flew aboard near Bird Island " had been feeding on fish eggs and ctenophores or comb jelly."

Behavior.—Seebohm (1891) writing of its habits in the Volcano Islands, says:

Mr. Holst found it very common on Sulphur Island and sends three examples, in each of which the pale bar across the wing formed by the grey margins of the greater wing-coverts is very conspicuous, which bar is said to be absent in *Bulweria macgillivrayi* from the Fiji Islands. These petrels flew about at night like bats in the twilight in great numbers, being extremely bold, sometimes touching the gun with the tips of their wings, but the rapidity of their flight made it very difficult to shoot them. Mr. Holst succeeded in dropping one of them and afterwards secured several more in the daytime, when they were found hidden away in pairs among the bushes and rocks all over the island, but he was unable to find any eggs.

Mr. Ogilvie-Grant (1896) writes: " The call of this bird is very fine and was frequently heard at night, a pleasant contrast to the harsh voices of the great shearwaters. It consists of four higher notes and a lower, more prolonged note, the whole repeated several (usually three) times and uttered in a loud, cheerful strain." Doctor Fisher (1906) observes: " The Bulwer petrel is quite gentle, and when first disturbed utters a penetrating but low moan, something like *who who*, dovelike in quality, but decidedly different from *oo-ow* of the uau kane (*Puffinus cuneatus*)."

Breeding range.—Islands in the eastern North Atlantic Ocean. In the Azores, Salvages, Madeira, and Canary Islands. Also on various islands in the North Pacific Ocean. On the Bonin and Volcano Islands, on Laysan, Necker, and Bird Islands, and on other islands in the Hawaiian group. Apparently the Pacific birds are not subspecifically distinct from the Atlantic birds. Breeding grounds protected in the Hawaiian Islands reservation.

Range.—Eastern portion of the North Atlantic Ocean and central and western portions of the Pacific Ocean from Japan and China to the Marquesas Islands.

Casual records.—Accidental in Greenland and in England (Yorkshire and Sussex, 5 records.)

Egg dates.—Canary and Madeira Islands: Fourteen records, January 7 to July 10; seven records, June 11 to 21. Necker Island: One record, May 31.

HALOCYPTENA MICROSOMA Coues.

LEAST PETREL.

HABITS.

The life history of the least petrel, the smallest of the family, long remained unknown. The type specimen, taken by Mr. Xantus, in May, 1861, near San José del Cabo, Lower California, remained unique until March, 1888, when Mr. Charles H. Townsend (1890) captured a second specimen, which "flew on board the *Albatross* in Panama Bay."

Nesting.—For all that we know regarding its habits we are indebted to Mr. A. W. Anthony (1898*b*) who discovered the breeding grounds of this rare species. He writes:

In early June I have found the least petrel migrating along the coast of Lower California in company with the Socorro and black petrels, and in late July have found them nesting on the small rocky San Benito Island, fifty miles off the coast of the peninsula. So far I have never found the least petrel nesting in burrows. They have always been taken from the crevices in rocky ledges or among the loose stones. The pearly white egg is laid on the bare rock. Usually several are found within a few feet if desirable crevices are numerous.

Regarding the islands and his interesting discovery Mr. Anthony (1896*a*) writes:

The San Benito Islands are small, rocky reefs only, with little vegetation, and being so far off shore are but little resorted to by gulls, cormorants, and similar species.

The second day on the island Mr. James M. Gaylord, the botanist of our party, reported finding a " half-grown petrel incubating an egg " on another part of the island. Scarcely daring to hope, but suspecting that it might be the almost mythical least petrel, he was instructed to bring it back with him when he returned from that quarter next day. As we had surmised, the specimen proved to be *Halocyptena microsoma*, which we subsequently found breeding in several parts of the island. All eggs of this species were taken either from under loose slabs of rock or crevices in the broken ledges, the former location seeming to be preferred. None were found in burrows, although several were opened in the colonies of this species. They all contained either *O. melania* or *O. socorroensis*.

Eggs taken from July 24 to 27 were in most cases fresh or but slightly incubated, though many were well advanced in incubation.

Downy young, and even incubated eggs were found on our return to the island September 8.

Again he (1900a) says:

In a rock wall about seven feet long and less than two feet high, I once found twenty-eight of these little petrels, but I have never found them in other islands of the coast.

Eggs.—The egg of the least petrel is well described by Mr. Anthony (1896a), as follows:

In shape the eggs of the least petrel were more inclined to be elliptical than either of the other species described, but were often elongate-ovate, short or even in some cases rounded ovate, as in the species of *Oceanodroma*.

They were pure white, with rosy flush before being blown, but dead white afterward. In many, if not in the majority of our specimens, a ring of very minute black specks encircled one or both ends. These specks came off upon the slightest touch, leaving slight stains or marks such as might be made by brushing away a spot of lampblack which had accidentally fallen on the shell.

Ten eggs of this species averaged in measurement 29.4 by 19.3 millimeters.

The measurements of 40 eggs, in various collections, average 23.4 by 19.4 millimeters; the eggs showing the four extremes measure **28.2** by **22**, **23** by 18.5, and 25.2 by **18** millimeters.

Young.—Mr. Anthony (1898b) says, of the downy young:

Young were taken as late as September 7 or 8 that were but a few days old. They were like the young of the three species of *Oceanodroma* I have mentioned, except for size. All are covered with sooty or slaty black down, through which the feathers appear when the bird is nearly or quite fully grown.

Behavior.—The same writer (1900a) gives an interesting account of the peculiar notes of the least petrel, which I quote in full, as follows:

As soon as the rocky ground at the base of the hills is reached, a strange note is heard, which seems to come from the loose rocks fallen from a small ledge above, and resembles the " whirring " of a rapidly revolving cog wheel. For about ten seconds the whizzing continues, when suddenly a note is dropped—there is a quick gasp, as for breath—and instantly the wheels begin to revolve again, having given one the impression that there is a broken cog in the buried machine. I have no idea how long the strange note might be continued. I have waited until my patience was exhausted, and always the same "cog" was slipped, at exactly the same interval, and the bird was as fresh as ever when I left it with its unfinished song. Another note of this species which is occasionally heard from the same rock pile and which gives one a clew to the author, is exactly like the cry of the two petrels above mentioned, but is higher pitched and more hastily uttered, giving one the idea of a smaller bird, as indeed it is, the least petrel (*Halocyptena microsoma*).

The least petrel should be easily recognized in flight by its small size, its wedge-shaped tail, and its uniformly dark color, without any white areas.

DISTRIBUTION.

Breeding range.—Known to breed only on San Benito Island off the Pacific coast of Lower California.

Range.—Pacific coast of middle America, from Lower California to Ecuador.

Egg dates.—San Benito Island: Twenty-four records, July 2 to 27; twelve records, July 25 to 27.

HYDROBATES PELAGICUS (Linnaeus).

STORMY PETREL.

HABITS.

The storm petrel or least petrel, as it was formerly called, is probably the original "Mother Carey's chicken" of the sailors. It is one of the smallest of the petrels and wanders over the north Atlantic Ocean chiefly on the eastern side. On the American coast it is said to occur on the Newfoundland banks and off the coast of Nova Scotia. It has been said to breed on Sable Island and at various places along the coasts of Newfoundland and Labrador, but such reports need confirmation, as there is not a single authentic American breeding record. It is abundant on the eastern Atlantic where it has long been familiarly known to sailors as a harbinger of storms, a mere superstition, of course. Much has been written about it, from which I shall quote.

Nesting.—Audubon (1840) and several later writers have quoted freely from Hewitson's observations, in his British Oology, from which I have selected the following passage:

Before leaving Shetland I again visited the island of Oxna, and though so late as the 30th of June, they were only just beginning to lay their eggs. In Foula they breed in the holes in the cliff, at a great height above the sea; but here under stones which form the beach, at a depth of three or four feet, or more, according to that of the stones; as they go down to the earth, beneath them, on which to lay their eggs. In walking over the surface, I could hear them, very distinctly, singing in a sort of warbling chatter, a good deal like swallows when fluttering above our chimneys, but harsher; and in this way, by listening attentively, was guided to their retreat, and, after throwing out stones as large as I could lift on all sides of me, seldom failed in capturing two or three seated on their nests, either under the lowest stone or between two of them. The nests, though of much the same materials as the ground on which they were placed, seem to have been made with care; they were of small bits of stalks of plants, and pieces of hard, dry earth. Like the rest of the genus, the stormy petrel lays invariably one egg only. During the daytime they remain within their holes; and though the fishermen are constantly passing over their heads (the beach under which they breed being appropriated for the drying of fish), they are then seldom heard, but toward night become extremely querulous; and when most other birds are gone to rest, issue forth in great numbers, spreading themselves far over the surface of the sea.

Mr. W. Eagle Clarke (1905a) gives a good account of the nesting habits of this species, as follows:

The storm petrel is very numerous during the summer, when they fly noisily about the islands during the nighttime. They breed on Eilean Mhor, and probably on the other islands, in abundance. Many chicks, some of them quite recently hatched, were found during our visit in September, and we saw young ones in every stage from a few hours' old (tiny balls of pretty lavender-grey down) to birds full grown and fully feathered, except that they had a bunch of down still present on the lower part of the abdomen. The old birds are entirely absent during the daytime, leaving even the small chicks to take care of themselves, and do not return until darkness sets in, when they tend their young and depart again early in the morning, probably to spend the day far out at sea in search of food. We opened out a number of their nesting holes at all hours of the day, but the old birds were always absent, except in one instance, where the young had only recently emerged from the egg. Occasionally they visited the lantern. They nest in the remains of the old building, in holes in turf, and under stones among grass. The nest is a mere mat composed of dry roots, grass, etc. I received a young one in full down, which had been taken on the 3rd October; probably the first egg of this pair had been taken or destroyed.

The fact that eggs have been taken at various dates between May and October has suggested the possibility that two or more broods may be raised in a season, but probably such is not the case.

Eggs.—Godman (1907) describes the egg as follows: " The egg is white, with a sprinkling of minute reddish-brown dots, frequently forming a distinct zone round the larger end."

The measurements of 44 eggs, in various collections, average 27.6 by 21.3; the largest eggs measure **30** by 22 and 28.5 by **22.5**; the smallest eggs measure **26.2** by 21 and 29.5 by **20.5** millimeters.

Rev. H. A. Macpherson (1898) says:

The task of incubation is shared by both sexes, but it is usual to find only one bird upon the egg. Probably the bird which is incubating is fed at night by its mate, which has passed the day at sea. The egg of the storm petrel is believed to be incubated for about thirty-five days. Mr. William Evans ascertained that eggs of this species when placed in an incubator chipped on the thirty-third day, while a chick hatched out upon the thirty-fifth day.

Young.—The same writer gives the following interesting account of the behavior and development of the young bird in confinement:

The late Mr. H. D. Graham once took two storm petrels about a fortnight old, covered with a profusion of down, on the 8th of September. They were at first fed with very small bits of fish, which they took reluctantly, but soon developed a great partiality for cod-liver oil, and "would suck a stick dipped in oil very willingly, clattering their bills and shaking their heads with evident satisfaction. I should conclude from this that the petrels feed their young with the oil which they have the power of ejecting from their bills." These nestlings became fledged about the middle of September—when about three weeks old—supposing that they were two weeks old when obtained, and became much dissatisfied with confinement, though they still retained a great deal of down upon their bodies. "Night and day their long, powerful wings were in incessant motion in their attempts to escape from the box. As soon as the lid is opened they raise themselves up until they can hook their bills on to the edge; and then, assisted by their wings, and scrambling with their claws, they hoist themselves up. When upon the top of the box, they would be satisfied for a little while, shake themselves, and dress their feathers. The instinctive love of motion, however, would soon return, and they go off on a voyage of discovery. They walk with great caution, keeping their heads down, and using their bills as walking sticks, hooking hold of any inequality to assist themselves along, and keeping themselves up, for they have a constant tendency to topple over on their faces; they also are of great service to feel their way, for their sight seemed very imperfect, and their eyes were generally closed. [This we might have anticipated, from the fact that this petrel passes the first few weeks of its existence in more or less complete darkness]. When informed by the bill that they are arrived at the edge of the table, the closed eyes open, and an anxious survey is taken of the depth below, and after considerable preparation and thought, the hazardous leap is taken, and a short flight performed in safety to the floor. These little birds seemed to have an irresistible instinct which led them to attempt to surmount every obstacle which fell in their way. When walking on the table every book and desk must be climbed by means of the hooked bill, with the assistance of claws and pinions.

Plumages.—Godman (1907) says that the young bird is "at first covered with long down of a sooty ash color, making the bird look like a long-haired mouse, as no bill or wings are visible. When the down is shed, the plumage of the young bird is exactly similar to that of the adult, with the exception that the greater wing coverts have a distinct, if narrow, margin of white. The scapulars and black tips of the upper tail coverts also have nearly obsolete white fringes." Morris (1903) describes the young bird somewhat differently; he writes:

The young bird is not quite so dark as its parents the first year. The breast has less white near the tail; the margins of the wing coverts are rusty brown. The tertiaries have little or no white on their edges.

Food.—Of the storm petrel's food Macgillivray (1852) writes:

The food of this species is said by authors to consist of oily and fatty substances, small crustacea and mollusca, fishes, animal matter of any kind, garbage thrown from ships, and even seaweeds. It frequently appears in the wake of vessels, especially before or during stormy weather, but also when it is calm; and then picks up portions of animal and vegetable substances, even fragments of biscuits, that are thrown to it. But, generally, its stomach and gullet are found to contain oily matter, which, on being seized, it vomits, like the other species of this family.

Godman (1907) has " seen them in great numbers feeding on the carcass of a dead whale."

Behavior.—Macgillivray (1852) gives the best account of the flight, saying:

In the open ocean they are met with by day as well as by night; but when breeding they are seen in the neighborhood of their haunts; that is, to the distance of twenty or more miles around, chiefly in the dusk and dawn, and during the day remain concealed in their holes. Stormy weather does not prevent their coming abroad, nor are they less active during calms. When the waves are high and the wind fierce, it is pleasant, even amidst the noise of the storm and the heavings of the vessel, to watch the little creatures as they advance against the gale, at the height of scarcely a foot above the surface of the water, which they follow in all its undulations, mounting to the top of the wave, there quivering in the blast, and making good their way by repeated strokes of their long, narrow wings; then sliding down the slope, resting a moment in the shelter of the advancing mass of water, gliding up its side, and again meeting on the summit the force of the rude wind that curls the wave and scatters abroad its foam bells. I have seen them thus advancing, apparently with little labor, and in such cases less effort, I think, must be required than when they have to encounter a gale before it has blown long enough to raise the waves, which afford it partial shelter. Their manner of flying is similar to that of the smaller gulls; that is, they glide lightly along with expanded wings, sailing or gliding at intervals and then plying their feathery oars. It is only when picking up their food that, with upraised wings, they hover over the spot, and pat the water with their feet; although many persons have described this as their ordinary mode of progression. In calm weather, when the sea is smooth, they hover, skim, and wheel around much in the manner of swallows, though with less velocity. They have, in fact, a striking resemblance to these birds and certainly merit the name of sea swallows, at least, as much as the terns.

Morris (1903) describes their vocal performance as follows:

When engaged with their nests they utter a very peculiar purring or buzzing sound, broken every now and then by a "click"; also toward evening a frequent shrill whistling noise. Meyer likens the note to the word " kekereck-ee." The voices of these birds may be heard, especially toward evening, under the stones, at a depth of three or four feet or more, where they breed on the beach, " distinctly singing a sort of warbling chatter."

In thick and stormy weather these and other petrels are often driven in near the coast or into harbors where they become exhausted and are easily caught; many are sometimes killed in this way by the fury of the elements; during severe gales and hurricanes large numbers are driven inland and picked up dead or in dying condition. Morris (1903) says that " these birds are made use of by the inhabitants of the Faroe and other islands to serve for lamps, a wick of cotton or other material being drawn through the body, and when lighted it continues to burn till the oil in it is consumed."

Winter.—During the latter part of the summer those which have finished breeding wander westward and northward over the Atlantic Ocean even to American shores. They are most frequently seen, from the coasts of Maine and Nova Scotia northward, during the month of August. As casual observers are likely to mistake them for the two commoner species, Leach and Wilson petrels, I suspect that they are often overlooked and may be much commoner than is generally supposed. The stormy petrel can be distinguished from the Leach by its smaller size, square tail, and white flank patches, and from the Wilson by its much shorter legs, which on the latter project beyond the tail in flight; the white in the under side of the wing is also conspicuous in the stormy petrel.

DISTRIBUTION.

Breeding range.—Mainly on islands in the northeastern Atlantic Ocean. North to Iceland and northern Norway (Lofoten Islands). On many islands around Great Britain (Shetland, Faroe, Orkney Islands, etc.). East in the Mediterranean Sea to Malta, etc. South to the Madeira Islands.

Range.—Extends across the North Atlantic Ocean to southern Greenland, Labrador, Newfoundland, and Nova Scotia. Migrates southward along the Atlantic coast of Africa and around the cape to Zanzibar on the east coast.

Casual records.—Accidental in Ungava (Koksoak River, July and October 9, 1882), Quebec (Godbout, May 18, 1885, and October 6, 1889), Nova Scotia (Sable Island, November 4, 1901). Accidental in the interior of Europe.

Egg dates.—British Isles: Thirty-four records, May 18 to July 24; seventeen records, June 6 to July 1.

OCEANODROMA HORNBYI (Gray).

HORNBY PETREL.

HABITS.

For over 60 years the only known specimen of this rare and well marked species remained unique in the British Museum. It was procured by Admiral Hornby when he was in command of the Pacific Station with headquarters on Vancouver Island, and is said to have been obtained in the seas off the northwestern coast of America. It was described by Mr. George Robert Gray in 1853, and, during all these intervening years, not another specimen ever came to light. It has been placed in the hypothetical list in our check list because there seems to be some doubt as to the locality where it was actually taken, the original label having been lost. I am including it in this work because it seems to me that the indications are that the type specimen *was* taken off our coast, that it has been seen there since, and that it may be taken again within our limits.

Dr. Edward W. Nelson (1887) was quite sure that he saw specimens of this petrel while crossing the North Pacific Ocean: he says:

> While on my way to and from the Aleutian Islands a petrel conspicuous by its white collar and under surface was seen repeatedly, and although none were secured, yet it was identified by its peculiar pattern of coloration. These birds were seen both in May and in October while crossing a part of the Pacific some 500 miles broad bordering the Aleutian chain.

I can not accept the suggestion, contained in Mr. Henry W. Henshaw's explanatory footnote, that the birds referred to were *Pterodroma fisheri*, for I am familiar with the latter species in life and I can not see how such a mistake could have occurred. *Pterodroma* is much larger than *Oceanodroma* and its behavior in flight is quite different. I know from personal experience in the rough and stormy seas of the North Pacific Ocean that observations are much interrupted in bad weather and that collecting is often impossible at such times, when unfortunately, the Tubinares are most abundant. Therefore, it is not to be wondered at that this and other rare species have so long escaped the collectors. Persistent and systematic work in that region might yield some very valuable and interesting results.

One of the most interesting results of the Brewster and Sanford expedition to South America was the rediscovery of this rare species, 60 years after the type was described.

Mr. Robert Cushman Murphy (1922) has published the following notes on these and other specimens of this rare petrel:

> In 1887 (*fide* Godman, Monogr. Petrels, p. 36, 1907) E. W. Nelson reported that he had seen numbers of Hornby's petrels, "both in May and October, while crossing a part of the Pacific, some 500 miles broad, bordering the Aleutian chain." Doubts were subsequently cast upon the identification, however, by Henshaw.
>
> In 1895 the National Museum of Chile, at Santiago, obtained two immature specimens, including a nearly full-grown bird with only a few traces of grayish-white down still clinging to its belly. These came from an inland region east of Taltal. They were not recognized as *Oceanodroma hornbyi*, and were described anew by R. A. Philippi as "*Procellaria (Oceanites) collaris*" (Verhandlungen des deutschen wissenschaftlichen Vereins zu Santiago de Chile, vol. 3, Pt. 1, pp. 11–13, plate). Philippi's account states:
>
> "Das Exemplar von Sturmschwalbe, dessen Beschreibung ich hiermit gebe, ist dadurch besonders merkwurdig, dass es inmitten des Landes, ostlich von Taltal, in Gesellschaft eines ganz jungen Vogelchens, welches noch mit dem vollen Flaum bekleidet ist, tolt gefunden wurde. Unser Museum verdankt es H. Dr. Darapsky.
>
> "Der vogel hat ganz die Grosse und Gestalt der ubrigen Sturmschwalben, von denen er sehr leicht durch folgende Diagnose unterschieden werden kann."
>
> The Latin diagnosis which follows, the recorded measurements, and the full page monochrome plate made from a crayon drawing leave no room for doubt

that the specimen described was *Oceanodroma hornbyi*, notwithstanding minor discrepancies in the amount of white pictured on the face and throat. The figure was drawn from a poorly mounted bird, which doubtless accounts for slight distortions of the color areas. Both of the specimens have been seen by Dr. Frank M. Chapman during visits to Santiago.

During the Brewster-Sanford South American expedition of the American Museum of Natural History, Mr. Rollo H. Beck collected 56 specimens of *Oceanodroma hornbyi* in the offshore waters of the Peruvian coast and proved that the species is a common bird in this region. Mr. Beck's specimens were all taken during June, 1913, between the approximate latitudes of Ancon (11° 47′ S.) and Cerro Azul (13° 4′ S.) in waters from 15 to about 200 miles from the shore. He first noted the species in the vicinity of Hormigas de Afuera Islets, 38 sea miles west of Callao, on June 4. On June 6, when about 200 miles off-shore, he obtained the first specimens, along with numerous examples of *Oceanodroma markhami* and other petrels. Thereafter he saw *O. hornbyi* frequently, chiefly beyond 25 miles from shore, often feeding and coming to his bait in groups of a score or so. His notes of June 25, on which date he collected 30 miles off Cerro Azul, contain the observation that in early morning, while the sun was still low, the white breasts of Hornby's petrels shone like silver as the birds darted back and forth among other species. After June 27 he changed his field of operations to the islands and inshore waters of the Pisco Bay region, and thenceforth saw the species no more.

All of Beck's specimens, the majority of which still remain in the Brewster-Sanford collection, are birds which had resting sex organs. Most of the individuals were completing or had recently completed the molt and renewal of the flight feathers.

In the same month of a later year, June, 1916, Dr. Frank M. Chapman also observed Hornby's petrel along the Peruvian coast. He has kindly supplied me with the following extract from his notes of June 23, 1916:

"Leave Pisco at 7.15, make the Boqueron in the face of a stiff breeze. At 8 a. m. we were about ten miles offshore, and the ocean swarmed with petrels; a large, black *Puffinus*, and a smaller one, in countless numbers were active, except one flock of several hundred resting on the water. Many gannets were diving from a height of from fifty to sixty feet. A few yellow-nosed albatrosses were seen—splendid, sweeping creatures. There were several white-rumped petrels and dozens of *O. hornbyi;* the latter the most erratic flier I have ever seen—like a bat, swift, and nighthawk in one. They were skimming here, flitting there, then suddenly swung off with the wind a hundred yards or more so quickly one nearly lost sight of them."

To these field notes Doctor Chapman has added the following comment, relating to the apparent absence of the species during the perior of the year which doubtless includes its breeding season:

"December 4–7, 1918, while en route from Callao to Mollendo, I sailed over this same area, but although on the lookout for them I did not see a single Hornby's petrel."

With regard to the breeding locality of *O. hornbyi*, we have only the information published by Philippi. This author's second paper relating to the species (Anales del Museo Nacional de Chile, vol. 15, sect. 1, pp. 90–92, pl. 42, 1902) is in part a reprint in Spanish of the German description cited above, with the addition of a colored plate. He states somewhat more fully that the mounted specimen in the Santiago Museum was obtained on the tableland east of Taltal, at a considerable altitude, in company with a dead chick of the same species, and that he therefore believes this region to be the petrel's breeding ground. The supposition surely seems to be supported by circumstantial evidence, and it would be altogether plausible were it not that mainland breeding sites are almost unknown among the Tubinares. If the petrels do actually nest in the Chilean mountains, their individual burrows are probably scattered over wide areas, for thickly populated colonies would soon be discovered and decimated by predaceous mammals.

Nothing further is known about the distribution or habits of this rare species, but I hope to see the Hornby petrel eventually restored to the American list on positive evidence. Nothing whatever seems to be known about its life history.

DISTRIBUTION.

Breeding range.—Unknown.

Range.—Known only from the "northwest coast of America" and from the coasts of Peru and Chile, as indicated above.

OCEANODROMA FURCATA (Gmelin).

FORKED-TAILED PETREL.

HABITS.

Among the *Tubinares* of the north Pacific Ocean this beautiful little petrel is one of the most widely distributed and most universally common species. On our cruise from Dixon Entrance to Unimak Pass some of these graceful little birds were almost constantly in sight, circling about the ship and flitting lightly over the waves in search of some tiny morsels of food. We also saw them frequently about the Aleutian Islands, as far west as Attu Island.

Nesting.—They were undoubtedly breeding on many, if not all, of the islands in the Aleutian chain, though we actually found only one small breeding colony. During that eventful afternoon on Tanaga Island, June 25, 1911, we wandered inland over a broad and marshy alluvial plain and up the valley of a little brook into the hills. We collected during that half day over 40 specimens of our new subspecies of ptarmigan, found and photographed several of their nests and spent some time hunting for nests of Aleutian sandpipers, and Northern phalaropes, both of which were breeding there quite commonly. Consequently we had but little time to devote to the forked-tailed petrels, desirable as they were; but, as we came to some steep grassy hills, Mr. Rollo H. Beck wandered off and discovered a small colony of this species. The hills were about a mile back from the bay and the nests were in typical petrel burrows in the soft soil of the steep grassy slopes near the base of the hill. Several burrows were dug out, but only one fresh egg was found, on which the incubating bird was caught. Apparently they were just beginning to breed, but further search was impossible for lack of time.

Dr. Leonhard Stejneger (1885) found a small colony of forked-tailed petrels breeding on Copper Island, in the Commander group, on July 12, 1883, where "the eggs, a single one in each nest, were deposited in deep holes in the steep basaltic rocks, 3 feet or more deep, and it was only with great difficulty that a few could be secured." This was apparently a departure from the usual custom of the species, for it usually closely resembles the Leach petrel in its nesting habits and is often intimately associated with it. Dr. Joseph Grinnell and Mr. Joseph Mailliard found these two species breeding abundantly together on St. Lazaria Island, a long narrow rock lying in the mouth of Sitka Bay, Baranoff Island, Alaska. They estimated that the Leach petrels outnumbered the forked-tailed by about four to one. Doctor Grinnell (1897) in describing the island, says:

It is irregularly shaped, approximately a quarter of a mile in length, by three hundred yards in width at its widest portion. It has the general outline of a huge rock with steep sides, but in the main it is crowned by a heavy growth of large firs and hemlocks. There is a rank growth of tall grass on those parts where there are few trees or none at all, and among the trees there are scattered clumps of salmonberry bushes, while the porous sod is carpeted by deer's feet and other low plants.

This island is the one in the vicinity of Sitka chosen by thousands of seabirds for a breeding ground. The exposed, broken precipitous sides of the island are the resorts of violet green cormorants, pigeon guillemots and California murres, while the glaucous-winged gulls and tufted puffins select the grassy banks and promontories above the cliffs. But the petrels, to be considered in the present paper, seem to prefer the dark forest, although their burrows are abundant wherever there is enough soil to hold them.

Mr. Mailliard (1898) describes their nesting habits as follows:

The burrows seemed to run in any and every direction except directly downwards. The area that I worked in was covered with bunch grass and low salmonberry bushes, the roots of the latter being greatly in the way. The peat was so loose and wet that it was difficult to clearly define the burrows, but it seemed certain that they frequently intersected when on the same level, and also that there were tiers of them on different planes and running diverse ways. I could, however, form no idea of the length of any particular one. Their depth varied from four to 18 inches from the surface of the ground. The diameter of the burrows was from about 2½ to 3½ inches, but frequently they were hollowed out in the interior to a greater size. The nests were merely small hollows in slightly enlarged portions of the galleries, with sometimes a little dry grass on the bottom, and were placed at irregular distances apart—frequently an *O. furcata* within a foot of a nest of *O. leucorhoa*, and then again perhaps several of one species in a succession at varying intervals. It was difficult to discern much removed material at the entrances to the burrows, the same ones being in all probability used year after year, the excavated earth having in the course of time become assimilated with the surrounding surface. It seemed as if one could dig down and strike burrows anywhere, and, in fact,

I gave up looking for the entrances proper, and simply dug up the peat in any spot that seemed likely to be free from roots. Unless violently disturbed, each bird would be found sitting upon its egg, or perhaps it would back away a few inches.

Doctor Grinnell (1897) says:

Most of the burrows each contained an egg, in which case one bird, either male or female, was sitting. In case there was a young one, neither parent bird was present. When there were neither egg nor young in the hole, both old birds were at home together.

The southernmost colony that I have seen described is on the Three Arch Rocks, off the coast of Oregon, of which Mr. W. L. Finley (1905) has written a very interesting account. Here he found this species breeding with Kaeding or Beal petrels, tufted puffins, western gulls, Brandt, Baird, and Farallon cormorants, California murres, and pigeon guillemots.

Eggs.—The single egg of the forked-tailed petrel is much like that of the Leach petrel, but somewhat larger. The surface is smooth but without gloss, and the color is dull white. There are usually plenty of minute dark specks, purple or purplish black in color, forming a cloud or a wreath about the larger end. Sometimes these specks are quite large and conspicuous, but more often very faint or indistinct. Some eggs show a few faint lilac spots.

The measurements of 40 eggs, in various collections, average 33.9 by 25.7 millimeters; the largest eggs measure **37.5** by 28.5 and 35.4 by **27.5,** and the smallest eggs measure **32** by 24.5 and 34 by **23.5** millimeters.

Both sexes incubate, relieving each other at night and morning.

Plumages.—The downy young when first hatched is covered with long, soft, thick down, foreshadowing the color of the parent, except on the chin and throat, which are naked. The color varies from "deep mouse gray" or "light mouse gray" above to "pale mouse gray below." The young bird is nearly fully grown before the plumage appears. Of the development of the plumage Mr. George Willett (1912) writes:

The first feathers to appear are those of the wings and tail, closely followed by those on the back of the head and throat. Then comes the beautiful gray covering of the back and upper tail-coverts, and shortly afterward the mature feathers replace the down on the chest. The last down to disappear is that on the lower abdomen. When this leaves the young is very similar in plumage to the adult bird. The tail, however, is not so deeply forked, the white patch on the throat is streaked with gray, the forehead is dark gray instead of brownish, and the general coloration of the back, wings, and tail is darker than in the adult.

Food.—The food of the forked-tailed petrel consists of soft, oily substances with perhaps a few minute particles of animal food which it picks up off the surface of the water. Turner (1886) says: " The Eskimo name of this bird is *O Ku ik*, and means oil eater. They assert that this bird skims the water for traces of oil which may have flowed from a wounded seal or whale, and that large flocks of them will follow the floating carcass of a seal for that purpose." Apparently oil is the principal food of this and other petrels for when caught or killed large quantities of oily juices flow from the mouths and nostrils, soiling the plumages beyond repair. The young are fed by squirting this fluid into their mouths.

Behavior.—The forked-tailed petrel in flight is not easily mistaken for anything else, as the soft, blended, pearl gray colors of its plumage are conspicuous and distinctive. The flight of this petrel, like others of its genus, is light, rapid, and erratic, flitting hither and thither close to the surface of the waves, often with its feet extended as if walking on the water. The following account, evidently taken from Doctor Pickering's journal, written off the coast of Oregon in April, 1840, is given by Baird, Brewer, and Ridgway (1884) :

Generally, they reminded him of Wilson's petrel, but their wings seemed longer and their movements appeared to be more rapid; in fact, they appeared to resemble the larger *Procellaridae*. Occasionally this bird sailed in its flight, but during the greater part of the time it moved by very rapidly flexing its wings in the same manner as Wilson's petrel. It proved to be not difficult to capture, and several specimens were taken with hook and line. The birds would dive a foot or two after the bait, and made use of their wings in and under the water, from which they evidently had not the difficulty in rising which is observable in the albatross. Their power of swimming seemed rather feeble, yet they alighted in the water without any apparent hesitation. The dead body of one of their companions having been thrown overboard, the other birds clustered about it with as much avidity as around any other food. This bird uttered a faint cry when it was taken on board.

Mr. Richard C. McGregor (1906) while anchored in Akutan Harbor in the Aleutian Islands, on August 19, 1901, witnessed a peculiar performance of this species in a dense fog at night, which he described in his notes as follows:

At about 9.30 a petrel was brought down (to my room) by the quartermaster; in a short time three more and then an auklet were produced by Davie (Q. M.). Going on deck I found *O. furcata* flying about the masthead light—there were probably five or six in sight. In a short time I had a dozen laid out. There was a moderate fog at first and as this thickened the birds increased in numbers. Fully a dozen were in sight like so many moths. They struck the rigging, bridge, and wheelhouse and fluttered to the deck in a dazed condition. The fox (a young animal caught by the men and kept on deck) soon had a dozen or more in and about his box, and the cats were running them over the deck. On all sides of the ship their cries were heard. They flew into the chart room, the fireroom, and down the ventilator to the main deck. Even from my room in the lower wardroom their cries are plainly audible.

Doctor Grinnell (1897) who was forced to spend a night on St. Lazaria Island, had an unusually good opportunity to study the midnight flight of the forked-tailed petrel on its breeding grounds, which he graphically describes as follows:

After the sun set and the long summer twilight began to make the woods a little gloomy, the petrels became more active. Their curious calls came from every direction in the ground, though as yet not a bird was to be seen. Presently a little stir in the grass called attention to a petrel which clumsily scrambled from his hole, and after the usual fumbling put himself in flight and betook himself speedily out to sea. Soon others appeared and others and others. The crows, their enemies, had by this time gone to roost, and as the gloom grew deeper the petrels became more numerous. Those which had been out to sea all day began to arrive among the trees, and were even more awkward than those leaving. They flew against branches and bushes and into my face, but all ultimately seemed to know where their respective homes were. The chorus of their cries was curious and depressing to one's spirits, and the chilly air was constantly being fanned into my face by their noiseless wings. The light-colored ghostly forms of the forktails were much more readily discernible than the dark Leach's.

The ground was alive with struggling petrels, and I picked up as many as I chose. As the twilight of evening slowly merged into dawn the height of their activity was reached. I walked from end to end of the wooded part of the island, and everywhere the petrels were equally numerous.

As I began to feel cold and likewise hungry, the novelty of these strange experiences naturally wore off. After considerable searching for dry fuel I started a smoldering little blaze, which lighted up the dusky surroundings, together with the flitting forms of the birds, thus disclosing a very impressive scene. But presently several of the petrels were attracted by the light and flew pell-mell into the fire, extinguishing the feeble flames in short order. After several similarly frustrated attempts, though partly on account of the damp wood, I gave it up.

As soon as the dawn became perceptibly brighter the petrels became quieter and fewer. Part went out to sea; others returned to their nests. By sunrise, at 2.30 a. m., not a petrel was to be seen nor a note heard where two hours before had been such a tumult of nocturnal forms and voices. The crows set up their saucy cawing and the western winter wrens and sooty song sparrows announced their presence with their clear musical trill.

The vocal performances of this species have been referred to above. They consist of a variety of soft twittering notes, given in flight while flitting about their breeding grounds, or faint squeaking notes when disturbed in their burrows or when handled. But, being nocturnal in its activity and being so intimately associated with other species, it is not easy to distinguish its note with certainty.

In its association with other species it is gentle and harmless itself, but it has many enemies. In the Aleutian Islands it falls an easy prey to prowling foxes, which dig out its nesting burrows, killing and eating both old and young; it has been practically exterminated on the islands where foxes are abundant. The mink and other predatory animals destroy large numbers. On St. Lazaria Island, Doctor Grinnell found evidence that crows were also destructive in digging out the burrows and eating the eggs. Probably gulls do their share also, as the burrows are often very shallow and in soft soil.

Winter.—This petrel seems to be a hardy species, wandering northward during the fall months throughout Bering Sea, along the coasts of Alaska and Siberia, and occasionally up some of the rivers. Nelson (1887) says: "The Eskimo find them after the sea is covered with ice. At such times they are usually near an air hole, and in several cases were captured alive, being too weak from starvation to escape." The main winter home of the species, however, is the north Pacific Ocean, where it is widely distributed, between the North American and Asiatic coasts.

DISTRIBUTION.

Breeding range.—Northern and eastern portions of the Pacific Ocean. From the Kurile and Commander Islands (Copper Island) all along the Aleutian chain (Attu, Agattu, Tanaga, and Atka Islands, etc.), on islands off the coast of southern Alaska (Sanak, St. Lazaria, and Forrester Islands, etc.), off the coast of Washington (Clallam County) and as far south as northern California (Whaler Island, Del Norte County, and off Trinidad, Humboldt County). Breeding grounds protected in Alaska, Washington, and Oregon reservations.

Range.—North Pacific Ocean, south along the coast to southern California (Orange County). North throughout Bering Sea, along both coasts, and through Bering Straits into Kotzebue Sound.

Casual records.—Accidental in the interior of Alaska (Tanana River, November).

Egg dates.—Southern Alaska: Sixteen records, June 10 to July 15; eight records, June 17 to 30. Washington and Oregon: Three records, June 7, 9, and 17. Aleutian Islands: Two records, June 25 and 30.

OCEANODROMA LEUCORHOA LEUCORHOA (Vieillot).

LEACH PETREL.

HABITS.

The most widely distributed and the best-known species of the genus *Oceanodroma* on American coasts is the Leach petrel. It is the only species known to breed on our Atlantic coast, in spite of numerous reports to the contrary. It is distinctly a bird of northern oceans, and its breeding grounds extend from the Aleutian Islands nearly to the Pacific coast of the United States and from the coast of Maine northward to Greenland on the Atlantic side. We ought to know something about its life history, but our knowledge of even this common bird is not complete.

Spring.—Concerning its arrival on its breeding grounds Mr. Arthur H. Norton (1881) has written the following:

In the early part of June, or even the latter part of May, these little birds come into the islands off the rugged coast of Maine. Some time is spent in investigating the accommodations, and as the time advances they enter one of the last year's tunnels or begin to excavate a new one. Both birds enter this subterranean tube and there work with a will, never coming forth to play in the sunshine or join in the terns' hurrying flight. So if we walk above their heads, we see them not; and knowing nothing about their habits we never suspect their presence. If we would learn of their ways, we must break into their burrows or await the coming of night.

On our breaking into their burrows they appear bewildered and seek darkness rather than flight; they utter no note of solicitude nor show signs of displeasure at this rude housebreaking, and can be taken in hand as easily as a pet chicken. They move with a staggering walk, or crawl, and get under the nearest object that affords protection from the light. When tossed into the air they take wing and fly far out over the ocean, never pausing to look back after the fate of their one egg.

As night comes on and the heat of day is succeeded by the cool of evening, we will hear, just after the tern's voice is hushed, a nasal squeak, in several syllables, delivered very rapidly and in a jerky way. It is the petrel on shore to spend the night in frolic or to propagate his race. Like his customs, his voice is peculiar, and musical in a way. On shore the petrel's voice is the only sound that accompanies the ocean's ceaseless roar through the solitude of night.

As morning approaches his notes become less frequent, and cease as the terns rise, and fill the air with their short cries.

Nesting.—In my various wanderings on the coasts of Maine and eastern Canada I have seen a number of breeding colonies of Leach petrels, but I shall not attempt to describe them all in detail. In the vicinity of Penobscot Bay, Maine, there are several large colonies on some of the outlying islands, but the inner islands are seldom visited for breeding purposes by this pelagic species, which makes its home on the open sea and loves to be within easy reach of the ocean swell. A picturesque and well-known breeding resort in this vicinity is on Spoon Island, which consists of two well-rounded hills connected by a low flat area of marsh and beach; its peculiar outline is easily discernible, far off to seaward, as the coastwise steamer passes around the south end of Deer Isle, though it stands in the outermost row of islands. The larger hill, presumably the bowl of the spoon, is perhaps a hundred feet high, rounded and bare of vegetation, except for its grassy slopes, over which are scattered many loose rocks and boulders or outcropings of its rocky foundations. But on this rocky hill sufficient soft loamy soil, full of vegetable mold, has accumulated to offer just the conditions wanted by the petrels for their burrows. On my first visit to Spoon Island, on June 19, 1899, the burrows were numerous, indicating a large colony of birds; we dug out some 30 burrows, 18 of which contained a single egg each, which were fresh, or nearly so, covered by an incubating bird. We failed to find a mated pair of birds in any of the nests, which is usually the case before the egg is laid, from which we inferred that the courtship period had passed and that all the eggs had been laid. I noticed that the entrances to many of the burrows were partially overgrown with vegetation, indicating that they had been occupied for successive seasons; undoubtedly such is the case; they are probably repaired, enlarged, or extended a little each year. The burrows varied in length from a little over 1 foot to 3 feet or more; the entrance, which was large enough to admit my hand, sometimes ran straight downward for a few inches, but was more often slanting inward from the side of some little eminence or on sloping ground; the passageway, which was often quite tortuous, usually ran along horizontally only a few inches below the surface, just beneath the roots of the grass. I could easily open the burrows by running my arm in and tearing up the sod. Sometimes the passages intersected or branched in several directions. At the end of the burrow was an enlarged chamber containing the nest, which was loosely made of dry grasses, bits of sticks, and weed stems, mixed with pieces of bark and sods. Sometimes the egg was laid on the bare, soft soil without any attempt at nest building. The nest cavity was so much larger than the nest that the bird, when exposed to view, could crawl away almost out of sight under the overhanging soil. The birds are always very stupid under such circumstances; they make no attempt to escape, but try to avoid the light by hiding under any shelter available; if thrown into the air, however, they fly straight out to sea with a wavy and uncertain flight.

My second visit to this island was made on July 12, 1915, and I was disappointed to find the petrel colony very much reduced in size; there were certainly not over 50 pairs nesting here; this may be accounted for by the fact that some fishermen had been camping on the island and keeping a dog there, which means death to petrels. I had hoped to find some specimens of downy young petrels, but I was too early; there were plenty of heavily incubated eggs, but I did not find any young. I did not, of course, want to dig out all of the burrows and perhaps break up the colony.

On Seal Island, Nova Scotia, in July, 1914, I saw a large and populous colony scattered over the heavily wooded portion of the island. In a large burnt area their burrows were scattered thickly among the stumps and on the edges of the spruce forest along the shores, where there was plenty of soft soil, the ground was fairly honeycombed with their burrows among the roots of the trees. This seemed rather unusual to me, as all the other colonies that I had seen were in open, treeless situations.

On St. Lazaria Island, near Sitka, Alaska, the Leach petrel breeds abundantly in company with a much smaller number of forked-tailed petrels. The bird breeding in southern Alaska has been recognized by several experienced naturalists as a distinct species under the name of *Oceanodroma beali*, but the characters ascribed to it hardly seem to warrant its separation as a species and perhaps not even as a subspecies. Mr. George Willett (1912) estimated that there were about 20,000 pairs of this species nesting in this reservation in 1912. He says:

It is by far the most abundant breeding bird on the reservation. Everywhere on the island where the soil is deep enough are found the burrows of this bird. The burrows and nests are similar to those of the last species but are found in thousands on the flat top of the island among the timber and brush, where *furcata* does not seem to occur. Also they evidently nest considerably later than *furcata*, as no very large young were seen and a few fresh eggs were noted as late as August 15.

Dr. Joseph Grinnell (1897) thus describes the nesting of the Leach petrel on this island:

The entrance to the burrows are semicircular and usually open out under some clump of grass or a bunch of leaves, so that it is partly hidden. From the entrance the burrow runs at an easy slant for a few inches and then parallel with the surface of the ground, from two to five inches below. The total length of the burrow varies greatly, being from one to three feet. It is seldom straight but usually very crooked. The birds in digging evidently follow the direction of least resistance. The débris is scratched out into a slight mound in front of the entrance. The cavity at the end of the burrow is about three inches in height by five inches broad, and contains on the saucer-shaped floor a slight lining of dry grass blades.

A still more populous colony exists in the Forrester Island reservation in the same region. I quote from Prof. Harold Heath's (1915) report in regard to it, as follows:

It is difficult to estimate the number of these birds nesting on South Island. The Indians sometimes call the place " the basket " since it is so full of holes, but when asked regarding the number of holes or birds their guesses ranged from ten thousand to two hundred and fifty thousand. In a rough way the island was measured into a number of plots and in each of these the number of nests was estimated. The result totalled not far from seventy-five thousand, or one hundred and fifty thousand birds, and this is certainly a conservative estimate.

Almost as soon as a landing was made small openings were noticed in the moss covering the rocks, and while these appeared surprisingly similar to those made by mice, a minute's work was all that was necessary to disclose their true character. Others were half hidden in the grass and among the underbrush, and from the central valley to the summits of both hills the soil was riddled with holes. In various places from four to seven were counted in a space a yard square, and one must tread cautiously indeed to escape breaking through the burrows at every step.

The burrow leads inward from the entrance for varying distances, two feet being about the average length. In extreme cases tunnels have been opened having a length of fully six feet, and from two to five birds occupy this in common, each nest being placed in one of the lateral offshoots from the main trunk. Such extensive residences have evidently been vacated by Cassin auklets, as one young bird of this species was found in a burrow with five petrels. The nest is a flat, thin pad composed of fragments of grass, bits of moss, and small twigs of spruce or salmon berry.

Eggs.—The Leach petrel lays a single egg and raises only one young bird each season. The egg is much like that of others of the same genus, varying considerably in shape and size. The shape is elliptical ovate, elliptical oval, or nearly oval. The texture of the shell is smooth, but not glossy. The color is pure white, dull white, or dirty cream white and it is often much nest-stained. Many eggs are spotless, but many others are finely sprinkled or more or less conspicuously wreathed with small and usually faint spots or fine scrawls of reddish, purplish, or lilac about the larger end.

The measurements of 55 eggs, in the United States National Museum collection, average 32.5 by 24 millimeters; the eggs showing the four extremes measure **35** by 23, 33 by **26, 30.5** by 23, and 33 by **22** millimeters.

The period of incubation has been variously estimated at all the way from two weeks to a month, but, as the stormy petrel egg has been demonstrated to require 35 days to hatch in an incubator, it is probable that the time required for the Leach petrel to incubate is not far from five weeks. Both sexes incubate, relieving each other during the night; the sexes of specimens taken on the nests show that this duty is shared about equally by both. It has been stated by several observers that one of the pair feeds its mate on the nest, but I think this hardly likely; it seems more reasonable to suppose that the bird which incubates during the day is relieved early in the evening and returns again to relieve its mate in the morning after having been feeding during the night. It is a weird experience to spend a night in a petrel colony during the breeding season. Night is their season of activity, birds are coming and going all the time, dark flitting, ghostlike forms, hardly discernible in the darkness, uttering their loud and peculiar cries, as they call to or greet their mates. They are awkward at first on leaving their burrows, stumbling about in the grass in their efforts to get on the wing, as they must find some little eminence from which to launch into the air. It is a wonder that the incoming birds can find their mates or their burrows in the darkness and the confusion of thousands of fluttering birds.

Young.—The young bird when first hatched is brooded by one of its parents for three or four days, after which it is left alone in the nest during the day and fed at night on the semidigested oily food which its parent regurgitates. Mr. Norton (1881) says of it:

This little creature is worthy of more than a passing notice. The observer is instantly impressed with the fact that this mass of down shields a living form. It does not sprawl like the helpless young of the passeres, but is nearly as helpless; by an effort it can stand, and raise its head to gaze at objects, but locomotion is beyond its feeble strength except in a very limited degree. It lays at full length with its feet placed by its side and the tip of the bill resting on the ground, usually asleep or in restful inactivity, while its rapid breathing testifies that it is not dead. If aroused, it raises its head with an air expressive of wonder, very often giving vent to its voice in a few low queaks. All of its movements are accomplished with the impulsiveness of childhood. It is pleasingly fearless, gazing at its captor, or making feeble efforts to secure a comfortable position in the hand, and when this is accomplished, pleased with the warmth, it will settle down for a nap.

Plumages.—The young bird is rather slow in developing and remains in the nest a long time, often well into September, or until it is fully fledged and ready to fly. When first hatched it is covered with long, soft, thick down varying from " hair brown " at the base to " smoke gray " at the tips. It becomes very fat and often exceeds the adult in bulk. The plumage appears first on the wings, tail and back, and then on the breast; the last of the down finally disappears on the lower belly. Doctor Grinnell (1897) says:

The feathers grow from the same follicles as the down, and in continuation with the latter. As the juvenile grows larger, the down wears off from the ends of the feathers and thus gradually disappears so that finally hardly a trace is left. This wearing away of the down is first noticeable on the wings, back, and breast, and is due to the bird's movements in the narrow nest-cavity.

The first plumage assumed is practically the same as that of the adult and subsequent molts do not show any well-marked seasonal differences. The annual molt of adults probably takes place in August and September.

Food.—The Leach petrel skims the surface of the ocean to pick up its floating food. It is particularly fond of animal oils or oily food and will follow in the track of a wounded seal or whale to feed on the traces of oil which have flowed from its wounds. It also follows living whales to pick up the bits of food which the feeding whale has left floating on the surface. It may also be seen flitting over the sea in wide circles in the wake of a ship to pick up what chance morsels of greasy food may have been thrown overboard. Fishermen cleaning fish at sea are soon surrounded by petrels which appear as if by magic as soon as the offal is thrown upon the waters; they are especially fond of the oily cod livers and can be easily tolled up to the boat by scattering such dainty morsels on the surface. When feeding thus they seldom settle on the water, as the albatrosses and shearwaters do, but hover close to the surface, rising over the waves, pattering occasionally on the water with their feet and pick up the smaller pieces in their bills or peck at the larger fragments. Their natural food includes shrimps and other small crustaceans, floating mollusks, perhaps small fishes occasionally, and probably many other forms of minute marine animals which are found swimming on the surface or in floating masses of seaweed.

Behavior.—The flight of the Leach petrel is swift, graceful, and strong, but not sufficiently distinctive to identify it with certainty. It can, however, be distinguished from the Wilson petrel, the other common petrel off our Atlantic coast, by its larger size and relatively shorter legs which are entirely hidden by the tail in flight, while the long legs of the Wilson petrel project conspicuously beyond the tail; the tail of the Leach petrel is markedly forked while that of the Wilson petrel is square. Mr. Walter H. Rich, who has studied these birds on the fishing banks, found them—

Instantly recognizable from the marked differences of wing action; the Wilson, with its apparently shorter, wider, and rather leaf-shaped wing and rapid fluttery, constant, mothlike flight, is unmistakable when contrasted with the slower, more irregular stroke of Leach petrel. The smaller species at once suggested to me the chimney-swift, while the fork-tailed species, with its apparently much longer wing, modeled after the pattern of that of the shorebirds and plied in much the same manner, recalled in its erratic flight and somewhat spasmodic wing action, a nighthawk gleaning its evening meal above the tree-tops. Another flight difference noted was the carriage of the wings when " scaling." The small petrel's wings were held flat and a trifle above horizontal, the tips slightly bent upward; while the fork-tailed species carried the wings down-bent, after the fashion of a shorebird when " sliding up " to the decoys.

The Leach petrel can not rise easily from the ground, as anyone who has spent a night on their breeding grounds can testify; here it flops along over the ground stumbling against everything in its way, half running and half flying; its legs are too weak to enable it to spring into the air and its long wings need more room in which to work to advantage; but when once under way its flight is full of grace and power. It swims easily and well, but it apparently never dives, though it frequently dips its head below the surface when feeding. Its reputed power of walking on the water is, of course, a myth; I doubt if its name was derived from its fancied resemblance to Saint Peter in this respect; it seems more likely to have been derived from a repetition of its notes.

Its various notes have been differently described by several writers. Audubon (1840) says that " they resemble the syllables *peur-wit, peur-wit.*" Mr. Rich writes me that the only note or call which he could " trace to this species was a twittering chuckle of perhaps a heavier and more guttural quality than that of the Wilson petrel." Dr. Frank M. Chapman (1912) refers to the note heard on Bird Rock at night as " a distinctly enunciated call of eight notes with a certain crowing quality; such a call as might be uttered by elves or brownies." The weird notes heard on the breeding grounds at night have suggested to some observers the phrases, "Got any terbacker," "Jonny get your hair cut" or "Go to Gehenna," but these seem to be very crude reproductions.

The midnight performance has been much more pleasingly described by Mr. Frank A. Brown (1911) as follows:

The flight of Leach petrels from the sea had begun, and, like erratic flying bats, they brushed my tent, my coat, flying almost full into my face, until the air seemed fairly alive with them, uttering their peculiar staccato, cooing sounds. To the monotonous chanting of these sounds, which came from the birds in swift, circling flight, in an hour I had dropped asleep, waking again at about midnight, to find the flight notes entirely succeeded by a different song, apparently proceeding from the ground, and some birds evidently but just separated from me by the side of my tent. Crawling on hands and knees with utmost care, I was unable to see the birds in the act of singing, although I could just make them out as they rose from the ground. The song, while of a similar tone, was absolutely different from the early evening, softer, somewhat liquid, and was nearly continuous. I judge it was uttered at the mouth of the nesting burrow. The cool night air of the ocean soon drove me again to my blankets, where I slept till the reddening drawn brought the first note of a stirring tern. But the petrels were gone, and the islands given over again to the legions of the day.

The gentle petrels have many enemies that attack them on their breeding grounds, where they are easily dug out of their burrows in the soft ground and are too stupid to escape. Dogs and cats, introduced as domestic pets, are the chief offenders. Between my two visits to Spoon Island fishermen camping on the island with a dog seriously reduced the numbers of the petrels nesting there. On Seal Island a Newfoundland dog, owned by the lighthouse keeper, spent much of his time hunting for and digging out petrel burrows. Apparently he did this purely for the sport of it, for we found the bodies of the petrels lying where he had killed them; perhaps the strong-smelling oily fluid which the birds ejected prevented his eating them, but did not discourage his digging out and killing them. After a few years of this persistent hunting I learned that this large and populous colony had been practically exterminated. Similar destruction was going on at Machias Seal Island until, through the efforts of the Audubon Societies, the dog was removed. On my recent visit to Bird Rock, in 1915, I found that the petrels had been exterminated by a cat. Mr. B. S. Bowdish (1909) calls attention to "the terrible slaughter of petrels by minks upon Western Egg Rock," on the coast of Maine. Dr. Joseph Grinnell (1897) found that the petrels of St. Lazaria Island had some formidable enemy, as he found "their remains, together with egg shells, scattered on many parts of the island." He suspected that "the hundreds of Northwest crows which breed on the island were accountable to some extent," and finally discovered one "which was evidently digging into a petrel burrow for either the egg or bird, or, more probably, both."

Winter.—The young are so late in maturing that the petrels can not wholly desert their breeding grounds until the latter part of September or in October, but as soon as the young are able to fly they start on their winter wanderings at large over both oceans, but probably mainly in the northern hemisphere. Mr. Ora W. Knight (1908) says that "a few stray specimens are reported in winter" off the coast of Maine, "but at this season a majority are wandering in distant oceans." Mr. Rich's notes show the appearance of the Leach petrel, "single birds or in twos and threes, until October 12, when I left the grounds, and somewhere between this latter date and October 23, my next return to Georges, the last petrel left these banks, since my record shows no further note of their presence. I am aware that there are records on inshore waters somewhat later than this date."

The following incident, related by Mr. I. I. van Kammen (1916), is interesting as indicating a flocking habit which I have never noted, though I have visited the same region:

During a recent cruise to the Pribilof Islands via southeastern Alaska two such flocks of "whale birds" were observed in company with schools of whales, and were noteworthy in that each flock consisted, in as far as I could see, of but one species of bird. The first of these, encountered about 25 miles off Cape Scott, B. C., on May 16, was the largest flock of whale-following birds that I have ever seen, and was made up entirely of dark-bodied shearwaters. The second flock, slightly smaller than the first, and seen off Yakutat, Alaska, on May 25th, were, if my identification be correct, Leach's petrel. Both of these flocks contained myriads of birds. They were visible at a distance of three or four miles and appeared as a dark cloud over the surface of the sea. As the vessel approached nearer it was seen that not only was the air filled with them but the water was supporting a still greater number. Their cries as they flittered or swam about were deafening. In both instances schools of about a dozen whales were being followed, and as they rose to the surface at intervals to spout the birds would rush in that direction with movements that bordered on a frenzy and with incessant screams. The fact that it seemed to be the sole aim of the birds to keep as closely as possible to the school tended to indicate that the whales were better able to locate the food supply. The cetaceans appeared to do all the hunting; the birds simply trailed behind to feed on what the former had found. Just what type of marine animal life serves to satisfy the tastes of both whale and bird is unknown to me, but it is undoubtedly tiny fish, crustaceans, and the like. That the excretory matter of the whale is also used by the birds is not improbable. The attraction, whatever it be, must remain very close to the surface of the sea, for it is readily picked up by the latter, either when flitting along the water and when resting on its surface.

DISTRIBUTION.

Breeding range.—Northern portions of the Atlantic Ocean. On the American side, from the coast of Maine (Casco and Penobscot

Bays) northward, on many suitable islands, as far as southern Greenland (probably to 65° North). In Iceland (Vestmanneyjan) and on
various islands around Great Britain (St. Kilda, the Blaskets, Outer
Hebrides, Flannan Islands, etc.). Northern and eastern portions of
the Pacific Ocean. From the Kurile Islands north to the Commander
Islands (Copper Island). Eastward throughout the Aleutian chain
(Attu, Kiska, and Amchitka Islands, etc.). Southward along the
coast of southern Alaska, at least as far as Forrester Island. The
breeding birds of the southern portion of the range, Washington,
Oregon, and California coasts, south to the Farallon Islands, have
been called *keadingi*, but are now referred to *beali*, both of which
are only subspecies of *leucorhoa*. Breeding grounds protected in
Alaska reservations.

Range.—North Atlantic Ocean. South nearly, if not quite, to the
Equator. East to the Cape Verde Islands and the coast of Africa
(Sierra Leone and Liberia). West to the coast of Brazil (Cape
San Roque) and the Lesser Antilles (Barbados). North Pacific
Ocean. South to southern California (San Clemente Island), south
of the Equator near the Galapagos Islands (13° 20′ South), and to
the Hawaiian Group (Midway Island).

Spring migration.—Atlantic dates: Atlantic Ocean, 3° 15′ South,
33° 40′ West, April 19; Atlantic Ocean, 13° 16′ North, 51° 34′ West
(near Barbados), May 4; Bermuda, May 1; New York, Fire Island,
May 4; Nova Scotia, Pictou, May 15; Quebec, Godbout, May 21.

Fall migration.—Atlantic dates: Quebec, Godbout, September 25;
Maine, Oxford County, October 21; Massachusetts, September 1 to
November 25; Rhode Island, Narragansett Bay, October 14; New
York, Long Island, October 22; New Jersey, Tinicum, December
18; Atlantic Ocean, 28° 36′ North, 31° 45′ West, September 9, and
10° 46′ North, 24° 38′ West, September 27.

Casual records.—There are numerous inland records as far north
as northern New Hampshire (Lancaster, October 1, 1897), as far
west as eastern New York (Catskill, October 19, 1874), and as far
south as southern Virginia (Petersburg). Casual in western Europe
from Norway to Portugal and in the Mediterranean Sea.

Egg dates.—Maine: Fifty records, June 8 to August 8. Southern
Alaska: Nine records, June 17 to July 15. Newfoundland: Four
records, June 20 to July 6. Saint Kilda: Four records, June 12 to
July 2.

OCEANODROMA LEUCORHOA KAEDINGI (Anthony).

KAEDING PETREL.

HABITS.

The bird which Mr. A. W. Anthony (1898*d*) described under the
above name is now recognized as the smallest of two or three

Pacific coast subspecies of *Oceanodroma leucorhoa*. It is a southern bird ranging north to the southern boundary of California and known to breed only on Guadalupe Island, Lower California, where Mr. Anthony found it. Since that time Mr. W. Otto Emerson (1906) described two new species, *Oceanodroma beali*, smaller than *O. leucorhoa* but larger than the others, breeding from the Aleutian Islands to southern Alaska, and *O. beldingi*, smaller than *beali* and decidedly grayer, breeding from Vancouver Island to northern California; to *O. kaedingi*, the smallest of all, he attributed a still more southern range. His species would thus show a gradation in size from north to south which might be expected. According to the ruling on which our check list was based *O. beali* and *O. beldingi* were not considered worthy of recognition, so the birds breeding on the Alaska coasts were referred to *O. leucorhoa*, and all those breeding on the Pacific coast of the United States were called *O. kaedingi*.

Recent investigations have shown, however, that all of these birds are only subspecifically distinct and that *beldingi* is a synonym of *beali*. Rather than attempt to discuss the matter more fully here I would refer the reader to what has been published on the subject by Dr. H. C. Oberholser (1917), Dr. Joseph Grinnell (1918), and Mr. Leverett M. Loomis (1918), three eminent authorities who have studied the question quite thoroughly.

As we know very little about the distribution and practically nothing about the habits of the Kaeding petrel, I shall not attempt to write its life history. Probably it does not differ materially from that of the Leach petrel. Mr. Anthony wrote me that on Guadalupe Island the Guadalupe petrel breeds early, April 20 or earlier, and that after they are through breeding the Kaeding petrels use the same burrows among the pines at the north of the island.

DISTRIBUTION.

Breeding range.—Known to breed only on Guadalupe Island off the Pacific coast of Lower California.

Range.—Pacific coast region of Lower California. North to extreme southern California (off San Diego). South to the Revillagigedo Islands (Clarion and Socorro Islands), and at sea to 5° 30′ North and 102° West.

OCEANODROMA LEUCORHOA BEALI (Emerson).

BEAL PETREL.

HABITS.

When the next edition of our check list appears the above name will probably replace the name of the Kaeding petrel, for reasons

stated in my account of that bird.   Both are apparently only subspecies of the Leach petrel.   This shifting of names will lead to much
confusion, but is a necessary correction of an evident error.   Much
has been written about the Kaeding petrel which must now be applied
to the newer name.

Nesting.—The main breeding grounds of the Beal petrel seem to be
on the islands included in the reservations off the coast of Washington, with a decided center of abundance in the Quillayute Needles.   On
one island in this group Mr. William L. Dawson (1908) estimated
that there were about 40,000 of these petrels breeding; he estimated
that there were somewhere between 55,000 and 100,000 of them breeding in the whole reservation.   Mr. Dawson has kindly sent me the
following interesting notes, describing his visit to the Quillayute
Needles, on July 20, 1906:

At 11.30 a party comprised of Mr. Albert Reagan, Mr. Herring, and myself
set out for the Quillayute Needles. The fog had cleared and the day was fine,
but it was found feasible to visit only one of the islets, the western one of a
central pair dubbed Huntington Rock upon the chart, but known to the Indians
as Dhuoyuatzachtahl, or The Rock Where One Catches Petrels; but we found
plenty to interest us here.

The rock is about 100 feet high, precipitous on three sides, but sloping and
climbable on the south. The top has an area of something over an acre, and
is rather unique for the abundance and uniformity of a rank grass which occupies the greater portion centrally. This grass has a triangular blade; i. e.,
with a stoutly projecting midrib, and grows to a height of two and a half feet,
its roots being embedded in a covering of its own waste to a depth of six or
eight inches more. Circling about the central bed was a border of turf all about
the edges of the islet, while a narrow stretch of dwarf salmon-berry bushes
occupied the extreme crest of the slope upon the north.

Upon arrival our attention was immediately called to the tiny entrances of
the petrel burrows in the turf, and we promptly fell to digging. There was
sufficient slope to the ground to afford the tenants a little start downward when
they emerged from their holes, but the tunnels were seldom driven into the
bank. Rather they pierced the turf, then ran under it horizontally at a depth
of two or three inches and for a distance of from two to three feet. It proved
to be easier to insert the hand and to rip the hole up from the inside than to
dig through the turf with the shovel. Since a fair proportion of the nests contained eggs, I enlisted the help of my companions and we soon ripped up fifty
nests. Of these 18 contained eggs, all but one being heavily set. Of the remainder all contained young except two, in which were two adults, doubtless male
and female enjoying a belated honeymoon. The young varied in age from
just hatched to a week or two old, the older ones in every case being accompanied by the parent bird.

When released the parent birds appeared dazed, but made off with a jerky
batlike flight to sea, with one exception, a bird which took a couple of turns
above the island before launching out. If placed upon the ground, however,
the bird usually poked about the grass in a nearsighted way looking for a hole,
and did not scruple to enter the home of a neighbor rather than remain under
surveillance. Or, again, the bird crept, half fluttered down hill for two
or three feet and then launched out to sea. After having waded through the

heavily grassed portion of the island once or twice, the thought occurred to us that there might be petrels there. Judge of our surprise, however, when we found the vegetable mold a perfect labyrinth of burrows. So light was the accumulation in density (once the growing blades were penetrated) and so abundant the birds that one had only to dig with the hands dog fashion and birds' eggs and young were the invariable result. The whole half acre of grass proper was a *seething mass of petrels*. Yet from all that host not a sound to betray their presence. The sun shone calmly and the breeze breathed benignly. Nothing disturbed the serenity of the day save the restless quaverings of the always hostile gulls. There was nothing to indicate that beneath our feet lay a buried city, not once populous and now deserted, but now teeming with life, a city of storm waifs, gathered from an expanse of a thousand watery leagues, a city perhaps more populous than any other colony of the class Aves within the limits of Washington, sitting silent where the eye saw only waving grass. The promise of the situation so wrought upon us all that we determined to return at evening some time later, and did so on the Monday evening following, July 23d. We arrived a little after 9 o'clock, provided with matches, bedding, and water, prepared to spend the night. We found the island still silent; but we used the remaining moments of twilight to determine the limits of the colony. At about 10 o'clock the first note was sounded—from the ground. In quality like a tiny cockerell, in accent like a glib paroquet, came the cry *Pettereteretterell, etteretteretterell.* The second phrase is slightly fainter than the first, and is therefore just suggestively an echo of it. After ten minutes, or such a matter, one sounded in the air. By and by came another and another. And so the matter grew until by 11 p. m. the air was aflutter with sable wings, and the island ahum with t's and r's and l's. This hour may be taken as being as typical as any, although the pace was more furious at 1 o'clock, when we roused for another observation. We had spread our blankets in the center of the grass field, regretful of the fact that the portion of the population *under* us must needs go supperless for that night. Perhaps, therefore, it was our presence which stirred the birds to unusual demonstrativeness, but I am not at all certain that this was the case, or that our presence affected the situation in the slightest degree.

The air was full at all times of circling birds, at least several hundred, probably several thousand. They flew about excitedly, much more nimbly than in daytime, but still erratically, incessantly clashing wings with their fellows, and now and then knocking each other down into the grass. Those which flew about uttered from time to time the characteristic cry, but those awing were but a small proportion of the total number in evidence. The grass swarmed with birds working their way down through to the burrows, or else struggling out, all giving from time to time the rolling cackle which is the accompaniment of activity, while from the ground itself came an attendant chorus of cries. Taken altogether there were thousands, perhaps tens of thousands, of birds in motion, and the total effect of the rustling and the cackling (or crowing) was a dainty uproar of large proportions, a never-to-be-forgotten babel of strange sounds. And in this fairy tumult not the least element was the peeping and whining of the chicks, both tended and untended. The characteristic cry is as given above, but it was frequently abbreviated to *Petteretterell, etteretterell.* This was the only sound heard save a rolling cry rendered staccato in r's and l's, and coming apparently from birds standing at the mouth of the burrows. The note is instantly suggestive of the name and if the notes of other petrels resemble this one, I should unhesitatingly say that the name is imitative, and that the classical explanation of " Little Peter walking upon the waves " is ingenious but improbable.

Concerning the number of birds in the colony it is difficult to form a judgment. We dug out fifty nests representing a hundred birds from the least populous portion of the colony, yet the area affected was no sensible portion of the whole, certainly not a hundredth, probably not a five-hundredth. Based upon this estimate alone the number of resident birds would run from ten to fifty thousand, and it might easily be much greater. I think the birds in the air simply represented the newcomers as they came in from the ocean to feed their mates, and who took a few turns about the island preparatory to settling down to business. Certainly the majority of the birds were at all times below ground, while the number in transition may be judged from the fact that at 1 o'clock, when I left the bed and crawled along the ground on hands and knees, I put my hands on two birds in the darkness.

At 4 o'clock the volume of sound had subsided, and not above a dozen flitting forms were seen, while at 6 o'clock there was no sign again to betray the presence of the sleeping myriad.

Prof. Lynds Jones (1908) has also visited this island and adds the following observations:

Many nests of both Kaeding's petrel and Cassin's auklet were uncovered by overturning the sod as the burrows were followed. While the burrows of the auklet were usually a litle farther from the surface and a little longer, the plan was the same. The mouth of the burrow extended almost vertically down 6 inches or more, until stones were encountered, then the burrow turned and ran parallel to the surface of the sod. Very few burrows were straight for any distance, but usually angled here and there apparently to avoid obstructions. Several feet from the nest end of the burrow there was always a side burrow branching off at a sharp angle, ending in an unused enlarged space. Nothing was ever found in this false burrow. The nest burrow of the auklets contained a bed of dry grass, but that of the petrel often contained nothing but fish bones. Very few of the auklets were at home on this island, possibly because there were no young in the nests, but at Alexander Island most of the burrows contained young birds and one parent. Unoccupied nests were few. In every petrel burrow there was at least one bird. If there was an egg the male bird was with it, but if there was no egg both birds occupied the nest burrow. We were unable to determine whether the office of incubation is assumed wholly by the male or whether it is shared by the female. Only males were found in the burrows with eggs. When either of these species was taken from the burrow and tossed into the air they took the shortest course to the water, usually vacillating somewhat as if confused by the sudden daylight. It seemed to us significant that the presence of these two species anywhere in this region would not be suspected away from their nesting burrows. None at all were seen during daylight on any part of the trip.

Only a few Beal petrels breed on the Farallon Islands. Mr. Dawson (1911) relates his experience with them, as follows:

Near us were several half-ruined stone walls, the relics of occupation by the eggers, or possibly by their predecessors, the Russian sea-otter hunters. These walls resounded nightly to the incessant cries of petrels as did every other wall on the island. On the evening of May 30, Leon Garland, one of the wireless operators, secured a white rumped petrel in his tent, whither it had been attracted by the light. On the morning of the 3d of June, Mr. Garland brought in another Kaeding petrel, which he had secured in one of these old stone walls near his tent, and he declared that the bird had been found sitting on an egg, although the latter was broken. Mr. Rowley joined forces with him and spent the best part of the day tearing down the walls of this and neighboring inclosures. Three more specimens were found along with considerable numbers of *homochroa*, which occupied the same area; and two eggs of each species, the first of the season, rewarded the search. Although precisely similar conditions obtain elsewhere, no other Kaeding petrels were encountered on the Farallons.

Eggs.—The egg of the Beal petrel is practically indistinguishable from that of the Leach petrel, as might be expected in a subspecies. It is dull white and nearly immaculate, or with a ring or sprinkling of minute dots of reddish brown or purplish about the larger end.

The measurements of 32 eggs, in various collections, average 31.7 by 20.3 millimeters; the eggs showing the four extremes measure **34** by 24, 33 by **24.5, 29.5** by 22.5, and 31.5 by **21.6** millimeters.

I have not seen the downy young but suppose that it is practically indistinguishable from that of the Leach petrel.

Little of interest is know of the life history of these birds outside of their breeding grounds, where they spend the greater part of the year wandering over the ocean wastes. They are frequently seen by navigators, but the various species are not easily recognized and it is only on the rare occasions when they are collected and recorded that we learn anything about their ranges and migrations. The general movement is, of course, southward in the fall and northward again in the spring.

DISTRIBUTION.

Breeding range.—Pacific coast islands from extreme southern Alaska southward along the coasts of British Columbia, Washington, Oregon, and California (at least as far as Mateo County and probably on the Farallones). This subspecies intergrades with *leucorhoa* somewhere in southern Alaska, perhaps in the Sitka region.

Range.—Unknown. Probably southward.

Egg dates.—Washington: Eighteen records, June 9 to July 11; nine records, June 11 to 18. California: Five records, May 30 to June 24. Alaska: Four records, June 29 to August 2.

OCEANODROMA MACRODACTYLA W. Bryant.

GUADALUPE PETREL.

HABITS.

This petrel seems to be confined in the breeding season to the island of the same name, off the coast of Lower California, and it does not seem to wander far from Guadalupe Island on its migrations. Its close resemblance to other forked-tailed species may have caused it to be overlooked, and we really do not know very much about its distribution.

Nesting.—Mr. A. W. Anthony (1898*b*) says of its nesting habits:

On Guadalupe Island a colony of *O. macrodactyla* were found breeding among the pines and oaks at about 2,500 feet above the sea. Well incubated eggs were taken March 24, and well grown young the middle of May. The range of variation in breeding in these three species of *Oceanodroma* presents an interesting study. The Guadalupe petrel, with a breeding season early in March, leaves the colony altogether by June 10, by which time *O. socorroensis* has not begun to lay, and *O. melania* is still later. I have found the last species incubating as late as September 8. I am quite sure that only one young is raised each year, though each species seems to have a rather long nesting season.

Little attempt is made at nest building by either the Socorro or black petrel, though a few sticks are often dragged into the burrow with an evident desire to construct something resembling a nest. The Guadalupe petrel, however, nearly always has a few dry oak leaves or pine needles at the end of the burrows I have opened, it making a much better attempt at nest building, owing perhaps to the fact that the burrows are dug among the trees where this class of nesting material is abundant, whereas the other species nest on barren islands and can not so readily obtain desirable material.

Mr. Henry B. Kaeding (1905) adds the following:

This species, peculiar to the immediate vicinity of Guadalupe Island, breeds sparingly on the island, eggs taken on the 25th of March being slightly incubated; the birds may be seen at sea near the island. The breeding habits of this petrel differ materially from the other petrels found breeding in these waters in that they lay their eggs at least 100 days earlier than the others, and also instead of selecting low, sandy or rocky situations for their burrows, are only to be found nesting in burrows at the extreme top of Guadalupe Island, at an altitude of over 4,000 feet above sea level, and in pine and cypress groves at that.

Mr. W. W. Brown's notes, published by Messrs. Thayer and Bangs (1908) give a different impression, as to the breeding dates; he took a series of a dozen adults and three downy young, between May 28 and June 17, also a single egg on the latter date; his notes state:

This species was abundant at night about its nesting burrows on the pine ridge at the northern end of the island. Most of the burrows that we opened were empty, the breeding season being about over; three, however, contained one young each, and one, one egg.

The burrows were of various lengths and usually led between or under heavy fragments of rock, making it very difficult, in many cases impossible, to reach the end. We found no adult birds in the burrows. After the young are hatched the old birds appear to come in only at night to feed them. The one egg we secured was in a deserted burrow fifteen inches long, and lay in a somewhat enlarged depression at the end. It was white with a faint wreath of reddish brown specks at the larger end.

The mortality among these birds from the depredations of the cats that overrun the island is appalling—wings and feathers lie scattered in every direction around the burrows along the top of the pine ridge. The species, however, is still breeding in large numbers in Guadalupe, and sometimes at night the air seemed to be fairly alive with petrels, their peculiar cries being heard on all sides.

Eggs.—The Guadalupe petrel lays but one egg, which in shape is between oval and elliptical oval. The shell is thin and smooth, but lusterless. When first laid it is pure, dull white, with a wreath of minute spots, of a faint reddish brown color and lavender about the larger end; some specimens have fine dots of pale lavender mixed with the reddish spots. After the egg has been incubated for a few days it becomes so nest stained that the original color and the spots are entirely obliterated. An egg in my collection is deeply stained, over all of its surface, an uneven reddish brown color, with accumulations of soil caked onto it in places.

The measurements of 50 eggs, in various collections, average 35.7 by 27 millimeters; the eggs showing the four extremes measure 38 by 27.5, 36 by 29, 31.5 by 26, and 33 by 24 millimeters.

Young.—The downy young is covered with long, soft, thick down of a "Benzo brown" or "light drab" color. Apparently the young bird molts directly from the downy stage into a plumage resembling the adult.

Behavior.—In its flight and behavior the Guadalupe petrel closely resembles the other species of the genus *Oceanodroma* from which it probably does not differ very much in habits. On account of its close resemblance to other species very little has been published regarding its habits except on its breeding grounds.

DISTRIBUTION.

Breeding range.—Known to breed only on Guadalupe Island, off the Pacific coast of Lower California.

Range.—So far as known, only in the vicinity of Guadalupe Island.

Egg dates.—Guadalupe Island: Twenty-two records, March 4 to July 2; eleven records, March 24 and 25.

OCEANODROMA CASTRO (Harcourt).

HAWAIIAN PETREL.

HABITS.

Although merely a rare straggler in North America, this petrel enjoys a wide distribution in the Atlantic and Pacific Oceans as far north as Madeira in the former and the Hawaiian Islands in the latter.

Nesting.—Lieut. Boyd Alexander (1898) found this species breeding in the Cape Verde Islands and noted that its burrows run farther into the ground and are more tortuous than those of *Pelagodroma marina*. Mr. Ogilvie-Grant (1905) found the Hawaiian petrel preparing to breed on Praya Island, in the Azores, of which he writes:

We procured a single specimen of Harcourt's stormy petrel, taken in a hole in the rocks on Praya Island on April 25th; on June 1st we picked up a dead specimen on Villa Islet, Santa Maria, but, at this season, the birds had not commenced to breed, and all their nesting-holes on that breeding-station were empty. The fishermen knew the bird well, and Senhor João S. G. da Camara kindly promised to procure specimens later on and forward them to England in spirits. This he did, the birds having been captured in September.

Mr. Ogilvie-Grant (1896) also found the species on 'the Salvages and makes the following statement regarding its breeding there:

Almost more interesting than the white-breasted species was the square tailed, white rumped petrel, of which we obtained but a single example, caught at night by our men on Great Salvage, though we saw several flying over the neighboring seas from the deck of our steam tug. This bird had not yet come ashore to breed, and the only egg we obtained was taken on Lime Island, Porto Santo, in the month of June. According to our Lanzarote pilot, this species breeds commonly on the Little Piton, and it was with great regret that we had to leave the Salvages without visiting this little island.

Mr. Leverett M. Loomis (1918) says of the breeding habits of this species on the Galapagos Islands:

A small breeding colony was discovered on August 13, 1906, on Cowley Island, a steep turfaceous islet about two hundred feet in altitude, situate east of Cowley Mountain, Albemarle Island. Two hard-set eggs, with parent birds, were secured, also an egg with a dried embryo. Mr. Beck's labels furnish the following particulars concerning them: One of the eggs, with living embryo, was deposited in a slight hollow in the soil of a small cave in a hillside amongst "lava boulders;" the other was placed on a little soil under a large "lava boulder" on a hillside. The egg with the dead embryo was found in a slight hollow in the soil at the end of a small cave in a hillside. Seven young birds in various stages of down were obtained in similar situations.

Eggs.—Godman (1907) says: "The egg of *O. castro* is white, without any gloss, with a more or less evident zone of reddish dots round one end, but these dots are never conspicuous." Rev. F. C. R. Jourdain has sent me the measurements of 32 eggs, collected from various sources; they average 33.57 by 24.82 millimeters; the largest eggs measure **36** by 26 and 35 by **26.1,** and the smallest eggs measure **30.8** by 24.1 and 31.2 by **23.2** millimeters.

Young.—Godman (1907) describes the nestling as "covered with long wooly down of a sooty brown color."

The Hawaiian petrel might be, and probably often has been, mistaken for the Leach petrel, which it somewhat resembles, but it can be recognized in flight by its less deeply forked tail and by the excess of white in the lateral, under tail coverts and flanks.

Behavior.—Lieutenant Alexander (1898), writing of its habits in the Cape Verde Islands, observes:

When the night shadows began to brood vaguely over this lone waste of an island the petrels came abroad and filled the air with their weird cries. They mustered strongly, flitting to and fro over the low-lying ground in hundreds. Among the number the most noticeable was *Puffinus assimilis*, as it glided like some large soft-winged bat over the small sandhills, and even sometimes brushing past our camp fire, forever uttering its weird cry " *karki-karrou, karki-karrou, karki-karrou,*" while amid these a similar but softer one would often strike fitfully upon the ear, coming from *Oceanodroma cryptoleucura*, as it flitted over the island, crying to its white-breasted relative " I'm a nigger, I'm a nigger, I'm a nigger." And the white-breasted petrel (*Pelagodroma marina*) replied by uttering grating notes like those of a pair of rusty springs set in motion.

As the night wore on the cries of these petrels died away, only to recommence, however, with redoubled energy just as dawn arrived, and then, as soon as the dusky light waxed clear, these voices ceased as suddenly as they had commenced, indicating that their owners had crept noiselessly into their dark retreats, there to remain till the heat had once more abated.

There are only three American records for this species, so far as I know, all of which were purely accidental inland records. Two were taken by Mr. William Palmer, at Washington, District of Columbia, on August 28, 1893, and one by Mr. N. H. Gano, at Martinsville, Indiana, on June 15, 1902.

DISTRIBUTION.

Breeding range.—Eastern portions of the North Atlantic Ocean. In the Maderia Islands (Porto Santo, Funchal, and the Desertas), Salvages, Azores (Praya Island), and Cape Verde Islands (Rombos Islands). On certain islands in the central Pacific Ocean. In the Galapagos Islands (Cowley Island) and the Hawaiian Islands (Kauai Island).

Range.—Northward from its Atlantic breeding range to Great Britain and Denmark; and southward to Saint Helena Island in the South Atlantic Ocean. In the Pacific Ocean north to Cocos Island off the west coast of Mexico, though it has been suggested that this and the Hawaiian birds are subspecifically distinct from each other and from the Atlantic birds.

Casual records.—Accidental in Indiana (Martinsville, June 15, 1902) and District of Columbia (Washington, August 28, 1893).

Egg dates.—Maderia Islands: Eleven records, November 13 to August 30; six records, April 29 to July 2. Galapagos Islands: One record, August 13.

OCEANODROMA MELANIA (Bonaparte).

BLACK PETREL.

HABITS.

Although this large, dark colored petrel is one of the commonest of the forked-tailed petrels seen off the Pacific coast of Mexico and southern California, it remained for a long time unknown and only within recent years have its breeding grounds been discovered.

Nesting.—Mr. A. B. Howell has sent me the following notes based on his experience with it:

Melania is the species of petrel most often seen quartering near, and occasionally following ships cruising along the coasts of southern and Lower California, but even so, it is seldom met with. While traveling rather extensively by boat in this region I have seen not more than a dozen individuals, and these were all more than five miles from shore. They were always flying methodically a foot or two above the waves, with slow and regular wing beats. In the region covered by the A. O. U. list they are known to nest only on the San Benito and Los Coronados Islands, Mexico. They have not been found regularly to occupy their nesting sites in advance of deposition of the eggs as in the case of *socorroensis*, though they may do so for several days; nor do they nest in colonies as do the latter, but are scattered over parts of an island wherever the nesting sites seem to be most to their liking. The usual situation chosen is a cranny beneath a boulder or a crack in a cliff, but they will occasionally take possession of an old burrow of the Cassin's auklet. I do not believe however that this form ever excavates its own burrow. On the Coronados in 1910, I found my first fresh egg June 17, and June 17, 1913, A. van Rossem and I found that incubation was slightly further advanced than this. The downy young to all intents are replicas of those of the socorros, except for being a shade larger. All that I know concerning the time of incubation is that it is in excess of 18 days. No nesting material is used. Nine times out of ten, when removed from the egg, the parent will vomit a short stream of orange-colored oil several times repeated, to the distance of four feet or more. She will savagely bite the finger of her captor, but of course is too small to inflict any pain, and will even seize her own wing in her rage. The oil has a peculiar pungence comparable to no other odor which I know, and by ornithologists, at least, is seldom considered disagreeable. This, by regurgitation, constitutes the food of the nestlings. After death, when in the collecting basket, great care is necessary to keep the oil from oozing out onto the chin and nape, for once it has saturated these parts, it is almost impossible to bring the feathers back to their original condition of smoothness.

Mr. A. W. Anthony (1896a) found this species nesting on the San Benito Islands about 75 miles off the coast of Lower California and some 20 miles west of Cerros Island, between latitude 28 and 30 degrees. He writes:

The San Benito Islands are small, rocky reefs only, with little vegetation, and being so far offshore are but little resorted to by gulls, cormorants, and similar species. Cassin's auklets had bred in considerable numbers, as their burrows testified, but at the time of our visit they had all left. Their burrows, however, had been appropriated by later arrivals, and during the four and a half days that we spent at the island Mr. Horace A. Gaylord and myself devoted most of our time to digging for petrels. Both black and Socorro petrels were taken from the burrows formerly occupied by the auklets, the former species outnumbering the Socorro about five to one. There was no attempt apparently on the part of the species to colonize by themselves, both being found in adjoining burrows. The Socorro petrel had evidently begun nesting somewhat earlier than its neighbor, the black, for while fresh eggs of the latter were the rule, very few fresh or even moderately incubated eggs of the Socorro were found, and several downy young were taken.

There was little, if any, attempt at nest building by either species, though in several burrows a small nest-like platform of little twigs was found upon which the egg was laid. But in most cases it rested upon the bare earth at the end of a more or less winding burrow, about three feet in length. Several eggs of both species were taken from under loose slabs of rock, but as a rule they preferred the burrows, which were in all cases, I think, those of Cassin's auklet.

On our return to the island, September 8 and 9, we found that the Socorro petrels had all left, but many young black petrels were found, as well as a few eggs which the birds were still incubating.

Eggs.—The single egg of the black petrel is nearly oval in shape, with a slight tendency toward elliptical oval. The shell is smooth and lusterless. The color is dull white, usually somewhat dirty and generally unspotted; some specimens show a faint suspicion of fine lavender or reddish dots about the larger end. The measurements of 61 eggs, in various collections, average 36.6 by 26.7 millimeters; the eggs showing the four extremes measure **38.5** by 25, 36.5 by **27.5**, and **32.5** by **24.2** millimeters.

Young.—The downy young looks much like that of the closely allied species; the chin, throat and malar region are naked, but the bird is elsewhere covered with long soft down, which is uniform " fuscous " in color, darker basally. I have seen small downy young only a few days old collected as early as July 4 and as late as September 5, on Los Coronados Islands. Subsequent plumage changes are probably the same as in other species of the genus.

Food.—Like other petrels, this species feeds on what it can pick up from the surface of the sea in the way of fatty, oily substances. Mr. Howell found the stomachs, of those he examined, filled with " oil and nothing else, except a small quantity of green, slimy stuff," which he thought might be " the remains of some small crustacean or a seaweed."

Behavior.—Mr. Anthony (1900*a*) writes, of the night flight of these petrels about their breeding grounds, as follows:

Hauling the boat out on the shingle, a few steps places us in the city of birds, a fact we discovered by breaking through into the burrows at almost every step, but the birds themselves are very much in evidence. Hundreds of inky black objects are dashing about with bat-like flight, now here, now there, with no apparent object in their wanderings. Like butterflies they come and go, flitting so near at times that one attempts to catch them as they pass.

Others are constantly coming from the burrows to join in the revel. Each, as it reaches the outer air, utters its characteristic call, flops along the ground a few feet, somewhat like an old felt hat before the wind, and is away, as gracefully and airy as the rest. Those in the air are constantly calling and from the ground under our feet come answering cries. The noise and confusion suggests a busy street in a city.

He (1898*b*) also says:

Both *O. melania* and *O. socorroensis* will at times dive a foot or more below the surface for a piece of meat that is sinking if they are hungry, but diving seems to be out of their usual line of business and is only resorted to when food is scarce. They seem to be unable to get below the surface of the water without first rising two or three feet and plunging or dropping, exactly as I have seen the black-footed and short-tailed albatrosses dive under similar circumstances.

In the same paper he speaks of the notes of the black petrel as follows:

On the first night of my sojourn I had scarcely fallen asleep, curled up on a rocky shelf just above the water, when I was suddenly recalled to my senses by a loud *Tuc-a-ree, tuc-tuc-a-roo* within two feet of my head. The call was repeated from a half dozen directions and as many bat-like forms were seen flitting back and forth in the moonlight along the cliffs and hillside. One or two attempts to shoot them proved utter failures, and the black forms soon moved out to sea, returning at intervals of an hour or so all night. The next afternoon I located one of the birds in a burrow under an immense rock, as I passed on my way to camp. It several times uttered a clicking note which I felt sure was that of a petrel.

He refers to the notes as harsher than those of the Socorro petrel. Mr. Howell writes to me:

They begin visiting their nests at 8.30 p. m. and are very active until shortly before dawn. Pitching in from the sea they come like big black bats rocking on the breeze and uttering their loud weird call. This I am unable to describe, except in that it consists of four notes. D. R. Dickey and A. van Rossem state that, during the night the bird at or on the nest utters a series of notes suggestive of the song of the wren-tit.

Mr. Howell also says that the black petrels suffer "considerably from the depredations of the duck hawks, as their dry remains on the islands bear mute witness."

DISTRIBUTION.

Breeding range.—Known to breed only on Los Coronados Islands and on San Benito Island, off the west coast of Lower California. May also breed in the Tres Marias group farther south off the Mexican coast.

Range.—Pacific coasts of California and Mexico. North to central California (Point Reyes, Marin County). South to southern Mexico (Acapulco) and to about 19° north in the Pacific Ocean.

Egg dates.—Lower California: Fifty-four records, May 30 to September 5; twenty-seven records, June 22 to July 23.

OCEANODROMA HOMOCHROA (Coues).

ASHY PETREL.

HABITS.

This is the smallest of the brown-rumped species of the genus *Oceanodroma*, and it is not strikingly different from the other small species. Its known range seems to be limited to the coast of California, and it is known to breed only on the Farallon Islands and on some of the Santa Barbara Islands. Mr. Walter E. Bryant (1888) says that it is " the last to arrive on the Farallon Islands " and the " rarest of the birds which breed there. They nest anywhere on the island in natural cavities, particularly those under loosely piled rocks. No nest is made and only a single egg is laid, although it sometimes happens that an egg and downy young will be found in the same place."

Nesting.—Prof. Leverett M. Loomis (1896) writes of this species on the Farallones:

Although these petrels were breeding abundantly in all parts of the island, every portion of it might have been passed over in daylight without a single individual being discovered, for apparently only brooding birds occurred, concealed in loose piles of stones, in stone walls, and under driftwood. After nightfall the petrels became active. They were especially conspicuous during the early morning hours of the 14th, when the auklets held their concert. As I stood in the dooryard of a keeper's house every few moments one or more would pass silently by, disappearing in the darkness. Their flight recalled that of a Goatsucker.

The strong musky odor of the petrels renders their discovery in the rock piles easy. It is only necessary to insert the nose into likely crevices to find them. With little practice one may become very expert in this kind of hunting, readily determining whether it is an auklet or a petrel that has its residence in any particular cranny. Sometimes the petrels are within reach, but usually the rocks have to be removed to get at them. When uncovered they generally shrink away as far as they can, but occasionally one will remain on its egg. When tossed into the air they fly without difficulty. Eggs with well-developed embryos were the rule, but there were also fresh eggs and downy young in various stages of growth. In seventeen specimens preserved the organs of reproduction, except in one female, displayed marked degeneration, showing that the breeding season was about over. Apparently nearly as many males as females were brooding. With a single exception, all the examples taken, including a partial albino, were very fat. It seemed strange to find these birds of the ocean rearing their young near the dwellings and within several rods of the siren. None of the feathered inhabitants of the island appeared to be alarmed at the blasts of this signal, repeated every forty-five seconds when the fog settled down.

Mr. William L. Dawson (1911) writes:

Either this species has notably increased of late, or else earlier visitors were inclined to underestimate its numbers. We found them well distributed throughout the main island. Not only are all the stone walls alive with them, but they occupy the minor rock-slides along with the Cassin auklet, and they even burrow in the level ground in front of the keepers' houses. In investigating the drift area on Franconia beach, we found almost as many petrels as auklets skulking under logs and planks. In point of abundance they are easily third, possibly second, on the island.

It is evident that these petrels have a lengthy season of courtship during which they spend their nights ashore, chiefly in their burrows, and return to the sea daytimes. This is followed by a "honeymoon" period of some duration, presumably a week or more, in which both birds remain ashore all the time. As soon as the egg is laid incubation begins, and the other bird retires to sea to forage. Precisely what the division of labor is from this point on as between male and female remains to be determined, but it is certain that the male is often found alone upon the egg.

Mr. Chester Barlow (1894a) describes a few nesting sites, as follows:

In 1892 I found an egg on the floor of a cave about ten feet from the entrance with the parent bird incubating it. The cave was dark and damp, and the egg was laid on a little moss growing on the ground. It was about to hatch. This year while climbing about on the summit on East End I secured a young auklet (*Ptychoramphus aleuticus*), and after examining it let it go into a crevice in the cliff. While watching it disappear I observed a forked tail of a bird vibrating as it breathed, and on tearing away the rocks found a petrel sitting on its fresh egg. The bird was sitting with its head as far into the crevice as possible, thus being protected from the light, but its tail was in view. The elevation was about 200 feet above the ocean.

I have found the petrels nesting beneath the stone walls within a few inches of Cassin's auklet, but have never found any sign of a burrow made by the petrel. In 1892 I took an egg from a petrel at the base of an elevated footpath of the West End, and carefully replaced the stones. This year on going by the place I remembered the incident and thought I would try again. On stooping down I detected the familiar musky odor, and soon had a fresh egg. It is possible that this was the same bird I found in 1892, and that it had clung to this nesting site these two years. Within a foot of this petrel was a pigeon guillemot (*Cepphus columba*) sitting on her two eggs. I found one egg about two feet in a crack in a cliff plainly in view, and it proved to be fresh. I suppose the bird did not discover she had selected such an open place to nest in until after she had laid the egg and daylight came, when no doubt she left for more secluded quarters.

Mr. Osgood discovered a petrel of decided tastes, as regards nesting, for on the brink of a cliff, beneath several loose boulders, she had constructed a nest, of coarse Farallon weed, perhaps four inches in diameter. It was naturally rough, but was undoubtedly constructed by the bird, as it was in such a position that a larger bird could not have gained access to it. It must be understood that the nest and egg were entirely concealed by numerous rocks, which had to be removed to permit of the photograph being taken. The egg was badly incubated.

In one instance I found an egg laid on an accumulation of pebbles, and again quite a collection of small granite chips were used. As in the former case, everything points to the bird gathering them.

The male incubates the egg as well as the female, as two males were found performing this duty. The mates of the birds incubating were never observed. I believe that when an egg is taken that the petrel does not lay a second egg the same season.

Eggs.—The single egg of the ashy petrel is much like that of the other small petrels. It is dull white or creamy white in color and either spotless or faintly wreathed with a circle of very fine reddish dots near the larger end. The measurements of 54 eggs, in various collections, average 29.7 by 22.8 millimeters; the eggs showing the four extremes measure **31.8** by 22.5, 30.3 by **24.4, 27** by 22.5, and 29 by **21** millimeters.

Young.—Mr. W. Otto Emerson's notes state that the young do not leave the nest until they are fully feathered and that they are fed on "small marine insects," which are probably regurgitated by the parents in semidigested form. Specimens of downy young, collected on the Farallon Islands on September 15, 1911, are covered with long, soft down, except on the naked chin and throat; the down varies in color from "fuscous" to "hair brown." The plumage appears first on the wings, back, and head, the down disappearing last on the breast and belly, after the wings are fully developed. The first plumage acquired is practically indistinguishable from that of the adult, so there is no noticeable sequence of plumages to maturity.

Food.—Very little is known about the food of this species, but Mr. Barlow (1894*a*) makes the following rather unsatisfactory remark: "The food of the petrel necessarily consists of fish or small shell-fish, with possibly a little marine algae by way of desert, but unfortunately no stomachs were examined."

Behavior.—Mr. Henry B. Kaeding (1903) describes the flight of this species as follows:

When flying about in the dim light the petrels resemble bats. Their flight is fluttering and zigzag and they frequently flit by the head of the watcher close enough for him to feel the wind of their wings. Often they run into the glass around the big light, or into the telephone wires that stretch from the lighthouse to the keepers' houses and the siren, and terminate their erratic careers then and there. Small, dainty, and velvety, they are the prettiest little birds imaginable, and would be perfect were it not for their habit of vomiting oil over everything when disturbed.

The same writer says of its notes:

These petrels, like others of their kind that nest farther south, are nocturnal in their habits during the breeding season, and seem to exchange places shortly after dark, the incoming birds replacing the mate on the nest after an exchange of courtesies and a chat over the day's happenings. These conversations are carried on in a queer little sing-song twitter, regularly punctuated with a gasp that resembles the exhaust of a Lilliputian engine. This twitter is characteristic of all petrels, varying with the species, and has been admirably described by Mr. A. W. Anthony.

Mr. Barlow (1894*a*) says the note was "a squeaky note uttered rapidly and in a low chuckling tone, and was prolonged for several seconds."

Very little is known about the migrations of the ashy petrel or where it goes after it leaves its breeding grounds, but probably it spends the winter wandering over the adjacent ocean.

DISTRIBUTION.

Breeding range.—The Farallon Islands and some of the Santa Barbara Islands (San Miguel and Santa Cruz Islands). Breeding grounds protected in Farallon reservation.

Range.—Coast of California. North to Point Reyes and south to San Clemente Island.

Egg dates.—Farallon Islands: Forty-two records, May 15 to July 13; twenty-one records, June 12 to July 2.

OCEANODROMA MONORHIS SOCORROENSIS C. H. Townsend.

SOCORRO PETREL.

HABITS.

In Godman's (1907) Monograph *Oceanodroma socorroensis* is treated as synonymous with *O. monorhis* (Swinhoe) from China; and Count von Berlepsch (1906) described it, from specimens collected on the San Benito Islands, as " the American representative of that Asiatic species " under the name *O. monorhis chapmani.* As I have not been able to examine sufficient material to warrant hazarding an opinion on the matter, I shall not attempt to argue the merits of the case.

The following notes by Mr. Henry B. Kaeding (1905) throw some light on the migration of this and other Lower California petrels:

It is interesting to note that during the trip south to Socorro Island, prior to May 1st, no petrels were seen except *Oceanodroma macrodactyla* at Guadalupe; but after May 1st the least, black, Socorro, and Kaeding petrels appeared, becoming more numerous during June, and apparently passing north to the breeding grounds from regions south of Socorro Island. Mr. Townsend secured but one specimen of *Oceanodroma socorroensis* at Socorro Island, and saw very few March 9th, so that it is probable that the bulk of the birds were still to the southward at that date.

Nesting.—Mr. A. B. Howell has contributed the following notes on the habits of the Socorro petrel which he found breeding on Los Coronados Islands:

In an aggregate of 1,500 miles by sea along the coasts of southern and Lower California I never saw a bird which I took to be of this species. By this I infer that they range farther out to sea than does *melania*, and it is probably more nocturnal in its foraging also, as they seem to be more greatly distressed by the light when removed from their burrows, which they visit only after nightfall. Mr. A. W. Anthony has recorded the fact that this species comes in from the sea, constructs and occupies the burrows for several weeks before the eggs are deposited, and this assertion surely holds good for the majority of cases, as both male and female can be found in a burrow long before the time for eggs; but there are exceptions to this rule, for A. van Rossem took several birds from fresh eggs out of burrows from which he had collected the original occupants but a few days previous. After laying, but one of the parents remains on duty, and I have found that, among birds incubating in the daytime, the males are slightly in the majority. Birds with partially white rumps are found in the same holes with unicolored ones and every degree of variation in this respect occurs.

On one of the small Coronados Islands about 200 pairs in 1913, and not quite so many in 1910, were nesting. Most of these occupied a small amphitheater in a compact colony, but this colonizing may have been because there is very little soft earth to be found on the remainder of the island. In this powdery loam the bird excavates a burrow about two feet long and a short distance below the surface, and turns usually either to the right or left a few inches from the opening. The entrance seems very small for the size of the bird is more than twice as wide as high. The tunnel is slightly enlarged near the end and here a flimsy platform is constructed of any bits of twigs and rootlets that are handy, though occasionally the egg rests on the bare ground. Observers have usually found that the nesting time of the Socorros is slightly in advance of that of the black petrels, and such A. van Rossem and I found to be the case in 1913, for during the latter half of June, slightly incubated eggs of the former was the rule, while those of the latter were nearer fresh. However, in 1910, on the Coronados, an egg of the present species was not found until June 22, while incubated eggs of *melania* were taken nearly a week before this.

Messrs. Grinnell and Daggett (1903) have given us a good description of Middle Island, in this group, where the petrels' nests were most accessible, as follows:

This island presents two jagged peaks about a hundred feet high, with a sag between the two. To one side of this saddle is a basin perhaps two hundred feet across, unevenly edged with ragged ledges. The bottom of the basin farthest from the saddle has been undermined by a subterranean channel connecting with the surf on the outside of the wall. Here one can look down thirty feet or more and see the water surging back and forth with the swell. The rest of the basin sloping up to the saddle is covered by disintegrated rock from the surrounding walls, and supports a scanty growth of dwarfed "buck-thorn" bushes. Where this bush is thickest a few inches of peaty soil has accumulated and this we found to be a favorite burrowing place for the petrels. Other parts of the island were also occupied, but in those places the burrows usually ended underneath or between heavy fragments of rock and so were mostly impossible to reach. We were first made aware of the presence of the colony by the strong and characteristic odor of petrel oil, for, of course, not a bird is to be seen above ground during daylight. Following the scent we soon found openings, generally more or less hidden by weeds or stones. A cursory survey showed that the basin was honeycombed with burrows. In the loose talus of the slopes they extended directly down into the ground, turning aside here and there to avoid pieces of rock, and ending, where further excavation had become impossible, in a cavity about twice the diameter of the main burrow. Those in the more level ground were often entirely concealed by wide-spreading bushes which had to be cut away before the entrance could be reached. Otherwise these latter were easy of access, for the peaty, fibrous nature of the soil rendered shallow burrows possible, and such were easily uncovered by sliding the hand in and lifting up the top soil. The terminal chambers were larger here than in the burrows among the rock fragments. Often two burrows crossed or united, but always the occupants were in separate terminal cavities. The shortest burrow did not exceed twelve inches in length, the first lifting up of the top disclosing a Socorro petrel and egg. The longest observed was in stoney ground, and zigzagged about so that in all its windings it extended fully six feet. The nest cavities sometimes showed a sparse flooring of fine twigs and grass, but just as often they were altogether bare of any lining.

Mr. A. W. Anthony (1896a) found both the black and the Socorro petrels breeding on the San Benito Islands, near Cerros Island off the west coast of Lower California, but, as his notes have been freely quoted under the former species, I shall not repeat them here. There is some doubt as to whether the Socorro petrel breeds at all on the island for which it was named and on which Mr. Townsend discovered it. Mr. Kaeding (1905) observes:

It is interesting to note in this connection that so far as we were able to ascertain, there are no sea birds nesting on Socorro Island at all, with the exception of the terns nesting on the outlying rocks. Mr. Townsend found burrows that he judged would be occupied later by petrels, but I am constrained to believe that these were the burrows of the land crabs, which swarm over the island. These crabs are so voracious and bold that it would hardly be possible for even a shearwater to withstand their attacks, and this is probably the reason why, although thousands of shearwaters nest on San Benedicte thirty miles away, none nest on Socorro, there being very few crabs on San Benedicte.

Eggs.—The single egg of the Socorro petrel is similar to the eggs of other small petrels; the shape is between oval and elliptical oval, generally nearer the former; the shell is smooth and lusterless. The color is dull dead white; Mr. Howell says that it " is sometimes pure white, but more often has a wreath of faint lavender dots and tracings about the larger end "; Mr. Anthony (1896b) refers to it as " usually freckled with reddish spots in a more or less complete ring about the larger end." The measurements of 18 eggs, in various collections, average 30.8 by 23.2 millimeters; the eggs showing the four extremes measure **34** by 24, 32 by **24, 29** by 22.5, and 30 by **22** millimeters.

Before the egg is laid both parents occupy the burrow. Incubation is performed by both sexes alternately, and after a few days the young is left in the nest alone during the day.

Plumages.—The downy young has the chin and throat naked, but is otherwise covered with long, soft down of a uniform, " deep mouse-gray " color. The young bird is nearly fully grown before any plumage appears; the wing feathers are the first to grow, and then the tail, both of which are complete before the contour feathers are acquired. The first plumage assumed seems to be indistinguishable from that of the adult. Messrs. Grinnell and Daggett (1903) refer to an interesting individual variation in the plumage of adults, which had also been noted by Mr. Anthony (1898c) ; about three per cent of the birds have more or less white on the upper tail-coverts, varying from a mere trace to nearly as much as in the Leach petrel; the normal color of these parts is, of course, uniform sooty.

Behavior.—Mr. Howell contributes the following notes on the habits of the Socorro petrel :

Unlike its larger relative, this form but rarely vomits oil when handled, but will often do so on the wing when released. This oil is practically the same as that of *melania*, but sometimes contains flakes of a white mucus matter, green slime, and occasionally a tiny rock lobster or crayfish. It has been stated that their food consists of these latter; and this is undoubtedly the case when they are easily obtainable, which is but part of the year. I believe, however, that they feed on a great variety of small sea life found at the surface and upon whatever floating oil they can gather. When released from the hand *socorroensis* launches in an uncertain fashion, twisting and turning after the manner that should be employed by a small drunken nighthawk. If placed on the ground they poke about confusedly among the bushes. In the hand one is impressed by their fragility and apparent weakness.

DISTRIBUTION.

Breeding range.—San Benito and Los Coronados Islands, off the west coast of Lower California.

Range.—Pacific coasts of Mexico and southern California. North to the Santa Barbara Islands and south to the Revillagigedo Islands. If this species proves to be identical with *O. monorhis*, its range should be extended across the Pacific to China and Japan.

Egg dates.—Lower California: Forty-eight records, June 4 to September 5; twenty-four records, June 22 to July 10.

OCEANITES OCEANICUS (Kuhl).

WILSON PETREL.

HABITS.

Contributed by Charles Wendell Townsend.

Few who have voyaged along the Atlantic coast or who have crossed to Europe have failed to see petrels or Mother Cary's chickens, as they are called. On untiring wing they skim the water, now on one side, now on the other of the vessel, all ready to gather in little bands in the wake and drop astern whenever delectable morsels are thrown from the cook's galley, and then it is that, like Peter of old, they walk upon the water.

Although the Wilson petrel has long been known as a common bird of the Atlantic Ocean, especially on the American side, its true distribution, including its breeding place, is but recently acquired knowledge. Alexander Wilson, who first described this species and who supposed it was identical with the stormy petrel (*Thalassidroma pelagica*), thought it bred in the Bahama and Bermuda Islands, as well as on the coast of Florida and Cuba. Audubon (1840) evidently confused it with the Leach petrel, for he says: "Wilson's petrel breeds on some small islands situated off the southern extremity of Nova Scotia." In 1881 Mr. William Brewster (1883) found in specimens he had shot in the Gulf of St. Lawrence between June 17 and July 25 no evidence of breeding. He also secured a young bird on June 18 which was at least two months old. He surmised, therefore, "that Wilson's petrel breeds in winter or early spring in tropical or subtropical regions and visits the northeastern coast of the United States *only in the interim between one breeding season and the next.*" His conjecture was a logical one and correct to a certain extent, but he did not put the breeding place far enough south. As late as 1884 Baird, Brewer, and Ridgway, in The Water Birds of North America, say of this bird: "Its breeding places have been and to some extent remain in doubt," and they instance records of its being resident about the Azores and of "eggs purporting to belong to this species said to have been taken near Madeira." They quote, however, Dr. J. H. Kidder's belief that these birds nest at Kerguelen Island, in 60° south latitude, and of his report of a nest and eggs of this bird found by Rev. A. E. Eaton on Thumb Mountain of that island. This discovery by the Rev. Mr. Eaton was the first definite knowledge we had of the true nesting of the species. The second edition of the American Ornithologist's Union Check List, published in 1895, gives Kerguelen Island as the only breeding place of this bird. Since then the Wilson petrel has also been found breeding on the South Shetland and the South Orkney Islands, as well as on the great Antarctic Continent itself, in South Victoria Land. Capt. Robert F. Scott (1905), of sad but glorious memory, says: "We twice saw it apparently exploring the great ice barrier, in latitude 78°, some 20 miles from the nearest water, where alone it would find its food." The mystery is solved; the Wilson petrel breeds only in the Antarctic regions in the summer months of the antipoles, namely December, January, and February, and migrates north during the antipodal winter and spends it in the northern summer. Its life is therefore one long summer, albeit a stormy and cold one.

Nesting.—Like most of the petrels this species prefers to nest in colonies. There is considerable variation in the nesting site and nest, dependent undoubtedly on the character of the country and the material at hand. Thus Wm. Eagle Clarke (1906) speaking of the South Orkneys, says:

There was no attempt at nest making, the egg was simply laid in a hollow in the earth in narrow clefts and fissures in the face of the cliffs, under boulders, and sometimes under stones on the screes sloping from the foot of the precipice.

The birds resort in thousands to the cliffs of Laurie Island, one of the South Orkney Islands, and nest all the way from 20 to 300 feet above the sea. Robert Hall (1900) thus describes the nesting of this species at Kerguelen Island:

The yellow-webbed Wilson petrel is a delicate creature that goes straight to sea in the early morning, and comes back to the rocks in the gloaming. Most of my time was spent among the stones below 1,000 feet, where this petrel is to be found in great numbers by diligent search. At 1,500 feet (Thumb Peak) one flew from the boulders in the daytime, which showed that a nest was there. Having returned from the sea into the harbours at dusk (8 p. m.) Wilson's petrel is then to be seen, flying to and fro before a ridge of rough-looking rocks. At 6 p. m. I observed (February 2) a gathering of from 50 to 60 birds off the South Head of Greenland Harbour. Generally they are unassociated until they come in toward night. They are seldom to be seen on land in the daytime, and I only noticed a bird flying up and down a part of a valley of stones, more than a mile from the sea, and a creek, which led from this highland, had encouraged the bird to go there. It reminded me of a martin collecting insects. Having sat down to finish a piece of buttered rye bread, I observed the bird alight on a jutting mass of loose stones, and this led me to remove the stones from the entrance to the nest and to discover a delicate egg.

At about 8 p. m. the croaking begins, for now the "night shift" has come in from the sea to go on duty. Many congratulations seem to be exchanged. Go straight to a wild-looking piece of the coast if you want nests. Look under large or small slabs of stone or within the crevices in the cliff-sides. Most of the nests are saucerlike and neatly put together with loose twigs. Your shovel will act as a lever to lift the slabs and expose them, when the sitting bird will move away to the farthest corner to escape the light, never offering to bite, although the act would be harmless. At 7 a. m. I have found the male bird sitting on the egg, indicating in this case, that it will sit out the day. A male also flew on board on one occasion during the night, which probably meant that it had a mate sitting on the nest. Thus the male possibly sits either day or night. At 8 p. m. I have taken both male and female from a nest which was on an earthen bank and had an entrance and an exit.

The nests of this species were built principally of azorella stalks. They were flat, in a shallow indentation beneath a stone, and had no definite tunnel running to them. The bird would sometimes scratch an entrance. A typical nest measured 7 by 5 inches, and the depth of the bowl was 5 inches. On handling a bird, it will (like other petrels) eject a fatty globule for a distance of 2 feet. I used to track the sitting birds between 8 and 10 p. m. by their strong but mellow note. One evening's search produced seven nests containing young and eggs. The eggs differ very slightly in size: Six measured 1.3 inches by 0.9 inch. On February 3d I found three eggs (fresh and hard set); on 7th, 8th, and 9th, four fresh eggs, seven young nestlings and two hard set eggs; on the 14th one hard set egg. The parents sit with the young during the night.

Dr. E. A. Wilson (1907) on January 9, 1902, at Cape Adare, South Victoria Land, found a still more elaborate nest. He says:

Two of these crevices could not be reached, but soon we saw a bird hover round and settle upon a large boulder. Hunting about for a burrow underneath we caught the sound of twittering, and traced it to a kind of mouse hole. This by dint of long and tedious picking with a sheath knife we enlarged till it admitted an arm up to the shoulder. The work was laborious, as the floor of the burrow was hard black ice and grit; but eventually we reached the nest. At the end of the little tunnel was a chamber containing a very comfortable nest thickly lined with Adelie penguin's feathers, and in it a somewhat remarkable collection. First we brought out an adult male alive, then an adult female, then two eggs, one clean and newly laid, the other old and rotten, and under all another dead and flattened *Oceanites*. Outside as we worked a fourth bird was hovering, which when shot proved to be an adult male.

Similar conditions were observed at the South Orkneys. Mr. Wm. Eagle Clarke (1906) says:

They appear to return year after year to the same nesting places, for both eggs and dead young birds of previous seasons were numerous in the tenanted holes containing fresh eggs.

He infers that an unusually cold summer may delay the nesting season so that the young are not sufficiently grown in the fall to withstand the cold, and great mortality results.

Eggs.—Only one set consisting of one egg is laid. Clarke (1906) thus describes the eggs: "An elongated oval, dull white peppered with tiny dots of reddish brown and underlying lilac, mostly accumulated round one end of the egg, but occasionally sprinkled all over the surface." Hall (1900) says the egg has "an almost true oval form, slightly wider toward one end, around which is a circle of pale pink spots." The measurements of 15 eggs, in various collections, average 32.2 by 23.2 millimeters; the eggs showing the four extremes measure **33.5** by 23.5, 33 by **24, 28** by 23, and 32.5 by **22.5** millimeters.

Young.—The period of incubation is not known. Both sexes incubate and, as already stated, both sexes have been found in the same hole at the same time, but it is probable, as in the case of the better known petrels, that one sex often remains on the egg in the day and the other in the night. The nestlings are thus described by Hall (1900): "The nestling was covered with a uniform greyish-black down. Bill black, legs bluish, tinged with faint yellow, toes faint black, nails black."

Food.—The food of the Wilson petrel consists by preference of the oily substances inseparable from the profession of the deep-sea fisherman. Fish "gurry" of all sorts seem to be relished by these birds, but they manifest the greatest eagerness when pieces of oily fish livers are thrown overboard. They will, however, seize upon any morsel that is cast from the ship's galley. Mr. Wm. Eagle Clarke (1906) says that "Great numbers were observed around a dead whale, picking up morsels of fat that fell from the bills of a host of giant and Cape petrels." Doctor Wilson (1907) says the food consists of minute crustaceans from the surface of the water. When picked up wounded or caught in their burrows the birds eject from their bill and nostrils a yellow or reddish oily fluid with a strong musty odor. This odor is very characteristic and clings to the skins of these birds in collections. Robert Hall (1900) says living birds when handled eject " a fatty globule for a distance of 2 feet." I have found this oily fluid in their stomachs and on one or two occasions a few bits of charcoal, on another a few small pebbles.

As already shown the Wilson petrel spends its nonbreeding season, its winter, in the northern summer. As the bird is very tame its habits may be studied at close range on almost any cod-fishing expedition a mile or more from the Atlantic seaboard of North America. When sailing or steaming along the coast or even in mid-Atlantic one rarely fails to see an occasional petrel flying close to the water beside or ahead of the boat or a few gathering in the wake, ever on the alert to pick up any morsel that may drop from the vessel. Day after day we may watch these tireless birds from any transatlantic steamer, but it is, of course, impossible to say how far the same birds follow the boat. On one or two occasions at night I have seen a petrel start up from near the bow of the vessel, wheel wildly over head and disappear in the darkness astern. Occasionally they drop on the deck. Whether the birds were asleep on the water or not is a matter of conjecture.

When a boat stops to fish the scattered wide-ranging petrels are at once attracted by the bait and " gurry" that are inseparable from this pursuit, and gather sometimes in considerable numbers. If fish are being cleaned, or if one purposely throws out bits of fish livers to attract the birds the gathering is often a large one. A large piece of liver may be seized upon by several birds until it is torn to pieces. It is not often that these birds actually settle on the water, but they do so at times and ride as lightly as phalaropes. As a rule the petrels pick up the food as they skim over the water either bounding with both feet together or pattering lightly over the water running or walking with alternate feet. In both cases they keep their wings spread, and support themselves largely on these. Both methods—feet together or alternate—are extremely graceful and fascinating to watch; in the first case the birds appear as if on springs and bound lightly from wave to wave. The wings are often held motionless and the birds appear to take advantage of the upcurrents of air deflected from the waves.

Behavior.—The flight of the Wilson petrel is graceful and swallow-like and the birds often winnow the air as if for insects. The stormier the day the more likely is one to see them close to the shore, but it is rare that they are seen flying over it except in their nesting region.

The following incident during an easterly June storm at Ipswich is described in The Birds of Essex County (1905):

The surf was breaking on the shallow beach as far out as one could see through the blinding rain and spray, but these birds, with wings set, would glide into the teeth of the wind and bound from wave to wave as if on springs, seeming every now and then to be overwhelmed in the surf, but appearing beyond the wall of foam steadily gliding and bounding to windward. A slight movement only of their wings was at times to be noticed, and an occasional pattering of their feet on the waves. Ever and anon they would wheel about like large swallows, flying to leeward, to turn again and glide and bound into the wind. Once or twice they flew for a moment over the beach itself, actually drifting past me on the shore side, as I stood in the water at the edge of the surf.

Mr. John Treadwell Nichols, who has studied extensively wide ranging oceanic birds, contributes the following:

Though sometimes found in large numbers where conditions are favorable or food is abundant they are not truly gregarious, and over wide stretches of ocean are usually met with singly or two or three together. Sailors generally believe that they do not rest on the water, but in calm weather the writer has occasionally seen numbers of them sitting on the surface like miniature gulls.

Though varying greatly in abundance, Wilson petrel is generally numerous close inshore off New York through the summer months. It regularly passes the Narrows and comes into New York Upper Bay, and occasionally one or two may be seen on the South Bay, Long Island. It probably is molting at this season, as on June 30, 1913, when the species was unusually abundant, flying rapidly about over the ocean off Mastic, Long Island, the nearer ones so far from shore as just to be seen readily with the naked eye, many of their feathers were scattered along the line of wash on the beach, particularly primaries, though others (including some tail feathers) were also found. * * * On this date it was estimated that from a point on the crest of the dunes at least 1,000 Wilson petrels were within binocular range at one time.

Capt. Herbert L. Spinney (1903) has recorded a diving habit in these birds seen near Seguin Island, Maine. He says: "They were feeding on the wash of the bait from a fisherman's hook, and were noticed a number of times to plunge beneath the surface of the water for the food they were after."

The following observations on the habits of this species made by Doctor Pickering in 1838, published by Cassin (1858), are of interest:

A storm petrel taken, which proved to be *Thalassidroma wilsonii*; and, although this species and others of its genus have been constantly seen during the voyage of the expedition, this is the first specimen that has been captured without having been injured, thus affording whatever facilities can be obtained on shipboard for observing its manners.

I was rather surprised to observe that this bird was not only entirely incapable of perching, but even of standing upright like birds in general, and as I have seen birds of this genus represented, unless by the aid of its wings. In standing, or rather, sitting, the whole of the tarsus (commonly mistaken for the leg), rests on the ground, and it walks in the same awkward position, frequently obliged to balance itself with its wings. With a more powerful exertion of its wings, however, it was enabled to run along on its toes, in the same manner that it does over the surface of the water. The absence of a hind toe, the nails being but slightly bent and flat, and, perhaps I may add, its evidently being unaccustomed to this description of locomotion, seemed to be the causes of its helplessness on its feet.

These birds have been numerous about us for some days past, and their coursing over the water with flitting wings reminds me of the actions of butterflies about a pool. One of them was swimming, or at least, resting on the surface. We have seen this species very frequently, indeed, almost daily, since leaving America, and scarcely any other sea birds, except in the immediate vicinity of the islands. It would seem that it scarcely ever visits the land, except for the purposes of incubation, and there can hardly be a better comment on its untiring power of wing than the popular fable amongst seamen, that it carries its eggs and hatches its young while sitting in the water. It does not sail in the continued manner of the gulls and some other sea birds, but moves by rapidly flexing its wings something like a bat, and was continually coursing around and in the wakes of the vessels, generally in considerable numbers, during much the greater part of the time that the expedition was in the Atlantic Ocean.

The voice of the Wilson petrel when the bird is picking up food from the water is a gentle peeping, which is repeated the more rapidly the more excited the birds become at the abundance of the feast. This is the only sound I have heard them utter on the New England coast, but various observers have written of the "twittering" and "cooing" sounds made on the nesting grounds. Wm. Eagle Clarke (1906) speaks of a "low whistle" and a "harsh screaming chuckle," and he says that: "These noises they keep up almost continuously after dark."

Although Wilson petrel seems to delight in stormy weather, there are times when even its native elements prove too much for it. A great storm raged on the coast of North Carolina on August 28, 29, and 30, 1893, and thousands of these birds were washed ashore dead and dying, unable longer to battle with the waves. The 10 miles of beach from Beaufort Harbor to Cape Lookout was literally strewn with them. The holocaust is described by T. Gilbert Pearson (1899) from information received from several reliable sources.

I have two birds of this species in my collection that were found floating dead in the water, but how they came to their death I do not know. One had a slit at the corner of the mouth, which may have been caused by the cruel sport in which passengers on vessels sometimes indulge, namely, the sport of fishing for these birds with hook and line. Sometimes a line with a button attached is used, and, as this skips along the waves in the wake of the vessel, there is a remote chance of the line becoming entangled with the wing or foot of a petrel.

When other sources of bait are lacking, petrels have sometimes been used, although one is scarcely large enough to bait two hooks. The superstition among sailors that it is unlucky to kill a "Mother

Cary's chicken" has, however, largely protected them. Capt. J. W. Collins (1884) thus describes the method formerly in use by fishermen desiring these birds for bait:

The most common and effective way of killing them was with a whip, which was made by tying several parts of cod line—each part 6 or 8 feet long—to a staff 5 or 6 feet in length. The petrels were tolled up by throwing out a large piece of codfish liver, and when they had gathered in a dense mass, huddling over the object which attracted them, swish went the thongs of the whip, cutting their way through the crowded flock and perhaps killing or maiming a score or more at a single sweep. By the time these were picked up another flock was gathered, and the cruel work went on until, maybe, 400 or 500 birds were killed, though perhaps it was seldom that so great a number was obtained at once.

Wilson petrels have a certain economic value as foretellers of bad weather, for they are more active just before storms, at least such is their reputation among sailors—and it is possible that on this account they derive their common name, "Mother Cary's chickens," from *Mater Cara*, the blessed Virgin. A group of petrels sitting quietly on the water on the other hand is said to be a sign of calm weather, although the contrary is sometimes affirmed.

Fall.—The fall migration of the Wilson petrel is, of course, the migration from their breeding place at the end of the Antarctic summer. Their winter habits and haunts in our northern summer have already been described.

The Wilson petrel resembles the Leach petrel in life, but can be distinguished from it in the following manner: The Wilson petrel is slightly smaller than the Leach and blacker—less rusty—although these differences are very slight and both birds appear to be black with white rumps. The tail of the Wilson petrel is rounded, that of the Leach slightly forked, but this again is a point that is difficult to make out. Murphy (1915) emphasizes the "notable different style of flight of Leach's as distinguished from Wilson's petrel." He says: "*Oceanodroma* flies with rapid, 'leaping' strokes, quite unlike the alternations of gliding and synchronous flutters which characterize the flight of *Oceanites*." The most diagnostic point, however, and the one that Wilson himself was the first to record, although a number of others have noted it independently, is the fact that the feet with their *yellow* webs extend beyond the tail in the Wilson, but the short, black-webbed feet of the Leach petrel are concealed below the tail.

DISTRIBUTION.

Breeding range.—Found breeding on Mauritius and Kerguelen Islands in the Indian Ocean; at Cape Horn, on Adelie Land, and on Victoria Land (Cape Adare); also on the South Shetland and

South Orkney Islands and South Georgia; also probably in the South Sandwich Islands, and on Bouvet Island.

Range.—All the oceans of the world except the North Pacific. North in the Pacific Ocean to about 5° or 6° South (rare north of the Equator). North in the Atlantic Ocean to the coast of Labrador, Resolution Island (62°), and Great Britain. Westward into the Gulf of Mexico (Vera Cruz and Louisiana coast). Eastward into the Mediterranean Sea (Sardinia). South to the Antarctic continent, the Great Ice Barrier (78° South), and Weddell Sea (72° South). Pacific Ocean birds have been named as a distinct subspecies.

Spring migration.—Northward in the Atlantic Ocean in March, April, and May. Recorded dates: South Georgia, March 15; Patagonia, Rio Gallegos, April 7; Brazil, Barra, April 27; Equator, April 25; Bermuda, May; North Carolina, Cape Hatteras, April 18; Barbados, May 8; Azores, May 21; New Jersey, May 9; Maine, May 28; Newfoundland, Cape Race, May 29.

Fall migration.—Southward in the Atlantic Ocean in September, October, and November. Recorded dates: Maine, September 17; Massachusetts, September 23; New York, October; Equator, October 14; Brazil, Fernando Noronha, October 16; South Orkneys, November 11; South Georgia, November 23.

Casual records.—Accidental in California (Monterey, August 24, 1910). Has wandered inland in North America to Pennsylvania (Columbia, August 29, 1893), to northern Ontario (Muskoka district), and to other less remote localities. Accidental in Spain, France, and Italy.

Egg dates.—Kerguelen Island: Four records, January 23 to February 11. Cape Horn: One record, January 2. South Orkney Islands: One record, February 12. Mauritius Island: One record, March 15. Adelie Land: Three records, December 1, 14, and 18.

FREGETTA LEUCOGASTRIS (Gould).

WHITE-BELLIED PETREL.

HABITS.

One accidental occurrence of this rare species on the coast of Florida is all that justifies us in recording this handsome little petrel as a North American bird. The following account of the capture is given by Baird, Brewer, and Ridgway (1884):

So far as we are aware, the black-and-white stormy petrel is only known to have been taken in a single instance within our waters, and its claim to a place in the fauna of North America rests entirely on the capture of these specimens on the Gulf coast of Florida. Seven examples of this bird are said to have been captured with a hook and line by the captain of a vessel while at anchor in the harbor of St. Marks, Florida. One of these was secured by Mr. John

Hooper, of Brooklyn, N. Y. They were observed about the vessel two days, after which none were met with.

There has been considerable doubt expressed as to the validity of this species. Godman (1907), who deals with the species under the name *Cymodroma grallaria*, admits that it is closely related to *C. melanogaster*, and says:

Dr. Bowdler Sharpe has suggested that *C. grallaria* might be the young of *C. melanogaster*, before the black appears on the center of the breast and abdomen. Salvin, however, did not indorse this view.

According to the evidence at present before me, I am inclined to agree with Salvin in separating the two species, for *C. grallaria* never shows any black on the abdomen, and all the white-banded specimens in the British Museum have the appearance of being adult birds. It seems, therefore, that the white edges to the dorsal feathers are a sign of adult plumage in *C. grallaria*, and of juvenile plumage in *C. melanogaster*.

Sufficient evidence to support either theory is lacking and the question can not be definitely settled until large series of specimens have been collected to show all the plumage changes from the downy stage to the fully adult plumage.

Nesting.—The following notes, sent to me by Mr. Rollo H. Beck, contain all that we know about the nesting habits of this rare species:

Though the fishermen of Juan Fernandez told me they had never found the nest of this bird I found the nests quite close to the beach on Santa Clara Island, which lies about 10 miles from the west end of Masatierra Island. The nests were usually in rock piles under a good-sized rock. The few nests examined were lined with straws or a few twigs from bushes. One nest with its downy occupant was plainly visible without moving the overshadowing rock. On January 19, 1914, the date of my visit, I found more nests with young birds than with eggs. As with other species of petrels the downy young of this species is left alone during the day.

Eggs.—The three eggs taken by Mr. Beck are probably the only eggs in existence. They vary in shape from oval to broad elliptical ovate. The shell is smooth, but without luster and the color is dull white, more or less discolored. One has a wreath of small purplish brown dots near the larger end and in one these dots form a cap over the whole of that end; the other has a larger cap of such dots with many minute dots scattered over the egg. The three eggs measure 34.5 by 24, 34 by 25, and 32.5 by 25 millimeters.

Plumages.—The downy young are apparently thickly covered with long, soft down of a " Quaker drab " color. There are several specimens in the Brewster-Sanford collection, collected by Mr. Beck, on Goat Island, Chile, on January 19, 1914. These are of different ages, but all still largely downy, though some are nearly fully grown. The new plumage, which shows under the down, is much like the adult plumage, except that the scapulars and the wing-coverts, particularly the latter, are broadly edged with white.

Behavior.—Comparatively little has been published on the habits of the white-bellied petrel. Gould (1865) says of it:

Like the *F. melanogaster*, the white-bellied storm-petrel is a fine and power-ful species, fluttering over the glassy surface of the ocean during calms with an easy butterfly-like motion of the wings, and buffeting and breasting with equal vigor the crests of the loftiest waves of the storm; at one moment descending into their deep troughs and at the next rising with the utmost alertness to their highest points, apparently from an impulse communicated as much by striking the surface of the water with its webbed feet as by the action of the wings. Like the other members of the genus, it feeds on mollusca, the spawn of fish, and any kind of fatty matter that may be floating on the surface of the ocean.

Mr. John Treadwell Nichols writes to me in regard to it:

In habits it resembles the Wilson petrel. It follows a ship for scraps, about which a little flock gathers, pattering on the water with their feet, their wings extended fluttering over their backs, so that they make a twinkling white spot in the distance. Its note, which I have heard at such times, is a funny little squeak.

Dr. E. A. Wilson (1907) writes of his experience with it in the Antarctic:

This petrel is to be recognized on the wing mainly by its small size and white belly, the chin, throat, and tail alone being black on the under part. We obtained no specimens, though we saw it on several occasions. On Septem-ber 18th, 1901, we had several in our wake, and again on September 20th we saw them continually dropping to touch the water with one foot, steadying themselves while they daintily took their minute crustacean food from the surface of the water. At these times their tails become much hollowed out on the dorsal surface, so that each half is at right angles to the other.

Mr. Beck has also sent me the following notes on the habits of the white-bellied petrel:

The first specimens of this form were noted about 150 miles offshore on the 400-mile trip across from Valparaiso to Juan Fernandez, and were found commonly within 100 miles of the islands. An interesting characteristic of this form is the manner in which it strikes the water with one foot. In a breeze or wind it was always the leeward leg that was used, the windward one being stretched out behind. As our schooner was always on the wind, the petrels usually had but little use for the leg on the southern side of the body. When the birds flew directly into the wind either one or the other or both legs might be used.

DISTRIBUTION.

Breeding range.—Known to breed only on Santa Clara and Goat Islands, near Juan Fernandez Islands, off the coast of Chile.

Range.—Southern temperate oceans. North in the Indian Ocean to the Bay of Bengal; in the Pacific Ocean to about 4° south; and in the Atlantic Ocean to about 33° south. Southern limits not clearly defined.

Casual records.—Accidental in northwestern Florida (Saint Marks).

Egg dates.—Juan Fernandez Islands: One record, January 19.

PELAGODROMA MARINA HYPOLEUCA (Moquin-Tandon).

NORTH ATLANTIC WHITE-FACED PETREL.

HABITS.

This handsome and well marked little petrel enjoys a wide distribution in the Atlantic and southern oceans. Its center of abundance seems to be in Australian and New Zealand seas, where there are several large breeding rookeries. It also breeds on the Salvages and on some of the Cape Verde, Azores, and Canary Islands in the Atlantic Ocean. Its slim claim to a place on our list is based on a single record of a straggler taken nearly 200 miles off the coast of Massachusetts. It was added to our list by Mr. Ridgway (1885), who published the following record:

On the 2d of September, 1885, there was captured on board the U. S. Fish Commission steamer *Albatross* (Capt. Z. L. Tanner, U. S. N., commanding), in latitude 40° 34′ 18″ N., 66° 09′ W., a specimen of the white-faced stormy petrel, *Pelagodroma marina* (Lath.). Mr. James E. Benedict, resident naturalist of the *Albatross,* writes me that it was " taken on the ship late in the evening of the 2d proximo," and that " it was in all probability attracted by the light and fell on the deck, from which it seemed unable to rise." He adds that no more of the same species were seen during the cruise, though petrels of other kinds were numerous around the ship.

Nesting.—Several interesting descriptions of breeding colonies of this petrel have been published from which I have selected two. Messrs. A. G. Campbell and A. H. E. Mattingley (1906) have given us the following full account of an Australian colony, probably the largest one known:

Opposite the entrance of Port Phillip Bay, and some 4 miles in from the actual Heads, lies a long, narrow strip of land known as Mud Island. The name is somewhat of a misnomer, for the island consists mainly of sand. The island, which is perhaps 3 miles around, stands sentinel over the entrance to the harbor of Melbourne, arresting the onrush of sand that would block the opening, piling it up in the shallows and in the banks that form its flanks. Mud Island is unique in being one of the few spots on the south coast of Australia where a species of storm-petrel (*Pelagodroma marina*) comes to breed. Through the kindness of Mr. S. P. Townsend, A. O. U., and in company with him and two friends, I was enabled to visit this rookery during the last week of the old year.

Passing over to some of the sand banks, we came across what was the real object of our summer visit—the petrel rookery. Little burrows, just large enough to put one's hand in, each with a little heap of sand outside, were seen among native spinach and saltbush, sometimes so thickly that every square yard held one of them. Inserting the hand, we could reach to the end, where a large chamber was found and a white-faced storm petrel sat quietly upon its egg. There was not a sound save our own voices, yet there must have been thousands of birds within earshot. Each was intent upon its task of incubation, now very near completion, for most of the eggs we examined were already chipping, and in three burrows we discovered a tiny, fluffy, grey chick. When brought out to the light the petrel, which is about 8 inches long, seemed very stupid, and scrambled away on being released. On the wing, however, it is the perfection of ease and grace. All the writers of the sea have made mention of storm petrels.

As it was now far past sunset and the Christmas moon was shining brightly, we decided to await the arrival of the other batch of birds—the mates of those sitting quietly in the burrows. Very little has been written about this species of storm petrel, so it was with eager interest that we awaited the progress of events. We marked 10 birds in the burrows, to see if this could give any clue to their habits. The same musty smell that pervades the mutton-bird rookery, arising from the natural oil with which the birds' plumage is greased, was noticed here, and it soon permeated our blankets and clothes. It was at 9.30 p. m. that the first storm petrel came in from sea and circled swiftly and silently close to the ground, as if searching for its own particular burrow. What a problem, especially if the night be dark, to find one's own home amid such tens of thousands of a similar nature. Bird followed bird every few minutes in silence, until about 10.30 the numbers had increased so that two or three could be seen at once. But where were the numbers scuttling about the ground and cutting the air in all directions amid noisy arguments and welcomes? Two hours later, still no great increase—ones and twos still passed our vantage point, flashing their white under surfaces as they occasionally turned in the moonlight, but none settling within sight, though the night was clear and bright. Not a sound until we beat or stamped upon the ground, when an impatient or hungry bird nearby would call from a burrow with a low, rasping voice as untuneful as all sea birds' notes are.

We estimated that at the very least there must be 50,000 nesting burrows in the sand rises about us, and we were forced to the conclusion that all the birds can not return every night. It appears as if some only, and that a very small proportion, return to change places with the brooding mate. Search as we would in the small hours of that moonlit morning, we could only find one burrow where two birds were at home. We then snatched an hour's sleep under the friendly shelter of a saltbush, and about 3.30 a. m. were awakened by two storm petrels, with low cries, running onto us from behind and taking wing. This illustrates the habit petrels have of running onto a mound, or throwing themselves from a cliff, before taking flight. Their long wings prevent them rising easily from flat ground. By daylight not a bird was to be seen. We visited our marked burrows soon afterwards, and often birds which were each labeled with a small piece of twine seven were still at home, two had changed shifts, and one burrow was empty. This corroborated somewhat our opinion that a small proportion only of the birds belonging to the rookery come in each night. The sitting bird must therefore be four or five days without food. We felt we had only touched the fringe of these interesting questions and that a longer stay on the island was necessary for their solution. But we had not the time to spare; we must be off.

Further visits to the petrelry were undertaken on the 16th and 17th February, and again on the 23d and 24th February, 1907, to extend and make more complete our observations on the breeding habits of " Mother Cary's chickens."

Wading across the lagoon the southern rookery was reached, and examinations of the white-faced storm-petrel's burrows revealed young birds in several stages of development. They were tiny fat little balls of slaty-grey down from out of which peeped a pair of beady black eyes situated behind a slender black bill which was surmounted by the long tube nostrils peculiar to the petrel family. Most nestlings were to be found more advanced, however. In many the abdomen had become covered with white feathers interspersed with down, the tail was beginning to show, and the primary wing feathers were prominent. It was noticed, too, that the white abdominal feathers had extended up to and over the pectoral muscles, whilst the markings from which the bird derives its vernacular name were showing up strongly through a few threads of down. In the next stage of growth the whole of the feathers were more strongly developed. The down, which freely covered the wings, back, flanks, nape, and crown in the previous stage, had almost disappeared, whilst the general contour of the burrowling resembled that of its parents, although it was still very fat. These birds had just been deserted by their parents and left to their own devices. Whilst lying out in the rookery at night some fully fledged birds were observed running and flapping about the rookery, stimulated by the pangs of hunger. It is owing to this that they gain sufficient muscular development both in the legs and in the wings to enable them in about a week's time to fly away one night with the adult birds, who no doubt assist and encourage them. At sea they use the feet almost as much as their wings, as they go tripping along over the billows. It is owing to this last-named fact that the members of the family to which they belong have been called petrels, after the Apostle Peter.

Up to the final stage the parents feed their offspring nightly with about a teaspoonful of fishy, oily paste, principally composed of "whale's food," a small species of crustacean found floating on the surface of the ocean. This they regurgitate, and when they enter their burrows a faint purring note of welcome is made by the nestling, evidently in anticipation of its evening meal. Opening its mouth wide over the head of its young one, which forthwith thrusts its beak into that of the adult and opens it, the parent bird brings up the dainty and juicy contents of its stomach. With this meal the young one has to be content until next night, but as it lives an indolent life, quietly ensconced in the cool shade of its burrow, it waxes exceeding fat, so much so that in some parts of the South Sea Islands, where these birds also nest, the natives, passing a dry rush through a dead young one's body, form thereby an excellent candle.

Mr. W. R. Ogilvie-Grant (1896) describes a breeding colony, which he found on the Salvages near Madeira, as follows:

On the afternoon of our arrival on Great Salvage we found an egg of this bird in what we at first mistook for a rabbit burrow, but it was unfortunately broken by one of the men. This, however, opened our eyes, and we subsequently found that large colonies of the white-breasted petrel were breeding on the flat top of the island, in burrows dug out in the sandy ground, and partly concealed by the close-growing ice plant. It was very unpleasant walking over these breeding grounds, which occupied considerable areas, for the ground was honeycombed with burrows in every direction, and gave way at each step, one's boots rapidly becoming full of sand. By thrusting one's arm into one hole after another, we soon procured a fine series of specimens, accompanied in most cases by an egg, for we had evidently hit off the breeding season, and most of the birds, having laid their single egg, were beginning to set. Most of the eggs were white, more or less finely spotted, and often zoned toward the larger end, with dark red and purplish dots, but some few were equally spotted all over the shell, while one was almost entirely devoid of markings. In shape they vary considerably, some being perfect ovals equally round at both ends, while others are slightly pointed at the one end. Both sexes take part in incubation, for out of twelve birds captured on the egg three were males.

Eggs.—Mr. Henry O. Forbes (1893) describes the single egg as " elliptical in shape. Ground color white, at one end covered with fine dots of heliotrope-purple and lavender-grey, with a few of seal brown interspersed, and at the other end sparsely with vinaceous buff. In some specimens the end is thickly dusted over with the finest vinaceous-rufus dots, while on the rest of the egg they are scarcely recognizable." Buller (1888) and Gould (1865) describe the eggs as " pure white." Campbell (1901) gives it as follows : " Texture of shell comparatively fine; surface occasionally has a faint trace of gloss; color, pure white, but about 50 per cent have numerous fine brownish freckles about the apex."

The measurements of 22 eggs, sent me by Rev. F. C. R. Jourdain, average 36.20 by 22.03 millimeters; the eggs showing the four extremes measure **37.4** by 26.5, 36.9 by **27.4**, **33.8** by 25.7, and 37 by **25.4** millimeters.

Young.—Several observers have noted that both sexes incubate. The period of incubation does not seem to be known. Mr. Robert Hall (1902) gives us the following good description of the downy young, partly fledged :

Except the chin and throat, the whole under surface is covered with a sooty-grey down averaging more than an inch in length. The down has fallen from the upper surface, excepting the crown and rump. The back is deeper slate colored than in the adult, and the wings, which are almost free from down, are of the same color; the hind neck is mottled with white; the face is deep slate colored; the lores white with dark tips; the chin, throat, and cheeks white; the feet slate colored, with a very light yellow mark between the toes; the bill is dark. The bulk appears to be twice that of the adult. Girth of nestling at shoulders 10.5 inches; of adult, 4.5 inches.

Plumages.—Godman (1907) says that " the plumage of full-grown young birds is like that of the adults as soon as the down is shed. The grey rump and upper tail coverts have wavy cross lines of grey and white, with a white fringe at the end of the feathers. One specimen has the lower flanks and under tail coverts freckled with greyish bars."

Food.—The only reference I can find to the food of the white-faced petrel is what I have quoted above from Campbell and Mattingley, that " up to the final stage the parents feed their offspring nightly with about a teaspoonful of fishy, oily paste, principally composed of ' whale's food,' a small species of crustacean found floating on the surface of the ocean."

Behavior.—Mr. Ogilvie-Grant (1896) makes the following reference to its flight:

> We first observed and recognized with pleasure these beautiful petrels as we neared the Salvages, when numbers were seen flitting along close to the surface of the sea, with their long legs dangling beneath them and just touching the water. Now they would be lost sight of in the hollows between the huge Atlantic rollers, now reappear, closely following the undulating waters with their graceful easy flight.

The same naturalist says:

> We never heard the call of this bird; those flying over the sea during the daytime were always perfectly silent so far as we heard, though they constantly passed close to our tug, and there was no lack of them. When caught on their eggs they uttered a short, grunting note, much like that given vent to by the domestic pigeon under similar circumstances.

Lieut. Boyd Alexander (1898), however, says that on its breeding grounds, in the Cape Verde Islands, it uttered "grating notes like those of a pair of rusty springs set in motion."

The white-faced petrel seems to have many enemies to check its increase in its thickly populated colonies. Lieut. Alexander (1898) noted that, in unearthing these petrels, several managed to escape. "They ran along the ground in a dazed condition, and before we could move them they were pounced upon and carried off by kites." Mr. Ogilvie-Grant (1896) "found quite a number of dead birds and sucked eggs, evidently the work of the mice already mentioned, as their droppings were to be seen all about the burrows, and the marks of their teeth upon the empty shells were unmistakable. The birds, some of which were quite freshly killed and almost untouched, were invariably done to death by being bitten at the nape of the neck, and in some cases part of the brain had been eaten. It seemed curious that these comparatively small mice should be able to kill a bird several times larger than themselves, and provided with a fairly strong, hooked bill; but no doubt the petrels get caught in the end of their burrow, and, being terrified, do not even try to defend themselves." Campbell and Mattingley (1906) write:

> Two enemies of the white-faced storm-petrel are found on the island—the harrier, and, worse still, the common rat, introduced by the guano-getters. If these rodents are not exterminated, it is only a matter of time when they will destroy the occupants of the rookery, since several freshly killed remnants of these fragile birds were found about.

Since the above was written the bird which breeds on the islands in the eastern Atlantic Ocean has been separated as a distinct subspecies, *Pelagodroma marina hypoleuca* (Moquin-Tandon). This is, of course, the subspecies which belongs on the American list. It seems better, however, to leave the life history as I have written it, for the species as a whole, than to leave out the full and very interesting accounts which have been written on the Australian bird.

DISTRIBUTION.

Breeding range.—The subspecies which belongs on the North American list breeds in the Salvage and Cape Verde Islands, in the eastern North Atlantic Ocean. Other subspecies breed on islands in Australian and New Zealand seas.

Range.—North Atlantic Ocean. Limits not well defined.

Casual records.—Accidental off the coast of Massachusetts (40° 34' north, 66° 9' west, September 2, 1885) and in Great Britain (Walney Island, Lancashire, November, 1890, and Colonsay, Inner Hebrides, January 1, 1897).

Egg dates.—Salvage Islands: One record, April 27. Cape Verde Islands: One record, March 15.

Order STEGANOPODES.

TOTIPALMATE SWIMMERS.

Family PHAËTHONTIDAE, Tropic-birds.

LEPTOPHAETHON LEPTURUS CATESBYI (Brandt).

YELLOW-BILLED TROPIC-BIRD.

HABITS.

The warm waters of the Gulf Stream, sweeping northeastward across the Atlantic, produce in the little Bermuda group semitropical conditions and bring thither this beautiful species of tropical origin, which finds here ideal conditions for rearing its young in the numerous recesses and cavities of the honey-combed limestone cliffs, so characteristic of these islands. Mr. A. Hyatt Verrill (1901) writes:

The most striking bird of the Bermudas is the yellow-billed tropic-bird (*Phaeton americanus*) ; or " Long Tail " of the natives. These beautiful creatures arrive about March 25th, and within a few days become exceedingly abundant. As many as 300 can frequently be seen at one time, flying about the cliffs or skimming the surface of the wonderfully colored water, the reflection from which causes their breasts to appear the most lovely and delicate sea-green. They are very tame and unsuspicious, flying close to moving boats and breeding everywhere, often within a few yards of houses or settlements.

The value of properly enforced bird protection is nowhere better exemplified than in the case of this bird. A few years ago the tropic birds were threatened with extinction from the Bermudas, whereas, since the passing of strict laws, prohibiting killing of birds or taking the eggs, they have rapidly increased, until at present the number breeding yearly on the islands is calculated at fully 5,000.

Spring.—Dr. Alfred O. Gross (1912) has made a most valuable contribution to the life history of this species, based on an exhaustive study of its breeding habits during two seasons at the Bermudas. He says of the migration:

The tropic birds migrate from the West Indies and, except for occasional stragglers, none are to be found in the Bermudas during the winter months. This annual migration flight is remarkable when it is considered that the birds must necessarily fly over open water for a distance of more than 600 miles without any landmark to guide them. The first tropic birds appear at the Bermudas during the latter part of February, according to the fishermen and local observers, but the great bulk of them do not arrive until the first weeks of March. Mr. Mowbray, superintendent of the Bermuda Aquarium, while making a voyage to Turks Island in 1909 saw on February 9 and 10 several groups of two or three individuals each, which were flying in a direct course for the Bermudas. This agrees with the supposed course of migration of the tropic birds and illustrates the keen sense of direction and orientation which they must possess. These birds would probably be admirable subjects for experimenting on orientation.

Nesting.—Of the nesting habits he writes:

Particular localities, especially on the south shore of the main island, seemed to be preferred by many of the birds. At Elys Harbor and Tuckers Town it was not unusual to find as many as 50–75 pairs nesting within a range of less than 100 yards. The tropic birds are not, however, strictly gregarious, for isolated nests about the islands of·the sound were very common. The so-called colonies probably exist because of many choice nesting sites, which chance to be situated in the particular locality, rather than to any gregarious or social instinct on the part of the birds.

The nature of the nesting site varies from that of the open places on the shelf-like ledges to that of the inner end of a narrow and circuitous passage, or the recesses of an obscure cave. In the two latter situations the presence of the adult bird may often be ascertained by inserting a long pole into the opening, which usually brings forth a shrill cry in response to the intrusion. At Tuckers Town nests were found in shallow excavations in the side of a high sand dune which ran along the shore. These cavities, which apparently were made by the birds themselves, were in each case at the base of some herbage, which to a certain degree shielded and protected the bird from the intense heat and light of the sun.

The height of the nest above the water varies greatly; it ranges from a point just above the high-water mark to one situated near the top of the highest cliffs, perhaps 75 or 100 feet above the sea. At Elys Harbor some of the nests were so low that during an unusually high tide accompanying a storm, they were overwashed by the waves and filled with heaps of sargassum and other sea weeds. The sargassum is found in many of the lower open nests, where it is deposited by the giant waves during the severe tempests of the winter months. No nesting material is ever collected by the birds, but the single egg is deposited on the bare rocks or else on the mat of sea weeds already present.

Mr. W. E. D. Scott (1891) describes an interesting cave colony, at Jamaica, as follows:

The cave where the birds were found had a very small entrance, about large enough for a man to crawl into, in the face of the cliff. This was approached only in the calmest weather, in a boat. The entrance led at once into a spacious chamber of irregular shape. Going directly back from the mouth the cavern was some sixty feet deep. It was at its widest point some seventy or eighty feet, and oval in shape as a whole. The bottom was covered with coarse sand and gravel, and boulders of varying size, evidently having fallen from above, were scattered thickly over this floor except at the extreme back of the cavern farthest from the sea. The height of the roof or ceiling, which was of an uneven rough surface, was about twenty-five feet, and many bats were hanging wherever the projections or inequalities afforded them opportunity. Toward the back of this chamber five birds were secured, each one sitting on a single egg. The place chosen for the nesting site, for this is all it can be termed, was in all these cases where two boulders on the gravelly floor lay close together, just leaving room on the ground for the birds to crawl between them. Two birds were obtained in like situations that had not laid, and may have been simply resting. The females were in every case the birds that were sitting on the eggs, and it was quite evident upon dissection that the single egg forms the complement in these cases. The birds taken from the holes in the cliff, and also those taken in this cave, were very tame, and were captured readily without attempting to escape. Later on the same day a bird was found with a single egg laid at the bottom of one of the holes in the face of the cliff.

Mr. Karl Plath (1913) states that he found nests, on the Bermudas, " in the deep grass and also under small cedar bushes." The data sent out with certain eggs would seem to indicate that bulky nests were made of grass, moss, and sea weed, but it seems more likely that the egg was laid on a bed of such material already in the cavity than that the material was carried in by the bird for nest-building.

Eggs.—The single egg of the yellow-billed tropic-bird is variable in appearance and often quite handsome. The shape is practically ovate or short ovate; some eggs are more pointed and some more rounded at the small end. The ground color is pinkish or dirty white, but this color is more or less completely (generally more) concealed by profuse, fine specklings or cloudings of various shades of "livid brown," "vinaceous brown," or "purplish drab" in an endless variety of patterns; some eggs are very light in color, some very dark and some are very much variegated; some are marked with heavy blotches or splashes of the above colors.

The measurements of 40 eggs, in various collections, average 54 by 38.9 millimeters; the eggs showing the four extremes measure 60 by 40, 56 by 41, 50 by 37.5, and 51 by 36.5 millimeters.

Apparently two young birds are raised by each pair in a season, the first eggs being laid early in April and the second sets late in June. The period of incubation is 28 days. Doctor Gross (1912), says:

Both the male and female birds take part in incubation, and during this period the egg is seldom left uncovered for more than a few minutes. The birds take their turns at the nest, thus giving each other an opportunity to feed. In one case an adult was seen feeding its mate while the latter was brooding the egg.

Young.—From Doctor Gross's (1912) extensive notes on the development of the young bird, I shall make only a few quotations; he found that "the length of time spent by the young tropic-bird in the nest extends over a period of 63 days, or about two months. The time required for incubation, previously noted, is about 4 weeks, making the complete period about 3 months. The adult birds remain in the islands about 7 months, which affords them ample time to rear two broods, but not more, during any one summer in Bermuda." Of the food and care of the young, he says:

The food of the young during the first 10 or 15 days consists of snails and soft marine animals. In some cases it seemed to be merely the regurgitated juices and semi-digested food from the gullet of the parent bird. When the birds are between 15 and 30 days old, more than 90 per cent of the food consisted of squids, the remainder being made up of small minnows and some unidentifiable material. During the latter half of the young bird's life fish constitutes a large part of the food, although many squids, some of considerable size, were present in nearly every specimen examined. The food is transferred from a pouch-like gullet of the adult to that of the young by process of regurgitation. This transfer of food is accompanied by a series of gulps, strains, and wrigglings of the head and neck on the part of both birds.

The adult birds remain very closely with the young during the first ten days. The little fellow is usually tucked in under the feathers of the adult and frequently sleeps with its head projecting through the feathers, just as a little chicken does when it is brooded by the old hen. When the little creature became restless the old bird uttered a series of low guttural sounds, which, I assume, were intended as disapproval.

The young birds are unable to fly well when they leave the nest although the wings have been exercised very frequently for some weeks. Those which I observed leaped into the water from the edge of the nest and then made their way out to sea by paddling. The young birds flopped their wings vigorously, as if attempting to fly, but were never able to rise from the water during the time I observed them. Such an event created considerable excitement among the adult tropic-birds, which assembled to witness the affair. The young bird while thus floating on the water may be fed by the adults, but more probably depends on its stored fat until it gains enough strength to fly and fish for itself.

Plumages.—Doctor Gross (1912) describes the downy young, as follows: "At the time of hatching, the young tropic-bird is to all appearances a ball of fluffy down with its dark colored beak and black feet standing out in marked contrast to the background of white. It is only the region about the beak, the underparts, and the middle of the back which are pure white, for the remainder of the plumage, especially the crown, sides of the back and regions of the wings, has a decided tinge of dull gray." Not much change takes place, except an increase in size, until the 16th day, when the first feathers appear in the scapular region; "by the end of the 35th day the wing feathers, including the coverts, are well expanded and now form, with the scapulars, a continuous band" and "by the 40th day the young is completely feathered, but down still shows about the region of the head and rump." The distinguishing features of this plumage are well illustrated in the photograph reproduced in the accompanying plate. Just how long this plumage is worn does not seem to be known, but probably the adult plumage is acquired before the end of the first year. Of the molts and plumages of the adult I have been unable to learn anything.

Food.—Regarding the food and feeding habits of the yellow-billed tropic bird, Doctor Gross (1912) writes:

The food of the tropic-bird consists chiefly of marine animals, which in the majority of cases are secured by diving. The birds go on long foraging flights, wandering, according to some observers, as far as 50 miles from land. On our return trip to New York in 1910 a lone individual was seen which was estimated to be 150 miles distant from Bermuda, and on June 25, 1911, I saw two of these birds which were 200 miles from land. These are probably extreme cases, but they serve to illustrate the unusually long excursions which the tropic-birds may make in their search for prey.

The food contained in the gullets and stomachs of 5 adult specimens was made up, for the greater part, of squids and fishes, especially small minnows. In one of the stomachs there were a few fragments of a crab and a sea urchin, as well as particles of material which could not be identified. Two of the five kinds of fishes found belonged to a species of flying fish (*Exocoetus furcatus* and *Exonautes exiliens*) which are common in the waters of Bermuda. It would be interesting to know whether or not these flying fish are captured while they are sailing above the surface of the water.

The adult birds are most active during the early morning hours; it is only occasionally that they can be seen feeding during the middle of the day, the heat at that time being, perhaps, great enough to account for the diminution in their numbers.

The numbers remained practically constant until about 8.30 a. m., when there was a uniform but rapid decrease, and by 11.00 a. m. there was only an occasional tropic bird to be seen flying about. The birds were again active during the few hours before sunset, but the numbers at this time never equaled those of the morning hours.

The diving of the tropic-bird is remarkable in that the plunge is usually made from a height of 50 feet or more above the surface of the water. The bird, after sighting its prey, poises a second or two in midair by rapidly vibrating the wings, meanwhile maintaining a gaze on its victim. It then turns quickly at right angles and, with wings flolded, darts through the air with the swiftness and precision of an arrow. Frequently this downward plunge takes the form of a spiral descent. It is uncertain whether this spiral course is the result of a voluntary act or not.

Behavior.—The flight of the tropic-bird has been likened to that of a large tern or a pigeon; it is entirely unlike any of the other *Steganopodes* in all of its movements and seems to belong in a class by itself; its flight is swift and graceful, accomplished by rapid wing strokes. It is decidedly an aerial species and its feet have become weak and abortive by disuse. Doctor Gross (1912) says of it:

The birds never walk upright, but the body is shoved along in a cumbersome manner by their diminutive legs. The wings are often brought into service for supporting and balancing the comparatively heavy body, which is scarcely raised above the surface on which the bird is moving. On first leaving the nest the adult bird leaps from the ledge and nimbly catches itself on the wing, but sometimes, especially after being irritated or excited, it may fall to the water before taking flight. When once poised in the air, the tropic-bird may be classed with the most graceful of sea birds. They have a very characteristic movement when flying, which is very unlike any other bird I know.

Mr. Plath (1913) writes:

They spend much time in the air, and may be seen flying in graceful curves, sometimes swooping in a spiral, with half-closed wings, to the surface of the water, and often alighting there after a skim over the waves. In the water they sit very high, with their tails held well above it. They frequently utter their peculiar cry, which varies—sometimes a rasping *t-chik-tik-tik* or *clik-et-clik-et;* again, the noise produced by several birds in the air reminds me of the noise of a greaseless axle on a wagon wheel.

Their manner of flight differs from most sea birds; the wings move much more rapidly, and at a distance one might easily mistake them for pigeons, as their long tails are not then conspicuous. Against the blue of the sky their plumage is dazzling; but see them against the dark background of a cliff, and they appear of a beautiful pale green, due to their glossy plumage reflecting the bright emerald of the water below.

Doctor Gross (1912) adds:

Among the enemies of the tropic birds are the colored natives, who molest the nests of the birds in spite of the stringent bird laws of the islands. It is probable the eggs collected are used as food. The robbing of nests for such purpose is said to be common in the West Indies. The wood rat (*Mus alexandrinus*), however, is responsible for some of the mysterious disappearances of the many eggs I had under observation. On one of my daily rounds to the nests on Two Rock Island I caught one of these rats in the act of sucking an egg. The greedy creature was allowed to finish his meal, after which he was killed and preserved as evidence against his kind. I saw no other rats in the act of molesting eggs, but no doubt they find the tropic-bird eggs a convenient source of food.

Winter.—During the winter the tropic birds retire from their more northern breeding grounds to the warmer climate of the West Indies and farther south. They spend much of their time on the wing, wandering far out to sea to feed; but as they must rest occasionally, they return to the islands, where they rest by day and roost at night in the caves and smaller cavities of the limestone cliffs. Mr. Scott (1891) says:

The birds appear every morning just after the sun is up and are then to be seen in the greatest numbers. By 10 o'clock they have either gone far out to sea to continue feeding or have retired to their roosting places in the cliffs. Their absence is noticeable from about the time in the morning indicated until just before sundown, when a few, not nearly so many as may be observed in the morning, are to be observed flying along outside of the cliffs. The native fishermen say that most of the birds return to their roosting places when it is almost too dark to see.

DISTRIBUTION.

Breeding range.—On the Bermuda Islands, some of the Bahama Islands (Great Abaco, Ragged Island Keys, Water Key, etc.), some of the Greater Antilles (Cuba, Jamaica, Haiti, Porto Rico, etc.), and some of the Lesser Antilles (Martinique, Dominica, St. Vincent, etc.).

Winter range.—Tropical and southern oceans, from the Bahamas and the West Indies southward, at least as far as Brazil (Fernando Noronha) and Ascension Island.

Spring migration.—Arrives in Bermuda from March 4 to 12 (sometimes in February).

Fall migration.—Leaves Bermuda from September 27 to November 1.

Casual records.—Occasionally visits Florida (Dry Tortugas, 1832, and Merritt's Island, April 21, 1886; seen at St. Marks, May 25, 1919). Accidental in western New York (Knowlesville, September, 1876) and in Nova Scotia (off the coast, September 4, 1870).

Egg dates.—Bahama Islands: Seventeen records, May 13 to June 16; nine records, May 14 to June 11. Bermuda Islands: Seven records, April 27 to August 12; four records, April 30 to May 12. Jamaica: One record, February 27.

PHAETHON AETHEREUS Linnaeus.

RED-BILLED TROPIC-BIRD.

HABITS.

The tropic-birds are well named, for they are always associated with those favored regions, where on the hot, sunny islands they find genial nesting sites and in the warm tropical waters fruitful feeding grounds. The red-billed species inhabits both oceans and is found as far north as the Lesser Antilles on the Atlantic side and as far as the Gulf of California on the Pacific coast.

Nesting.—Dr. E. W. Nelson (1899) gives the following account of the nesting habits of the red-billed tropic-bird on the west coast of Mexico:

Soon after landing on Isabel, a tropic-bird was found sitting on its solitary egg at the end of a little hole in the rock close to the beach. The hole was only about 15 or 18 inches across and about 3 feet deep, so that there was no difficulty in taking the bird by hand after a little maneuvering to avoid its sharp beak. During a stay of about 24 hours on this island at least 20 nests containing eggs or young were examined. A single egg is laid directly on the rough rock or loose dirt forming the floor of the nesting site, which is always located under the shelter of overarching rock, but varies greatly in situation. The inner ends of holes in cliffs facing the sea were favorite places, but as the number of such situations was limited, the birds were forced to utilize small caves and even rock shelters. In one locality five or six nests were placed on loose earth at the bottom of rock shelters so situated that I could walk directly up to them and pick up the birds. Whenever a nest was approached the parent screamed and fought viciously, ruffled its feathers and looked very fierce, but made no attempt to escape. They protested with beak and voice when pushed about, but as soon as I went away a few yards they would shuffle back to resume their former position over the egg. The young, even when quite small, were equally fierce in resenting any intrusion. One nest was found on the beach under the edge of some great rocks that had fallen from the adjacent cliff. It was only 5 or 6 feet above high tide and would have been overlooked but for the angry cries of the old bird when she heard me walking over the roof of her habitation. At sunrise the old birds were found sitting side by side at the mouths of their nesting places waiting to enjoy the first rays of sunlight. Half an hour later one of each pair started out to sea, while the other resumed its place on the nest.

Col. N. S. Goss (1888a) found them nesting on San Pedro Martir Island, in the Gulf of California, where "the birds breed in holes and crevices on the sides of the steep cliffs that overhang the water; many were inaccessible." The nests "were without material of any kind," the egg being laid upon the bare rock. In the Galapagos Islands Mr. Rollo H. Beck (1904) says that "on Daphne Island they were common; several of their nests were in small caves in the sandstone cliffs, being quite similar to the nests of duck hawks in the islands along the Lower California coast. Usually they select some crevice among the loose rocks for a nest, although on San Benedicto Island of the Revillagigedos very often a burrow of the wedge-tailed shearwater is used."

Eggs.—The red-billed tropic-bird, like the other species, lays but one egg, which in shape is short ovate, ovate or a little elongated. What few eggs I have seen resemble eggs of the yellow-billed species, but average a little larger and are more prettily marked, more evenly and clearly speckled or spotted with "livid brown" or "purple drab." Mr. H. H. Bailey (1906) says: "The coloring of a series of eggs in my collection varies from a creamy dirty yellow ground color, spotted with a darker yellow, to a dark red ground color, spotted with a darker red." Certain eggs look very much like eggs of the prairie falcon or duck hawk.

The measurements of 40 eggs, in various collections, average 56.4 by 41.7 millimeters; the eggs showing the four extremes measure **63.2** by 46, 63 by **46, 50.5** by 39.5, and 51.5 by **36.5** millimeters.

Mr. Bailey (1906) says:

Both birds take turns in incubating and caring for the young, and during this period the bird in the cavity is fed by its mate. The female, and sometimes both birds, is found in the cavity for three or four days before the single egg is deposited. While graceful on the wing, this bird is most awkward on its feet, and when alighting to look for a nesting site drags itself along like a bird with both legs broken. * * * Two cases of removing their young happened while I was on White Rock, both of them similar. Two old birds and their single young were found in a cavity, and I took one old bird to skin that night, expecting to get the remaining parent and young the next morning. On returning the next day, great was my astonishment to find the two birds gone, and still further was it taxed when I found, after careful search, the two birds in another cavity twenty to thirty feet away.

Plumages.—The downy young is covered below with short, thick, white down, and above with long, soft, silky down varying in color from "ecru drab" to "pale drab gray." The first plumage to be acquired is, in a general way, similar to that of the adult; there is more black on the head, forming an occipital crescent; the black bars on the back are broader; there are no long, central tail feathers; and the bill is yellow instead of red. How long this plumage is worn, or at what season the adult plumage is assumed, I do not know.

Food.—Mr. E. W. Gifford (1913) says of the food of this species:

The food of the red-billed tropic-bird, as shown by the stomachs examined, consists of fish and squids. These were very often disgorged by both young and old when they were taken from their burrows. This species dives for its food somewhat like a tern.

Behavior.—Of its voice, he writes:

Red-billed tropic-birds could be recognized at almost any time by their cry, which is long and shrill and consists of a lot of short, high, rasping notes given in quick succession. Birds flying about the nesting-places often gave it, and birds disturbed on the nest also gave it. The young, when taken from the nest, uttered the same cry, and I have even heard a young bird only a day or so old give three or four notes of it when handled.

Doctor Nelson (1899) says that "when disturbed on the nest their cries are very shrill and strident, consisting of a series of short, harsh, clicking, or rattling sounds something like the noise of an old-fashioned watchman's rattle."

The flight of the tropic-birds is said to be not unlike that of the terns, with rapid wing strokes; they must be graceful birds on the wing with their long tail feathers streaming in the wind. They are said to soar very high in the air at times, far above the boobies and frigate birds. Mr. Beck (1904) thought that "their flight and call as they wheeled and darted about the high cliffs closely resembled that of the white-throated swifts in California." He also says:

"In this section of the world the tropic-bird wanders as far away from land as the frigate bird. We found both this species and the red-tailed tropic-bird more than 600 miles from any island."

Mr. Gifford (1913) writes of the activities of the red-billed tropic-bird as follows:

During the breeding season at Daphne Island I saw birds circling about holes on the hillsides without beating their wings. Whenever they came opposite certain holes they would flutter their wings to check their flight, and come to a standstill for an instant, as though about to alight, but they would continue their circle. This was repeated ten or twelve times before the bird finally entered the hole. On Hood Island they usually went directly to their holes without hesitation.

Only twice in the archipelago were these birds seen on the water; once I saw three off Daphne Island, and on another occasion one off Mount Pitt, Chatham Island. In the latter case the bird flew as we passed and shook itself just after getting out of the water. As far as we observed, the tropic-birds are practically immune from the attacks of man-o'-war birds. On one occasion only did I see man-o'-war birds harrass a tropic-bird, and then without success.

DISTRIBUTION.

Breeding range.—On some of the Lesser Antilles (St. Vincent, Grenada, Bequia, Carriacou, etc.), off the coast of Venezuela (Orquilla and Los Hermanos Islands), and off the coast of Brazil (Fernando Noronha). And on the Pacific coast, from the Gulf of California (San Pedro Martir Island) southward along the coast of Mexico (Tres Marias Islands), on the Galapagos Islands and on the coast of Peru (San Lorenzo).

Winter range.—Tropical oceans, from the West Indies (Jamaica) south to Brazil (Fernando Noronha and Abrolhos Islands) and Ascension Island; also from Lower California (Espiritu Santo Island) south to Chile (Taltal).

Migrations.—Not well marked and data very scanty.

Casual records.—Accidental in Bermuda (April, 1901), on the Newfoundland Banks (August, 1876), and in the Cape Verde Islands (January 23, 1832). Wanders north on the Pacific coast to southern California (San Pedro Channel, August, 1916).

Egg dates.—Tres Marias Islands, Mexico: Eighteen records, March 6 to April 23; nine records, April 9. Galapagos Islands, four records, March 6.

SCAEOPHAETHON RUBRICAUDUS (Boddaert).

RED-TAILED TROPIC-BIRD.

HABITS.

This, the most beautiful of the tropic-birds, is the rarest of the three in North American waters. It is an inhabitant of the tropical regions of the Pacific and Indian Oceans, occurring, as a straggler only, on the coast of Lower California.

Gould (1865) says of it:

This bird is very generally dispersed over the temperate and warmer latitudes of the Indian Ocean and South Seas, where it often hovers round ships, and occasionally alights on their rigging. During the months of August and September it retires to various islands for the purpose of breeding; among other places selected for the performance of this duty are Norfolk Island, off the coast of Australia, and Raines Islets, in Torres Straights, from both of which localities I possess specimens of the bird and its eggs. As I had no opportunity of observing it, I avail myself of the following information communicated to me by Mr. Macgillivray:

"This tropic-bird was found by us on Raines Islet, where, during the month of June, about a dozen were procured. Upon one occasion three were observed performing sweeping flights over and about the island, and soon afterwards one of them alighted. Keeping my eye upon the spot, I ran up and found a male bird in a hole under the low shelving margin of the island bordering the beach, and succeeded in capturing it after a short scuffle, during which it snapped at me with its beak, and uttered a loud, harsh, and oft-repeated croak. It makes no nest, but deposits its two eggs on the bare floor of the hole, and both sexes assist in the task of incubation. It usually returns from sea about noon, soaring high in the air, and wheeling round in circles before alighting."

Nesting.—The red-tailed tropic-bird is the common breeding species on the islands of the Hawaiian group, where Dr. Walter K. Fisher (1906) has given us the following information regarding it:

The red-tailed tropic-bird is fairly common on Laysan, where it nests under the shelter of bushes and not infrequently several will congregate beneath colonies of *Fregata aquila*, occupying the ground floor as it were. The bird has a vicious temper, and if one attempts to disturb or to take it from the egg, it sets up a horrible and discordant screaming, which soon grows unbearable. The sharp beak with serrated edges is not to be despised and the enraged bird will sometimes use it to good advantage. The bow's'n birds keep up their strident cries so long as one meddles with them, but if left undisturbed will soon quiet down. Whenever we inadvertently passed near one hidden under a chenopodium bush, we soon became aware of its presence by its cry of defiance.

The nest is merely a hollow in the sand, with a few grass straws and leaves gathered in the bottom. The single egg is brooded by both parents, each of which sits upon it with the wings slightly opened. We found one white, downy nestling and most of the eggs were considerably incubated.

We saw only one red-tailed bow's'n bird near the French Frigate Shoals, but on Necker they were rather common. Contrary to the very pronounced nesting habits on Laysan, the species here has accommodated itself to the rocks and lays its egg in any rounded cavity. One nest I examined consisted of old torn feathers, a few stray sticks, and similar rubbish. The birds sat facing the wall and were as noisy as usual when disturbed.

Mr. Edward Newton (1861) has published the following notes on this species:

Round Island lies about twenty-five or thirty miles northeast of Mauritius, and is about a mile and half long by a mile wide. The land rises at once from the sea to about the height of a thousand feet, and is consequently very steep. Here the red-tailed tropic-bird (*Phaeton rubricauda*, Bodd.) breeds in very large numbers. They are the tamest birds I ever saw and do not know what fear is. They never attempt to leave their single egg or nestling at one's approach, but merely stick out their feathers and scream, pecking at one's legs with their beaks. It is the fashion on the island for visitors to remove the old bird from its egg by a slight shove, and then placing the foot gently on its head to draw out the long tail feathers. It resents this insult by screaming and snapping, but never tries to escape by flying or shuffling along the ground; in fact, like all birds which have their legs placed so far behind, they can not rise off a flat surface but require a drop of a few feet to give them an impetus. One that had an unusually tight tail I lifted up and held in the air by that appendage, and it flapped in my hand until the feathers gave way, when it flew off, but having left a young one behind, returned almost to my feet in two minutes or so as if nothing had happened. They do not appear at all particular in the choice of a place to deposit their single egg. They make no nest, but the shelter of an overhanging rock or the protection of the arched roots of the Vacoa (a species of *Pandanus*) seems preferred. On one occasion I found an old lady asleep on her egg, and she was extremely indignant at being stirred up and having her tail stolen. It is curious that I did not see a single egg without its owner sitting on it, and perhaps one may hence presume that they feed at night. In some places their nests were excessively numerous, their eggs or young occurring every few yards. There were to be found about as many young as eggs, some of the former almost as large as their mothers, and nearly able to fly, but I did not see a single immature bird that had started in life on its own account, though I have no doubt many had already done so. Most of the eggs had been incubated some time; in fact on blowing fifty or so of them I hardly think that I found half a dozen fresh, the majority being within a few days of hatching. I was rather short of baskets for carrying eggs, and consequently I did not get as many as I might have done. Certainly I had been told that the eggs might be picked up by the thousand, but I had not believed the statement. This species is much finer and larger than the yellow-billed one (*P. flavirostris*, Brandt). Of this there were a few about the island, but I did not find a single egg or see a bird on the ground.

Eggs.—The single egg of the red-tailed tropic-bird is similar to that of the foregoing species, but it is somewhat distinctly spotted, speckled, or scrawled on a clearer background, producing a handsomer effect. I can not improve on the following description by Doctor Fisher (1906):

The egg is particularly handsome, being thickly sprinkled with specks, spots, and even blotches of reddish brown (liver brown), in most of the specimens rather evenly distributed over the egg, but with an irregular dark area at the larger pole in some specimens. The ground color is a dirty white, almost obscured by the fine marks. Some examples have few spots, only fine sprinkling, so that the general tone of the egg at a distance is vinaceous. One specimen is almost white, while two others are very heavily washed at the blunt end with deep reddish chocolate. The eggs are ovate and a typical specimen measures 67 by 45 millimeters.

The measurements of 36 eggs, in various collections, average 65.5 by 46.6 millimeters; the four eggs showing the four extremes measure 73.5 by 46.5, 67 by 51, 59 by 43, and 64 by 41 millimeters.

Plumages.—I have never seen the downy young. What few immature birds I have seen would seem to indicate that the adult plumage, including the red tail, is acquired during the second winter. Gould (1865) describes the immature bird as follows:

The young birds for the first year are very different from the adults, being of a silky white without the roseate blush, with the whole of the upper surface broadly barred with black and with the black of the shafts of the primaries expanded into a spatulate form at the tips of the feathers.

Food.—He also makes the following reference as to the food of this species: " The contents of the stomach consisted of the beaks of cuttlefish." I have not been able to find any other references to its food, which probably does not differ materially from that of other tropic-birds.

Behavior.—Doctor Fisher (1906) refers to its flight as follows:

To see these birds at their best one must watch them flying about in the bright sunshine when their pale, salmon-pink plumage shines as though burnished, and the satiny feathers stand out like scales. The two long, red tail-feathers are possessed by both sexes, and the female is only a trifle less pink than the male. Usually when flying about they were quiet, and progressed by short, nervous wing beats, never attempting to sail. Occasionally, however, they swooped about our heads and made the neighborhood lively.

I regret that, as I have never seen the red-tailed tropic-bird in life, I can not add anything to the life history of such an attractive bird.

DISTRIBUTION.

Breeding range.—Warmer portions of the Indian and Pacific Oceans. East to the Galapagos Islands. South to the Kermadec Islands. West to Mauritius. North to the Bonin Islands and Laysan Island. Also on many intermediate islands.

Winter range.—Practically the same as the breeding range, extending north in the Pacific Ocean to the Linschoten Islands and Kruzenstern Rocks and south into New Zealand seas.

Casual records.—Taken once near Lower California, Guadalupe Island, April 23, 1897. This and the Laysan bird are now considered subspecifically distinct from the birds of the Indian Ocean and Australian seas (*Scaeophaethon rubricaudus rothschildi* [Mathews]).

Egg dates.—Bonin Islands: Five records August 15 and 27, September 14, and December 1. Galapagos Islands: One record, March 6. Laysan Island: One record, May 23. Mauritius Island: One record, September 15. Lord Howe Island: One record, December 3.

Family SULIDAE, Gannets.

SULA DACTYLATRA Lesson.

BLUE-FACED BOOBY.

HABITS.

The blue-faced booby is an inhabitant of the tropical oceans, breeding as far north as the West Indies, in the Atlantic, and as far as San Benedicto Island, off the coast of Mexico, in the Pacific Ocean. Its principal breeding grounds seem to be on the islands of the Hawaiian group in the mid-Pacific.

Nesting.—Dr. Walter K. Fisher (1906) has given us the following account of the nesting habits of this species on Laysan Island:

On Laysan the masked, or blue-faced booby lives only on the sedgy slope facing the ocean, exposed to spray-laden winds and close to the booming surf. On the inner slopes of the island the species is entirely absent, being replaced by its somewhat smaller congener *Sula piscator*. We found *cyanops* most plentiful on the northeast, east, and southern exposures, where the narrow littoral slope is broadest, but on the west side, where a little bluff replaces the seaward slope, the birds are absent. The homes of these boobies are not crowded, but are scattered here and there over the greensward and from a distance are easily recognized by a little round patch of sand and the sentinel bird. Two limy, white eggs are laid on the bare sand, with usually no semblance of a nest, or occasionally there may be a little dried sedge scratched about the eggs or young.

Dr. Thomas H. Streets found this booby breeding on Christmas Island, though not very abundantly. He says (1877) : "They build no nest, but scratch a slight concavity in the fine coral sand, where the egg is deposited." He speaks, however, of a nest he found on Palmyra Island, which "was well constructed of grass."

Mr. A. W. Anthony (1898*f*) writes of their nesting habits in the Revillagigedo Islands as follows:

On May 19 we found some colonies of blue-faced boobys on Clarion Island, in which there were fresh eggs and young birds, and even a few well-grown young were seen. The nests were mere hollows in the coral sand, anywhere from just above high tide to the top of the island, at 500 feet altitude. The nests were all vigorously defended by the birds, who greeted our approach with deafening shrieks and threatening bills. Indeed, their bill is not to be despised. It is as sharp as a bayonet and is wielded with no little force, as my shins could testify after an hour's collecting among the nests. If the Webster boobys required a kick to drive them from their nests, the blue-faced required a charge of dynamite. I have repeatedly put my foot under a sitting bird—gently to save the eggs—and thrown her as far as I could—with vigor to save my shins—but before I could grab the eggs, was driven back by a shrieking demon in snowy white that charged at me with agility surprising in so large a bird. On one occasion a bird came in from out at sea and with a scream threw itself between me and a sitting bird I was approaching, constantly moving about so as to interpose its body between its nest and the threatening danger. The defense being so spirited and gallant I concluded that the eggs were far advanced in incubation.

I several times found the present species sitting on large sea shells, which in shape and size somewhat resembled their eggs. The "boobies" seemed perfectly contented with the substitute, and I often supplied them with the shells after taking their eggs. These they immediately tucked under their breasts with their bills, and accepted the change as a matter of course. One nest, from which I took one egg, was supplied with two shells. Both were tucked away, but next day I found that one had been discarded. Others which were incubating two eggs accepted two shells in exchange and were sitting on them ten days later, when we left the island.

Eggs.—The set generally consists of two eggs, though sometimes only one. The shape varies from ovate to elongate oval or short fusiform, according to Doctor Fisher (1906). The ground color is very pale blue or bluish white, but the egg is generally completely covered with a thick coating of calcareous deposit which is dull white in color and often much nest stained; the surface is smooth and soft; the coating is easily scraped off, showing the bluish tint beneath it.

The measurements of 41 eggs, in various collections, average 67 by 46 millimeters; the eggs showing the four extremes measure 77 by 47, 65.2 by 48.5, and 60 by 40 millimeters.

Young.—Both sexes incubate, and while one is sitting the other often stands on guard nearby. They are exceedingly tame or stupid, merely hissing at the intruder when approached. Doctor Fisher (1906) says:

It is a curious fact that although there are two eggs, only one young is reared. Often all signs of the second egg were removed, as if the young had hatched and had been devoured by a parent or some marauding *Fregata*. But more frequently there would be one nestling and one egg. Sometimes this egg was spoiled, sometimes contained an embryo. In one case I found two newly hatched young, one of which had already been trampled to death. Professor Nutting saw one large nestling and one small, still alive, but I doubt if it lived long. The presence of only one young bird has been noted in the eastern Pacific at Clipperton Island by R. H. Beck, and Rothschild mentions the same fact for Laysan. The voracity of the bird first hatched is probably responsible for the death of the second.

The young bird nearly always keeps its head under the parent, although the greater part of its body may be exposed to the sun. Both old birds take turns in sitting on the eggs or watching the nestling. Occasionally both will be seen standing guard together in an absurd statuesque pose, or gazing seaward or at the sky on the lookout for winged marauders. From time to time they utter a very hoarse strident cry.

The young are fed on semidigested food; the process is described by Doctor Fisher (1906) as follows:

The young one inserts its head fairly into the throat of the parent, in a decidedly gruesome manner, and catches the disgorged food. In fact, the young one's head went so far into the parent's throat that I became solicitous for its safety. Flying fish, swallowed whole, seem to be their favorite food, judging by remains scattered about nests and a stomach examined.

When the old birds exchange places, one slips off the nestling and the other immediately takes its place, as if fearing an attack from a frigate bird. The boobies appear to exhibit affection for their young. I have seen them gazing at the fuzzy-white ball with evident pride in their otherwise stolid countenances, and on one occasion saw an old bird carefully lay dry sedge over the exposed and not too heavily feathered hind parts of the young.

Plumages.—The young is covered with soft, thick, yellowish-white down. The immature, or first year, plumage is described by Dr. Thomas H. Streets (1877) as follows: " The brown color of the back and upper surface of the wings has a grayish tinge; the head and neck all around dark brown, as in *S. leucogastra*, except that the dark color does not extend as far down in the breast as in the latter." There is not sufficient material available to show the subsequent sequence of plumages, but apparently the fully adult plumage is not completed until the second winter or later.

Food.—Mr. A. J. Campbell (1901), referring to the flight and feeding habits of this booby, quotes the following observation of Mr. F. M. Hobbs, of Norfolk Island:

I think the gannet is the clumsiest on the ground of all the birds which frequent this locality, but once it gets on the wing, it seems one of the proudest. I have often watched them from the whaling boats darting down after their prey. They descend at a wonderfully rapid rate, and must go to a considerable depth below the surface of the water, for they keep under for a long time. The flying fish seem to be their favorite food, but I have never seen a gannet pursue them while they (the fish) are flying.

Its most troublesome enemy seems to be the man-o-war bird, as the following incident, related by Dr. Homer R. Dill (1912) will illustrate:

Not far from this spot we saw a man-o-war bird pursuing a booby which had just returned from fishing, with a crop full of fish. At first it seemed as though the booby would outfly its pursuer, but its load was too heavy. The man-o-war bird overtook the booby, seized it by the tail, raised itself in the air, and turned the booby completely over. Being thus rudely overturned the booby lost control and quickly disgorged the contents of its crop, and the man-o-war bird actually caught the fish as it came from the booby's mouth.

Behavior.—Messrs. Snodgrass and Heller (1902), referring to the habits of the blue-faced booby in the Galapagos Islands, say:

The most common note uttered by the adults was a loud quack. Occasionally a sharp whistle was heard, but no special significance to this sound was observed. The species was observed fishing at sea, 300 miles from the island, and it is probable that the birds, in pursuit of food, daily travel more than 100 miles from their breeding grounds.

DISTRIBUTION.

Breeding range.—On some of the Lesser Antilles (the Grenadines, [Battowia and Kick-em-Jenny]) and off the coasts of Venezuela (Los Hermanos Islands), Colombia (Gorgonall Islands) and Yucatan (Alacron Reefs). Formerly on the Bahama Islands (Santo Domingo Key).

Birds which breed in various islands in the Pacific and Indian Oceans, from the coast of Mexico westward have now been subdivided into other subspecies.

Winter range.—Practically the same as the breeding range, within 30′ of the equator.

Casual records.—Said to be accidental in southern Florida. Taken once in Louisiana (Avery Island, August, 1915).

Egg dates.—Mexican Islands: Twelve records, March 20 to May 21; six records, April 26 to May 21.

SULA NEBOUXII Milne-Edwards.

BLUE-FOOTED BOOBY.

HABITS.

This species is one of several tropical and semitropical forms which have been included in our check list because they are to be found in Lower California, but nowhere else within our limits. I have never been able to understand why this region should be included within the limits covered by our check list, for politically and geographically it is a part of Mexico and faunally it is much more closely allied to that country than to our own. Including this remote and narrow strip of Mexico adds to our list a number of otherwise foreign species and subspecies, which few American ornithologists are ever likely to see.

Our information regarding the blue-footed booby comes from those fortunate ornithologists who have visited the islands in the Gulf of California and off the west coast of Mexico and the Galapagos Islands. Our attention was first called to it by Col. N. S. Goss (1888a) who found it breeding abundantly on San Pedro Martir Isle in the Gulf of California. It was described and named in his honor, as a new species, under the name *Sula gossi*, but it was subsequently discovered that the species had been previously described as *Sula nebouxii*.

Courtship.—Mr. E. W. Gifford (1913) gives the following account of the interesting courtship of this species:

At Finger Point, Chatham Island, in the middle of February, there were several blue-footed boobies standing about in the vicinity of some old nests three or four hundred feet above the ocean. Whenever a bird alighted, there was a great deal of squawking and bowing and waddling carried on by it and its mate. In latter March during the mating-season at Tagus Cove, Albemarle Island, they were quite demonstrative, the mated birds seeming to talk to each other, and managing to keep up an incessant racket. One of them as a rule did considerable strutting about, lifting its feet very high with each step, and appearing to us very ridiculous. They made a very elaborate bow uttering one or two short notes at the same time. With the breast almost touching the ground, the neck stretched upwards, and the wings outspread but held vertically, the ceremony of bowing would last for about half a minute.

Nesting.—In the same paper he refers to the nesting habits of the blue-footed booby as follows:

The nest of this species was like that of the Peruvian booby, a mere depression in the earth in which two eggs were laid. On Hood and Champion Islands blue-footed boobies nested in the vicinity of the shore, sometimes along the tops of cliffs, at other times close to the water. The birds at Hood Island in September, 1905, were nesting beside white glazed rocks and in the broiling sun, with no shelter whatsoever. Many of them were sitting on their nests with mouth open panting with heat and thirst. On Daphne, they nested on the sandy floor of the crater, which is three or four hundred feet deep, and very hot, as it is protected on all sides from the wind. Only one pair was seen nesting outside the crater. At Tagus Cove they nested on the broad ledges and tops of the low tufaceous cliffs.

The following notes on the time and place of breeding of the blue-footed booby, taken in conjunction with the observations of other expeditions, point to an almost continuous breeding season. We found eggs, young in the down, and fully fledged young at Hood Island, in September and October; both naked young and young assuming juvenal plumage at Hood in February; eggs, birds in down, and well-feathered young at Champion in October; young in the down at Champion in February; naked young at Brattle in October; eggs and downy young at Daphne in November; large young of various ages at Daphne in July; fresh eggs at Tagus Cove in March; and one large young one at Tower in September. There are two young hatched; but by the time they reach the partially-feathered state, seldom more than one has survived.

Mr. H. H. Bailey (1906) found the species breeding abundantly on Isabella Island, off the west coast of Mexico, of which he writes:

All around our camp, which was pitched under the low bushes bordering the little bay, were pairs of boobies, one or the other of the pair covering the eggs while the mate stood close by. This, however, was during the middle of the day, the fishing being mostly done before ten a. m., and after four in the afternoon, during which time one or the other of the birds always remained on the eggs to keep the gulls from stealing them. The poor boobies had a hard time of it here, as the man-o'-war birds nested just back of them in the bushes, and lucky was the booby who passed in the entrance of the bay without having to disgorge part, or may be the whole, of its day's catch to this robber. Numbers of nests were on the sandy beach just above high tide while others were still farther back under the shrubbery and below the man-o'-war birds, and still another colony was situated on the top of the rocky southwestern side of the island. All the birds were very tame, and I think had not been molested since the expedition of the Biological Survey in 1897, as Mr. Beermaker on landing in search of guano deposits in March, 1904, had not found them breeding at that time, nor had he disturbed them in any way. When I first started in to get a series of eggs, I used my foot to remove the booby from them, but after the first few attempts I found that the sharp beak whenever it came in contact with my leg drew blood, and almost penetrated through my cowhide boots, so I soon abandoned this method. Two eggs were generally the complete set and but three sets of three were discovered while on the island, and in some cases highly incubated single eggs were found. In case of the latter I am inclined to think the gulls had stolen one of the eggs after incubation had commenced. No nest was made, a slight hollow being scratched in the sand or earth, while those on the rocky side of the island simply deposited them on the bare rock or on the little drifted earth that happened to be on its surface. During the moonlight nights these boobies could be seen going and coming, and I have no doubt their best catches were made at this time, as they were then unmolested by the man-o'-war birds. Single fresh eggs gathered by the crew were made into omelets, but the flavor was rather rank.

Dr. E. W. Nelson (1899) relates an amusing experience with these birds in the same colony, as follows:

About 10 o'clock the following night a visit was paid to the nesting boobies. The night was calm, and taking a lighted candle I walked out a short distance to an opening in the bushes where there were twenty or thirty nests. The females were found on their eggs with the males standing close beside them. When the strange visitor appeared in their midst the birds set up a continuous series of hoarse cries and, like so many moths, seemed to become fascinated by the light. They started up on all sides, and trooping within the circle of bright light, began to run around me in a ring about 20 feet in diameter. They ran in single file from right to left and presented a most ludicrous sight. Occasionally one fell on its breast, whereupon the others scrambled over the fallen bird until it regained its feet and rejoined the procession. One of the number was suddenly possessed with a desire to run around one of my legs, and, although seized by the head several times and tossed out among its companions, persisted in returning to the same place and continuing its gyrations.

Eggs.—The blue-footed booby lays usually one or two eggs, rarely three, perhaps more commonly two. In shape they are usually elliptical ovate or elongate ovate. The shell is more or less rough or uneven, due to its chalky covering. The color of the shell is very pale blue or bluish white, which is generally mainly concealed by a thin chalky coating, which is dirty white and often much nest stained.

The measurements of 62 eggs, in various collections, average 62.7 by 42.5 millimeters; the eggs showing the four extremes measure **69** by 44, 68.5 by **48, 57.8** by 41.2, and 63.5 by **38.8** millimeters.

Young.—Incubation seems to be performed by the female alone, but she is constantly attended by her mate, except when he is off fishing, and is fed by him at the nest, as it is necessary for the eggs to be guarded from their various enemies. Mr. Gifford (1913) says: "The half-fledged young exhibited considerable pugnacity. When one was shoved into a neighbor's domain a fight ensued, the birds seizing each other by the beak and then having a tug-of-war for perhaps a minute."

Plumages.—The downy young is pure white. Two young birds in the United States National Museum, in one of which the head and neck is still covered with white down, show the development of the juvenal plumage. In this plumage the head and neck is variegated or washed with " pale brownish drab "; the variegated effect is produced by the paler tips of the feathers, which are long and narrow; the back and wing coverts are "sepia," with whitish edgings on all the feathers, producing a whitish interscapular saddle; the breast is pale brownish, shading off gradually into the color of the neck; the under parts are variegated or mottled with dusky, particularly on the flanks. How long this plumage is worn or at what age the adult plumage is assumed does not seem to be satisfactorily shown by the material available.

Food.—The food of this booby consists principally and probably wholly of fish. Mr. Gifford (1913) describes the methods employed as follows:

The fish were almost invariably caught by diving, although an occasional flying fish was chased and caught while in the air. It was a common thing to see blue-footed boobies fishing in flocks, often all diving simultaneously. They dive with wings half closed and neck rigid and straight, striking the water with great force. As all would not get fish when diving in a flock, there was usually considerable squabbling over captures. One day a booby was seen to enter the water obliquely at a very small angle, appearing quickly on the surface again and continuing its line of flight without a pause.

Behavior.—The same writer says of its actions:

When offshore and on a journey, the blue-footed boobies frequently flew in single file, all following the undulations of the leader. On the south coast of Albemarle Island, in May, they were noted flying toward Brattle Island each evening. Single birds met with offshore usually circled about the schooner. The birds noted about the bays and coves had the habit of continually looking downward when flying, apparently in search of fish.

When not fishing, the blue-footed boobies frequently congregated on the low black lava points which jut into the sea, the assemblages varying from two or three to thirty or forty. Single birds and pairs are often seen standing on the ledges and on the tops of sea cliffs. On south James they were seen in the mangroves. It was not unusual to find them asleep in broad daylight. An entire flock, however, was never caught napping, two or three birds always being awake and on the lookout.

As to the migrations and the habits of the blue-footed booby when absent from its breeding grounds, I can not find that anything has been published.

DISTRIBUTION.

Breeding range.—From the Gulf of California (San Pedro Martir Island) south along the west coast of Mexico (Tres Marias Islands), the Revillagigedo Islands (Clarion Island), the Galapagos Islands, and on the coast of Peru (Lobos de Tierra Island).

Winter range.—Mainly near its breeding grounds. Ranges south to Chile.

Egg dates.—Mexican islands: Twenty-nine records, March 7 to May 21; fifteen records, April 10 and 11.

SULA LEUCOGASTRIS (Boddaert).

BOOBY.

HABITS.

The common brown booby, or white-bellied booby, often called the brown gannet, is a widely distributed species among the islands of the tropical seas of both hemispheres. At the present time it is known to be a North American bird merely as a straggler or an occasional visitor on our coasts, though its breeds abundantly at various localities in the West Indies.

Nesting.—According to Audubon (1840) it formerly bred on one of the Dry Tortugas; I quote from his account of this colony as follows:

About eight miles to the northeast of the Tortugas Lighthouse lies a small sand bar a few acres in extent, called Booby Island on account of the number of birds of this species that resort to it during the breeding season, and to it we accordingly went. We found it not more than a few feet above the surface of the water, but covered with boobies, which lay basking in the sunshine and pluming themselves. Our attempt to land on the island before the birds should fly off proved futile, for before we were within fifty yards of it they had all betaken themselves to flight, and were dispersing in various directions. The nest of the booby is placed on the top of a bush, at a height of from four to ten feet. It is large and flat, formed of a few dry sticks, covered and matted, with sea weeds in great quantity. I have no doubt that they return to the same nest many years in succession and repair it as occasion requires. In all the nests which I examined only one egg was found, and as most of the birds were sitting and some of the eggs had the chick nearly ready for exclusion it is probable that these birds raise only a single young one, like the common gannet or solan goose.

This account of Audubon's has been discredited by some modern writers, who think he must have been mistaken as to the owners of the nests, because this species is known to nest only on the ground and to lay two eggs instead of one. But, as Audubon studied the birds at close range and shot some 30 specimens, which he described and figured accurately, I see no reason for doubting his statement; moreover, Baird, Brewer, and Ridgway (1884) write that "Peale found it breeding on nearly all the coral islands visited" by the Wilkes exploring expedition, and that "the nests were constructed of sticks and weeds on bushes and low trees, and were generally found to contain but one egg."

The best modern account of the habits of the booby on its breeding grounds is by Dr. Frank M. Chapman (1908a). His studies were made on Cay Verde in the Bahamas, which he describes as follows:

Cay Verde lies on the eastern edge of the Columbus Bank, 30 miles southeast of Little Ragged Island. It is about 0.5 mile long by 0.25 mile in greatest width, the longer axis lying approximately north and south, and, roughly estimated, contains some 40 acres. On the west and south, or shallow, bank sides there are steeply shelving beaches, where under favorable conditions a landing may be easily made. On the eastern side the deep blue waters of the ocean break directly against the characteristic water-worn limestone rock, of which Cay Verde, in common with other Bahama Islands, is composed. At the northern end, where the islet terminates in a point, this rock is but little above sea level. Southward it gradually increases in height and, with pronounced irregularities in coast line, reaches a blufflike elevation of 75 feet at the southeastern extremity of the islet.

About one-eighth of the surface of the island is covered with a dense growth, chiefly of sea grape (*Coccolobis uvifera*), but with a liberal mixture, mainly about the borders, of a "prickly-pear" cactus (*Opuntia*) and sea lavender (*Tournefortia gnaphalodes*). Where sufficient soil has accumulated the remainder of the island supports a growth of coarse grasses, sparse on the higher and rockier portions, more luxuriant in the lower portions, particularly about the margins of a small salt pond, the size of which was dependent upon conditions of tide and wind. There is no fresh water on the cay.

He remained on the island from April 9 to 11, 1907, and wrote a full account of his observations, from which I quote in part:

A partial census of eggs and young led to the conclusion that there were about 1,500 pairs of boobies nesting on Cay Verde. They were distributed in several groups, where the comparatively level surface and sandy soil furnished favorable nesting conditions. In most instances the young were covered with down, with the brown second plumage more or less evident in wings and tail. A few birds of the year were already awing, and several nests contained fresh eggs. For the greater number of birds, however, the nesting season, as Bryant has stated, evidently begins in February.

The booby's nests on Cay Verde were usually slight hollows in the ground, with often a scanty lining or rim of dried grasses, but in some instances even this humble preparation for housekeeping was lacking, and the eggs were laid without pretence of nest.

About 98 per cent of the boobies nesting on Cay Verde had young, some of which were newly hatched, while a few were on the wing, but the largest number were beginning to acquire flight feathers. Of the nests, 35 contained eggs, of which 21 held 2 eggs, while in 14 there was but 1, but possibly in some, if not most, of these another egg would have been laid. As a rule, therefore, there were 2 eggs, this confirming previously recorded observations on the nesting habits of this species. On the other hand, 2 young were the exception. Of 740 nests counted by Doctor Mayer on the east side of the cay, only 2 contained young, and both pairs were well grown and approximately the same size.

Examination of the eggs contained in sets of two showed that either there was a marked difference in the development of the embryos or that one or both eggs were infertile. For example, of 13 nests containing 2 eggs, in 3 nests both were bad; in 10 both were good; but with every good pair there was about a week's difference in the age of the embryo. In 6 nests, each containing one young and one egg, 5 of the eggs were decomposed.

With those boobies which lay 2 eggs, apparently a week intervenes between the laying of the first and second egg, and to this unusual irregularity, in connection with the high percentage of infertility, we attribute the discrepancy between the number of eggs laid and the number of young reared.

Dr. Alexander Wetmore has contributed the following notes on another interesting colony of this species:

Off the west coast of Porto Rico, seven leagues from the port of Aguadilla, lies the small island of Desecheo, hot and dry for a large part of the year, but swept occasionally by tempestuous downpours of rain. The island is little more than an isolated rock rising from the restless waters of Mona passage with its treacherous changing currents, profound depths all about cutting it off from other land connection. In shape it is roughly an ellipse a mile and a half long and three-fourths of a mile wide with abrupt rocky shores and steep slopes rising into two pointed hills, the highest about three hundred feet above the sea. Three or four small indentations boast a rough gravelly beach where with care a landing can be made in the surf and behind these are small semicircles backed by water-worn cliffs on the landward side and floored with sand and huge rocks fallen from the overhang above. The thin soil of the island supports a considerable growth of vegetation, bound with thorny creepers into an impassable jungle, with only small grass-grown openings offering a pathway. The West Indian birch (*Bursera simaruba*), with its trunk and limbs curiously shortened, thickened and gnarled in the struggle for life, is the common tree, while growths of three species of cactuses are common.

On this interesting island, boasting of but eleven resident avine forms, the booby (*Sula leucogastra*) has chosen its home and here in June, 1912, I spent a few days in studying the habits of these ungainly birds. Between eight and ten thousand of them at a conservative estimate occupied the rookeries, spread over the entire island, but they were so distributed on the steep brush-covered slopes that a more accurate census was impracticable. Though they were seen at the top of the higher of the two hills, the greater number were found within four hundred feet of the beach, gathered usually in groups. By my fishermen they were said to nest from late June until October, but these dates are very uncertain. The young now were nearly all caring for themselves, though a few showed traces of down feathers clinging to the tips of the feathers about the head, and I would consider February or March a more probable date for their nesting. A few were seen playing with sticks and straws as though contemplating nest building, but the sexual organs of those taken were little developed. Birds in all possible intermediate plumages were seen and immature specimens were much more common than the fully adult with smooth dark brown heads and white underparts.

The young birds were averse to flying when they could avoid it, but preferred to scramble away under the bushes awkwardly, falling over sticks and stones in their haste. Even the adults could not take flight from a level surface, but had to launch themselves from the cliffs and sail down for a distance before being able to rise with strong wing beats. From the limbs of the trees they flew readily, but on the ground I captured several by merely pinning them down with my gun barrel. They showed little real fear of me and many stood their ground, snapping and hissing, and it was a point of wisdom to keep beyond reach of their sharp powerful beaks. It rather gave me the shivers occasionally to see one flounder and flop through and over a bed of prickly pear, but the birds seemed careless of the thorns. Numbers were seen with spines or even small lobes of cactus hanging to the feet or wings, and the dissemination of the plants by this means can be readily pictured. At a gunshot there was a great rush among those near by, and the air for a few minutes would be filled with them circling and crossing, frequently almost within reach. The confusion among them would cease gradually, and they would soon be all around again, eyeing me curiously or forgetful of my presence, busy with their own affairs. On the rough limestone blocks above the sea they sat in rows in the blazing sun, rather upright, occasionally waddling along a foot or two, but usually motionless. Birds came and went during the day, flying out to sea to feed, sometimes at considerable distances off shore, but they were most active in the morning and evening. The common call note was a loud *quack quack quack*, and at night, whenever I awoke, there was always much commotion among them.

Eggs.—From the foregoing quotations it would seem as if two eggs was the normal set with the common booby, but apparently sometimes only one is laid. The eggs vary considerably in shape and size, but usually they are elliptical ovate, elongate ovate, or elliptical oval. The underlying color of the shell is pale bluish white, but it is usually completely or nearly covered with a thin layer of white calcareous deposit. In some eggs this deposit is uneven, broken, or rough, but usually it has a smooth, clean, lustreless surface.

The measurements of 40 eggs, in the United States National Museum and the writer's collections, average 59.4 by 40.2 millimeters; the eggs showing the four extremes measure **65.5** by 41, 62 by **42.5**, **52.5** by 40, and 56.5 by **34.5** millimeters.

The male assists the female in the duties of incubation, but the period of incubation seems to be unknown. The behavior of the birds during the incubating and brooding period is fully described by Doctor Chapman (1908a) as follows:

One or both of the adults remain, as a rule, with the young. On March 9 the birds awoke at 5.15 a m., when for the ensuing 10 or 15 minutes there was a subdued kind of quacking, and some birds were seen flying. At 5.30 several hundred birds left the rookery in a body to go a-fishing, this being the first general movement. Individuals returned at intervals during the day and evidently changed places with the bird left at the nest, which in turn went out to feed and to gather fish for the young. There was no concerted return movement until dusk, when flocks of birds came in from the sea, the last comers not arriving until after dark. In the meantime the man-o'-war birds had retired, and it is not impossible that the boobies have acquired the habit of " staying out late " to avoid being robbed of their food by the man-o'-war birds, which at times attacked them as they approached the cay and forced them to disgorge.

Sitting or brooding birds spend the night upon the nest with the mates standing at their sides, but the close resemblance of the sexes rendered it impossible to distinguish them at this time. When the young is too large to be brooded, it passes the night on the ground between the two parents, which stand on either side, all three with their heads tucked under their scapulars.

When perched on rocks about the border of the island, boobies showed a decided fear of man and generally flew before one had approached to within 30 yards of them; but when on their nests they were conspicuously tame, the degree of tameness being related to the advance of the nesting season. A bird with newly hatched young would not, as a rule, leave the nest unless actually forced to do so, and it would strike so viciously at anyone approaching that it was well not to venture within its reach. This was the extreme development of parental instinct, which now gradually diminished as the young increased in size. Evidently as a result of excitement caused by our presence, the birds which remained to defend their young threatened us with their bills, picked up bits of sticks or grasses only to drop them and pick them up again, and even struck at their own young in a confused and aimless manner. The young also had this habit. The report of a gun occasioned but little alarm among the boobies, some of which, with their young near my feet, did not fly when the gun was discharged.

In spite of the apparent sociability expressed by their communal habits, the boobies immediately resented trespass on their home site by one of their own kind. Where the nature of the ground permitted, their nests were placed with more or less regularity 6 to 8 feet from one another. As long as a bird re-- mained within its own domain, having a diameter of approximately 6 to 8 feet, it was not molested; but let it or its young advance beyond these limits and they were promptly attacked.

So closely, however, are the birds confined to their own little areas that difficulties of this kind are rare, and under normal conditions peace reigns in the rookery. But when, as we walked through the rookery, the birds, in escaping from the larger evil, forgot the lesser one and inadvertently backed onto a neighbors' territory, the unusual cause of the trespass was not accepted as an excuse and they found the " frying-pan " worse than the " fire," as the enraged owner, with bristling feathers, furiously assailed them with open bill, sometimes taking hold. At these times and whenever the birds were alarmed, they gave utterance to hoarse, raucous screams or screeches, though as a rule they were comparatively silent.

Young.—Regarding the young birds he says:

The young booby is born practically naked, and since exposure to the sun before the downy plumage is developed would result fatally, it is constantly brooded, one parent immediately replacing the other when the brooding bird is relieved. Brooding continues even when the white down is well developed and the young bird, then too large to be wholly covered by the parent, lies flat on the ground, the head exposed, the eyes closed, apparently dead. This relaxed attitude is also taken by young which are not sheltered by the parent, and we were not a little surprised on several occasions when about to examine an evidently dead bird to have it jump up, and with a trumpeting call, blare at us with open mouth. Nor do they rely only on the voice for defense, but use the bill effectively, and, as has been remarked, they possess with the adult, the somewhat ludicrous habit of venting their feelings by picking up bits of stick and grass.

Compared with other rookeries I have visited, the mortality among young boobies on Cay Verde—aside from the prenatal mortality already referred to— was surprisingly small. This I attribute to the isolation of the cay, which permits the birds to rear their young with little or no intrusion by man, whose presence, even as a visitor, results in great confusion and consequent death among the young of ground-nesting colonial birds.

The young were fed on squids and fishes, which, in a more or less digested condition, they obtained by thrusting their heads and necks down the parent's throat, a manner of feeding common to all the Steganopodes with whose habits I am familiar (including *Pelecanus, Fregata, Phalacrocorax,* and *Anhinga*). I have not, however, seen *Phaethon* feeding its young, and it would be interesting to know whether this tern-like member of the order has a similar method of administering food.

Evidently but one brood is reared, since approximately three months must elapse after the egg is laid before the young can fly and care for itself.

Plumages.—The young booby is hatched naked, but the down soon begins to sprout in the various feather tracts and shortly clothes the whole body, head, and neck, except the naked face, with a pure white, soft, woolly covering. The juvenal, or first real plumage, appears first on the wings, the primaries coming first; the tail soon follows, so that all the flight feathers are developed at an early age and considerably in advance of the body plumage; the latter appears first on the breast. Doctor Chapman (1908*a*) describes the juvenal plumage as follows:

In the succeeding specimen the second or juvenal plumage is essentially complete, except upon the foreneck, where it is just emerging. This bird is almost uniform grayish-brown above; the upper tail coverts are slightly browner; the exposed portion of the remiges and rectrices show a somewhat frosted effect; the primaries are decidedly blackish; the lower breast and abdomen are grayer than the dorsal plumage; the upper breast (with which the throat feathers would apparently agree) is decidedly browner.

This plumage is apparently worn for about a year or until the first complete postnuptial molt. I have seen young birds in this wholly brown plumage in July, September, January, and March and have seen birds molting out of this plumage and into the white-bellied adult plumage in May, in July, and in September. Young birds therefore probably become indistinguishable from adults when about a year and a half old.

The small amount of material available for study makes it difficult to arrive at any satisfactory conclusions as to the sequence of plumages and molts of this species. I have seen but one adult in full molt; this is a July bird in which the primaries are in such condition that the bird must have been practically incapable of flight.

Food.—The food of the booby consists almost entirely of fish, chiefly flying fish and mullets, many of them of large size, which it is very expert in catching by diving. Audubon (1840) says:

The expansibility of the gullet of this species enables it to swallow fishes of considerable size, and on such occasions their mouth seems to spread to an unusual width. In the throats of several individuals that were shot as they were returning to their nests, I found mullets measuring seven or eight inches, that must have weighed fully half a pound.

Mr. Austin H. Clark (1903), writing of the habits of this species on the Venezuela coast, says:

They seemed to approach the land solely for the purpose of feeding, after which they withdrew to open water. Just off Carúpano there was a certain spot to which every day came hundreds of sea birds of many species to fish. Over one-half of this congregation were common brown pelicans and most of the rest were these gannets. Overhead soared a score or more frigate birds, while various gulls and terns composed the remainder. All the larger members of this vast flock acted in perfect unison, wheeling about until a sufficient altitude was obtained, all diving with a great splash, then all slowly rising again to repeat the performance.

Single boobies may often be seen fishing in company with solitary pelicans, imitating in every way the actions of their larger companions, diving at the same time, and rising simultaneously. Mr. Outram Bangs has suggested to me that perhaps the booby, being smaller and more active, finds a good fare in the fish which the uncouth pelican fails to catch.

Dr. Henry Bryant (1861) says of its feeding habits:

The booby is, I think, the most expert diver that I am acquainted with; no matter in what position it may be, whether flying in a straight line, sailing in a circle, just rising from the water, or swimming on the surface, the instant it sees its prey it plunges after it. I have frequently seen one dive from the wing, rise to the surface, and dive in rapid succession five or six times; and on taking flight again, dive before it had risen more than two or three feet from the surface, and perhaps catch a dozen fish in the space of a minute.

There is nothing graceful in its style; it is apparently work and not pleasure.

On one of the keys I visited, called Booby Key, near Green Key, I saw a great number of a species of *Anolis* of a dark, almost black color, entirely unlike any seen elsewhere, but they were so timid and active in their movements that I could not procure a specimen. The stomach contained a great many varieties of fish; among them a cottus, a parrot fish, flatfish of two species, and some large prawns; but their principal food seemed to be flying fish and a species of hemirhamphus.

Behavior.—Audubon (1840) describes its flight, as follows:

The flight of the booby is graceful and extremely protracted. They pass swiftly at a height of from twenty yards to a foot or two from the surface, often following the troughs of the waves to a considerable distance, their wings extended at right angles to the body; then, without any apparent effort, raising themselves and allowing the rolling waters to break beneath them, when they tack about, and sweep along in a contrary direction in search of food, much in the manner of the true petrels. Now, if you follow an individual, you see that it suddenly stops short, plunges headlong into the water, pierces with its powerful beak and secures a fish, emerges again with inconceivable ease, after a short interval rises on wing, performs a few wide circlings, and makes off toward some shore. At this time its flight is different, being performed by flappings for twenty or thirty paces, with alternate sailings of more than double that space. When overloaded with food they alight on the water, where, if undisturbed, they appear to remain for hours at a time, probably until digestion has afforded them relief.

The booby is usually a silent bird, but when excited it is said to utter loud and raucous cries which have been likened by various observers to the croak of a raven, the honk of a goose, or the hoarse quack of a duck.

Undoubtedly the booby's worst enemy is the man-o-war bird, to which it pays frequent and regular tribute, but Audubon (1840) says: "Their principal enemies during the breeding season are the American crow and the fish crow, both of which destroy their eggs, and the turkey buzzard, which devours their young while yet unfledged."

Winter.—After the young birds are able to fly the boobies leave their breeding grounds and begin their fall and winter wanderings up and down the coasts, following the schools of fish, on which they feed. These wanderings, which can hardly be called migrations, sometimes take them as far north as Massachusetts.

DISTRIBUTION.

Breeding range.—The Bahama Islands (Cay Verde, San Domingo Key, Berry Islands, etc.); some of the West Indies (Porto Rico,

Jamaica, St. Thomas, Dominica, St. Vincent, Battowia, etc.); the Cayman Islands; off the coasts of Venezuela (Los Testigos and Los Hermanos Islands), Honduras (Belize and Swan Islands), Costa Rica (Uvita Island), and Brazil (San Paulo and Fernando Noronha); and in the tropical Atlantic Ocean (St. Paul Rocks and Ascension Island). Birds which breed on islands in the western Pacific and the Indian Oceans are probably subspecifically distinct. Breeding grounds protected on Desecheo Island reservation, Porto Rico.

Winter range.—The Caribbean Sea, Gulf of Mexico, and Atlantic Ocean, from the Bahamas and Florida south to the Straits of Magellan and Ascension Island.

Casual records.—Has wandered to Massachusetts (Cape Cod, September 17, 1878), Bermuda (October 3, 1847, and September 26, 1875), and Louisiana (below New Orleans, two taken in September, 1884).

Egg dates.—Bahama Islands: Sixteen records, January 14 to June 12; eight records, April 15 to May 19.

SULA BREWSTERI Goss.

BREWSTER BOOBY.

HABITS.

This species is in much the same class geographically as the blue-footed booby; neither would be included in our fauna except for the inclusion of that extra-limital strip, Lower California. It somewhat resembles *Sula leucogastris* and takes the place of that species on the Pacific coast of Mexico.

Nesting.—It was first described by Col. N. S. Goss (1888*a*), who found it breeding on San Pedro Martir Isle in the Gulf of California; he says of its breeding habits:

The birds were not wild, but their nesting places as a whole were not in as exposed situations as those of the blue-footed; they seemed to prefer the shelves and niches on the sides of the rocks. They lay two eggs, and in all cases collect a few sticks, seaweed, and often old wing or tail feathers; these are generally placed in a circle to fit the body, with a view, I think, to keep the eggs that lie upon the rock from rolling out. There is but little material on or about the isle out of which a nest can be made.

The birds must commence laying as early as the 10th of February, for I found in many cases young birds from half to two-thirds grown—white, downy little fellows with deep bluish black skins—that, in places where they can, wander about regardless of the nests where they were hatched.

Mr. H. H. Bailey (1906) gives us the following account of the habits of the Brewster booby on the west coast of Mexico:

This species was common along the coast of San Blas, roosting on the small rocks near the shore and on a large white rock some ten miles west of San Blas, called Piedra Blanca, but on none of these rocks did they breed. All the birds in this section belonged to the colony breeding on White Rock, and many traversed the sixty miles back and forth daily from their nesting and roosting place on the rock to their feeding grounds near the coast. Never did I see a blue-footed booby in this section; hence my assertion that the Brewster boobies went east and south from their colony to fish, while the blue-footed boobies went northward. Thousands of these boobies were roosting on White Rock and some few had been laying previous to our arrival, but as the workmen had robbed the nests as fast as eggs had been deposited, the birds had become disgusted and stopped laying for the time being, although they still continued to use the rock as a roosting place. It was the guano from this countless flock of birds, which probably had been breeding there for centuries, that the men were engaged in collecting. During the day when not fishing they roosted on the sides of the island, and when the men left the top to come down to supper at six, they returned to the top of the island to roost and make their so-called nests. Many an evening, as I sat at my skinning table or in front of camp waiting for supper, have I watched these birds as they came in from their day's fishing excursion. From about five o'clock on, as far as the eye could reach, could be seen small flocks of from four to twenty making for the island, and after circling half around it, would generally alight on the top, but a few preferred to roost in the caves in the cliffs of the island.

Numerous visits to the top of the rock were made at night after specimens, and a series of some seven pairs were procured by walking up to them while asleep and selecting individual birds as I chose. I had seen colonies of birds before, but none like this, and the sight certainly made one take a long breath. The whole island surface was literally covered with birds, some with their heads and necks stretched out along their backs, sound asleep, some picking up bits of bone, long wing feathers, grass, and small chips of stone and guano to form nests with, while others sat on little piles of heaped-up guano with the neck stretched upward watching the approach of a bird about to alight, as if hoping it might be its mate. They always seemed to roost in pairs, each pair always separated, as were also the nests, by enough space to be out of reach of their neighbor's sharp beaks. It was truly a weird sight in the starlight, and the low, hissing sound from the birds that were awake, with the shadowy forms floating through space, reminded one of a graveyard.

One of the most amusing sights I ever saw was the regular "Mexican cock fight," between males of this species. This combat was, I imagined, over the unmated females, or some single male trying to steal a female from another, and started in this fashion: A male in alighting commenced to strut around, craning his long neck and uttering a low, hissing sound, and on coming near to some mated pair, or some other male also trying this mode of courting, would suddenly stop. Both males now squatted low on their short legs, their breast sometimes touching the ground, while their long necks were craned upward in a double bow. No regular cock fight could be more complete or interesting. While they did not use their feet, their long wings and sharp beaks were thrust out at their rival, and occasionally they met with open beaks, which became locked together in the struggle. Sometimes one would catch the other by the wing, while he retaliated by getting his adversary by the neck, these cases often proving fatal to one or the other of the combatants. Over all this scene was the ever-present smell from the guano, which one must get accustomed to if he would study bird life on an island in the Pacific. Birds with broken wings, as well as those with little strength, were at daybreak quickly put out of the way by the Caracaras, and the gulls made part of their morning meal of these poor unfortunates.

Dr. E. W. Nelson (1899) describes a breeding colony of this species as follows:

Only a few of these boobies were seen about the Tres Marias until an islet was visited off the northwest shore of Maria Cleofa. This islet rises from 150 to 200 feet above the sea, with cliffs on all sides. The summit is mainly rolling, with an elevated, sloping bench on one end. At this time, May 30, many thousands of boobies were breeding on the bare top of this rock. Ths eggs were laid directly on the surface, with no sign of a nest. The sun was intensely hot and heated the rocks so that they were uncomfortably warm to the touch. The birds did not sit upon the eggs during the hottest hours, but while standing to avoid contact with the heated rocks kept in such position that the eggs or young were shaded from the sun, and thus had their vitality preserved. While trying to secure photographs of this breeding ground a few of the old birds flew away, and it was surprising to see how quickly the newly-hatched young succumbed to the heat when the parents left them exposed to the rays of the sun. The nests were spaced at intervals of 4 or 5 feet, so that the old birds were safely out of reach of one another. Although so gregarious in their breeding habits, they appeared to have but little regard for one another. It was amusing to see the savage way in which the nest owners assisted intruders of their own kind out of their territory. While we were walking among them some of the birds would often waddle off to one side, and in so doing necessarily trespassed on their neighbors. The latter at once raised a hoarse shrieking and set upon the outsiders with wicked thrusts of their beaks, which continued until the victims took wing and escaped.

We were also subjects of this proprietary rage, and had our legs nipped every now and then, despite all efforts to walk circumspectly. Our progress over the breeding ground was accompanied by a wave of horse nasal cries that sometimes became almost deafening. Many of the birds were valiant upholders of their rights and sturdily refused to leave their nests, which they defended vigorously, all the time uttering loud cries of rage.

Eggs.—The Brewster booby lays ordinarily two eggs, but sometimes only one. The eggs vary in shape from ovate to elliptical ovate. In appearance they are indistinguishable from the eggs of other boobies; the color, bluish white, is obscured by a chalky coating, which is dirty white, rough and often much stained.

The measurements of 45 eggs, in various collections, average 61 by 41.1 millimeters; the eggs showing the four extremes measure **66** by 42, 65 by **45**, **53.6** by 40, and 59.7 by **37.5** millimeters.

Plumages.—The young booby is hatched naked, but soon becomes covered with pure white down. The series of young birds in collections is too limited to throw much light on the sequence of plumages to maturity, but apparently an immature plumage is worn for at least a year; this plumage is described by Doctor Nelson (1899) as follows: "Dorsal surface uniform dark brown slightly paler than back of adult; entire lower surface still paler and more dingy brown. Feathers over much of body, especially about head, neck, and lower parts, narrowly edged with grayish brown, giving a faint wavy barring." A male bird in this plumage was taken on April 23, which was evidently a bird of the previous year, and several others like it were seen. Apparently the immature plumage is worn for at least a year; but nothing further seems to be known about the molts and plumages of this species.

Nothing more seems to have been published regarding its life history and probably not much more is known. It probably does not differ materially from other boobies in its habits.

DISTRIBUTION.

Breeding range.—Islands off the Central American coasts, from the head of the Gulf of California (San Pedro Martir and Georges Islands) south to Costa Rica (Cocos Island).

Winter range.—Practically the same as the breeding range, but including the Galapagos Islands.

Egg dates.—Mexican islands: Twenty-one records, March 7 to May 18; eleven records, April 1 to May 1.

SULA PISCATOR (Linnaeus).

RED-FOOTED BOOBY.

HABITS.

This is another widely distributed species on the tropical coasts and islands of the Atlantic, Pacific, and Indian Oceans, which is perhaps even better known than the common booby. As an American bird its status is rather unsatisfactory and it seems to have a very slim claim to a place on our fauna. It undoubtedly occurs occasionally, perhaps more often than we suppose, on the coasts of Florida, but the only specimen from that region, so far as I know, is one of somewhat doubtful status presented by Audubon to the Philadelphia Academy. This is an immature bird in variegated plumage; it may not be this species at all; moreover there is considerable doubt as to its having been taken in Florida.

Nesting.—Dr. Walter K. Fisher (1906) has given a good account of the breeding habits of the red-footed booby in Laysan Island, from which I quote, as follows:

Unlike its relative, the masked gannet, this species always builds in bushes, never on the ground. At Laysan it is found in colonies of scattered individuals on the inner slopes of the island, usually well down toward the lagoon. The nest is simple, scarcely more than a slightly hollowed platform composed of twigs and sticks of chenopodium, on the tops of which the structure is usually placed. In the newer nests a few leaves are scattered under the egg. These leaves were a rude index to the age of the egg, for when dry and crisp the bird had been sitting some time, but when fresh, as was frequently the case, the egg was only newly laid.

Both male and female sit on the eggs, and occasionally one is seen perched on the side of the nest while the other is brooding. The birds are rather loath to leave their egg, and when disturbed ruffle their feathers and utter a very harsh cry, making use of their beaks if occasion offers. They are singularly beautiful birds despite their vicious yellow eyes, as the white plumage is set off by bright blue skin about the bill, and by coral-red feet.

Dr. Thomas H. Streets (1877), writing of the birds of the Fanning Islands, in the North Pacific Ocean, says:

On Palmyra Island, their principal breeding-place, the period of their incubation was over at the time of our visit in December, but the young were not yet fledged. The latter were very numerous; they covered the trees and bushes, and looked like great balls of snow-white down. The nests are rudely constructed of coarse twigs, and are built on the low trees.

We arrived at Christmas Island one month later, in January, and there we found the gannets still sitting on their eggs; few or no young were to be seen. This difference is probably induced by the physical conditions surrounding them. One of the islands is situated almost directly on the Equator, exposed to the fiercest rays of a tropical sun; it is devoid of fresh water, and it rarely or never rains; the vegetation is scanty and stunted, and life in general has a very unequal struggle for existence. On the other island, Palmyra, a condition of things directly opposite to these exists. The gannets of Christmas Island have a very curious habit, which, as far as our observations extended, is confined to those of that island. Under their nests, which were quite low on account of the stunted condition of the shrubbery, were mounds one and two feet high, built of twigs, and in some instances solidly cemented together by their excrement. It probably affords them diversion during the monotonous period of incubation to break off all the twigs within reach of their bill, and to drop them under their nests. These mounds furnish evidence of the nests being occupied for several successive years, for the lean bushes could not furnish a sufficient amount of twigs to build them up in a single breeding season.

Eggs.—The red-footed booby lays ordinarily only one egg, but, according to published accounts, two eggs are very often found in a nest. Only a single brood of one or two young is raised in a season. The shape varies from "elliptical ovate" to "elongate ovate," in average specimens, but extremes are "cylindrical ovate" or "short ovate." The color of the shell, where it can be seen, is pale bluish white, but the egg is so completely covered with a thick, rough coating of calcareous deposit that the underlying shell is nearly or quite concealed. This outer coating, which was originally white, is usually much nest stained and dirty; it is rough and lumpy and badly scratched, cracked or peeled off in spots, giving the egg a far from attractive appearance.

The measurements of 38 eggs, in various collections, average 62.7 by 41.4 millimeters; the eggs showing the four extremes measure **72** by **48.5, 59** by 40.5, and 69 by **35** millimeters.

Plumages.—Incubation is shared by both sexes and the period of its duration is said by Campbell (1901) to be 45 days. The young bird is hatched naked, but soon becomes covered with a coat of white down. By the time that the young bird has become fully grown the down has been replaced by the first plumage; the wings are the first to develop and enable the young bird to fly at an early age. This juvenal plumage is too variable in shade to definitely name the colors, but in a general way it is sooty brown above, including the wings and tail, and lighter or drab below; there is no white in this plumage at first. The changes that take place subsequently are not well understood, nor is it definitely known how long it takes to complete the changes. Until more material is collected for study we can make only a provisional guess at what takes place. Apparently some progress is made during the first year, either by a prenuptial molt or by a more or less continuous molt during the year, for young birds seem to acquire considerable white before they are a year old. Probably no white is acquired before the first prenuptial molt, which seems to be quite extensive. Doctor Fisher (1906) describes a young bird, which was probably about a year old, as follows:

Whereas the adult is pure white, except the dark grayish-brown quills and greater wing coverts, this immature bird, in much-worn plumage, has the head and neck hair brown, the feathers edged with whitish; throat the same; jugulum white; a sepia band across breast; abdomen white; back deep bister, the feathers edged with wood-brown; wing coverts and tertials sepia, edged with light brown; rectrices same, tipped with white; remiges brownish black. The immature individuals must belong to a late brood of the previous year.

At the next molt, the first postnuptial, another brown plumage somewhat darger than the first is acquired on the upper parts, with probably an increasing amount of white on the under parts, head, and neck; probably the white tail, rump, and under tail coverts are assumed at this molt, but perhaps not until the next molt, the second prenuptial.

In this second nuptial plumage, in which the tail, lower back, rump, vent, and both tail-coverts are white, birds have been frequently found breeding. Mr. M. J. Nicoll (1906) noted that on Glorioso Island "at least 90 per cent of the gannets are brown-plumaged birds with white tails." Although these white-tailed brown birds are generally conceded to be *Sula piscator* and are so labeled in collections, I have always had a lurking suspicion that they might represent a distinct species and that perhaps Mr. C. J. Maynard (1889) was justified in naming them *Sula coryi*.

Probably during the following year, the third year of the bird's life, the adult plumage is fully acquired; I have seen one bird, apparently about three years old, collected on July 25, which is in worn adult plumage except for some dusky mottling on the back. This bird, which had not yet molted, would probably have assumed the fully adult plumage at the next molt, the third postnuptial. I have seen immature birds undergoing the postnuptial molt as early as July 25, as late as October 9, and at various intermediate dates. Adults I have seen molting in June and in August. Undoubtedly the postnuptial molt is complete, and probably the prenuptial molt includes everything but the wings.

Food.—The food of the red-footed booby consists of various fishes and squids.

Behavior.—Mr. E. W. Gifford (1913) writes of the habits of this species as follows:

When a bird alighted at its nest or beside its mate it craned its neck and, swinging its head from side to side, uttered a long, harsh, cackling call consisting of a short guttural note repeated fifteen or twenty times in quick succession. This call resembled somewhat the call given by the man-o'-war bird when on the nest, only that it was harsher. At Cocos Island the birds in the trees kept up a continual loud cackling noise.

When these boobies were asleep or pluming themselves in some tree, a person could walk right up to them before being noticed. They usually straightened up with a startled expression, often uttering a short squawk of surprise. If one continued to disturb them they would squawk vociferously and try to fly away, frequently floundering about among the branches.

The flight of the red-footed booby is more graceful than that of the blue-faced and the Peruvian, and somewhat resembles that of a large shearwater. When in the vicinity of Cocos Island and of Clarion Island, flocks of red-footed boobies were seen flying away from the islands in the morning and toward them in the evening. The flocks contained from six to fifteen birds. The birds fly with the same gentle, wave-like rise and fall that characterizes the flight of other members of this genus. The wing-strokes occur on the rise; on the downward swing the bird sails, in calm weather often going several yards very close to the surface of the water. The members of a flock are practically synchronous in every action.

In fishing, the red-footed booby pursues the same tactics as the blue-footed, diving, with wings half closed and rigid, from a height of twenty or thirty feet. On one occasion, however, I saw one catching flying-fish on the wing by swooping into schools which were skimming along above the water.

Winter.—At the close of the breeding season the birds disperse and scatter out over the ocean, congregating at times in large numbers where schools of fish are to be found. A striking picture of their winter activities is furnished by Mr. Outram Bangs (1902) as follows:

On February 12, 1895, occurred the second terrible " freeze " of that memorable winter. At the time I was at Oak Lodge, on the East Peninsula of the Indian River, opposite Micco. For several days thereafter the weather continued to be very cold and unsettled, with high winds that drove the water out of the Indian River to such an extent that it was impossible to cross it in a boat, and culminated on February 16 in a northeasterly gale accompanied by rain, of a violence seldom attained on the east coast of Florida in winter. About 10 o'clock of that morning (February 16, 1895), Mrs. Latham came into the workshop where I was skinning my morning's catch, thankful to be indoors again out of the storm, and told me she had just been at the beach and had seen a great many birds there, among them what she thought were gannets, fishing in the breakers. I instantly took my gun and started along the trail through the palmetto hummock, fighting my way foot by foot against the fury of the wind and rain. On arriving at the beach I was greeted by the wildest scene imaginable ; huge breakers were rolling in over the shallow water and falling on the beach with tremendous noise; the rain, driven by the gale, came in sheets, but in spite of it the cutting white sand was blown with such force against my face and hands that I had repeatedly to turn my back to the storm.

Vast numbers of herring gulls, royal terns, and Bonaparte gulls sat huddled together in bunches on the upper beach, not daring to trust themselves to the elements. These great gatherings of gulls were very tame and allowed me to walk up close to them, and when they did take wing, skimmed only a short distance along the crest of the beach and lit again, huddled together as before.

High up overhead an occasional frigate bird swept by on motionless wings, cutting directly into the teeth of the gale, or driving before it with apparent indifference. The stolid pelicans, unmoved by the storm, proceeded as usual up and down the line of breakers, in little companies, with the same measured flight as in the finest weather, rising and falling as the huge breakers rolled under them.

But to me most interesting of all was a sight I had never before witnessed on the beach, although I had visited it every day; as far as the eye could reach, up and down the line of surf, were great numbers of boobies flying back and forth and every now and then collecting over some school of small fish and diving from a height like a party of boys following each other off a spring-board. There were hundreds, perhaps thousands, of them. There were probably but two species, though of three styles of coloration. A comparatively small number were adults of the common booby (*Sula sula*), easily identified by their brown backs and heads and white bellies; next in numbers were young birds in wholly grayish brown plumage, but outnumbering both these together was a small white species with conspicuous blackish flight feathers. All these were of about one size.

For two hours I lay flat on the beach, hoping to get a shot, but though the boobies came often to within a hundred yards of me and sometimes gathered and fished in front of where I lay, none came quite close enough to shoot, keeping just outside the breakers. At the end of this time they began gradually, in small parties, to fly out to sea, till all had gone. From the way these birds behaved I do not think they were driven in by stress of weather, because all the time they were off the beach they were very busy fishing, and when they had done they gradually left again, flying out to sea, though the storm had not abated. It is my opinion, rather, that the boobies know by experience that during such a storm there is good fishing on the east Florida beach and come there to enjoy it.

DISTRIBUTION.

Breeding range.—On some of the West Indies (Porto Rico, Little Cayman, Dominica, Battowia, Kick-em-Jenny, etc.) ; off the coasts of Venezuela (Los Testigos and Los Hermanos Islands) and Honduras (Half-moon Cay, and Little Swan Island) ; in the tropical Atlantic Ocean (Trinidad and Ascension Islands) ; on various islands in the Pacific Ocean (Revillagigedo, Galapagos, Laysan, Fanning, Philippine Islands, etc.) ; and in the Indian Ocean (Glorioso Island and Raine's Islet).

These Pacific birds may prove to be subspecifically distinct from the Atlantic birds. Said to have nested once on Atwood's Key in the Bahama Islands.   Breeding grounds protected on Desecheo Island reservation, Porto Rico.

Winter range.—Practically the same as the breeding range.

Casual records.—Accidental on the coast of Florida (Micco, February 16, 1895.)

Egg dates.—Mexican islands: Twenty-four records, April 29 to December 10; twelve records, May 2 to 18.   Swan Island, Caribbean Sea: One record, March 31.

MORUS BASSANUS (Linnaeus).

GANNET.

HABITS.

Day after day we had gazed, from the hilltops of the northern Magdalens, across the waters of the stormy Gulf of St. Lawrence toward the distant Labrador coast, where we could see looming up on the horizon a lofty reddish mass of rock, the goal of our ambitions and the mecca of many an American ornithologist, Bird Rock.   At last the day came sufficiently smooth for us to risk the trip in our tiny craft, the only boat available.   To visit and storm that almost impregnable seabirds' fortress is risky enough in a seaworthy vessel, for storms come up without much warning and the waves thunder at the base of its almost perpendicular cliffs with such fury, that only during the calmest weather can a landing be effected with safety on a narrow beach.   At the time of our visit the present comfortable landing had not been completed.   It is now no longer necessary to be hoisted up in a crate, a hundred feet or more to the top of the rock.

Gannets were seen flying past us toward the rock, as they returned from their fishing grounds and as we drew near we could see a swarm of white birds circling about it.   The setting sun shone full upon its towering cliffs of red sandstone, deeply cut or carved by the elements into ledges and shelves of varying sizes and shapes; the broader ledges seemed covered with snow and it was hard to believe that such wide bands of white were really colonies of nesting gannets.   The whole side of the rock seemed to be covered with birds; wherever there was room for them the gannets were sitting on their nests on the wider ledges; clouds of noisy kittiwakes were hovering overhead or nesting on the smallest shelves of rock; razor-billed auks were breeding in the crevices near the top of the rock and the murres, Brunnich, and the common, were sitting in long rows upon their eggs on the narrower ledges.   Such was the home of the gannet as I saw it in 1904.

The history of the gannet colonies of Bird Rock is interesting as showing the effect of human agencies in the extermination of bird life.

It begins with Jacques Cartier's account of his voyage to Canada in 1534, at which time there were apparently three islands in the group, of which he says, according to Gurney's (1913) rendering of Hakluyt's translation: " These ilands were as full of birds as any medow is of grasse, which there do make their nestes; and in the greatest of them there was a great and infinite number of those that wee cal margaulx, that are white and bigger than any geese." There is very little doubt that the birds he referred to were gannets. For three centuries the persecution of these birds was not sufficiently severe to reduce materially their numbers, for when Audubon (1897) visited Bird Rock in 1833 it was a most wonderful sight, as the following graphic description, taken from his journal for June 14, 1833, well illustrates:

About ten a speck rose on the horizon which I was told was the rock. We sailed well, the breeze increased fast, and we neared this object apace. At eleven I could distinguish its top plainly from the deck, and thought it covered with snow to the depth of several feet; this appearance existed on every portion of the flat, projecting shelves. Godwin said, with the coolness of a man who had visited this rock for ten successive seasons, that what we saw was not snow, but gannets. I rubbed my eyes, took my spyglass, and in an instant the strangest picture stood before me. They were birds we saw—a mass of birds of such a size as I never before cast my eyes on. The whole of my party stood astounded and amazed, and all came to the conclusion that such a sight was of itself sufficient to invite anyone to come across the gulf to view it at this season. The nearer we approached the greater our surprise at the enormous number of these birds, all calmly seated on their eggs or newly hatched brood, their heads all turned to windward and toward us. The air above for a hundred yards, and for some distance around the whole rock, was filled with gannets on the wing, which, from our position, made it appear as if a heavy fall of snow was directly above us.

At that time the whole top of the rock was covered with their nests and it was regularly visited by the fishermen of that vicinity, who killed the gannets in large quantities for codfish bait. The stupid birds were beaten down with clubs as they tumbled over each other in their attempts to escape. Sometimes as many as 540 of them have been killed by half a dozen men in an hour, and as many as 40 fishing boats were supplied regularly with bait each season in this way, the birds being roughly skinned and the flesh cut off in chunks.

When Dr. Henry Bryant visited Bird Rock on June 23, 1860, the colonies were very much reduced in numbers, although the lighthouse had not been built at that time and the gannets were nesting over all of the northern half of the flat top of the rock. He estimated that there were at least 100,000 birds in this colony and about 50,000 that were nesting on the side of the rock. Mr. C. J. Maynard visited the rock in 1872, three years after the lighthouse was built, and found the colony on the summit reduced to 5,000 birds. In 1881 Mr. William Brewster reported only 50 pairs still nesting on the flat top of the rock, and since that time they have abandoned it entirely, resorting only to the safer locations on the ledges. In 1887 the total number of gannets nesting on Bird Rock was estimated at 10,000, and at the time of our visit in 1904 we estimated that their numbers had been reduced to less than 3,000 birds. Fortunately, they are now protected by the lighthouse keeper, and will probably not be further reduced in numbers by persecution on their breeding grounds, but the soft sandstone cliffs of Bird Rock are gradually wearing away and it is only a question of time when their old home will disappear, and it is doubtful if they can find another suitable and safe substitute for it.

Though not so well known as Bird Rock, the island of Bonaventure, off the Gaspé Peninsula in the Gulf of St. Lawrence, is fully as important as a breeding resort for gannets, for it contains by far the largest colony of these birds on the American coast. Gurney (1913) records this colony as containing about 7,000 gannets. It has a similar formation of red sandstone cliffs some 300 feet high and may, at some remote period in the past, have formed a part of a chain of cliffs or islands of which Bird Rock is now the surviving outpost. There are many broad ledges on Bonaventure Island which are practically inaccessible, offering attractive nesting sites for thousands of gannets, where for many years to come they will be safe from molestation. Gannets are said to have nested on Funk Island many years ago, but after the extermination of the great auk the gannets probably shared a similar fate. Another colony of recent existence was on Perroquet Island, of the Mingan group, off the south coast of Labrador. Mr. William Brewster noted several hundred birds there in 1881, but they disappeared soon after that. We saw a few gannets flying about these islands in June, 1909, but were told that they were not breeding there, having been driven away by constant persecution. Bird Rock and Bonaventure have both been set apart as reservations by the Canadian Government, where these birds will be permanently protected.

Spring.—The northward migration of the gannets begins in April and extends well into May, following the earliest movement of herring and other fish on which it feeds. They arrive on their breeding grounds in the Gulf of St. Lawrence in May, many of the older birds being already paired. Love making and nest building begin at once and eggs are laid late in May or in June.

Courtship.—I have never seen the courtship of the gannet, but Dr. Charles W. Townsend has sent me the following interesting notes on what he calls the courtship dance, although, at the time of his observations, the breeding season was well advanced. He says:

I spent many hours in the summer of 1919 under most favorable conditions near the great gannet nesting ledges on the cliffs of Bonaventure Island; I saw the dance repeated by hundreds of pairs many times and I came to the same conclusion that Professor Fisher did in the case of the Laysan albatross, namely, that it was originally a courtship dance and that it was continued from habit and from the joy of it, in the same way that the song sparrow continues to sing long after the nesting season.

Let me describe a typical performance: As the sexes are alike in plumage, they can not be distinguished apart. One of them—we will assume it is the male—is swinging around in great circles on rigidly outstretched and motionless wings. He passes within a few yards of me and swings toward a shelf crowded with birds brooding their downy black-faced young. Alighting on the edge, he elbows his way along the shelf, notwithstanding the angry looks, the black mouths suddenly opened, and the vicious pecks of his neighbors. All of these he returns in kind. Arrived at the nest, he is enthusiastically greeted by his mate, who, disregarding the young bird beneath her, rises up to do her part in the dance. The birds stand face to face, the wings slightly raised and opened, the tail elevated and spread. They bow towards each other, then raise their heads and wave their bills as if they were whetting these powerful instruments, or as if they were performing the polite preliminaries of a fencing bout. From time to time this process is interrupted as they bow to each other and appear to caress each other as each dips its pale-blue bill and cream-colored head first to one side and then to the other of its mate's snowy breast. With unabated enthusiasm and ardor the various actions of this curious and loving dance are repeated again and again, and often continue for several minutes. After the dance the pair preen themselves and each other, or the one first at the nest flies away, and the new arrival waddles around so as to get back of the nestling, and the strange process of feeding takes place.

This dance is not only performed by pairs, as first described, but not infrequently individuals perform a *pas seul;* it may be because he or she is wearied with waiting for its mate. The wings are slightly raised and opened, the tail elevated and spread, the bill pointed vertically upwards and waved aloft, then dipped to one side under the half-open wing and then to the other, the bill raised and waved again, and so on over and over again. Owing to the great volume of sound from the ledges, it is impossible to distinguish any individual performer, and I was unable to tell at what point in the dance and to what extent the song was important. The sound is like that of a thousand rattling looms in a great factory, a rough, vibrating, pulsing sound—" *car-ra, car-ra, car-ra.*"

Nesting.—An account of the nesting conditions as we saw them on Bird Rock and on North Bird Rock, will serve to illustrate the two common methods of nesting, which are also typical of the species elsewhere. On Bird Rock the nests were all on the ledges on the sides of the rock; the broader ledges were well covered with nests several rows deep, and many smaller shelves were occupied by as many nests as they could hold. The nests varied greatly in size and in style of construction from practically nothing to well-made nests 18 inches in diameter and 5 inches high; probably the nests are added to from year to year by more or less extensive repairs, so that the oldest nests become quite bulky. As a rule, they were fairly well made of fresh seaweed, kelp, or rockweed, in many cases still wet, as if recently pulled up by the birds, but more often partially dried. There were usually a few straws and feathers in or about the nests, and in one case a large piece of canoe-birch bark had been brought in, probably as an ornament. The nests at that date, June 24, all contained eggs, a single egg to each nest, and some of the young had hatched. There was always more or less filth about the nests, broken eggs, decaying fish, and excrement, the ledges often being whitewashed with the latter.

We found primitive conditions still prevailing on North Bird Rock, about three-quarters of a mile from the large rock; this had been cut into three parts by the action of the sea, two flat-topped rocks with perpendicular sides, joined by a rocky beach and an inaccessible pillar of rock separated by water. We climbed up the steep sides of one of the rocks and as we looked over the top of the cliff we saw, in miniature, what might have been seen on Bird Rock 50 years ago, a wildly scrambling mass of great white birds, frightened by our sudden appearance and stumbling over each other in their haste to get away. The whole flat top of the rock was covered with their nests, set about 3 feet apart, leaving just room enough to walk among them, and sufficiently separated for each sitting bird to be beyond the reach of its nearest neighbors, a necessary precaution, for gannets are quarrelsome birds and frequently steal the nesting material from neighboring nests. These nests had evidently been occupied year after year for many seasons, new material being added each year, until a considerable pile of soil had been accumulated by the gradual decay of the nest material and the new portion of the nest occupied only the top of the mound. The nests, described by the earlier writers, on the flat top of Bird Rock showed similar signs of age. Gurney (1913) gives an interesting list of the miscellaneous articles that have been found in gannets' nests and says of their increasing bulk: "Gannets' nests have ever been regarded as substantial edifices—although only intended to receive one egg—in truth, their size attracted attention centuries ago, when in a fissure, or leaning against the rock; Mr. J. M. Campbell has obliged me with a photograph of one 5 feet in height, but they are not all equally large, and some do not measure 18 inches across."

Eggs.—The gannet lays only one egg, which is not large for a bird of its size, varying in shape from elongate ovate to elliptical ovate. The pale bluish white ground color is almost wholly concealed by a thick calcareous deposit, which is dull white at first but soon becomes nest stained and much soiled by mud and dirt from the birds' feet.

The measurements of 44 eggs, in various collections, average 77.6 by 47 millimeters; the eggs showing the four extremes measure **86.5** by **53.5, 70** by 47, and 80 by **37** millimeters.

The period of incubation is variously given by different observers as from 39 to 44 days, and, as Mr. Gurney (1913) suggests, probably 42 days is about the average. Both sexes incubate. The absence of any bare hatching space on the belly of the gannet is due to the peculiar method in which the bird incubates. Mr. J. M. Campbell, of the Bass Lighthouse, has given a very good account of this, which Mr. Gurney (1913) quotes, as follows:

Alighting on the edge of the nest, the bird shuffles on to the shallow depression, carefully adjusting the huge webs of both feet over the egg until it is completely concealed from view. The body is then lowered over the feet until the breast feathers but barely cover them, giving one the impression that the bird is not sitting sufficiently far forward on the nest. From this habit the eggs, originally chalky white, soon become stained and discolored.

Young.—The following account of the hatching process is also taken from the writings of the same excellent observer:

On the 5th of June the young solan was seen emerging from the shell * * * The young bird, on making its exit from the egg, appeared to use at first the little horny excrescence on the tip of the upper mandible for the purpose of rupturing the inner membrane, mere pressure being afterwards sufficient to chip the shell. This is invariably effected at the broad end, a little deeper than one would cut a breakfast egg. The chipping was continued slowly, bit by bit; first a small portion of the tough membrane was ripped, then the opposing shell pressed out. After a short rest, the bird wriggled a little farther round—the bill always in view—and again renewed the attack, until fully two-thirds of the circumference had been cut. The claws of one of the feet now made their appearance over the lower edge of the fracture, and, by dint of pressure of the whole body, the remaining third of the shell was snapped, and out tumbled a black, sprawling object, helpless, blind, bare as the palm of one's hand, and whining like a puppy dog.

The very young gannet when first hatched is naked and livid gray in color, an unattractive object, fat, shapeless, and helpless. It is carefully brooded by its devoted parent, for it must be shielded from the hot sun and protected against the rain and cold fogs until, in the course of about three weeks, its protective coat of soft, white down completely covers the body. It is well fed by semidigested food from its parents' crop and increases rapidly in size, until it equals or even exceeds the adult bird in weight. When feeding a very young bird, the parent practically scoops the little fellow into her mouth, but when larger the youngster is able to dive into the cavernous throat and fish for himself. When old enough to eat solid food the young bird is fed on fresh fish deposited near the nest by its parents. When about six weeks old the plumage appears and by the end of September the flight stage is reached. Concerning this interesting and critical period in the life of the young gannet, I can not do better than quote what Mr. Gurney (1913) has to say about it, as follows:

When the young gannets are twelve or thirteen weeks old, instinct tells their parents that they are quite fat enough for their own good, and that any more stuffing with fish will make them too unwielding to fly. Accordingly it would seem that they desist from feeding their young for the last ten days before they quit the ledges. As a matter of fact, it must be an exceedingly necessary precaution, for if too heavy, the young gannet, when it launches itself for the first time into space, would often not get clear of the rocks. When the day comes for the mighty plunge to be made, spreading wide their great sails of wings, the young gannets may be seen to half fly, half fall, into the abyss below. This does not take place until the month of September has commenced, and then numbers of them are to be seen quitting the safety of their ledges. A singular, not to say absurd sight, it is to stand, as my son and I did, on the Bass Rock and watch their awkwardness and hesitation, like that of a timid human bather about to take a first header into the water. I reckoned, when I was there in 1906, that between August the 29th and September the 4th, two hundred and fifty young gannets made the plunge, and with it took their departure from the Bass Rock.

For some days before their actual departure the young gannets may be seen continually flapping their long black wings, which is done, it is to be presumed, to relax the joints and strengthen the ligaments; ten or twelve young gannets may be viewed going through this performance at the same time on the ledges. Notwithstanding so much preparation, some make a bad start, and I was told at Ailsa Craig, where there is a belt of rock-strewn shore to be crossed, that they not infrequently fall on to it. In squally weather others lose their balance and are carried by a gust of wind down into the sea before they are ready. But even if they do meet with either of these mishaps, they are not necessarily left to die, for old ones—very likely not their own parents—will sometimes provide for them.

The flight, or, rather, descent, of the young gannet from its natal ledge is a very unsteady performance, yet on the whole it is well sustained, so that the bird has probably achieved a distance of half a mile before the final descending curve into the sea takes place, which ends with a mighty splash caused by impact with the water. The otopyn, or natural effection, of which Gilbert White wrote so eloquently, is now past and over, and the young one must shift for itself as best it can in the world of waters. When once launched, the young gannet is comparatively safe, except that it is now in some measure at the mercy of the tide. In the sea it remains, drifting hither and thither for the space of two or three weeks. It is apparently unable to rise from the water, and all evidence points to its receiving no food whatever except the sustenance contained in its own subcutaneous layer of grease, which is considerable enough to impart nutriment to the rest of the body. Besides the tide, it has to reckon with any high wind, but September is generally a tranquil time of the year and young gannets from Ailsa or the Bass soon work their way out to sea.

Having reached the sea, we shall be safe in assuming that the young gannet will be nearly four months old before it voluntarily essays a second flight. Even this is much less than is the case with the young albatross. Then a new phase of its life begins; it rises from the water with a newly found power, henceforth to find its own livelihood by those beautiful plunges which are the admiration of all who see them.

Plumages.—The naked young gannet, even when first hatched, shows some signs of sprouting down, and when about 10 days old it is completely covered with long white down, except on the face, which remains naked and black. When about 3 weeks old the tail and wing quills begin to sprout, followed by the black juvenal plumage of the scapulars and back, and the full first plumage is assumed at an age of 9 or 10 weeks. This is the plumage in which we see the young birds in the fall, nearly black above, sprinkled with small triangular spots of white, one on each feather, and much lighter below, where the feathers are largely white. During the first winter and spring a gradual change takes place, by fading, wear, molt, and growth of new feathers. Mr. Gurney (1913) has described this very well from observations made on a captive bird. He writes:

At what I considered to be four months old the white spots upon this young gannet were less numerous and were becoming distinctly smaller, being presumably worn by abrasion. At five months its entire plumage had grown darker. At six months there was not any further change worth registering; nor at seven months. At eight months all its feathers were darker, and the molt had set in, shed feathers being pretty numerous in its enclosure. At nine months its new tail-feathers were growing—very large and very stiff when compared with the limp rectrices which they replaced. At the same time new feathers were discoverable upon the back, and these were black with small white spots on the tips of a few only. Some white color was apparent at the back of the neck also. At ten months the white on the neck had spread and was beginning to cover the throat and breast, and at eleven months the whole of the underparts were white.

Describing the plumage of the second year, he goes on to say that when 12 months old its forehead retained—

Many dark speckles, but there were no longer many spots of white to be seen on the back. By the time it had reached 16 months there was not a spot of white on my young gannet's back, which was nearly black, but two-thirds of its head and neck were now quite white. Although the molt seemed to be finished, it was evident that there was still some change of color going on, either by fading or abrasion. The only part of its body which remained in the spotted plumage now was the lower part of the belly. At 17 months the head and neck were nearly white. At 21 months the lesser upper wing coverts and a part of the scapulars were white also, and three white spots of some size were visible on the back. At 22 months a shade of yellow came out on the head and neck. At 23 the white spots or blotches on the back were the size of a florin, and several new ones had appeared upon the wing coverts. At 24 the blotches were still larger, and at 25 months the bird, which had been in excellent health until the last fortnight of its life, unfortunately began to droop and died— August 7th, 1908—and my observations came to an abrupt end.

When a gannet is about 26 months old it exhibits a yellow occiput and a partly black back, forming a handsome conjunction of colors. When 28 months it should have, if the normal molt has been adhered to, nearly acquired its complete white plumage, but there still remain a few small patches of black on the lower part of the back and upon the wings. The black tail is the last portion of the immature plumage to be shed; in a molt which is normal, the two middle rectrices, which are the longest of the twelve, being the final ones to go.

I have examined a large number of young gannets in first and second year plumages (I have a series of 26 immature birds in my own collection), all of which agree substantially with Mr. Gurney's observations. During the first year young gannets are extensively mottled on the under parts, with an increasing amount of white in heads, necks, and under parts toward spring; the upper parts are slate colored with a hastate spot of white at the tip of each feather. These slate-colored feathers with the white spots are characteristic of the first-year plumage; but they are renewed on the back, rump, and lesser wing coverts at the first complete molt, when the bird is about a year old, so that they appear also during the first part of the second year; however, the white tips disappear by wear during the fall, and before winter the young bird has a solid black back. A few white feathers appear in the lesser wing coverts at about this time.

During the second winter, then, the young gannet has a solid black back in which an increasing number of white feathers appear toward spring, showing first in lesser wing-coverts, then in the scapulars, and lastly in the back. The head, neck, and under parts, which are largely white in the fall, become increasingly white during the winter and spring; and the yellowish suffusion comes in on the head. The secondaries are still all black and the tail feathers all dusky. By the next summer, when the young bird is two years old, the back and wing coverts are about half white and half black, in a variegated pattern of wholly white and wholly black feathers. Many birds in this plumage are seen in the breeding colonies and are probably breeding.

At the following molt, which begins as early as June, when the bird is two years old, white feathers begin to appear in the secondaries and in the tail, the white feathers in the upper parts increase and the black feathers decrease until the bird is three years old. The summer and fall molt, at this age, probably produces the fully adult plumage in many individuals; but in many cases, perhaps in all, traces of immaturity, such as black secondaries, alternating or scattering through the wings, and black central tail feathers, persist through part of all of the fourth year.

I have seen birds which I call 40 months old in this plumage, but, as late winter and early spring specimens are lacking, I can not say whether these last black feathers are shed before the bird is four years old or not. Certainly at the four-year old molt, if not before that, the plumage becomes adult. During all of this time the young bird has been undergoing an almost continuous molt, represented by two semi-annual molts, much prolonged during the earlier years so that they nearly overlap, but later becoming restricted to a postnuptial and a prenuptial molt in older birds. There is much individual variation in the time required for the various changes.

The adult gannet undergoes a complete postnuptial molt in August and September, which is sometimes prolonged into November, and a partial prenuptial molt, involving the contour feathers and perhaps the tail, during March, April, and May. There is no conspicuous seasonal change in plumage, except that the yellow suffusion on the head is richer and more extensive in the spring and is much paler or entirely lacking in the fall.

Food.—The food of the gannet consists entirely of fish, which it obtains by diving in a most spectacular manner. A flock of feeding gannets bombarding a school of herring is a most interesting sight and not an uncommon sight on the New England coast late in the fall. At that season a few gannets are almost always in sight circling high in the air off the coast, looking for migrating schools of fish. As soon as a school is discovered and one or more gannets begin diving, others begin drifting in from all sides, until, in an incredibly short time, a great cloud of birds has gathered; how the welcome news is transmitted so quickly and so far is a mystery; where less than a dozen gannets were in sight a few minutes before, there are now two or three hundred. Over the unlucky school of fish is a bewildering maze of soaring, circling birds, pouring down out of the sky in rapid succession, plunging into the water like so many projectiles and sending columns of water and spray many feet into the air like the spouting of a school of whales. In the center of the mass are the plunging birds hurling themselves at their prey with tremendous force; all around them on the water are the birds which have just risen to the surface to swallow their prey or to rest before trying again and in the air birds are constantly rising, circling, and soaring for the next plunge. It is a lively scene for a while, but it does not last long, as the fish soon become frightened and seek safety in the depths, when the gannets scatter to look for another school.

Dr. Charles W. Townsend (1905) describes the process in detail as follows:

The gannet flies rapidly over the water and begins to soar at a height of from 30 to 100 feet, often rising just before the plunge. At the plunge the head is pointed down, the tail up; the wings are partly spread so that the bird appears like a great winged arrow. The speed of the descent is great, and the wings are closed just before reaching the water, which spurts up to a height of from 5 to 15 feet. After the waters have subsided following the splash and all is still, the bird suddenly and buoyantly comes to the surface, the head and neck stretched out first. It then sits quietly on the water for half a minute or so to finish swallowing the prey and to rest, and then slowly and laboriously rises to windward, with its long neck and tail stretched to their full extent. Gaining a height of thirty or more feet, it swings around to leeward and is soon soaring and plunging again. Of eight observations made with a stop-watch on the length of time that this bird remained under water after the plunge, the limit was 4 and 7 seconds, the average being 6¼ seconds. I also timed them in three descents from height of perhaps 60 feet and found it to be 1¼, 1½, and 1 second, respctively, from the beginning of the descent to the time when they struck the water. This would indicate that the bird actually throws itself downward and not merely drops by gravitation, as the distance traveled is too great for such a quick descent by gravity alone. This is apparent without actual measurement, and is also shown by the fact that the birds sometimes descend quickly at an angle, two often aiming at the same spot. How they avoid annihilating each other seems marvelous. The height of the descent is, of course, very difficult to judge, but my estimates are based on comparisons with the masts of schooners equally distant. The height of the splash was compared with that of spar buoys near the fishing grounds. As with all other sea birds at a distance, observations were made with a telescope.

The gannet is well protected against bodily injury in its terrific plunges by a strong elastic cushion of air cells under the skin of its breast, which softens the shock of impact as it strikes the water. The gannet is a voracious feeder and undoubtedly consumes an enormous number of fish; it is not partial in its choice, though it feeds largely on herring and mackerel where they are abundant in schools; it also takes capelin and other species as well as small codlings. I have heard it said that gannets may be easily killed by fastening a fish on a floating board, for which they will dive and break their necks, though this hardly seems credible. Audubon (1840) describes a method of feeding which I have never seen. " At other times I have seen the gannet plunge amidst a shoal of launces so as scarcely to enter the water, and afterwards follow them, swimming, or as it were moving, on the water, with its wings extended upwards, and striking to the right and left until it was satiated."

The gannet has a peculiar habit of disgorging whatever fish it has recently eaten when disturbed and forced to fly; it goes through a series of preliminary motions, pumping its neck up and down, straining, gaping, and retching until the fish is finally forced out of its mouth and deposited on the ledge near the nest, where it is left to decay or dry in the sun. These fish are often as much as a foot in length and generally partly digested. I am not sure whether this habit is caused by fright or by a desire to get rid of unnecessary weight; probably the latter, as it is a very docile or very stupid bird and not easily frightened away. It is easily approached with a little caution, and I even caught one in my hands, but usually if I came too near the disgorging process would begin, it would move awkwardly away, uttering a variety of loud guttural croaks or grunts, until it could flop off over the edge of the cliff, spread its long, black-tipped wings and sail gracefully out into space a sudden transformation from an ungainly, awkward, stupid fowl to an elegant, soaring seabird, riding at ease on its broad and powerful wings, one of nature's triumphs in the balancing of forces.

Behavior.—The flight of the gannet is a magnificent performance as it soars aloft on its long, pointed, black-tipped wings, its spearlike head and beak, and its slender tapering tail offering little resistance to the air, as it sweeps in great circles far above the sea until almost lost to sight in the blue sky. When traveling it flies close to the water, flapping its wings and sailing at intervals with wings fully outstretched, after the manner of the pelicans. It is well built for speed and its flight is powerful and long sustained. Its peculiar shape, forming an almost perfect cross while soaring, serves to identify it, as far as it can be seen.

The vigorous plunge of the gannet from a great height, often over a hundred feet, together with the momentum of its heavy body, gives it a decided advantage over other diving birds in reaching great depths. There have been some remarkable stories told of the depths to which gannets dive, based on their having been caught in fishermen's nets set at known depths. Mr. Gurney (1913) mentions a number of such cases from which I infer that gannets frequently dive to a depth of 60 or 70 feet and occasionally over 100. It is hardly conceivable that the gannet can penetrate to any such great depths as these by the impetus of its plunge; it must, therefore, swim downward, probably using both wings and feet for propulsion. The gannet is not only an expert diver, displaying great agility below the surface, but it is also a strong swimmer above, where it propels itself rapidly with alternate strokes of its great paddles. A wounded gannet is not an easy bird to catch.

I have never heard gannets utter any vocal sound except on their breeding grounds, where they are often quite noisy; they indulge in a variety of soft guttural notes among themselves in conversational tones, and when disturbed a series of loud, grating grunts and croaks, sounding like the syllables "*kurruck, krrrrruck*" or "*gorrrrok, gorrrrok*," the base accompaniment of the never ceasing chorus of sounds in the mixed colonies of Bird Rock. Macgillivray (1852) describes the notes as follows:

> Their cry is hoarse and harsh, and may be expressed by the syllables *carra, carra*, or *kirra, kirra*, sometimes it is *crac, crac*, or *cra, cra*, or *cree, cree*. The cry varies considerably in different individuals, some having a sharper voice than others, and when unusually irritated they repeat it with great rapidity.

Gannets quarrel considerably among themselves on their breeding grounds, but I can not find any evidence that they ever molest the other species that breed near them. Morris (1903) describes—

> A battle between a gannet and two full-grown male swans, the latter both attacking at the same time, and following up the contest most vigorously with the former, who defended himself most resolutely for a very long time, and ultimately defeated the swans, beating them both off, and laying them pros-

trate, totally disabled, helpless, and seemingly seriously injured. The gannet, much exhausted by the protracted struggle, was easily caught alive, and very little the worse for fighting.

Gannets have never been considered as game birds and the flesh of the adults must be very strong and unpalatable, but there is plenty of evidence to show that the fat young birds have been largely used for food, particularly in the European colonies. As they are naturally long-lived birds, they would have increased more rapidly than they have done if it were not for this and other natural causes which have kept their numbers in check. They are naturally sluggish and somewhat deaf, so that they are easily caught when asleep on their nests or on the water. Mr. Gurney (1913) says that they are frequently choked and killed by attempting to swallow gunnards, " whose spinous dorsal fin may easily become wedged in the gannet's throat." They are sometimes killed by plunging into boats containing freshly caught fish, or they become entangled in fishermen's nets or are caught on hooks baited with fish. Undoubtedly many gannets, as well as other sea birds, starve to death during prolonged periods of rough weather when it is difficult or impossible for them to catch fish. Mr. Gurney (1913) mentions such a disaster, stating that the French ornithologist, M. Baillon, " saw the dead birds lying spread along the shore, and testifies to there having been about 200 gannets, with some 500 razorbills, gulls, etc., on an extent of 4 miles, near the mouth of the Somme."

Winter.—As soon as the gannets leave their breeding grounds they begin their autumn wanderings and southward migrations. They have been seen on the Massachusetts coast in August, but the main flight passes along the New England coast during September and October and extends as far south as the Gulf of Mexico. I have specimens in my collection taken off Cape Cod in both December and January and a few birds winter regularly about Long Island, but usually by November most of the gannets have gone farther south, their movements being governed largely by the migration of the herring. They winter regularly about Florida and in the Gulf of Mexico, where they find an abundant food supply.

DISTRIBUTION.

Breeding range.—The Gulf of St. Lawrence (Bird Rocks and Bonaventure and a rock off the south coast of Newfoundland near Cape St. Marys). Formerly near Yarmouth, Nova Scotia, on a rock near Grand Manan, Bay of Fundy, and on Perroquet Island, off Mingan, Quebec. On several islands and rocks near the British Isles (St. Kilda, Bass Rock, Ailsa Craig, etc.) and near Iceland (Sulusker, Eldey, and Grimsey). Breeding grounds protected on reservations in the Gulf of St. Lawrence, Bird Rocks, and Bonaventure.

Winter range.—North Atlantic coasts. On the American side rarely from Massachusetts (Cape Cod) regularly from Virginia, mainly at sea, south to Cuba, the Gulf of Mexico, and Mexico (Vera Cruz). South on the other side to the Azores, Canary Islands, and Africa (Morocco).

Spring migration.—Mainly off shore. Early dates of arrival (north of Cape Cod, where it may winter): Massachusetts, Lynn, April 8; Nova Scotia, Pictou, April 20. Late dates of departure: Cuba, Cape San Antonio, May 20; Florida, Ormond, March 31; Virginia, Smith's Island, May; New York, Long Island, May 25; Rhode Island, Block Island, May 16; Massachusetts, Essex County, May 18 (latest June 7).

Fall migration.—Early dates of arrival: Massachusetts, Essex County, August 28; Rhode Island, September 10; Block Island, October 4; New York, Montauk Point, October 5.

Casual records.—Accidental inland, mainly near the Great Lakes, as far north and west as Ontario (Toronto, December 19, 1908, and Ottawa, October 14, 1909), Indiana (Michigan City, November, 1904) and Michigan (Ann Arbor, October 18, 1911). Recorded on the Labrador coast at 65° north, and in Greenland. Occasional on Louisiana coast (Rigolets, December 9, 1886).

Egg dates.—Gulf of St. Lawrence: Twenty records, June 4 to July 25; 10 records, June 16 to July 1. British Isles: Sixteen records, May 9 to June 11; eight records, May 18 to June 7.

Family ANHINGIDAE, Darters.

ANHINGA ANHINGA (Linnaeus).

WATER-TURKEY.

HABITS.

In the swamps and marshy lakes of Florida, where the shores are overgrown with rank vegetation and the stately cypress trees are draped with long festoons of Spanish moss, or in the sluggish streams, half choked with water hyacinths, "bonnets" and "water lettuce," where the deadly mocassin lurks concealed in the dense vegetation, where the gayly colored purple gallinules patter over the lily pads and where the beautiful snowy herons and many others of their tribe flourish in their native solitudes, there may we look for these curious birds. We may expect to find them sitting quietly, in little groups, in the tops of some clump of willows on the marshy shore or on the branches of some larger trees overhanging the water, with their long necks stretched upwards in an attitude of inquiry or held in graceful

curves if not alarmed; perhaps some may have their wings outstretched in the sun to dry, a favorite basking attitude. If alarmed
by the sudden appearance of a boat one may be seen to plunge headlong into the water, straight as a winged arrow, and disappear; soon,
however, a snake-like head and neck may be seen at a distance rapidly
swimming away with its body entirely submerged. The anhinga is a
water bird surely enough, but I could never see any resemblance to a
turkey, and I can not understand how this name happened to be
applied to it. The name " darter " or " snake bird," both of which are
descriptive, seem much more appropriate.

Spring.—Throughout the southern portion of its range, in the Gulf
States and in tropical America, the water-turkey is a resident throughout the year, but it migrates a short distance northward, up the
Mississippi Valley and to the Carolinas, in March, avoiding the salt
water and frequenting the inland marshes and ponds.

Courtship.—Audubon (1840) observes that during its courtship the
movements of its head and neck—

Resemble sudden jerkings of the parts to their full extent, become extremely
graceful during the love season, when they are reduced to gentle curvatures.
I must not forget to say that during all these movements the gular pouch is
distended, and the bird emits rough guttural sounds. If they are courting on
wing, however, in the manner of cormorants, hawks, and many other birds, they
emit a whistling note, somewhat resembling that of some of our rapacious birds,
and which may be expressed by the syllables *eek, eek, eek*, the first loudest,
and the rest diminishing in strength. When they are on the water, their call-
notes so much resemble the rough grunting cries of the Florida cormorant that
I have often mistaken them for the latter.

Nesting.—My first experience with the nesting habits of the
water-turkey was in the extensive marshes bordering the upper
St. Johns River in Florida. The river at this point is spread out
over a marshy area about 3 miles wide with a narrow open channel and a series of small lakes or ponds in the center. Except in
these open places the water is very shallow, from 1 to 3 feet deep,
with a treacherous muddy bottom, making wading impossible. The
marsh consists of broad areas of saw grass among which are numerous tortuous channels overgrown with a rank growth of coarse
yellow pond lilies, locally known as " bonnets," through which we
had to navigate by laboriously polling a shallow, pointed skiff. The
channels are still further choked by small floating islands, made up
of bushes and rank aquatic vegetation, which drift about more or
less with the changes of the wind. There are also many permanent
islands overgrown with willows, which serve as rookeries for thousands of Louisiana herons, little blue herons, anhingas, and a few
snowy, black-crowned and yellow-crowned night herons. Least
bitterns, red-winged blackbirds, and boat-tailed grackles nest in the
saw grass; coots, purple and Florida gallinules frequent the " bon-

nets," and large flocks of white ibises, wood ibises, cormorants, and a few glossy ibises fly back and forth over the marshes, especially at morning and evening.

Here we found, on April 18 and 21, 1902, several small breeding colonies of water-turkeys in small isolated clumps of willows or on the borders of the larger willow islands inhabited by the various herons. There were never more than 8 or 10 nests in a group, which were placed from 5 to 15 feet above the ground or water and were very conspicuous; we generally saw the anhingas sitting in the tree-tops and sometimes saw them on their nests as we approached. The nests were easily recognized, as they were always loosely built, often quite bulky and irregular in shape and always showed a large quantity of brown, dead leaves mixed with the sticks in the body of the nest. The nests were generally carelessly built, mostly of willow twigs and coarse sticks, mixed with the dead leaves, which gave them a ragged appearance; they were profusely lined with green willow leaves. The date of laying must vary considerably, for we found eggs in all stages of incubation, from incomplete sets of fresh eggs to full sets of four or five, and young birds, some recently hatched and others nearly grown.

In the locality described above the anhinga's nests were segregated in groups on the outskirts of heron rookeries or were in small rookeries by themselves, but they are often found mingled with various other species in the large rookeries. In the great Cuthbert rookery in southern Florida, which occupies a small mangrove island in Cuthbert Lake, we estimated, on our first visit on May 1, 1903, that the population consisted of about 2,000 Louisiana herons, 1,000 white ibises, 600 Florida cormorants, 200 anhingas, 100 little blue herons, 18 American egrets, and 12 roseate spoonbills; the total, about 4,000 birds, was really a wonderful population for so small an island, and I have no doubt that the estimate was well below the actual figures. The water-turkeys' nests were scattered among the ibises and cormorants nests in the red mangroves and mostly over the water; they were similar to those described above and in most cases contained from three to five eggs, though there were also young of various ages.

Mr. Charles R. Stockard (1905) describes the nest of this species, as he has found it in Mississippi, as "rather loosely constructed of sticks and very shallow, suggesting at once the architectural style so commonly employed by the herons," apparently unlined and without leaves. Other writers have referred to nests lined with willow catkins, cypress needles, and *Tillandsia*. The water-turkey returns to the same nesting site and probably uses the same nest year after year, which may account for the presence of dead leaves in the nest, the remains of previous years' linings.

Eggs.—The full set usually consists of four eggs, sometimes only three and sometimes five. The eggs are often laid at irregular intervals, as the young in a nest are frequently of widely different ages. The eggs have been described as resembling other eggs of the Steganopodes, but to me they look quite different and easily recognizable. The shape varies from "ovate," slightly elongated, to "elliptical ovate" or "elongate ovate." The ground color is pale bluish white, which is usually more or less covered with a very thin coating of chalky deposit, rarely roughly or thickly covered with it; this is generally quite smooth, and after the egg has been incubated for a while it even becomes quite glossy. The color is always more or less concealed by brownish, buffy, or yellowish nest stains, which will not wash off; some eggs are uniformly stained a rich cinnamon or buff color over the entire surface.

The measurements of 42 eggs in the United States National Museum average 52.5 by 35 millimeters; the eggs showing the four extremes measure **57.5** by 35, 54 by **37.5, 47** by 33.5, and 53.5 by **33** millimeters.

Young.—The young remain in the nest or near it until they are fully grown and able to fly, using both bills and feet to climb out of the nest and over the surrounding branches. Audubon (1840) says on this subject:

At an early age the young utter a low wheezing call, and at times some cries resembling those of the young of the smaller species of herons. From birth they are fed by regurgitation, which one might suppose an irksome task to the parent birds, as during the act they open their wings and raise their tails. I have not been able to ascertain the period of incubation, but am sure that the male and the female sit alternately, the latter, however, remaining much longer on the nest. Young anhingas when approached while in the nest cling tenaciously to it until seized, and if thrown down they merely float on the water and are easily captured.

Plumages.—The young snake bird, when first hatched, is naked and yellowish buff in color, very different from the jet-black young of cormorants, but it soon becomes covered with a short, thick coat of soft buff-colored down, which contrasts prettily with its black bill. The peculiar snake-like attitude of the head and neck give the young bird a very curious appearance at this age. Audubon (1840) says of the development of the young:

When they are three weeks old, the quills and tail feathers grow rapidly but continue of the same dark-brown color, and so remain until they are able to fly, when they leave the nest, although they still present a singular motley appearance, the breast and back being buff-colored, while the wings and tail are nearly black. After the feathers of the wings and tail are nearly fully developed, those of the sides of the body and breast become visible through the down and the bird appears more curiously mottled than before.

In the juvenal or first winter plumage the sexes are practically alike; the flight feathers of the wings and tail are plain dusky; the belly is dark brown and the breast and neck lighter brown, sometimes pale "cinnamon" on the chest; the upper parts are brownish black with a limited amount of the silver-gray markings so conspicuous in adults on the back, scapulars, and wing-coverts; these markings are more restricted and less brilliant than in adults and are bordered with brownish. I have seen young birds, still partially in down, in which these silver-gray markings were well developed. A prenuptial molt occurs during the first spring, which involves part or all of the body plumage, the tail and perhaps also the wings. This molt brings progress toward maturity, but the wings and tail are still plain dusky, lacking the characteristic corrugations of the latter or having them only faintly suggested; there is an increase in the silver-gray markings of the upper parts and more black appears in the belly, but the head, neck, and chest are still light brown in both sexes.

At the first postnuptial molt, during the following summer and fall, a plumage approaching the adult is assumed and the sexes become differentiated. This is a complete molt at which the adult wings and tail are assumed and at which the male acquires the black chest, neck, and head; but signs of immaturity still remain in the shape of scattering brown feathers, which give the head and neck of the young male a mottled appearance. The fully adult plumage is not completed until the following spring, when the young bird is nearly two years old.

The adult winter plumage is similar to the adult nuptial plumage, except that the scattering light-colored plumes of the head and neck are lacking, also the elongated dark mane of the hind-neck. The prenuptial molt is nearly complete; the tail is molted in April, beginning with the central rectrices; I have seen birds in early summer which had apparently fresh remiges, but I have never seen them actually molting these feathers in the spring. The postnuptial molt is probably complete, though I have not fully traced it and can not say just when it occurs.

Food.—Audubon (1840) found in the stomachs of this species "fishes of various kinds, aquatic insects, crays, leeches, shrimps, tadpoles, eggs of frogs, water-lizards, young alligators, water-snakes, and small terrapins," certainly a varied bill of fare. He also relates the following incident to illustrate its voracity:

One morning Doctor Bachman and I gave to an anhinga a black fish, measuring nine and a half inches by two inches in diameter; and although the head of the fish was considerably larger than its body, and its strong and spinous fins appeared formidable, the bird, which was then about seven months old, swallowed it entire, head foremost. It was in appearance digested in an hour and a half, when the bird swallowed three others of somewhat smaller size. At another time we placed before it a number of fishes about seven and a half inches long, of which it swallowed nine in succession. It would devour at a meal forty or more fishes about three inches and a half long. On several occasions it was fed on plaice, when it swallowed some that were four inches broad, extending its throat, and compressing them during their descent into the stomach. It did not appear to relish eels, as it ate all the other sorts first, and kept them to the last; and after having swallowed them, it had great difficulty in keeping them down, but, although for awhile thwarted, it would renew its efforts, and at length master them. When taken to the tide-point at the foot of my friend's garden, it would now and then after diving return to the surface of the water with a cray-fish in its mouth, which it pressed hard and dashed about in its bill, evidently for the purpose of maiming it, before it would attempt to swallow it, and it never caught a fish without bringing it up to subject it to the same operation.

Fish undoubtedly form the principal part of this bird's diet and it is especially well adapted to catch them, with its skill as a diver, its speed under water and its long neck, controlled by highly developed, special muscles and armed with a spearlike beak, which may be darted in any direction swiftly and accurately. Mr. N. B. Moore's unpublished notes on this species in Florida show that it does not fish exclusively in fresh water, for he frequently saw it diving in the tidal waters of a bay between two oyster bars.

Behavior.—Though ungainly in appearance and somewhat awkward in its movements when perched on a tree, it is really a graceful bird on the wing with splendid powers of flight; it clings somewhat clumsily to the branch on which it sits, but its totipalmate feet hold it securely, as it spreads its broad wings in the sun to dry them or flaps them vigorously for exercise, its ample tail serving to balance it. As it launches into the air it is evident that the broad expanse of wings and tail, in proportion to its small, compact body, are amply sufficient to sustain it in rapid, strong, and protracted flight. The neck is outstreached, usually to its full extent, but sometimes with a partial fold near the body, the tail is spread as a rudder and the wings are moved rather rapidly as the bird forges steadily ahead in a straight line. Like other Steganopodes, it sets its wings and scales at intervals, when it suggests, in appearance and manner, the flight of a Cooper's hawk. One of the favorite pastimes of a flock of waterturkeys is to indulge in aerial exercise by rising from their roost, mounting high in the air and soaring in circles gradually upwards until almost out of sight, suggesting in their movements the flight of the Buteos. After gazing in admiration at such a spectacle the observer may be suddenly surprised to see one after another of the birds fold its wings and dart downwards, swift as an arrow.

In the water it is even more at home than in the air, where it swims gracefully and swiftly on the surface or sneaks away with its body submerged and only its snake-like head and neck showing in sinuous curves; sometimes only its bill is seen cutting the smooth surface and making scarcely a ripple. In pursuit of its prey it does not plunge from the air into the water, but dives from the surface, disappearing like a flash with the least possible effort or commotion, like a master diver with perfect control of its movements in its favorite element. Under water its long slender body is propelled by the powerful feet alone, the wings tightly folded and the broad tail guiding its movements.

Audubon (1840) says of its roosting habits:

The anhinga is altogether a diurnal bird, and, like the cormorant, is fond of returning to the same roosting place every evening about dusk, unless prevented by molestation. At times I have seen from three to seven alight on the dead top branches of a tall tree, for the purpose of there spending the night; and this they repeated for several weeks, until on my having killed some of them and wounded others, the rest abandoned the spot, and after several furious contests with a party that roosted about two miles off succeeded in establishing themselves among them. At such times they seldom sit very near each other, as cormorants do, but keep at a distance of a few feet or yards, according to the nature of the branches. Whilst asleep they stand with the body almost erect, but never bend the tarsus so as to apply it in its whole length, as the cormorant does; they keep their head snugly covered among their scapulars, and at times emit a wheezing sound, which I supposed to be produced by their breathing. In rainy weather they often remain roosted the greater part of the day, and on such occasions they stand erect, with their neck and head stretched upwards, remaining perfectly motionless, as if to allow the water to glide off their plumage. Now and then, however, they suddenly ruffle their feathers, violently shake themselves, and again compressing their form, resume their singular position.

Aside from the whistling notes, referred to above as a part of their courtship performances, their only utterances are the rough, grunting call notes, much like the sounds made by cormorants. Even these are not often heard, as the birds are usually silent. I have never noticed anything worthy of comment in their behavior toward other species; they seem to be peaceful and harmless neighbors in the large, mixed rookeries where they breed; and, so far as I know, they seem to have no serious enemies. They attend strictly to their own affairs, have their own favorite haunts and usually flock by themselves. They are practically useless for food and their plumage is not in demand.

Winter.—At the approach of winter the water-turkeys withdraw from their northern breeding grounds and spend the winter in Florida and the Gulf States. At this season they become more gregarious and are often seen flying about in large flocks.

DISTRIBUTION.

Breeding range.—Tropical and subtropical regions in North and South America. In the United States, north to south central Texas (Bexar County), eastern Arkansas (Helena), southern Illinois (Cairo and Mount Carmel), and southern North Carolina (near Wilmington). Southern limits of South American breeding range not well defined, but the species ranges south to southern Brazil, Paraguay, and northern Argentina, and it probably breeds throughout most of its range. Said to breed on the coast of Peru.

Winter range.—Includes most of the breeding range, at least north to central Arkansas (Newport), central Alabama (Greensboro), and probably southern Georgia.

Spring migration.—Migrates into South Carolina in March (earliest, March 13, usually common by March 21).

Fall migration.—Latest dates: Illinois, Cairo, August 31; South Carolina, Otranto, August 31.

Casual records.—Has wandered as far west and north as California (Imperial County, February 9, 1913), Wisconsin (Kelley Brook, spring, 1889), and Ohio (Lowell, November, 1885).

Egg dates.—Florida: Fifty-four records, February 15 to June 16; twenty-seven records, March 16 to April 29. Louisiana and Texas: Eight records, April 14 to June 2; four records, April 21 to May 27.

Family PHALACROCORACIDAE, Cormorants.

PHALACROCORAX CARBO (Linnaeus).

CORMORANT.

HABITS.

Contributed by Charles Wendell Townsend.

On the northern Atlantic seaboard the term shag is used for both this and the double-crested species, and the two are not distinguished by the ordinary observer. Although not as common here as the double-crested bird, it has an almost world-wide distribution, and breeds in the northern part of the Northern Hemisphere from Nova Scotia, Labrador, and Greenland to the British Isles and Kamchatka, and winters as far south as Long Island, southern Africa, Australia, and New Zealand. The bird is said to be very intelligent, easily domesticated, and to become attached to its masters. In the time of Charles the First, fishing with trained cormorants was a regular sport in England, and this species was employed. Rings around the neck, as in China at the present day, were used to prevent swallowing the prey, although in well-trained birds this was unnecessary.

Although the cormorant does not now breed south of Nova Scotia, in the time of Audubon it nested at Grand Manan. Nuttall (1834) says, " They breed, and are seen in the vicinity of Boston on bare and rocky islands, nearly throughout the year." Earlier still, when the first settlers came to this country, they were abundant along the New England coast, where now they are uncommon. Thus William Wood (1634) writes:

Cormorants bee as common as other fowles which destroy abundance of small fish, these are not worth the shooting because they are the worst of fowles for meate, tasting ranke and fishy; againe, one may shoot twenty times and misse, for seeing the fire in the panne, they dive under the water before the shot comes to the place where they were; they used to roost upon the tops of trees, and rockes, being a very heavy drowsie creature, so that the Indians will goe in their Cannoes in the night, and take them from the Rockes, as easily as women take a Hen from roost.

Spring.—The birds arrive early on the breeding grounds and begin nesting before the snows of winter have disappeared. Frazar (1887) says that in southern Labrador it is sometimes the case that the frozen foundations of the nest give way under the summer heat, and the domicile and its contents are projected into the sea. He found large young in the nests at Cape Whittle, as early as June 19th.

Courtship.—The courtship of the cormorant is spectacular and is performed both on the rocky ledges and cliffs and on the water. In the former situation the male approaches the female with an awkward waddle or hop and sinks down before her on his breast. In both situations the neck is stretched up to its full extent, with widely open beak and the brilliant inside lining of the mouth displayed. The tail is cocked up and the head stretched back and down until it touches the back. Selous (1901) says that " in this attitude he may remain for some seconds more or less, having all the while a languishing or ecstatic expression, after which he brings his head forward again, and then repeats the performance some three or four, or perhaps half a dozen times."

Nesting.—Rocky cliffs are chosen by these birds for their nesting colonies, and, as a rule, they prefer the elevated stations while the double-crested species nests for the most part on low rocks or on the lower portions of the cliffs. At Whapatiguan, the breeding place in southern Labrador made famous by Audubon, this species was found by Bryant (1862) to nest on the higher parts of the cliffs, while the double-crested nested lower down, although he found that the highest nest of all belonged to the double-crested species. Frazar (1887) at this place observed the double-crested nests all over the cliff, but those of *carbo* close to the top only. Brewster (1884) visited a colony of 20 pairs at Wreck Bay, Anticosti, and says the nests were situated " on the projections of a vertical limestone cliff some 15 feet below the summit and at least 100 above the sea." Audubon's (1840) description of the colony at Whapatiguan is classic; he says:

We saw no nests of this species placed in any other situations than the highest shelves of the precipitous rocks fronting the water and having a southern exposure * * *. On some shelves eight or ten yards in extent, the nests were crowded together; but more usually they were placed apart on every secure place without any order; none, however, were below a certain height on the rocks, nor were there any on the summit.

Yarrell (1871) speaks of an island in county Cork, Ireland, where a colony of 18 pairs of cormorants had built their nests in Scotch fir trees not under 60 feet in height. He also speaks of their nesting in trees in Norfolk and Sicily.

The cormorant has not reached the point in evolution where sanitation and cleanliness about the dwelling place are considered important. A cormorant colony can be smelt from afar, and the vile, fishy odor clings to the clothes and remains long in the memory. Rocks, sticks, bushes, nests, eggs, everything is daubed with the chalky, slimy excrement. The nests are placed close together, or scattered wherever there are suitable ledges on the cliffs. In construction the nest is a bulky affair composed of twigs and branches of trees, grass stalks, pieces of mountain cranberry and curlew berry vine, seaweed, and fresh evergreen boughs. It measures about 10 inches inside and 20 to 24 outside and 3 or 4 inches high. Some of the nests, however, are fully a yard across and a foot high and are built upon the nests of preceding seasons.

Eggs.—The eggs are four or five in number and occasionally six, and one set only is laid. They are somewhat larger than those of the double-crested species and are more rounded or ellipical in shape. They are of a faint green or blue color overlaid with a thick, chalky coating which soon becomes soiled a dirty yellowish color.

The measurements of 42 eggs, in various collections, average 64.8 by 40.9 millimeters; the eggs showing the four extremes measure **70.5** by **43.5, 61** by 39.6, and 62 by **38.5** millimeters.

Young.—Audubon (1840) graphically described his pleasure in watching a cormorant family at Whapatiguan: "The mother fondled and nursed her young with all possible tenderness, disgorged some food into the mouth of each, and coaxed them with her bill and wings. The little ones seemed very happy, billed with their mother, and caressed her about the breast." They grow rapidly and are fed by both parents who convey the partially digested fish in their capacious gullets. Into these the young thrust their heads and necks and forage to their hearts' content.

Plumages.—The young are not objects of beauty, as they appear to be all legs, feet, and head and are naked and of a dark leaden color; this also is the general color of their bill, eyes, and feet. Later they become clothed with a sooty colored down. When three or four weeks old, before they are able to fly, they take to the water and at this time, according to Lucas (1897) the external nostrils, which have been open, become closed as in the adult. The juveniles, when fully feathered, have a brownish gray back, a dark brown breast, and in the first winter plumage the belly is nearly white. In this respect they differ from double-crested cormorants, which have a light-gray breast shading down to black on the lower belly. With good glasses I have been able to distinguish the two species at the distance of a mile. In the full adult plumage both sexes are alike, and are blue black below and bronzy slate-brown above. There is a broad band of white on the throat below the bare gular sac, there are scattered linear white feathers on the side of the head and upper neck, and there are patches of white feathers on the flanks. These white patches, but particularly the white feathers of the throat, are excellent field marks to distinguish this bird from the double-crested cormorant. The fowlers of Belfast Lough, Ireland, according to Patterson (1880) speak of the flank patch as "the watch that it carries under the wing." The bill is grayish-black; yellowish white on the edges of both mandibles and at the base of the lower mandible. The iris is a light bluish green with a dull olive bare space above and a bright red space below. The gular sac is yellow, not orange as in the double-crested species. The feet are grayish black.

The distinctive white patches are worn by both sexes but for a brief time during the nuptial season. Yarrell (1871) reports some observations on this point on captive birds in the gardens of the London Zoological Society; the white feathers on the side of the head and neck began to appear January 4th, arrived at greatest perfection February 26th, began to disappear on April 2d, and were gone by May 12th; the white patches on the thighs began on January 24th, were complete in five weeks, began to disappear on June 16th and were almost entirely gone on July 30th. It is probably that three or four years are needed before the full adult plumage is attained.

Food.—The cormorant is an expert on the wing and in the water, and its habits are very similar to those of its double-crested cousin. Its food consists entirely of fish, which it is able to follow under water with great speed and seize with its powerful hook-like bill. When it appears on the surface it sometimes throws the fish up into the air in order to get a better hold; its gullet is so wide that its swallowing capacity is large. Most of the fish it captures are of no economic importance to man, but in some cases, no doubt, a toll is taken of useful fish. On Cape Cod I have seen cormorants perched on the fencing of fish weirs, and it is probable that they are not considered desirable visitors by the fishermen. With us the cormorant is rarely seen away from the sea, although there are records from Lake Ontario. Stead (1906) says of it in New Zealand that it "is with us largely an inland bird, frequenting fresh-water lakes and rivers." Yarrell (1871) writes that they follow the course of rivers many miles inland.

Behavior.—The flight of the cormorant is heavy and heron like, with slow flapping of its broad wings. It often flies close to the water, and I have seen it touch the surface with its wing tips at each stroke From a flat station like a beach, or the water on calm days, it has considerable difficulty in rising, and strikes with its feet together in great hops several times before it can get away. From a cliff or buoy it launches itself into the air and descends in a great downward curve nearly to the water, sometimes even splashing the surface before it gets impetus enough to rise again and fly away. The stronger the wind to which it opposes its aeroplanes, the less is the depth of the curve. The reverse process of alighting on a cliff, and particularly on a small perch like a buoy, also calls for much skill on the part of the bird, and is interesting to watch. The cormorant flies with considerable velocity upwind toward its buoy, sets its wings, and with neck outstretched and feet dropped, it sails upwards toward its perch. If it has not calculated exactly right it may fail to accomplish the feat; whereupon it swings around to leeward and tries again. I watched a cormorant try four times one calm March day off Rockport on Cape Ann before it succeeded in alighting on the spindle on the salvages. Cormorants, in migration or when flying to and from their feeding grounds, maintain no regularity of flock arrangement. An irregular flock is common, as is also a perfect V-shaped formation, a long file, or a rank. In the latter case each successive bird in the rank is generally slightly behind his neighbor on one side. Although the flight is usually heavy, with slow wing beats, the birds are swift flyers in strong winds and, at times, soar like gulls or hawks to a great height.

On the water they are rapid swimmers, and they often swim with their body depressed so that the back is level with the surface. When alarmed they sink still lower so that only the head and neck are exposed. They not infrequently swim with the head and neck extended forward under water for the purpose of looking for fish. Under the surface they are especially at home, and progress with great swiftness. As the cormorant dives for fish he springs upward and forward and enters the water in a graceful curve with wings pressed close to the sides. Headly (1907) says: " The cormorant uses his feet alone to propel him [in diving] striking with both simultaneously, and holding the wings motionless, though slightly lifted from the body. The position of the wings must have given rise to the idea, common among fishermen, that the cormorant flies under water * * * but when you see him in a tank you can have no doubt that the legs are the propellers." Selous (1905) made observations on wild birds seen under advantageous circumstances in a cave in the Shetlands and confirms the statement that the wings are not used in diving. Cormorants are also able to dart down from a height as from a cliff and dive into the sea. This they are apt to do when shot at or otherwise disturbed.

The position of the cormorant on a perch is very characteristic by reason of the long neck which takes on an **S** curve, and the long tail which points diagonally downward or is slightly elevated to clear the ground. The gait of this bird is a waddle of the most marked description. It may be seen asleep on rocks or sandbars with head buried in the scapulars and the tail elevated. At their nesting places in cliffs they support themselves on the vertical faces by their claws and tail like woodpeckers. The most characteristic attitude of the cormorant, however, is the spread-eagle one with wings widely open. This attitude is assumed on trees or buoys, on rocks or sand and even on the surface of the water—sometimes for minutes together. On one occasion I timed an individual who sat thus on a rock for ten minutes. The position is generally supposed to be assumed for the purpose of drying the wings, but, if so, it is not assumed by other water birds, who content themselves with flapping and shaking their wings. I have seen cormorants assume the spread-eagle position on foggy, rainy days, and I am inclined to think that the habit is derived from the same ancestors that bequeathed it, to the vultures, for cormorants and vultures are now believed to be allied.

The cormorant is not a song bird, and, as far as I know, he utters his feelings only in harsh, guttural croaks.

Although Longfellow has made us familiar with the "fierce cormorant," this bird seems to get along peaceably with other birds. As already stated it nests in communities with the double-crested species. G. M. Allen (1913) quotes from the notes of B. F. Damsell the interesting case of a cormorant that took refuge in an oak tree from the attacks of two kingbirds. From the tree it fell to the ground and was found to have a broken wing that had healed.

Man, as always, is the cormorant's worst enemy, although its flesh and eggs are so fishy that they are but indifferent eating. I have already quoted William Wood on the subject. Josselyn (1674) gives a similar verdict and describes more in detail the Indians' method of capture. He says:

I have not done yet, nor must not forget the *cormorant*, Shape or Sharke; though I can not commend them to our curious palats. The *Indians* will eat them when they are fley'd, they take them prettily, they roost in the night upon some Rock that lyes out in the Sea, thither the *Indian* goes in his Birch-*Canow* when the Moon shines clear, and when he is come almost to it, he lets his *Canow* drive on of its self, when he is come under the Rock he droves his Boat along till he come just under the *Cormorants* watchman, the rest being asleep, and so soundly do sleep that they will snore like so many Piggs; the Indian thrusts up his hand of a sudden, grasping the watchman so hard round his neck that he can not cry out; as soon as he hath him in his *Canow* fast, he clambreth to the top of the Rock, where walking softly he takes them up as he pleaseth, still wringing off their heads; when he hath slain as many as his *Canow* can carry, he gives a shout which awakens the surviving *Cormorants*, who are gone in an instant.

Bewick (1884); says:

At other times and places, while they sit in a dozing and stupified state, from the effects of one of their customary surfeits, they may easily be taken by throwing nets over them, or by putting a noose around their necks.

Kumlien (1879), reports that the primaries of this bird were formerly in great demand by the Eskimos of Cumberland Sound for their arrows.

Winter.—The fall migration of the cormorant along the Atlantic coast begins in October and the birds winter in favorable localities along the shore. One of these is Rockport on the end of Cape Ann. Here three or four individuals, the pitiful remnant of a much larger number, may generally be seen fishing about the Salvages—rocky islands in the outer harbor—and alighting on spar buoys and spindles.

DISTRIBUTION.

Breeding range.—Probably now extirpated as a breeding bird in North America; a few may still breed in Greenland. Formerly bred from central western Greenland (Godhaven, 69° north) and Baffin Land (Cumberland Sound) south to Newfoundland, southern Labrador (Whapitaguan) and the Bay of Fundy (Grand Manan). In the eastern hemisphere this form breeds in Iceland, on the Scandinavian and north Russian coasts, east to the Kola Peninsula, and south to the Faroe Islands, Scotland, England, Ireland and Wales. The birds of continental Europe and Asia are now regarded as subspecifically distinct.

Winter range.—From southern Greenland, throughout its breeding range, and southward along the Atlantic coast, regularly to New York (Long Island) and occasionally to Maryland (Chesapeake Bay) and South Carolina (two specimens taken). On the other side of the Atlantic the winter range extends to the Canary Islands.

Spring migration.—Has been noted in Rhode Island (Newport) as late as May 15, and in Massachusetts (Amesbury) as late as June 18.

Fall migration.—Arrives in Rhode Island (Seaconnet Point) as early as September 15, and New York (Long Island) as early as September 22.

Casual records.—Accidental inland: Ontario (Toronto, November 21, 1896), and New York (Oneida Lake, November 15, 1877).

Egg dates.—Labrador: Twelve records, June 1 to 30; six records, June 16 to 20. British Isles: Seven records, April 22 to May 25; four records, April 28 to May 19. Greenland: April 28 to July 25 (Hagerup).

PHALACROCORAX AURITUS AURITUS (Lesson).

DOUBLE-CRESTED CORMORANT.

HABITS.

Among the passing flocks of wild fowl which migrate along the New England coast, one occasionally sees a flock of large black birds flying high in the air in a regular V-shaped formation like geese, or in single file, or rarely in an irregular bunch. At first he may mistake them for geese or brant on account of their size and manner of flight, which is heavy and strong, with rather slow wing strokes, but if he watches them carefully he will see them set their wings and scale along at occasional intervals, by which he recognizes them at once as cormorants or "shags." There are two species of "shags" found on this coast, the double-crested and the common cormorant, of which the former is much the commoner.

Courtship.—On the flat top of Percé Rock, which stands only a few rods from the shore of Percé, Quebec, is a large breeding colony of double-crested cormorants and herring gulls, and the top of the rock is about level with the heights of Cape Cannon, the nearest point. On June 19, 1920, while watching this colony from that point through a powerful telescope, I had a good opportunity to study the courtship or nuptial greeting of this species. Many birds were standing by their mates on the nests; others were constantly coming or going. The incoming bird, presumably the male, bows to his mate and walks around her with his neck upstretched and swollen, opening and closing his bill. Then approaching his mate he begins caressing her with his bill; she steps off the nest; then both begin a series of snakelike movements of heads and necks, almost intertwining them. Finally he passes his head over, under, and around his mate, apparently caressing her from head to tail, and he or she settles down on the nest.

Nesting.—Many of the birds must reach their breeding grounds on the south coast of Labrador by the middle of May or earlier, for we found their nesting operations well under way during the last week in May, and they are said to begin nest building before the snows of winter have passed away. They must be very common all along this coast, for in a 75-mile cruise from Esquimaux Point to Natashquan, Doctor Townsend and I saw three breeding colonies in 1909. These were all on low, bare, rocky islets well off the coast. The first colony visited, on May 26, was on Seal Rock, off St. Genevieve Island, a low-lying rock of less than an acre in area. From a distance we could see the large black birds sitting all over it, but as we approached it in a small boat they all flew off, and after circling about us a few times, to satisfy their curiosity, they settled down on the water to watch us. We counted 204 nests in various stages of construction, closely grouped together on the higher portions of the rock, which was thickly covered with excrement, making the rocks quite slippery and filling the small water puddles with a putrid, vile-smelling mixture. Some of the nests had well-made foundations of sticks, but most of them were made wholly or largely of seaweed, kelp, rockweed, grasses, feathers, and bark; they were generally lined with grasses or seaweed, and many were decorated with green sprigs of fir, spruce, cedar, or laurel; a few were still further ornamented with gull's feathers, birch bark, or dead crabs, and one had a long curly shaving in it. A typical nest measured 22 inches in diameter outside and 9 inches inside; they were usually built up 4 or 5 inches, but one was 9 inches high. Many of the nests were incomplete or empty, but most of them contained from one to five fresh eggs. Two similar colonies containing about 75 pairs each were noted a little farther along the coast. We watched them through our high-power glasses and saw them building their nests; most of the seaweed was obtained near by, the birds diving for it in deep water and bringing it up in their bills; the sticks and green twigs were, of course, brought from the mainland several miles away. Although they were not breeding in the interior anywhere we frequently saw these cormorants flying up the rivers, probably in search of fishing grounds.

The most southern breeding resort of the double-crested cormorant that I know of on the Atlantic coast is at Black Horse Ledge, a precipitous crag of rough black rock, towering 60 or 70 feet up out of the ocean off Penobscot Bay, Maine. I visited this rock on June 19, 1899, where I had some difficulty in landing and climbing up its steep sides. I had seen eight or ten cormorants fly off as I approached and the top of the rock was filthy with their excrement and swarming with flies, but no nests had been built. Mr. Ora W. Knight, who told me about the colony, said that a few pairs bred there nearly every year, but did not lay their eggs until late in June or in July. A few pairs of herring gulls also nest on this rock.

The most populous summer resort for this species that I have ever seen is Lake Winnipegosis in Manitoba, a large shallow lake, about 120 miles long and averaging about 15 feet deep, with numerous rocky shoals and low reefs of loose boulders. The whole country around the lake is low, flat, and largely marshy, a fine country for water fowl of many species. The waters of the lake are teeming with fish, mostly white fish, pickerel, and pike, which furnish an abundant food supply for thousands of cormorants, grebes, loons, and pelicans. Numerous small islands and rocky reefs furnish convenient nesting places, which are well patronized. During a short cruise of less than a week we saw no less than five breeding colonies of double-crested cormorants, ranging in size from 45 to 1,500 pairs. The largest colony that I have ever seen was visited on June 18, 1913, on a small triangular island near the northern end of the lake. As we approached the island and anchored in the lea of it, preparing to land, an imense cloud of the large black birds poured off the rocky shores and began circling around us in a bewildering maze, and mingled with them were a few of the great white pelicans, which were also breeding on the island. It was an impressive sight. The birds were much tamer than usual, for when we landed they were still sitting on their nests on the farther side of the island behind a little ridge, but they went scrambling off in haste and confusion as soon as we were in plain sight. The cause of their tameness was soon apparent for we were surprised to find that nearly all of the nests contained young; this was rather remarkable, for none of the other colonies contained any young at all and nearly all the eggs we had collected were fresh or only slightly incubated. Perhaps this was the oldest colony, for it was by far the largest, and had been occupied by the earliest arrivals. In an average space 3 yards square I counted 25 nests and by roughly measuring the whole occupied area I estimated that there were between 1,500 and 2,000 nests in the colony. The island was about 50 yards long by 40 yards wide, consisting of a mass of boulders piled up quite high at one end with an accumulation of bare soil in the center, probably the result of generations of guano deposits. Except for a bare space in the center where the pelicans were nesting, the whole island was covered with cormorants' nests nearly down to the water's edge, even on and among the boulders. The nests were made of sticks, dead weeds, canes, and flags, most of which had been picked up as drift material along the shore; they were lined with straws, grasses, and often with green leaves and fresh twigs; some were decorated or lined with gulls' feathers. One large nest measured 14 inches in height and 18 by 22 inches in diameter; most of the nests were much smaller than this and some of them consisted of only a few sticks and straws. The nests and their surroundings were far from atractive as the whole island was slimy with excrement and reeking with dead fish; the odor was almost unbearable. Some of the nests still held eggs but the great majority held young of various ages, from naked, helpless, newly-hatched chicks to well-developed, half-grown young, covered with jet black down and squawking vigorously.

Although I have never seen the double-crested cormorant nesting in trees, as is the universal custom with its southern representative, the observations of others indicate that it frequently does so in the southern portion of its range in the interior of the United States. Mr.

R. M. Barnes (1890) has described a large herony, formerly existing in Illinois, in which these cormorants nested with great blue herons and American egrets, all three species building their nests in trees, just as they do in Florida. More recent information on the nesting of double-crested cormorants in Illinois is given us by Mr. Frank Smith (1911). Mr. Arthur H. Howell (1911) describes a recent colony in Arkansas, as follows:

A large colony, probably the only large one now remaining in the State, breeds in a rookery at Walker Lake, Mississippi County, in company with great blue herons and water-turkeys. When I visited this rookery the first week in May, 1910, I found the cormorants sitting on their nests in the tops of the tall cypresses growing in the lake. The nests, of which there were between 100 and 200, were placed in crotches either close to the trunks or some distance out on the limbs and were compactly built of green cypress twigs with a few strips of bark as a lining. Most of the nests examined contained three or four bluish eggs, but in one were four little naked coal-black cormorants a few days old. The number of nests in a single tree varied from 1 to 6—usually 3 or 4—and in many instances the cormorants shared the tree with several great blue herons. Specimens taken in this colony are referable to the northern form, and this is probably the southern limit of its breeding range.

Mr. P. A. Taverner (1915) found a colony of about 30 pairs near the Gaspé Basin in Quebec, where the nests were built in trees, mostly small birches, growing from the top and upper face of a bluff overlooking the sea at a height of about 150 feet, a most unusual situation.

Eggs.—The double-crested cormorant lays ordinarily three or four eggs, frequently five, rarely six, and I have taken one set of seven. They vary in shape from elongate ovate to cylindrical ovate. Their color is very pale blue or bluish white, more or less concealed by a white calcareous coating which is thinner than in some other species, and they are often badly soiled or nest stained.

The measurements of 40 eggs in the United States National Museum and the writer's collections average 61.6 by 38.8 millimeters; the eggs showing the four extremes measure **65.5** by 40, 63 by **42, 56** by 38, and 57.5 by **36.5** millimeters.

Young.—The young when first hatched are purplish black in color, naked, blind, and helpless. Their downy covering begins to grow when they are about 10 days old, and at the age of about three weeks they are fully covered with thick, short, black down. The plumage appears first on the wings and scapulars; the wings and tail are practically fully grown before the body plumage is fairly started, which does not appear until the bird is fully grown; the head and neck are the last portions to become feathered when the bird is about six weeks old. A populous colony often contains young birds of all ages from naked helpless chicks to full sized birds, and presents a most interesting, if not an attractive, picture. Such a colony is the filthiest place imaginable, for no other birds can equal cormorants in this respect. The nests and their surroundings become thoroughly whitewashed with excrement, which also accumulates in slimy pools swarming with flies; the nests are often alive with fleas, lice, and other vermin; and the odor of decaying fish scattered about adds to the nauseating stench. Among such unhealthful surroundings the young cormorants begin life and seem to flourish. At first they are too weak to even hold up their heads, and the heat of the sun on the black, naked bodies often brings fatal results, if they are left too long without the brooding care of their parents. Even when older and covered with black down, they seem to suffer greatly with the heat, panting with wide open mouths, the gular sacks vibrating rapidly as if in distress; perhaps this action may be caused by fear rather than by suffering, but it strongly suggests the panting of a dog on a hot day.

The young are fed by their parents until they are fully grown and able to fish for themselves; at first the helpless youngster sips the semidigested liquid food from the tip of the old bird's bill; later on he learns to thrust his head and neck deep down into the parental throat where he finds a more substantial supply of food; and finally when he has learned to eat solid food his fish are brought to him whole. The young remain in the nests until about fully grown, but after their wings and tails are grown and while their bodies are still downy they begin to wander about and gather in groups near the shore; they walk about freely, exercising their wings and legs, but do not attempt to enter the water; if one falls into the water by accident, it makes no attempt to swim and soon becomes thoroughly water soaked and chilled. Mr. Hersey once rescued one from such a predicament, which seemed to be benumbed and lay flat on the rocks as if dead, although it had been in the water but a few seconds. As soon as the body is fully feathered the young bird takes to the water and soon learns to swim; probably it learns to catch fish before it can fly, which accomplishment is not acquired until it is about eight weeks old.

Plumages.—The first winter plumage is complete in September, being acquired gradually from the downy stage, as explained above, and is worn with but slight progress toward maturity during the following winter and spring. The plumage of the back suggests the color pattern of the adult, each brown feather being bordered with brownish black, but it is dull and lusterless, instead of glossy greenish black; the under parts are dull brown, lighter on the throat and belly than elsewhere; the colors become lighter and duller as the season advances, by wear and fading. The progress of the molt into the next plumage is very variable; some vigorous individuals begin to molt as early as February, but with most birds this does not begin until late in the spring or in the summer; the latter is probably the

normal time at which the first postnuptial molt takes place. This
molt is complete, though much prolonged, and produces the second
winter plumage, which is similar to that of the adult when complete.
It is often not completed, however, until the latter part of the winter,
when the bird may be said to be in its second nuptial plumage. This
is similar to the adult nuptial plumage except that the crests are
lacking on the sides of the head. Up to this time the young bird has
been undergoing an almost constant change and development of
plumage and it is now ready to breed.

The plumage changes of the adults are simple; a complete postnuptial molt in the late summer produces the winter plumage and a
partial prenuptial molt early in the spring produces the nuptial
plumes on the sides of the head which are characteristic of the mating
season and constitute the only marked difference between the nuptial
and the fall or winter plumages. These nuptial plumes are apparently shed during the nesting period, as they are seldom seen after
the season is well advanced.

Food.—The food of the double-crested cormorant consists almost
entirely of fish, which it obtains by diving from the surface or swimming below it, at which it is an adept, capable of making great speed
under water, diving to great depths and remaining under for a long
time. I have seen it stated that cormorants use their wings in flying
under water, but I doubt if they do so regularly; their long slender
bodies and powerful totipalmate feet are highly specialized for rapid
swimming, without the aid of wings. On the New England coast
they are frequently seen flying up the larger rivers and tidal estuaries
to fish, where they live largely on eels. Mr. George H. Mackay
(1894) makes the following interesting statement regarding the food
of this species in Rhode Island:

All the double-crested cormorants (*P. dilophus*) obtained had eels (*Anguilla
vulgaris* Turton) in their throats. In four of the birds the heads of the
eels had been apparently torn off and they rested in the throat in every instance in the form of a loop or ox bow, the two ends being nearest the stomach.
In the fifth and largest bird an eel in perfect condition, measuring sixteen
inches long and one inch in diameter, rested lengthwise in the throat with
the tail at the mouth. Those taken from the other four birds were seven to
ten inches long. It would therefore seem that eels constitute a large part of
their food in this locality, at least at this time. I also picked up on the top
of the rock an eel in a partially dried condition, minus its head, which was
probably seven or eight inches long before the head had been torn off. It was
in the form of an ox bow or loop, having dried as it was probably ejected.

He also speaks in the same paper of finding their ejected pellets
of fish bones on a rock off Seaconnet Point, Rhode Island:

On the flat top of the rock I found and saw a large number of curious balls
(and brought fourteen away with me) varying from an inch to two inches in diameter and composed almost entirely of fish bones, chiefly the bones of young
parrot-fishes (Labroids) and drums (Sciaenoids) firmly cemented together

with gluten, hard in the dried specimens and soft and gelatinous in those more recent. One of the largest of the former, which was five and a quarter inches in circumference and quite black, while all the others were of a light color, contained three crabs (*Cancer irroratus* Say—*Panopeus sayi* Smith) in a fairly perfect condition, with some of the claws still remaining in place, showing that they were probably swallowed whole. I am consequently inclined to the opinion, in the absence of absolute facts, that these birds, like the owls, have the power of ejecting indigestible substances.

Mr. Taverner (1915) says of their fishing habits:

In the morning as soon as the sun is well up the cormorants fly in through the narrow channel separating the basin from the bay, their numbers increasing until about nine o'clock, when most of the birds are to be found fishing in the shallow water at the head of the basin. On first coming in they alight in the water, look about a minute, and then disappear with an easy gliding dive. They generally remain under the water for about a minute. If they have been successful in their fishing, their prey can be easily seen when they reappear. They catch a fish crossways, and it takes a little manipulation and sundry jerks of the head to get it placed properly in the mouth; then there is an upward flirt of the bill and the fish is swallowed. A few gulps are given and the bird is ready to repeat the operation.

He says of their food:

With the exception, then, of a few wandering birds, the cormorants feed either along the sea coast, as at Percé, or in the tidal mouths of the rivers. We collected some thirty stomachs from such localities, but none of them contained salmonoid remains. The food contents were mostly capelin, flounder, herring, and an occasional eel and tom cod.

Of the thirty-two stomachs examined, five were empty, one so nearly so as to make the contents unrecognizable, and two were from nestlings with contents regurgitated from the parents' throat and, having been subject to double digestive action, were not recognizable.

Of the remaining twenty-five, sixteen contained sculpins, five herring, one each capelin and eel, and two tom cod or allied fish. Nearly all had *ascaris* and other parasitical remains. The evidence indicates that these were incidentally obtained from the flesh of the original hosts. In many stomachs there were fragments of eel-grass, crustaceans, molluscs, and pebbles, but in small quantities and evidently derived from the stomachs of the prey or taken accidentally with it.

Behavior.—Except for an occasional hoarse grunting croak, when alarmed, I have never heard the double-crested cormorant make any vocal sound whatever and believe it is usually silent. Its flight, which I have previously described, is characteristic of the genus, slow and heavy, with occasional periods of scaling. When flying from a spar buoy, one of its favorite perches, it drops downward at first nearly to the water and flies along close to the surface, rising in an upward curve to its next alighting place. On bright, sunny days it frequently stands on some convenient perch in an upright position, with its wings outstretched in spread-eagle fashion, enjoying a sun bath. Unless facing a strong wind it experiences considerable difficulty in rising from the water, pattering along its surface for a long distance.

Winter.—As soon as the young birds are large enough to fly they gather into great flocks and prepare for the fall migration, which begins in August. They are deliberate in their movements, loitering along the coast for two or three months. In Massachusetts the main flight passes between the middle of September and the first of November. The south Atlantic and gulf coasts are the principal winter resorts of the double-crested cormorants, where they mingle with their close relatives, the Florida cormorants, and lead a similar roving life.

On the North Carolina coast Mr. T. Gilbert Pearson (1919) says that this is the common cormorant in winter and that "as evening comes they congregate in flocks of from ten to forty individuals, and in solid ranks, go flying low over the water to some favorite 'lump' of shell or small sandy island on which to roost." Once he "dug a hole in the shells of a miniature island, where, lying concealed, he was enabled to watch unobserved the hundreds of cormorants which came there to roost. Without exception the flocks all pitched in the water a short distance away, and later swam leisurely ashore."

Mr. Arthur T. Wayne (1910) says that, on the coast of South Carolina, "every afternoon these birds fly out to sea to pass the night, and at break of day flock after flock may be seen returning to the tidal creeks and sounds in quest of food."

DISTRIBUTION.

Breeding range.—Temperate North America, east of the Rocky Mountains. East to the Gulf of St. Lawrence (from Cape Whittle to Percé Rock). South to the coast of Maine (Penobscot Bay), west central Ohio (near Celina, formerly at least), central Illinois (Havanna and Persia, on Illinois River), northeastern Arkansas (Walker Lake, Mississippi County), central northern Wyoming (Buffalo), and northern Utah (Great Salt Lake). West to above point and south central Alberta (Buffalo Lake). North to central Mackenzie (Great Slave Lake), central Manitoba (Lake Winnipegosis) and James Bay. Utah records may refer to *albociliatus* or the two forms may intergrade here. Breeding grounds protected in the following reservations: In Quebec, Percé Rock; in North Dakota, Stump Lake; and in Arkansas, Walker Lake.

Winter range.—Mainly on the Atlantic and Gulf coasts from New Jersey to northern Florida and Louisiana. Has been recorded as far north in winter as eastern Maine (Calais) and Michigan (Grosse Isle).

Spring migration.—Northward along the coast and throughout the interior. Early dates of arrival: New York, Long Beach, March 31; Massachusetts, Plymouth County, March 26; Quebec, Godbout, May 19; Illinois, Mount Carmel, March 1–7; Michigan, Ann Arbor,

April 12; Manitoba, Shell River, May 13. Late dates of departure: New Jersey, Sea Island City, May 23; New York, Montauk Point, May 15; Rhode Island, Newport, May 17; Massachusetts, June 18; Missouri, St. Louis, May 22; Louisiana, Lake Catherine, April 14.

Fall migration.—Reversal of spring routes. Early dates of arrival: Massachusetts, Essex County, August 22; New York, Montauk Point, August 26; New Jersey, Wildwood, August 30; Missouri, October 5. Late dates of departure: Quebec, Montreal, November 1; Massachusetts, Essex County, November 24; New York, Onondaga Lake, November 30; Pennsylvania, Erie, December 14; Michigan, Ann Arbor, November 25; Illinois, Chicago, November 20.

Casual records.—Wanders occasionally to Bermuda (October 10, 1847, February 8, 1848, etc.)

Egg dates.—North Dakota and Minnesota: Thirty-one records, May 12 to July 11; sixteen records, May 23 to June 15. Manitoba and Saskatchewan: Eighteen records, June 4 to July 21; nine records, June 14 to 18. Quebec: Six records, May 26 to June 30. Utah: Five records, April 9 to May 17.

PHALACROCORAX AURITUS FLORIDANUS (Audubon).

FLORIDA CORMORANT.

HABITS.

About the mangrove keys of southern Florida, principally in that broad expanse of shallow water known as the Bay of Florida, between Cape Sable and the Keys, this smaller form is exceedingly abundant and one of the characteristic birds of the region. It is decidedly gregarious in its habits, flying about in large flocks and roosting in immense numbers on certain keys, to which it regularly resorts, the mangroves becoming thoroughly whitewashed with the accumulated droppings of hundreds of cormorants. These roosts are occupied by day as well as by night and it is an interesting experience to row around one of them in a small boat and see the great black birds pour off the trees down to the surface of the water and go flying off in large flocks. They are much tamer than their northern relatives, as they are seldom molested. They are called "nigger-geese" by the natives, who consider the young good eating, but even the negroes and conchs do not care for adults.

Courtship.—As I have never witnessed the nuptial performance of this species I must quote the following graphic account from the pen of the illustrious Audubon (1840):

The Florida cormorant begins to pair about the first of April, and commences the construction of its nest about a fortnight after. Many do not lay quite so early, and I found some going through their preparations until the middle of May. Their courtships are performed on the water. On the morning, beautiful but extremely hot, of the 8th of that month, while rambling over one of the keyes, I arrived at the entrance of a narrow and rather deep channel, almost covered by the boughs of the mangroves and some tall canes—the only tall canes I had hitherto observed among those islands. I paused, looked at the water, and observing it to be full of fish, felt confident that no shark was at hand. Cocking both locks of my gun, I quietly waded in. Curious sounds now reached my ears, and as the fishes did not appear to mind me much, I proceeded onward among them for perhaps a hundred yards, when I observed that they had all disappeared. The sounds were loud and constantly renewed, as if they came from a joyous multitude. The inlet suddenly became quite narrow and the water reached to my arm pits. At length I placed myself behind some mangrove trunks, whence I could see a great number of cormorants not more than fifteen or twenty yards from me. None of them, it seemed, had seen or heard me; they were engaged in going through their nuptial ceremonies. The males, while swimming gracefully around the females, would raise their wings and tail, draw their head over their back, swell out their neck for an instant. and with a quick forward thrust of the head utter a rough, guttural note, not unlike the cry of a pig. The female at this moment would crouch as it were on the water, sinking into it, when her mate would sink over her until nothing more than his head was to be seen, and soon afterwards both sprung up and swam joyously around each other, croaking all the while. Twenty or more pairs at a time were thus engaged. Indeed, the water was covered with cormorants, and had I chosen I might have shot several of them. I now advanced slowly toward them, when they stared at me as you might stare at a goblin, and began to splash the water with their wings, many diving. On my proceeding they all dispersed, either plunging beneath or flying off. and making rapidly toward the mouth of the inlet. Only a few nests were on the mangroves, and I looked upon the spot as analogous to the tournament grounds of the pinnated grouse, although no battles took place in my presence. A few beautiful herons were sitting peaceably on their nests, the mosquitoes were very abundant, large, ugly blue land crabs crawled among the mangroves, hurrying toward their retreats, and I retired, as I had arrived, in perfect silence. While proceeding, I could not help remarking the instinctive knowledge of the fishes, and thought how curious it was that, as soon as they had observed the cormorants' hole none had gone farther, as if they were well aware of the danger, but preferred meeting me as I advanced toward the birds.

Nesting.—The most northern breeding colony of the Florida cormorant that I have heard of was well described by Mr. T. Gilbert Pearson (1905) as he found it during the early days of June, 1904, in Great Lake, among the cypress swamps of eastern North Carolina, and surrounded by a heavy forest, far from the haunts of man. On his former visit to the lake he had found 150 pairs of cormorants breeding here, but the colony has decreased in numbers since. I quote from his description of the colony as follows:

The colony at that time was found to be in the height of the breeding season. The heavy nests of sticks and twigs occupied low-spreading cypress trees standing solitary here and there in the water, usually from fifty to one hundred yards from shore. A number of the trees were occupied by the domicile of a single pair of birds; others contained two, three, five, seven, or eight nests; one tree held sixteen and another thiry-six cradles of these great birds. One hundred and twenty-one homes of the cormorants were counted, twenty-eight trees in all being used for their accommodation.

Alligators gather about the colony, probably to feed, in part, upon the fragments of food which fall from the nests above. Six were counted at one time within easy rifle range of the boat. One of the young, while climbing along a slender limb, lost its balance and fell with a splash into the water. It immediately dived, and, coming to the surface about twenty feet away, began swimming up the lake with long and rapid strokes. By the time I had descended to the boat with my cameras the bird was fully fifty yards away. To our horror, a large alligator had given chase, and was rapidly approaching the swimmer. We immediately started in pursuit, and, after an exciting chase, rescued the young cormorant; but not until the alligator had made two unsuccessful snaps at his intended victim, which escaped only by diving with marvelous quickness just at the proper instant.

Mr. C. J. Pennock (1889) described a somewhat similar colony, nesting in large cypress trees in an inland pond, near St. Marks, Florida. His account of the immense size of the trees chosen and the unusual height of the nests is well worth quoting:

The nests were placed for the most part on the horizontal limbs well out from the body of the tree, some, however, well up in the tops of the trees. Eight trees were occupied, and ninety-seven nests were counted. The largest tree was at least six feet in diameter at a height of eight feet from the ground, and carried its size in good proportion well up to the lower limbs, which we estimated to be over sixty feet from the ground. This tree contained twenty-three nests, but none of the others had over sixteen nests. The lowest nest was over fifty feet from the ground, the majority were over sixty feet high, and on the large tree referred to several nests must have been one hundred feet high. This tree, by the way, was not molested by our party; the combined girth of the strap and a pair of long arms not being sufficient to compass it by fully six feet.

I think the above two instances are rather unusual, although illustrating the nesting habits of the Florida cormorant in inland lakes, for this cormorant evidently prefers to frequent the shores, bays, estuaries, inlets, and mouths of rivers, where it is more frequently found nesting in low red mangrove trees or bushes on islands. On my first visit to Cuthbert Lake, near Cape Sable in southern Florida, we found, on May 1, 1903, a colony of about 600 Florida cormorants nesting on a small mangrove island with large numbers of Louisiana and little blue herons, American egrets, white ibises, roseate spoonbills, and water-turkeys. The cormorants' nests were on the extreme outer edge of the red mangroves which grew well out into the water of the lake. The nests were closely bunched in compact colonies on the very tops of the trees or bushes, from 6 to 10 feet above the water, which was from 2 to 3 feet deep at this point. They were well made of sticks, compactly interwoven, and were lined with green leaves, but, like all cormorants' nests, they were very filthy; the nests and the trunks, branches, and leaves of the trees were completely whitewashed with excrement, which peeled off in large flakes, where it had become dry, making climbing very unpleasant. Most of the nests contained two or three eggs each, but in some cases we found newly hatched young, black, naked, and feeble. The old cormorants were quite tame and soon returned to their nests even within 10 feet of us. Their only note was a loud guttural croak or grunt, which seemed to roll up through their long necks with a hollow, rattling noise. I visited Cuthbert rookery again on March 29, 1908; the herons were incubating on full sets of eggs, but the cormorants had not begun to lay at that time. Apparently the Florida cormorant does not ordinarily lay its eggs before April, probably early in that month in the southern portion of its range and later farther north, but evidently not until May in the Carolinas. Its nesting habits seem to vary considerably in different localities, as do those of its relatives, but, as far as I know, it never nests on the ground. Some observers state that it uses no lining in its nest, but, as most cormorants do line their nests with grasses, leaves, or other soft substances, it is probably exceptional when it fails to do so.

Eggs.—The Florida cormorant usually lays three eggs, sometimes only two, or rarely four; except for an average difference in size, they are not distinguishable from those of its northern relatives. The measurements of 41 eggs, in the United States National Museum and the author's collections, average 58.2 by 36.8 millimeters; the eggs showing the four extremes measure **64.5** by 38.5, 62 by **39, 50** by 35, and 53 by **33** millimeters.

Food.—The feeding habits of the Florida cormorant are similar to those of the northern subspecies. Mr. John T. Nichols (1918) speaks of seeing " a school of porpoises breaking not far from our anchorage," with "three or four cormorants following them closely, screaming and making short flights, diving close after them." He refers to this as a common habit, perhaps for the purpose of securing pieces of fish left by the porpoises. According to Mr. T. Gilbert Pearson (1919), " In the summer of 1905 H. H. Brimley saw an immature bird disgorge a portion of a large water snake (*Natrix taxispilota*)."

In other respects the life history and habits of the Florida cormorant are not essentially different from those of the double-crested cormorant, though it is less migratory and, except in the northern portion of its breeding range, is practically resident.

DISTRIBUTION.

Breeding range.—On the Atlantic coast from North Carolina (Craven County) southward, along both coasts of Florida and the coast of Louisiana; on some of the Bahama Islands (Great Abaco,

Andros Island, and probably others) ; and on the Isle of Pines. Has been recorded as breeding in southern Illinois and Ohio, but these birds are now considered referable to *auritus*, though perhaps they may be intermediate.

Winter range.—Practically resident throughout its breeding range. Winter range includes most of the Bahamas, the Greater and Lesser Antilles, and the coasts of Texas, Honduras, and Yucatan. Withdraws from the Carolinas in winter.

Egg dates.—Florida; thirty-six records, March 5 to June 21; eighteen records, April 3 to May 14.

PHALACROCORAX AURITUS CINCINATUS (Brandt).

WHITE-CRESTED CORMORANT.

HABITS.

The northwestern race of the double-crested cormorant is restricted in the breeding season to the northwest coast region from southern Alaska to Oregon. Reported records of its breeding in the interior are probably erroneous and refer to the eastern subspecies, or to the Farallon cormorant; such errors may have arisen from the fact that in high nuptial plumage a few white feathers are occasionally found in the crests of the eastern bird. All of the subspecies of *Phalacrocorax auritus* habitually shed their crests during the season of incubation, the long curling plumes serving merely as courtship and nuptial adornments. The species can always be distinguished, however, from the other Pacific coast species by the conspicuous yellow gular sac.

Nesting.—The best known breeding resorts of the white-crested cormorant are in the great sea-bird reservations off the coasts of Washington and Oregon, which have been so well described by Mr. W. L. Dawson and Prof. Lynds Jones in their various writings. I can not do better than to quote freely from one of Professor Jones's (1908) excellent papers on the subject, as follows:

The proper study of the white-crested cormorants (*Phalacrocorax dilophus cincinatus*) was made during our stay on Carroll Islet. The reader has already seen enough pictures of the rocks and islands characteristic of this coast to become familiar with the precipitous sides, jagged outlines, verdure-clad top, and crumbling ledges. The accompanying halftone pictures will give some idea as to what parts of Carroll Islet these cormorants select as nesting sites, and illustrate certain details which the camera was able to record. These pictures represent two somewhat different kinds of nesting places, and fairly represent the life of these birds during the breeding season.

Figure 2 is a representation of nearly the entire colony which occupied a sharp ledge jutting out from the northeast corner of the island, a ledge with a sharp and jagged summit ridge, as the picture shows. This was the only colony of this species found in such a situation. Figure 1 represents a part of one of the other and apparently more usual nesting site of this species—a rather narrow ledge of broken shelving rock at the foot of a precipice or over-hang. Apparently any relatively flat space sufficiently large to accommodate the nest may be utilized, either upon the sharp ledge or precipice's foot. A careful scrutiny of any of the nests shown will reveal the fact that one of the prime requisites in a nesting site for the individual nest is that on one side the ground or rock must fall abruptly away. It is on this side that the excrement forms a limy smear, often extending many feet below the nest. The uphill side of the nest is always relatively clean.

Nests are made of coarse sticks arranged much after the manner of a hawk's nest, cupped to the depth of five or six inches, and with a lining of grassy material which covers scarcely more than the bottom of the depression. The sticks used were such as might have been found upon the island, and the grass seemed to correspond to that within a short distance of the colony. There was no evident attempt at concealment in any case, nor was there any clear indication that any nests were placed with a view to shelter either from the weather or from the scorching rays of the sun. The evident distress of both old and young birds when exposed to the direct sunlight would certainly afford excuse enough for seeking a shady nook among the rocks. The very young birds were nearly baked when left uncovered for any great length of time. One such died under our eyes, evidently from the heat.

The varying ages of the young—none of which were yet feathered—and the fresh eggs in a nest which showed no signs of having been a victim of the pilfering crows, both point to the conclusion that there must be a great deal of individual variation in the time of nesting of these birds. It is true that nests containing fresh eggs may represent a second set after the loss of the first one, but the fact that none of the young birds were anywhere near ready to leave the nests seem conclusive that only one brood is reared in a season. The nesting season was too far advanced to afford any opportunity for studying nest building or egg deposition.

The colony shown in Figure 1 was shared by a few California murres who occupied the spaces between nests which were level enough to keep an egg from rolling into the water, or off from the ledge. There was no apparent discord in such a mixed colony, even though the murres were within reach of the weapons of the cormorants. In one other place the same conditions prevailed. I could discover no reason for regarding this as a case of true communalism. If there was any benefit derived from this association it must have been to the advantage of the murres.

Besides these two nesting sites there were a few small ledges on the ocean side of the island where we found nests of this species, usually not more than two or three nests together. Here there was some distant intimacy with Baird cormorants, but the different manner of nesting of these two species precludes the possibility of any competition between them.

The perpetual noises made by the birds of the island seriously interfered with any careful study of the various notes of these cormorants. When the old birds were disturbed or alarmed they gave vent to a spluttering squawk and often a low grunting. The young yelped something like a puppy, particularly when they were calling for food. They were usually silent when crouching away from danger. The very young birds showed no fear, but the older ones clearly did.

Eggs.—The eggs of this subspecies seem to be scarce in collections. They are apparently indistinguishable from eggs of the other subspecies. A small series of 9 eggs collected by William L. Dawson on the coast of Washington average, in measurements, 62.4 by 40.8 millimeters; the eggs showing the four extremes measured **64.2** by **42, 59.4** by 40.2, and 60.7 by **40.2.**

Behavior.—It hardly seems necessary to go into further details of the life history of this bird, about which comparatively little has been published, as it is the rarest and the least known of the four subspecies. There is no reason for thinking, that it differs essentially in its habits from its better known relatives.

Winter.—Mr. William H. Kobbé (1900) say of its winter habits, near Cape Disappointment, Washington:—

This cormorant is a very abundant species during the entire year, but especially so in the winter and spring. They are rather wary birds to hunt, but may always be shot while sitting upon the stakes which support the fish pots. They sometimes perch upon these poles for hours and oftentimes may be seen with their wings half spread, by which means they dry them. Although the birds remain throughout the summer, I did not find them nesting upon the numerous cliffs of the cape and am certain they do not breed in this locality.

DISTRIBUTION.

Breeding range.—Northwest coast region. From the coast of Washington (The Olympiades) northward throughout southern Alaska to Kodiak Isand and the base of the Alaska Peninsula (Lake Iliamna). Aleutian Islands records are open to question. Breeding grounds protected in the following reservations: In Alaska, St. Lazaria, and Forrester Island; and in Washington, Flattery Rocks, Quillayute Needles, and Copalis Rock.

Winter range.—Practically resident in its breeding range.

Egg dates.—Washington: Four records, June 3, 12, and 20, and July 10.

PHALACROCORAX AURITUS ALBOCILIATUS Ridgway.

FARALLON CORMORANT.

HABITS.

This name is somewhat misleading, for this is the least abundant of the three species of cormorant known to breed on the Farallon Islands; it is much more abundant at many other places; and it is widely distributed from southern Oregon to Lower California, breeding on the islands along the coast and in many lakes in the interior. It has a much wider range and is much better known than the northern subspecies, the white-crested cormorant. Its life history is so similar to that of the eastern double-crested cormorant that it would involve a useless repetition to give much more than a brief account of some of its characteristic breeding colonies.

Nesting.—Mr. W. Otto Emerson, in his notes sent to Major Bendire says that on the Farallon Islands they begin to assemble about the first of April or earlier if the season is favorable.

They gather about the old rookeries and collect great pieces of dry kelp and Farrallone weed to repair their old nests; they may be a month or more about the nests, adding bit by bit to the home; sometimes all leaving for a fishing trip to sea, then back again, sitting around the nests or on them; purloining one from another's nest to add to its own; bits of sea-moss and broken sticks are stuck in the nest here and there. By the first of May some of the nests contain eggs, both sexes sharing the work of incubation, one staying on the eggs to protect them from the thieving gulls, while the other is off fishing. I found these cormorants to be the tamest of the three species on the island; one can get up to within two feet of the nests.

The tameness of the Farallon cormorant has been referred to by several writers and a number of good photographs of birds on their nests have been taken at short range; this trait is not shared by the eastern subspecies which is usually so shy that it is difficult to come within gunshot of one on its nest.

Mr. Milton S. Ray (1904) describes the nests of this species, on the Farallon Islands, as follows:

The weed nests were like those of the gull but much larger and shallower, measuring twenty inches across, the cavity being nine in width and three in depth. I counted but forty-seven nests in the colony, which shows that the number of these birds, now the least abundant cormorant on the islands, is continually decreasing. On subsequent visits we noticed the birds did not relay in the nests from which we had taken eggs. The gulls did not molest the eggs and young in this rookery, for the reason the old birds did not give them a chance, they settling back on the nest as soon as we passed it. While it was interesting to watch these avian snakes in their summer home, the decaying remains of numerous fish about the colony and the swarms of seal-flies rendered it a pleasant place to be away from.

A vast breeding colony of this cormorant was found on San Martin Island, Lower California, by Mr. Howard W. Wright (1913); he made a careful estimate of the area covered by this colony and figured that it occupied about 1½ square miles; then allowing one nest for each 100 square feet, based on a count in an average measured area, he concluded that the colony contained the astonishing number of 348,480 nests. This is certainly the largest colony of cormorants of which we have any record. He says:

We became very much interested in estimating the amount of fish these birds consumed per day. We noted the amount each young cormorant threw up when molested, and found on several occasions a bunch of fish as big as a man's two fists. This mass was generally composed of surf fish, smelt, and sardines. I have heard of other estimates of from three to six sardines a day for a cormorant, so I consider a half pound of fish a day very conservative.

Allowing half a pound of fish a day for each of the 1,800,000 birds, the entire population would consume four hundred tons a day or about ten thousand tons a month. The fishing was done in San Quentin bay, exclusively, but in that bay and in Hassler's Cove, on the island, fish were found very plentiful, and always hungry, showing that the birds do not seriously lessen the number of fish.

Referring to the early morning flight witnessed at this island, he writes:

From the hills there poured a steady stream of cormorants, flying about eight or ten abreast. This stream poured from these hills continuously and reached as far as we could see, toward the bay of San Quentin. The stream was like a great black ribbon that waved in the breeze and reached to the horizon. It was truly a wonderful sight. The birds kept coming as though there were no limit to their numbers.

At about seven-thirty a stream began to return, each individual heavily laden with fish. The ribbon of birds was now double—one part leaving and the other returning. The flow of birds was continuous during the daylight hours of each day we were there. The flow was unbroken—simply one steady stream going, all day, and a steady stream returning.

A colony found by Dr. Joseph Grinnell (1908) on an island in Salton Sea was evidently much like inland lake colonies of the eastern subspecies. He says of it:

A census of cormorant's nests showed 147 containing eggs, besides many others partly built. The nests were tall, compact structures composed altogether of angular shrub-trunks, and lined with mesquite barkstrips and old feathers. The outer basal sticks and the surrounding rocks were all whitewashed with excrement. A typical nest was 414 mm high and 552 mm across, slightly saucered. The tendency seemed to be to locate the nests on prominent rock ledges or pinnacles. The number of eggs in a nest ranged from one to six, commonly four or five.

Several writers report inland colonies nesting in trees. One of the most interesting of these is described by Mr. Corydon Chamberlain (1895) as follows:

Early in March of the present year I visited Lakeport (California), a small town on the west shore of Beautiful Clear Lake in Lake County. Big Valley lying on the south side of the upper basin of the lake is a forest of large white oaks. The trees extend down toward the lake as far as the moist soil will support them. Some trees standing within a hundred yards of the low water mark are wholly or partially dead, as though the unfavorable moisture of the soil had early completed the work of senile decay. In such a place where they were within easy reach of their feeding grounds, the cormorants occupied a rookery that had been in use many years.

We landed on a gravelly beach (the only one for several miles) among some willow bushes and poplar trees. A number of cormorants fluttered excitedly from the poplars and flew away in a frightened manner. Under these trees we found pieces of carp which the birds had dropped and the whole place had a vile smell. About two hundred yards beyond us were two trees covered with cormorants. Both of these trees stood apart from the great body of the forest and one of them was dead, only the trunk remaining, and that, though bleached, was charred deeply on one side. The other had some bunches of leaves about the body and a few more trailing from the ends of some branches, but the upper parts were white, seemingly dead, but really covered with the limey excrement of the birds. South of the trees in the edge of the forest were several containing nests but none having the bare appearance of the two described. There were probably a hundred nests in this rookery all built in the very highest places in the trees. I found no nest lower than 75 feet from the ground, while the average height was about 80 feet. These measurements were made with a tape from the treetop. One tree, which contained a few nests, looked to be considerably over a hundred feet high, though I did not climb it to verify my estimation.

Of the two trees described the dead one contained a single nest and the other one 19. As I climbed the latter tree all the cormorants left their nests and perches and went wheeling around until I descended, when they immediately settled down on their empty nests seemingly as contented as ever. Of the 19 nests in the tree all but one contained complete sets of eggs, the usual number being four, though sets of three and of five were common. All of the sets were incubated slightly, though not enough to cause trouble in blowing. The nests were solid, well-built affairs, having a width of from 15 to 20 inches and a depth of about 6 or 8 inches. They were built of oak twigs and the stalks of marsh weeds as a base, some of the oak twigs having leaves on them; and dead tules and other green weeds from the lake as a lining. Some had a further lining of green oak leaves. The birds continue to put on nest materials after the eggs are laid. Some birds could be seen flying around with great ribbonlike tules streaming from their mouths.

Mr. A. B. Howell writes to me:

June 8, 1912, C. C. Lamb and I found them breeding abundantly at Buena Vista Lake, California. Their nests were either near those of the white pelicans or in the standing dead timber in the mouth of the Kern River, and held eggs in various stages of incubation. At Salton Sea they also breed in the dead trees in the water near the shore, and as the sea is receding rapidly, the height of the water from year to year may be gauged accurately by the position of the old nests on the shore.

Eggs.—The eggs of the Farallon cormorant can not be distinguished from those of the double-crested cormorant, though eggs from northern latitudes average larger than those from southern localities. The measurements of 71 eggs, in the United States National Museum, average 62.9 to 38.8 millimeters; the eggs showing the four extremes measure **69.5** by 40.5, 68.5 by **42.5, 54** by 37, and 67.5 by **36** millimeters.

The sequence of plumages, the behavior and other details of the life history of the Farallon cormorant are apparently similar to those of the double-crested cormorant. It is a common and well-known bird throughout its range. Together with the Brandt cormorant, with which it is often associated, it is a familiar feature at all seasons along the California coast, frequenting all suitable fishing grounds about the islands or perching conspicuously on buoys, posts, or floating timbers about the harbors.

DISTRIBUTION.

Breeding range.—Pacific coast region of United States and Mexico. On inland waters from southern Oregon (Lake Malheur and Klamath

Lakes) to western Nevada (Pyramid Lake) and southern California (Salton Sea). On islands off the coast from northern Oregon (Three Arch Rocks) southward along the coasts of California and Lower California to the Revillagigedo Islands. The breeding birds of Great Salt Lake may be intermediate between this and the eastern form. Breeding grounds protected in the following reservations: In Oregon, Three Arch Rocks, Klamath Lake, and Malheur Lake; and in California, Farallon.

Winter range.—Includes most of the breeding range, except perhaps the more northern inland resorts, and extends to the valley of the Colorado River and the Gulf of California.

Egg dates.—Farallon Islands: Twenty-seven records, May 9 to July 12; fourteen records, May 30 to June 28. Los Coronados Islands: Eighteen records, March 27 to June 3; nine records, April 3 to May 10. Oregon, California, and Nevada: Twelve records, February 5 to June 6; six records, April 20 to May 20.

PHALACROCORAX VIGUA MEXICANUS (Brandt).

MEXICAN CORMORANT.

HABITS.

This small, but handsome, cormorant is a tropical species which extends its range northward over the Mexican border and into the southern part of the Mississippi valley. It has also been found breeding in some of the West Indes. It is the only one of the North American species of cormorants that I have not seen in life. Comparatively few ornithologists have studied its habits and still fewer have published anything about it, so its life history will be rather meager. It seems to be rare north of Texas and Louisiana, but on the coasts of southern Texas and Mexico it is a common bird of the salt water lagoons, rivers, and inland lakes, much resembling in appearance and behavior the well known Florida cormorant.

Nesting.—It is apparently not a migratory species, being a resident throughout the year over practically all of its range and having a much extended breeding season. Dr. E. W. Nelson (1903) has given us the best account of its habits and I shall quote freely from his notes. On Christmas day, 1902, he discovered a breeding colony of Mexican cormorants on Lake Chapala, Mexico, of which he writes:

In the afternoon a long line of whitened bushes growing in the open water some distance away was pointed out by our host who said he had passed there a short time before and found a lot of cormorants nesting in them. I could scarcely credit this but the whitened appearance of the bushes showed that the birds used the place as a roost at least and I decided to investigate. As we poled near enough we saw that the bushes, or small trees, which projected twelve or fifteen feet from the water were full of cormorants and many could be seen standing on nests. We stopped the boat when within one hundred yards and after removing our clothing slid cautiously overboard into from three to four feet of water. Camera in hand Goldman and I stalked the birds to within about forty yards and secured a few exposures. The bushes extended in a narrow belt for about two hundred yards in the otherwise open water and in them were perched between two to three hundred birds. At our first stop the outstretched necks and changing position of some of the birds gave evidence of their uneasiness and as we waded still nearer most of them flew clumsily down into the open water. After moving out a hundred yards beyond the line of bushes they formed a black line on the water where they remained as long as we stayed in the vicinity. When the birds became alarmed at our approach they began a curious guttural grunting which came in a low continuous chorus from those left in the bushes as well as those in the water. These notes sounded much like the low grunting of a lot of small pigs while feeding. As we waded among the bushes the birds which had remained by their nests pitched off into the water one after the other and swam out to join the main flock; or took wing, and after a short detour, came circling close overhead, uttering at short intervals their guttural notes of alarm or protest.

The nests were strong platforms placed on forking branches and measured about 15 inches across and 4 to 6 inches deep, with a shallow depression in the top. They were composed entirely of small sticks compactly arranged, as is shown in detail in the accompanying photographs. From one to half a dozen nests were placed in a bush and we planted our tripods in the muddy bottom, and, standing nearly waist deep in the water, secured good pictures before calling up the boat and getting aboard. As the bushes were scattered, we had no trouble in poling about and examining the nests at leisure. Most of them were just completed and contained no eggs. Quite a number had a single egg and in a few cases two eggs were found. A series of 18 eggs were taken. They are rather small for the size of the bird and have a pale-green ground color overlaid with the usual chalky white deposit which gives them a greenish-white shade.

Mr. J. H. Riley (1905) found a colony of this species breeding in the Bahamas, of which he writes:

A colony of these cormorants was breeding in some tall mangroves in the large salt-water lake on Watlings Island. Most of the young were found sitting on the edge of the nests, that were 15 to 20 feet up, or on the limbs out of the nest. Some of the young were already in the water with their parents, though they could not fly, apparently. A few nests contained heavily incubated eggs. This was on July 11. A few cormorants were seen on the salt pans around Clarence Harbor, Long Island, but as none were shot here their identity is in doubt, though they appeared to belong to the same form as those shot on Watlings. The young are eaten by the inhabitants and are said to be very good. The numerous downy skins found along the shores of the salt lakes on Watlings would indicate that young cormorant is quite an item in the domestic economy of the islanders.

Eggs.—The Mexican cormorant usually lays four or five eggs, similar to other cormorants' eggs in shape and texture. The ground color is pale bluish white, but it is almost entirely concealed by a thin coating of white calcareous deposit and the eggs are often nest stained. The measurements of 41 eggs, in various collections, average 53.7 by 33.8; the eggs showing the four extremes measure **58** by 35, 57.5 by **37**, **47.5** by 33.5, and 50 by **29** millimeters.

Plumages.—I have never seen the naked or the downy young of this species, nor can I find any description of either in print. The nesting season is so prolonged and variable that it is usually impossible to even approximately guess at the ages of immature birds in collections, but apparently the sequence of plumages to maturity is similar to that of other cormorants. In the fresh juvenal plumage, in which I have seen birds in November, January, and April, the head, neck, and under parts are deep, rich, dark brown, " Vandyke brown," or " warm sepia," paler on the throat and darker on the crown, flanks, and lower belly. This plumage is probably worn for about a year, but it wears and fades out to much paler colors, nearly to white on the throat and belly. The upper parts are much as in the adult, but duller and browner, with less conspicuous black edgings on the back and scapulars. The fully adult nuptial plumage is not acquired until the second breeding season. Adults in winter plumage are similar to those in breeding plumage, except that they lack the white plumes about the head and neck, where there is also more brownish mottling. I have seen adults in full nuptial plumage in July, August, September, November, and December. There is probably one complete molt each year and one partial molt; the tail is apparently molted twice.

Behavior.—Doctor Nelson (1903) writes of the behavior of Mexican cormorants as follows:

Last March we camped on a small river at the bottom of a deep canyon in central Michoacan; this stream runs a tortuous course between high rocky walls and at short intervals breaks into foaming rapids. Our camp was on a narrow sandy flat at the water's edge, under the overhanging branches of some small mahogany and other trees that had secured a foothold in the talus at the foot of a cliff. As we lived here unsheltered except by the foliage, the happenings among the wild life of this solitary place were under constant observation. Among the interesting daily events was the passage up the river each morning of several Mexican cormorants, always flying singly, their glossy black plumage gleaming in the intense sunlight as they turned. They were evidently on their way to some fishing ground higher up, and several hours later—usually about midday—came back following, as in the morning, all the wanderings of the river, and giving a touch of completeness to the wild character of the surroundings.

In the summer of 1897 we found them in abundance about the lagoons and rapids of the coast country in southern Sinaloa, and especially at some shallow rapids in the Rosario River a few miles above the town of Rosario. During the early part of the rainy season the river was low and at the place mentioned a short descent in the boulder-strewn bed of the stream made a stretch, forty or fifty yards long, of brawling rapids. Every morning dozens of cormorants flew up stream to the rapids from the mangrove-bordered lagoons near the coast. They flew low along the water, sometimes singly and sometimes in small parties, usually keeping side by side in a well-formed line when two or more were together. For a time most of them perched about on the numerous projecting stones in the river, preening their plumage and sunning themselves; others swam idly in the slow current about the rapids. At such times the brilliantly green masses of foliage bordering and often overhanging the water, the swift dark stream broken by jutting rocks on which were the numerous, black, sharply outlined forms of the cormorants, and overhead the crystalline depths of the morning sky of the rainy season made a wonderfully beautiful picture.

When a considerable number of cormorants had congregated they seemed to become suddenly animated by a common purpose and followed one another in swift flight to the foot of the rapids. There most of the assembled birds alighted and formed a line across a considerable section of the river. Then with flapping wings, beating the surface of the water into foam, the black line moved up stream, the birds showing much excitement, but keeping their places very well. The surface of the water was churned to spray by the strokes of so many powerful wings and feet, yet in the midst of the apparent confusion the birds could be seen darting to one side or the other, or spurting a few feet ahead on the line, and sometimes disappearing for a moment below the surface, but nearly always securing a fish. When they reached the head of the rapids the birds flew heavily to their perching stones, or swam slowly up the quiet surface of the river. After a short rest the line would reform and again beat up the rapids and this was repeated until the birds had satisfied their hunger.

The cormorants evidently fully appreciated the advantages of thus working in company, so that a fish trying to escape from one bird would almost certainly become the prey of another. The purpose of beating the surface of the water with their wings was evidently in order to alarm and confuse the fish so that they would dart blindly about and become more easily captured. I have seen parties of gannets doing the same thing in the midst of fishes off the Tres Marias Islands.

When the cormorants were gorged they deserted the fishing ground for the day and streamed back down the river to the lagoons, where they perched motionless for hours in large mangroves or other trees along the edge of the water.

The west coast lagoons are long lakelike bodies of brackish water varying greatly in size and proportion but nearly always fringed by a more or less dense growth of mangroves. These are low, rarely rising over twenty-five or thirty feet, and as the leafage begins at the water's edge they present a solid wall of dark green, back of which often rises the larger growth of scattered forests. Here and there among the mangroves occur dead and weathered trees, or, lacking these, wide branching living trees which project over the water. These are favorite congregating places for the Mexican cormorants which, with their somewhat grotesque outlines, form a conspicuous figure of the bird life in such localities. These birds are not considered game by the Mexicans and this combined with the high price of ammunition, is sufficient to protect them from wanton killing so that they are not often disturbed and will permit a canoe to approach within easy gunshot before they clumsily take flight. They are heavy-bodied and awkward and frequently fall from the perch into the water and try to escape by swimming in preference to flight. When driven to take wing from such a perch they commonly make a broad circuit and returning pass near the canoe and turn their heads in evident curiosity to examine the cause of the alarm. Their flight like that of other cormorants is steady and rather labored, and as they circle about an intruder they often glide for some distance on outspread wings, turning their long outstretched necks toward the object of their curiosity and presenting almost as grotesque an appearance as the snake-bird."

Mr. H. H. Bailey (1906) saw numbers of cormorants which he took to be of this species fishing near the surf on the west coast of Mexico. Mr. C. William Beebe (1905) says that "their food in the barrancas is partly vegetable, not exclusively fish." What we know about the behavior and voice of the species is included in the above quotations and I regret that I can add nothing more to its life history. There seems to be no fall migration and its winter home and habits are probably the same as at other seasons.

DISTRIBUTION.

Breeding range.—Tropical North and Central America. North to northwestern Mexico (Guaymas), southeastern Texas (Brownsville), southern Louisiana (Lake Arthur), Cuba, Isle of Pines, and Bahamas (Watling Island). South to Nicaragua. South American birds are subspecifically distinct.

Winter range.—Resident throughout its breeding range.

Casual records.—Has wandered north to Colorado (near Denver, October 15, 1899); Kansas (Lawrence, April 2, 1872); and southern Illinois (near Cairo, spring 1879).

Egg dates.—Texas: Eighteen records, February 8, October 12 and 16. Mexico: Four records, May 10, 12, and 20 and December 25. Louisiana: Three records, May 29.

PHALACROCORAX PENICILLATUS (Brandt).

BRANDT CORMORANT.

HABITS.

This large, heavy, well-marked species is perhaps the best known, the most abundant, and the most characteristic cormorant of our Pacific coast, being found in all suitable localities from southern Alaska to Lower California. It is mainly a resident throughout its range, where its heavy, lumbering form is a familiar figure on the coast at all seasons, sitting for hours on any convenient perch over the water in lazy indolence, congregating in large numbers in its favorite roosting places on outlying rocks or gathering in great black rafts on the water where fishing conditions are favorable.

Nesting.—For breeding purposes it congregates into large colonies on rocky islands or on the more inaccessible rocky cliffs of the mainland, where it is beyond the reach of marauding enemies, except its most persistent and most successful foe, the western gull. While cruising among the Santa Barbara Islands we found many a large breeding colony of Brandt cormorants, visible many miles distant as a conspicuous, whitewashed space on some prominent rocky slope or promontory; as we drew near we could see that the white surface was dotted with hundreds of black specks, which later we could recognize as cormorants sitting on their nests, spread closely and evenly over the gently sloping rocks.

Brandt cormorants seem to prefer to nest on the flat top of a rocky island, on a gradually sloping incline or more often still on a high rounding shoulder of rock. They never seem to nest on the inaccessible perpendicular cliffs, such as are chosen by the Baird cormorants. The nests seem to be easily accessible and they are so, provided one can make a landing on the island, but this is generally not so easy, for these rounding shoulders of rock often terminate in steep and slippery sides washed by dangerous breakers. The nests are not very different from those of the Farallon cormorant, except that they never use sticks in their construction, which the other species usually does utilize. But the birds themselves are much shyer and can be easily recognized by the blue gular pouch, which is very conspicuous during the breeding season. The nest is made of various seaweeds and sea mosses, which the birds may be seen gathering by diving in the vicinity of their breeding grounds; the nest is used for successive seasons, fresh material being added each spring to the foundation of rotted débris and guano; they are often placed so near together that there is barely walking space between them.

Two interesting colonies of Brandt cormorants, near Monterey, California, are described by Prof. Leverett M. Loomis (1895) from whom I quote in part as follows:

Two rookeries were discovered; one at Point Carmel and the other at Seal Rocks. June 25th I visited the former, which is situated on a rock or little islet in the ocean at the extremity of Point Carmel, about fifteen yards from the mainland. This rock rises perpendicularly some forty or more feet above the water. At first sight it does not seem that it can be scaled, but closer inspection reveals that a foothold may be had in the seams and protuberances on its water-worn sides. Only on days when the sea is very calm can the rock be landed upon, and then only from the sheltered channel separating it from the mainland. Fortunately, it happened that the sea was quiet the day of my visit. The following day a party of Stanford University students were unable to land on account of the heavy surf.

We first took a view of the rookery from the mainland. The cormorants were very tame, remaining on their nests while we clambered down the sloping rocks and while we stood watching them on the same level only a few yards away. They were safe, however, from its precipitous walls of rock, effectually cutting off further advance. They were equally tame when the boat drew near as we approached from the water.

The clefts in the sides of the rock were occupied by Baird cormorants and the top by Brandt's. There were comparatively few of the former, but of the Brandt cormorants there were upwards of two hundred pairs. Their nests covered the top of the rock, every available situation being occupied. The surface was so uneven that all the nests could not be seen from one spot. Standing in one place I counted one hundred and eighteen.

All the nests of the Brandt cormorants on the rock contained eggs (apparently in an advanced state of incubation), with the exception of eleven, which had young birds in them. In ten, the young were just out of the shell. In the remaining one they were as large as "spring chickens." The eggs in seventy-seven nests were counted by a companion. Twenty-one contained four eggs each; thirty-six, three eggs; fourteen, two eggs; three, five eggs; three, one egg. The most frequent numbers were therefore three and four, probably the ordinary clutches.

Sardines were lying in little bunches near the nests, apparently placed there as food for the birds that were setting.

The smell from the accumulated excrement was sickening. The sides of the rock were so daubed that it appeared to be white toward the top. Flies swarmed about the rookery.

It was not until I fired my gun that the brooding birds began to desert their eggs. The Baird cormorants were the first to go. Many of the Brandt cormorants lingered on the edge of the rock while I walked about among the nests, only a few steps away. Finally all were driven to the water, where they formed a great raft. They began to return as soon as I left the top of the rock.

The rookery at Seal Rocks was much larger than the one at Point Carmel. The rocky islet upon which it was located is considerably greater in size and much lower in elevation than the Point Carmel islet. From the mainland, less than a hundred yards distant, no nests were in sight, all being on the side toward the ocean, hidden from view by a sort of dividing ridge. The Del Monte drive passes along the shore directly opposite the Rocks. It is a much frequented roadway, and the summer visitors have greatly persecuted the birds with firearms, forcing them to seek shelter for their nests behind the projecting rock.

My first visit to the rookery was made July 2d. As at Point Carmel, a landing could be effected only on the shore side of the islet. The resident population was composed exclusively of Brandt cormorants. Their nests were crowded so closely together on the uneven surface of the rock that room to place the foot was not always readily found. Some of the nests were on little points of rock, others in crevices, every available spot being utilized. Most of the eggs had hatched. The young were in different stages of growth, varying in size from those just out of the shell to half-grown ones. The larger left the nests when approached, and huddled together on the edge of the islet well above the reach of the surf. There was such a complete mixing up of babies that the old birds must have had some trouble in sorting them out when they returned, for immediately after I landed most of the adults retreated to the water, congregating in a great raft a short distance away. A few of the bolder remained behind for awhile. Several, apparently females, kept close by their young until I approached within ten feet of them, when their courage failed and they took flight, leaving the young to shift for themselves. Two of the larger young birds sought refuge on an outlying rock, separated from the islet by a little channel. They had apparently never been in the water before. They succeeded, nevertheless, in swimming across the channel and climbing up the steep sides of the rock, although a number of times they were buried out of sight by incoming waves.

A vibratory movement of the gular sac, apparently occasioned by fear, was noticed in a number of adults and half-grown young. Most of the adults observed on the rookery appeared to have lost the nuptial filaments.

The general form of the nests was circular, except where wedged in between rocks. They appeared to be constructed entirely of eel grass (*Zostera*). Those containing the larger young were trampled down. Two typical, untrampled nests yielded the following measurements: Outer diameter 22 by 19, inner diameter 10 by 10, depth 4 by 4, height 5¼ by 7.

Not many fish were lying about the nests. There were too many hungry mouths to be filled for a store to accumulate as at Point Carmel rookery. It was evident that sanitary measures were not in vogue, for the decaying bodies of several birds were suffered to remain and add to the almost intolerable stench of the excrement deposits. Quantities of feathers were scattered about and there were myriads of flies. Some of the flies accompanied us in the boat most of the way to Point Pinos, much to our annoyance.

Referring to this species on the Farallon Islands, Mr. Milton S. Ray (1904) writes:

Bandt cormorant is the commonest and biggest species of the island cormorants. Besides the large rookery on the more gradual slopes on the north side below Main Top Ridge, extending from near the water to well up the hillside, there are large colonies nesting on Saddle Rock and Sugar Loaf. We gained our first view of the rookery on West End when we crossed the ridge on the morning of May 30. Right below us, with scarcely foot-space between the nests, was the great city of cormorants. I counted 156 nests; on June 3 they had increased to 187, and they were still building. The weeds that trail over the rocks form most of the nest material, and these become more or less dry by the end of May and are easily detached by the birds; in fact a strong wind will frequently rip up a whole mat like bed. In make and size the nests of this species are like those of the preceding. I noticed considerable sea moss among the nest material, which is undoubtedly uprooted by the birds themselves, but it was not in such variety as I had been led to believe. Quarrels over nest material were of frequent occurrence among the birds of the rookery, but the most arrant robbers came from the settlement on Sugar Loaf, where the weeds do not grow. It was a queer sight to see one of these great lumbering-flighted cormorants come flapping into the colony, and after some opposition succeed and go awkwardly sailing off with a long stringing bunch of weeds.

All day long the great rookery was a scene of activity; everywhere the ponderous clumsy birds, using to the best of their ability what skill nature had endowed them with, were fashioning their weed-homes, while scores of setting birds ever and anon would rise to stretch their stiffened wings or to greet their mates returning fish-laden from the sea.

Eggs.—The Brandt cormorant lays from three to six eggs, usually four, and only one brood is raised in a season. The eggs are not distinguishable from those of other cormorants of similar size. The ground color is pale blue or bluish white, which is more or less completely concealed by a white calcareous coating, which becomes very much soiled during the process of incubation. The shape varies from "elongate ovate" to "cylindrical ovate." The measurements of 41 eggs, in the National Museum and the writer's collections, average 62.2 by 38.6 millimeters; the eggs showing the four extremes measure **68.5** by 39.5, 68 by **40.5, 56** by 39, and 61 by **36** millimeters.

Plumages.—The young cormorant, when first hatched, is blind and naked, an unattractive object covered with greasy black skin. The down soon appears, however, and before the young bird is half grown it is completely covered; the down coat is "clove brown" above, slightly paler below, mottled with white on the under parts and wings. The feathers of the wings and tail appears first and are fully developed before the body plumage is acquired; the down disappears last on the head and neck, after the young bird is fully grown. The brown plumage of the first winter succeeds the downy stage and is worn for nearly a year, fading out to a very light color on the breast in the spring. There is a partial molt during the first spring, but no very decided advance toward maturity is made until the first complete molt the following summer. At this first post-nuptial molt a plumage is acquired which is somewhat like the adult, but there is still much brown mottling in the head, neck, and under parts. During the following spring there is still further advance, the nuptial plumes are partially acquired and the young bird is ready to breed; but the fully adult nuptial plumage is not acquired, I believe, until the next, the third, spring. The partial prenuptial molt of adults, at which the long nuptial plumes of the neck and back are acquired, occurs in February and March; and the complete post-nuptial molt extends from August to October. Both old and young birds in any plumage can be distinguished from the Farallon cormorant by the outline of the feathered tract bordering the gular sac; in the Brandt cormorant the gular sac is invaded by a pointed extension of the feathered throat area, whereas in the Farallon the gular sac has a broad, rounded outline.

Food.—Like other cormorants, this species feeds almost exclusively on fish, which it obtains by diving. As it is a maritime species, it lives on salt-water fishes, many of which it obtains near the bottom and often at considerable depths. Professor Loomis (1895) took some fish from the gullets of these cormorants which were identified as " a species of rock cod (*Sebastocles paucispinis*)." He also says: " Great rafts of these cormorants collected on the bay whenever ' the feed came in.' At a distance these gatherings present a very peculiar appearance. The water seems to be thickly set with black sticks, often covering an area of several acres."

Mr. A. B. Howell writes me:

The throat is capable of great expansion. I have seen an adult down a fish, after repeated attempts, which seemed surprisingly large for the size of the bird. They forage in very deep water. I have seen them bring up seaweed where I was assured that there was none to be had within a 150 feet of the surface.

Behavior.—Mr. Dawson (1909) says:

It is a familiar figure on the stringers of salmon traps, as well as on isolated piles or the old abandoned wharves on the lower Sound. If the bird is not exactly of a mind to fly at the first alarm from the passing steamer, it stands with wings half open, that, should necessity arise, no time may be lost in making good its escape. Again, a group of them will sit on a low-lying reef, or even on a floating log, with wings half extended, "drying their clothes" in the sunshine. The wings as well as the feet are used under water, but we can not guess why the cormorants more than other aquatic species should be averse to wet plumage.

The chief enemy of the Brandt cormorant in its breeding grounds is that persistent robber of all the sea birds on the California coast, the western gull. The cormorant is big and strong enough to defend its eggs and young against its weaker foe, but the omnipresent gulls are so numerous, so persistent, so active, and so ever on the alert to seize a favorable opportunity, that a brood of young cormorants is successfully raised only at the price of eternal vigilance. Fortunately the cormorants are prolific layers and persevering in their attempts to raise a brood, for the stupid birds are so often driven away from their nests by some chance intruder that the active gulls, which are not so easily frightened, clean out all the eggs in a colony so frequently that it is a wonder that the cormorants are not discouraged and exterminated.

The cormorants are harmless and peaceable neighbors among the various species which share their breeding grounds—murres, gulls, pelicans, and other cormorants. At other seasons of the year they also associate with other species. Mr. Loomis (1895) says:

Sometimes solitary cormorants returning to their rookery joined the files of migrating California murres, and frequently single murres were observed bringing up the rear of strings of outgoing cormorants. On one occasion a California brown pelican was seen at the end of a line of cormorants.

Winter.—In their winter resorts they often congregate in enormous rookeries or roosts. They winter as far north as Puget Sound and are common southward all along the coast in winter. A long line, or a **V**-shaped flock, of great, black birds winging their heavy flight to and from their feeding grounds is a familiar sight about the islands and the rocky bays.

DISTRIBUTION.

Breeding range.—Pacific coast of North America. From southern Alaska (Forrester Island) southward all along the coast to southern Lower California (Magdalena Bay). Breeding grounds protected in the following reservations: In Alaska, Forrester Island; in Washington, Flattery Rocks and Quillayute Needles; in Oregon, Three Arch Rocks; and in California, Farallon.

Winter range.—Includes most of the breeding range, extending from northern Washington (Puget Sound) to southern Lower California (Cape San Lucas).

Egg dates.—California: Fifty-eight records, April 3 to July 15; twenty-nine records, May 28 to June 20. Lower California: Four records, March 28 to April 23.

PHALACROCORAX PELAGICUS PELAGICUS Pallas.

PELAGIC CORMORANT.

HABITS.

I have never been able to recognize any constant characters by which the two northern forms of the pelagic cormorant, *pelagicus* and *robustus,* could be satisfactorily separated. And if the two forms are subspecifically distinct, the breeding ranges of the two have never been satisfactorily separated. The birds of southern Alaska seem to be identical with those of the Aleutian Islands and the birds of the American coast of Bering Sea seem to be similar to those of the Asiatic coast. Therefore *Phalacrocorax pelagicus robustus* seems to have no standing. For these reasons and because I am unable to satisfactorily separate the references between the two forms, I prefer to treat them both together, for certainly their life histories are similar. I shall use the name pelagic cormorant to cover both forms.

Nesting.—Throughout the whole length of the Aleutian chain we found this small, slender cormorant sitting in little groups on the rocks about the promontories or flying out to meet us and to satisfy their curiosity by circling about our boat; they seemed far from timid and were but little disturbed by our frequent shooting for they returned again and again to look us over. Here they breed in colonies on the highest, steepest and most inaccessible rocky cliffs, safe from the depredations of foxes and men and shrouded in the prevailing fogs of that dismal region. The nest is placed on some narrow ledge on a perpendicular cliff facing the sea; it is made mainly of seaweeds and grasses, is added to from year to year and becomes quite bulky.

On the Siberian coast their nesting habits are similar; Dr. J. A. Allen (1905) quotes Mr. N. G. Buxton's notes as follows:

At this place, and six miles farther south, at Matuga Point, there are several rocky islets with precipitous sides where thousands of them nest. Their nests are placed in the most inaccessible places on top of ledges and projections. The nests are large and bulky and composed of kelp and seaweed. The eggs are chalky-white, with a bluish tinge. Five to seven constitute a clutch. The eggs are not palatable on account of the strong flavor, although the Koraks gather and eat them. The height of the nesting season is reached by the 10th of June. The males assist in the work of incubation.

In southern Alaska the pelagic cormorant was found breeding abundantly at various localities by all of the expeditions sent to these regions. Dr. Joseph Grinnell (1909) quotes Mr. Joseph Dixon's notes, referring to South Marble Island in Glacier Bay, as follows:

> There were at least a hundred cormorants breeding on the island and from one hundred and fifty to two hundred more were merely roosting there. Only breeding birds were seen during the day, but about 7 o'clock the other black nonbreeders began to arrive in bunches of from four to seven. They left about 4 o'clock in the morning. The nests were attached to the sloping marble just before it dropped off into salt water and were from fifteen to seventy-five feet above the high-tide mark. Most of the nests were not finished, but four contained one egg each. The nests were compactly built of moss gathered nearby, and not of seaweed. The white patches on the flanks and the two crests were very noticeable in the breeding birds, and most of the males also had the white, slender plumes on their necks. The nonbreeders had no white flank patches.

Mr. George Willett (1912) says that at St. Lazaria Island "the nests are built of sticks and seaweed, lined with grass and seamoss. Many of the breeding birds have little or no white on the flanks, and in many cases the nuptial plumes on the neck are not present or are very poorly developed."

Eggs.—The pelagic cormorant is said to lay anywhere from three to seven eggs, but the usual numbers run from three to five, the larger numbers being exceptional. They are "elliptical ovate" or "elongate ovate" in shape. The color is very pale blue or bluish white, which is more or less concealed by a thin calcareous deposit, originally white, but usually somewhat nest-stained. The measurements of 41 eggs from the supposed breeding range of *pelagicus*, average 58.3 by 37.4 millimeters; the eggs showing the four extremes measure **63** by 38, 61 by **41, 53.3** by 37, and 56 by **35** millimeters. The measurements of 43 eggs from the supposed breeding range of *robustus*, average 57.5 by 37.2 millimeters; the eggs showing the four extremes measure **63** by 39, 62 by **39.5, 51.5** by 36, and 55.5 by **34** millimeters.

Plumages.—The period of incubation is 26 days. The young bird is naked when first hatched, but before it is half grown it is covered with short thick down of a dark, sooty gray color. The wings and tail appear first and are fully grown before the down disappears. In the first plumage young birds are very dark colored, "blackish brown" above and clear uniform, "clove brown" below, but lighter and somewhat mottled on the head and neck. This plumage, which is somewhat glossy on the back when fresh, becomes duller and paler during the fall and winter by wear and fading. Dr. Leonhard Stejneger (1885) has made some exhaustive studies of the molts and plumages of this species, based on the examination of fresh material. I can not do better than to quote from his conclusions, as follows:

It will be necessary first to remark that these birds raise two broods during the summer. This is not to be understood as a positive statement that the same parents rear two sets of young every year—although I believe that most of them do—but simply that I have found the colonies of this species having eggs and downy young at two different times. The first season commences early in May, the young of this brood being fully fledged in the latter part of July. In the middle of this month, however, the colonies again contained all stages, from fresh eggs to newly-hatched young. During the first days of August I found downy young of almost the same age and still without feathers, while on the 21st of August, 1882, I visited a numerous colony at Poludjonnij, Bering Island, in which the oldest young were about half fledged. These would not be able to fly before the first week of September. Between the two periods, young in all stages of development will be found in the colonies, but proportionately few in number. It will thus be seen that it is safe to assume that the difference in age between the earliest and the latest born young in one year amounts to three months, at least.

We are now prepared to understand that we can find two birds undergoing the corresponding molt at times as much apart as the birthdays of the same two birds. If the first molt occurs, say, ten months after the bird broke the shell, the bird born in the middle of May will molt in the middle of March next year, while the one born in the middle of August will not molt before the middle of June next year. And this conclusion is borne out fully by the observed facts. As will be seen from the details relating to the birds collected by me, as given below, I shot birds in the latter part of February, both younger and older, which were just in the first stage of molting, while, on the other hand, I have a skin before me in full molt from young to adult plumage, as late as July, a discrepancy hardly to be accounted for, except by the above explanation.

When about ten months old, the first plumage, which is of the dark grayish sooty color, with some green and purplish reflections in the fresh plumage, changes into the resplendent garb of the adult, from which it then is undistinguishable, except by not having the bright colors of the naked parts of the face and by lacking the white feathers on the neck and thighs. In the following spring, or when about twenty-three months old, it begins to breed.

The above conclusions seem to be substantiated by what material I have examined; I have seen young birds molting into adult plumage in May, June, July, and September, showing that the molt is much prolonged or very variable, probably the latter. Adults have a complete postnuptial molt during the summer and early fall and a partial prenuptial molt in February, March, and April. The highest nuptial plumage, including the white flank patches, the two crests on the head, and the white filaments on the neck and back, is worn during March, April, and May; the white filaments are very brittle and soon disappear; they are seldom seen in museum specimens, as they are easily lost in skinning. The winter plumage is duller or browner than the nuptial and lacks the special adornments mentioned above.

Food.—The food of the pelagic cormorant consists principally, perhaps wholly, of fish. Prof. Harold Heath (1915) says: " Several times at sea these birds were seen feeding on herrings."

It can be distinguished from other species by its size and shape, as well as by the white flank patches, if present. As a diver and a swimmer it is an expert, though it seldom rests on the water. It must be exceedingly swift in the pursuit of its finny prey. Being more slender and more elegant in form than the other cormorants, the flight of this species is rather more graceful than the others. It is a rakish looking craft in the air with its long, slim neck and long tail, but its flight is not swift; its wing strokes are rather rapid, interrupted by intervals of scaling. Dr. Frank M. Chapman (1902) publishes the following interesting note by Mr. J. D. Figgins on the feeding habits of this species:

When the gulls, by their discordant cries, proclaim the discovery of a school of fish every cormorant within hearing distance flocks to the scene, and in many cases so thoroughly appropriate the school to their own use that the gulls are compelled to seek other feeding grounds, as they do not relish diving into a mass of cormorants. The cormorants make no attempt to fish on their own account, but wait until the gulls discover the game and then appropriate it.

Cormorants are usually silent birds and this species is no exception to the rule. Mr. Joseph Dixon (1907) says: "They make a particularly groaning sound when on the nest that sounds like someone moaning in pain. We could hear it quite a ways out before we landed and could not imagine what it was."

Behavior.—These cormorants, which build their nests on inaccessible cliffs, have few enemies to contend with, except the winged robbers of their eggs and young. Mr. George Willett (1912) writes that on St. Lazaria Island:

Owing to the depredations of the crows, very few of these birds succeed in raising an entire brood, and I believe there are many who are unable to raise a single young. When frightened from the nest, they very foolishly fly a considerable distance to sea and often remain for several minutes at a time. This opportunity is quickly seized by the crows, and in an almost incredibly short time the cormorants' nest is empty.

Doctor Stejneger (1885) refers to a wholesale destruction of this species in the Commander Islands, as follows:

During the winter of 1876–77 thousands and thousands were destroyed by an apparently epidemic disease, and masses of the dead birds covered the beach all around the islands. During the following summer comparatively few were seen, but of later years their number has again been increasing, though people having seen their former multitude think that there is no comparison between the past and the present. From Bering Island the reports are similar, with the addition that the stone foxes would not eat the corpses.

Fall.—The natives in the vicinity of Bering Sea depend largely on the flesh of these cormorants at certain seasons for food; their skins were formerly used for clothing and their nuptial crests and plumes served as ornaments. Mr. L. M. Turner (1886) writes:

During severe weather of the winter and fall these birds resort to the high rocky ledges or the single rocks which jut from the sea. Some of the rocks are fairly covered with these birds, and these appearing like a lot of black bottles standing on the rock. The natives of all parts of the country use the flesh of this bird for food. Some of the Aleuts, especially those of Attu, prize the flesh more than any other bird. They formerly obtained many of these birds with a kind of net which was thrown over the birds when sitting on the shore rocks, being driven there by the severity of a storm, so that the birds could not remain on the outer rocks without being washed off.

Winter.—Mr. W. H. Kobbé (1900) writing of the winter habits of this species near Cape Disappointment, Washington, says:

The violet-green cormorant is only found upon the cape during the winter months, when it is very abundant. It arrives in the fall and departs rather late in the spring. During its stay upon the cape it associates with the white-crested cormorant, and the two species may often be seen perched upon the fish-trap poles in large flocks. Both species frequently fly into the fish pots from which they are unable to escape ,since they are unable to fly vertically upward. It is an easy matter for the birds to fly from the poles downward into the square pot formed of netting, but after they once get in they are forced to remain and are generally killed by the fishermen.

DISTRIBUTION.

Breeding range.—Coasts and islands of Bering Sea and northern Pacific Ocean. From Norton Sound (Sledge Island) and St. Lawrence Island southward along the coast to southern Alaska (Forrester Island) and perhaps farther. Westward throughout the Aleutian Islands and Commander Islands. Southward through the Kurile Islands to Japan (Yezzo). Northward along the Asiatic coast of Bering Sea to northeastern Siberia (East Cape) and westward on the Arctic coast of Siberia to Cape Irkaipij, Cape Kibera Island and Koliutschin Island. Seen in summer and may breed in Kotzebue Sound. Birds breeding near the south end of Vancouver Island are probably referable to *resplendens*. Breeding grounds protected in the following reservations: In Alaska, Bering Sea, Pribilof, Aleutian Islands, St. Lazaria, and Forrester Island.

Winter range.—From the Aleutian, Pribilof, and Commander Islands southward throughout the remainder of the breeding range and beyond it south to Puget Sound and to China.

Spring migration.—Arrives in northeastern Siberia, Gichiga, as early as May 13, in Norton Sound, Alaska, by June 5, and at St. Lawrence Island, June 2.

Fall migration.—Leaves northeastern Siberia about the second week in October and Norton Sound, Alaska, in October or November.

Casual records.—Taken at Point Barrow, Alaska, June 8, 1898.

Egg dates.—Southern Alaska: Twenty-four records, June 16 to July 31; twelve records, June 29 to July 19. Aleutian Islands: Four records, June 20 to July 4.

PHALACROCORAX PELAGICUS RESPLENDENS Audubon.

BAIRD CORMORANT.

HABITS.

The Baird cormorant is clearly distinct, subspecifically at least, from the northern subspecies of *Phalacrocorax pelagicus* and it has been suggested that it might be even a distinct species. To what extent the northern and southern forms intergrade and what the limits of the respective breeding ranges are I must leave to others to investigate and decide; but for the purposes of this life history I shall assume that the birds which breed from the coast of Washington southward are *resplendens*. Much of what I have written about the life history of *pelagicus* would apply equally well to the smaller southern form, so I will not repeat it.

Nesting.—The nesting habits of the Baird cormorant are similar to those of the pelagic, but very different from those of its neighbors on the California coast, the Farallon and Brandt cormorants. The latter two are almost absurdly tame, whereas Baird is very shy about its breeding grounds. The two larger species breed in large colonies and build their nests on the flat tops of the rocky islands or on the broader and more accessible ledges, whereas the slim, little Baird cormorant almost always builds its nest on the narrowest and most inaccessible, little shelves or crannies on the face of some steep, rocky cliff, usually breeding in small scattered groups or singly. The Baird cormorant also uses no sticks in the construction of its nest.

Prof. Lynds Jones (1908) gives the following account of the nesting habits of the Baird cormorant on Carroll Islet, off the coast of Washington:

The nesting places of this cormorant were small ledges or grottoes in precipices. Therefore the most of them were nesting on the ocean side of the island, and at various elevations. Nests were usually placed not nearer together than several feet, possibly because of the character of the rock face. The birds were uniformly more timid than the white-crested. Their single barklike cry was not often heard, even when they were disturbed or frightened.

None of the nests examined contained sticks, but were wholly composed of dry grass, with occasionally a few feathers in the lining. All of the nest except the outside was clean, but the outside was characteristically covered with lime, and the rocks below the nest for many feet were white with the same substance. In fact, the nesting places of these birds could be discerned at considerable distances by the white streaking of the dark gray rocks. All along the coast, when we approached the rocky shores, evidences of these birds were scattered along the rocks.

Mr. Walter E. Bryant (1888), writing of this cormorant on the Farallon Islands, says:

They are less common than the two foregoing species, with which they do not associate. The nests are built usually in the most inaccessible places, and at all altitudes; some were found so close to the water's edge that they were splashed by the highest waves beating against the rocky shore. The same rookeries are used from year to year, and the same nests are occupied after being robbed, the owners simply adding a few more pieces of weeds before laying. They congregate in colonies of eight or ten pairs, nesting on natural shelves of perpendicular or overhanging rocks. Three or four eggs are laid in a nest of the same material as is used by the other cormorants. Incubation commences after the first egg is laid, in order to keep it protected from the gulls. The birds may be seen on the nests for days before the first egg is laid.

Eggs.—The eggs of the Baird cormorant are practically indistinguishable from those of the pelagic cormorant, though, strangly enough, the eggs, of which I have measurements, average larger. The measurements of 40 eggs, in various collections, average 61.7 by 40.4 millimeters; the eggs showing the four extremes measure **65** by **40** and **51** by **36** millimeters.

Behavior.—Referring to the behavior of Baird cormorants, Mr. W. Leon Dawson (1909) writes:

Cormorants plunge into the wildest waters as fearlessly as sealions, and they carry on their fishing operations about the shoulders of booming reefs, which humans dare not approach. After luncheons, which occur quite frequently in the cormorant day, the birds love to gather on some low-lying reef, just above the reach of the waves, and devote the intervening hours to that most solemn function of life, digestion. There is no evidence that the birds discuss oceanic politics on these occasions; the benevolent assimilation of a twelve-inch cultus cod is presumed to be ample occupation for union hours.

When the birds of a colony quit their nests they launch out swiftly, wagging their head from side to side if the danger is above them. They may join the puffins and gulls for a few rounds of inspection, but oftener they settle in the water at some distance from the shore, a large company of them looking and acting very much like a flock of black geese. It requires quite an effort on the bird's part to rise from the water, but this is done with a single motion of the wings, unassisted by the feet, as would be the case with heavy ducks and loons. If the shag has been diving it may burst out of the water with the acquired impetus of the chase, and once under way its flight is swift and vigorous and not altogether ungraceful.

Winter.—An interesting account of a winter resort of this and other cormorants on an island off the coast of Lower California is given by Mr. A. W. Anthony (1906) as follows:

The first cormorants will arrive at the island as early as 4 o'clock, and taking up their station well back from the beach will be joined by the next flock. The black patch on the gray sand extends its outposts until it meets the brown borders of the pelican colony on the one side and the snowy expanse of gulls on the other, completely surrounding them and forcing later arrivals of gulls and pelicans to start other camp grounds farther along.   These again are over-taken and surrounded until by dusk the entire side of the island will be one solid mass of closely packed birds, the white of the gulls and brown plumages of the pelicans standing out in striking contrast to the inky blackness of the cormorants, which form over three quarters of the mass.   The species all flock separately so far as is possible, and the result is a patchwork of white and gray separated by broad zones of black; even the Brandt and Farallon cormo-rants roost apart, with the somewhat rare Baird cormorant still further re-moved, perching on the low cliffs and rocks along the beach.   Stragglers arrive until late in the night; the gulls in fact do not all get home until the first of the early risers begin to leave at daybreak.   The departure is even more grad-ual if possible than the arrival of the night before, and it is not until the sun is two hours high that the last of the cormorants leave for the fishing grounds.

The following quotation from Mr. C. I. Clay (1911) will illus-trate the remarkable diving ability of this species:

We were one and one-half miles southwest from Trinidad, Humboldt County, California, and about one-half mile off shore.   Mr. Francisco had set a net the night before near a blind rock and in twenty fathoms of water.   We were taking in the net when a Brandt cormorant came to the surface in its meshes, then a second one and a third.   Although the Baird cormorants were common everywhere on the ocean there were none in the net.   On closely questioning the fisherman, he informed me Brandt cormorants were caught almost daily in from five to thirty fathoms of water while using the deep water nets, but were never taken in over forty fathoms of water, while the Baird cormorant (I had taught him the difference between the two species) were often taken in as much as eighty fathoms of water.

I saw several Baird cormorants rise to the surface of the water with pieces of kelp in their bills in places where Joe informed me the water was over eighty fathoms deep.   Brandt cormorants were not seen far offshore, though they were common among the rocks near shore.   Is it a superiority in diving or a desire to obtain a certain kind of food that prompts the Baird cormorants to go down deeper than Brandt cormorants while on their feeding grounds?

DISTRIBUTION.

Breeding range.—Pacific coast of North America.   From extreme southern British Columbia (Sidney Island, near Victoria) southward all along the coast to extreme northern Mexico (Los Coronados Islands).   Breeding grounds protected in the following reservations: In Washington, Flattery Rocks, Quillayute Needles, and Copalis Rock; in Oregon, Three Arch Rocks; and in California, Farallon.

Winter range.—Includes most, if not all, of the breeding range and extends southward to, at least, the central Mexican coast (Cape San Lucas and Mazatlan).

Egg dates.—California: Sixty records, May 3 to July 15; thirty records, May 29 to June 19.   Los Coronados Islands: Thirty records, April 17.   Washington and Oregon: Seven records, June 10 to 21.

PHALACROCORAX URILE (Gmelin).

RED-FACED CORMORANT.

HABITS.

Walrus Island, one of the Pribilof group in Bering Sea, the home of the red-faced cormorant, is without exception the most interesting bird island I have ever seen. Although situated only 7 miles to the eastward of St. Paul Island, it is well isolated and protected by the prevailing fogs and storms of that forbidding region, for it is only during the calmest weather that a landing may be effected on its rugged shores. It is a small, low, rocky islet of less than 5 acres in area, not over a quarter of a mile long, and less than 80 yards wide, formed mainly of flat volcanic rock and lava in a series of shelves and low cliffs extending in an irregular outline down to and into the water. Portions of the island are covered with great masses of water-worn boulders of various sizes, piled up indiscriminately by the action of the sea, under which hundreds of paroquet, crested, and least auklets, as well as tufted and horned puffins, find suitable nesting sites. The accumulation of guano for many generations, perhaps for centuries, has formed sufficient soil on the higher portions of the island to support a luxuriant growth of grass in compact tufts. Here the ground is so honeycombed with the nesting burrows of tufted puffins that it is impossible to walk without constantly breaking into them; here also a large colony of glaucous and glaucous-winged gulls build their nests among the tufts of grass. But all of these are as nothing compared with the vast hordes of California and Pallas murres which resort to this wonderful little island to breed. All around the rocky shores every available bare spot above high-water mark is literally covered with them, thousands and thousands of them, sitting as close as they can sit on the rocks, on the cliffs, and on the bare ground above them.

The day we landed, July 7, 1911, was perfectly calm and the sea was as smooth as glass; we stepped out of our dory onto a flat shelf of rock as easily as if it were a wharf. As we walked out among the murre colonies they scarcely moved enough to allow us to pass and it was not until we almost stepped on them that they decided to leave and went pouring off in swarms down into the water. They soon returned and circled about the island, a constant, steady stream of whirling birds. A cloud of great white gulls were hovering overhead screaming constantly and downy young gulls were running about in the grass. The lively little auklets were chattering beneath the rocks or scrambling out from under them to fly off to sea. Grotesque puffins, disturbed in their burrows, made ludicrous attempts to escape by bounding along the ground in an effort to fly. Amidst all the noise and confusion the stolid red-faced cormorants sat unmoved upon their nests, on the wide shelves of rock projecting from the low cliffs, their rich glossy black plumage glistening with metallic tints of purple, blue, green, and bronze, offset by the brilliant scarlet face and the gular sac of clear smalt blue, a striking feature in the scene, a picture of dignified indifference. All about them murres were sitting on their eggs and the well-made nests of Pacific kittiwakes were often near them. They seemed to live on good terms with their neighbors though they took no part in the exciting events going on about them; they were busy brooding over their young and it was only when we almost touched them, as they stood craning their necks at us in awkward stupidity, that they finally flew off in silence.

Although the common name of this species is aptly descriptive, it might also be well applied to other cormorants; I have always thought the old name *bicristatus* peculiarly fitting for the red-faced cormorant, for its two conspicuous crests, one on the crown, and one on the occiput, make it more strikingly double crested than *dilophus*, or *auritus*, as it is now called. Much confusion seems to have existed, among the earlier writers on the birds of Bering Sea, as to the species of cormorants noted in this region, but between *pelagicus* and *urile* there seems to be sufficient difference to distinguish these two species at all ages. The extent of the naked skin on the face and forehead of *urile* is distinctive in the adult; its larger size, stouter bill and heavier head are characteristic at all ages; and even the downy young are different in color.

Nesting.—The breeding season begins early, two or three weeks earlier than with the other sea birds of Bering Sea, with the possible exception of the glaucous and glaucous-winged gulls. Eggs, well incubated, were taken by Elliott as early as June 1, 1872, and young, about a week old were secured by Palmer on June 13, indicating that egg laying must have begun about the middle of May or earlier. At the time of our visit, July 7, 1911, nearly all the nests contained young of various ages; a very few nests held heavily-incubated eggs, probably laid about the middle of June or later, these may have been second layings where the nests had been robbed by gulls. Probably the last of the young do not leave the nests until well on toward the end of August, extending the breeding season over three or four months.

The nests are placed on broad flat ledges of rock on the steepest cliffs, where they are often inaccessible, though on Walrus Island the cliffs are so low that the nests are easily reached. Other writers have stated that they are exceedingly filthy about their nests, but my experience was quite to the contrary; the nests that I saw were the handsomest, neatest, and cleanest cormorants' nests that I had ever seen. The nests were large, well built, and securely plastered onto a firm foundation; some were made almost wholly of green grass and sods, evidently gathered in the center of the island; others were made partially or wholly of various pretty seaweeds, sea ferns (Sertularidae) and sea mosses, fresh and neat in appearance and of various shades of brown, pink, and purple, probably obtained at considerable depths by diving; some of the nests were profusely decorated with gulls' feathers. One typical large nest measured 20 by 16 inches in diameter outside, was built up 6 inches high, and hollowed in the center about 3 inches; another, small nest, measured 14 by 12 inches outside, 3 inches high, and nearly 3 inches deep.

Eggs.—The eggs are small in proportion to the size of the birds; the measurements of 47 eggs, in the United States National Museum and the writer's collections, average 60.3 by 37.6 millimeters; the eggs showing the four extremes measure **65.5** by 38.5, 62 by **41.5, 53.2** by 36.2, and 62.3 by **33** millimeters.

The ground color is pale bluish white, which is almost wholly concealed by a rough calcareous deposit, more or less nest stained and soiled. They are much elongated in shape, varying from elliptical ovate to cylindrical ovate.

Young.—The incubation period is about three weeks. When first hatched the young are naked, blind, and quite helpless, a dark, livid, purplish brown in color. They grow rapidly and like other members of the family are fed on semi-digested regurgitated food, for which a more solid diet of small fish, crabs, and shrimps is substituted as they grow older. Within a few days after hatching, down begins to appear on the dorsal tracts and the young bird is soon well covered with dark-gray down mottled with white on the belly.

Plumages.—Mr. William Palmer (1899) has described in detail the development of the downy and juvenal plumages in this species. At the end of six weeks the young cormorants are practically fully grown and ready to fly, the wings and tail being fully developed before the contour plumage is completed. The full adult plumage is not acquired until the fall of the second year; young birds in the dull brownish plumage and lacking the brilliant colors of the facial parts frequent the breeding grounds when one year old but they probably do not breed until the following season. Young birds in this plumage closely resemble the young of other species, but they can be distinguished by the narrow frontal naked space or by the outline of the feathering surrounding the gular sac.

Behavior.—The red-faced cormorant can not be readily distinguished at a distance from other species of the genus; its flight is similar, slow, strong and direct, with rapid wing-beats and occasional intervals of scaling, and with head, neck and feet outstretched to the fullest extent. Like other cormorants it is strongly impelled by curiosity to fly out to meet an approaching boat and to circle about it several times, though generally a little beyond gunshot range. While flying about an intruder or when its home is invaded it sometimes utters a loud, guttural and rolling note or croak, but as a rule it is a peculiarly silent bird.

Winter.—After the breeding season is over, in September, the red-faced cormorants leave their breeding grounds to wander about the shores of Bering Sea, as far south as the Aleutian Islands, during the winter months. Even the severe winter storms which rage so furiously among those desolated rocky islands fail to drive this species from its inhospitable home, where it proves a blessing to the hardy natives. During severe winters when other bird life is scarce these birds are much in demand for food and furnish a convenient supply of fresh meat for soups and stews; the flesh of the young birds may be fairly palatable, but the old birds could hardly be tolerated if anything else were obtainable.

Dr. E. W. Nelson (1883) says:

These birds appear to be a fitting accompaniment of the bleak, barren coast found so frequently along the northern shore of Bering Sea. The dark cliffs, with scarcely a trace of vegetation, and the cold rocks, relieved here and there by banks of snow in the ravines, are rendered still more wild and inhospitable in appearance by the presence of these large, awkward, sombre-colored birds, which circle silently back and forth in front of their cliffs, fitting inhabitants of the remote and cheerless wilds where their home is made.

DISTRIBUTION.

Breeding range.—Bering Sea region. On the Pribilof Islands, perhaps on the western Aleutian Islands, on the Commander Islands, and on the coast of northeastern Siberia as far north as North Cape. Breeding grounds protected in the Pribilof Reservation, Alaska.

Winter range.—From the vicinity of the Pribilof, Aleutian, Commander, and Northern Kurile Islands, southward to Japan and Formosa.

Casual records.—Ranges to Norton Sound (Saint Michael) and the Diomede Islands.

Egg dates.—Aleutian and Pribilof Islands: Four records, June 17 to July 7.

Family PELECANIDAE, Pelicans.

PELECANUS ERYTHRORHYNCHOS Gmelin.

AMERICAN WHITE PELICAN.

HABITS.

The day we reached Big Stick Lake, after a 30-mile drive over the rolling plains of Saskatchewan, was cold and blustering; the lake looked forbidding enough, for its muddy waters were covered with white caps and heavy breakers were rolling in on the pebbly beach before a strong northerly gale; but we could not resist the temptation to visit a small island, which lay less than 200 yards offshore, and over which a cloud of white gulls were hovering. The chief attraction was a great white mass of birds standing on one end of the island, conspicuous as a snow bank in spring, but recognized at once as a flock of pelicans. I had never seen a breeding colony of white pelicans and, as our driver assured us that the water was shallow enough to drive to the island, we decided to attempt it. Our horses plunged bravely on through the rough water, which nearly flooded the wagon, the flying spray drenched us to the skin and nearly took our breath away as it was blown into our faces by the gale; but we arrived safely at the end of our short drive none the worse for our chilly shower bath, and we were well repaid for our trouble. Clouds of California and ring-billed gulls were rising from the little island and beating the air above it in a bewildering maze; numerous ducks flew from the grassy knolls and a lot of yelping avocets added their cries to the constant chorus of gulls' voices. But the pelicans stood silent and dignified until they decided to leave and then, as if by one common impulse, they all rose at once with a great flapping of long black-tipped wings; they seemed heavy, awkward, and ungainly at first, but they soon gained headway and showed their marvelous mastery of the air, as they swung into line forming one large V-shaped flock; they circled around the island two or three times, with slow and dignified wing beats in military precision, or all scaled in unison like well-drilled soldiers; and finally, when satisfied that they must leave and when fully arranged in proper marching order, they all followed their leader and departed northward over the lake; the last we saw of them they were flying in a long straight line, just above the horizon, their black-tipped wings keeping perfect step and their snowy plumage showing clearly cut against the cold gray sky even when miles away. It was a fascinating spectacle to stand and gaze at that departing flock of magnificent birds and to dream of nature's wonders, the marvels of creation, which only those may see who seek the solitudes of remote wilderness lakes.

We were doomed to disappointment, however, for not a pelican's nest was to be found on the island; we felt sure that they would have eggs at this late date, June 14; possibly they had been disturbed; but more likely they were merely wandering about in flocks, as we had seen them elsewhere. Later in the season, on July 18, 1906, Doctor Bishop and Doctor Dwight visited this island again and found a small breeding colony of white pelicans with a few double-crested cormorants; there were ten nests of the pelicans with two eggs each, and four with only one each, surrounded by a thickly populated colony of California and ring-billed gulls. The pelicans' nests were made of sticks and feathers. Doctor Chapman visited this island on June 10, 1907, and found a great colony of 3,000 pelicans nesting there; the young were just appearing at that date, showing that they were unusually late in nesting the previous season.

Nesting.—The first breeding colonies of white pelicans that I found were in Lake Winnipegosis, Manitoba, where they were nesting on small islands with double-crested cormorants, ring-billed gulls, and common terns. The largest of these was examined on June 19, 1913.

A long white reef was seen in the distance, which, as we drew near, seemed to be covered with birds; the mass of loose boulders which formed its foundation, and was prolonged into a point at one end, was black with nesting cormorants; a fine stony or pebbly beach formed a point at the other end, over which a cloud of screaming terns were hovering, and in the center, where the soil had accumulated to a considerable height, we could see the great, white solemn forms of numerous pelicans sitting on their nests, or standing beside them. While making a landing in our canoe the scene suddenly changed to one of action, as the cormorants began pouring off their nests and out over the water, and the pelicans rose with one accord; not a single bird was left on the island, but the whole great regiment formed in one vast flock and circled around the island again and again in a dense, black cloud, with nearly a hundred of the great white birds in the center; it was a magnificent sight not soon to be forgotten. They swung close over our heads several times within easy gunshot, and my boatman could not resist the temptation to send two of the large, beautiful creatures tumbling into the water with a mighty splash. Although ungainly in form and massive in size, weighing from 15 to 20 pounds and stretching from 8 to 10 feet in alar expanse, the white pelican is really a glorious bird, the spotless purity of its snow-white plumage offset by its glossy black wing feathers and enriched by its deep orange bill and feet.

On landing we found that the common terns were nesting in a densely populated colony of from 500 to 800 pairs on the gravelly beach at the eastern end, and the double-crested cormorants, about 300 or 400 pairs of them, were occupying the bare ground and the rocky point at the western end. On the high bare ground in the center we counted 46 nests of white pelicans, mere depressions in the bare earth, with usually a more or less complete rim of dirt and rubbish raised around the eggs. The usual number of eggs was two, but three or four nests contained three eggs each and one held six, probably laid by two or perhaps three birds; some nests held only one egg, and there were a few single eggs lying around on the ground or under the rocks. We saw one pelican's egg in a cormorant's nest with four eggs of the latter. The nests of the two species were often close together, showing that they are friendly neighbors.

Dr. Joseph Grinnell (1908) visited Echo Island in Salton Sea on April 20, 1908, where he found an interesting breeding colony of some 2,000 white pelicans, the most southern colony recorded at that time. He gives the following accurate description of the nests:

The nests varied greatly in size and composition, according to location. A nest on the drift line just at highest water mark was a tall, steep-sided affair, like the pictures I have seen of flamingos' nests. Appropriate material was plentiful, consisting of sections of plant stems, chips, and chunks of pumice. Planks and railroad ties sometimes interfered with the symmetry of the nests. The finer material had evidently been heaped up by the bird as she sat on the nest, for the nests were often surrounded by radiating spoke-like grooves, plainly bill marks. The material is thus pulled towards the sitter, but not from a farther distance than 828 mm. from the center, beyond which the bird is evidently not able to reach. The spacing of the nests in the colony, quite regular in places, seems to be dependent on the reach and conflicting interests of the inhabitants. The sets of eggs were never closer together than 828 mm., usually 1,380 mm. apart. The ground between the nests was usually absolutely clear of even the finer fragments, these having been scraped up onto the walls of the nests. On the hill slopes the nests were more scanty, for material was scarce. Some were made wholly of angular pumice or dried mud fragments, some of brush stems, and some of just soft earth. But their diameter was an almost constant quantity, between 414 and 532 mm. The depression was 46 to 69 mm. deep, so that there was nearly always a well-defined rim to the nest. The higher nests, those in the drift, were mounds as much as 276 mm. tall.

In the Klamath Lake region of southern Oregon, now a reservation, the white pelicans nest in very different situations. Mr. William L. Finley (1907) has thus described their nesting sites:

Extending for several miles out from the main shore was a seemingly endless area of floating tule islands, between which flowed a network of channels. These islands furnished good homes for the great flocks of pelicans that return each spring to live about these lakes and rivers that teem with fish. The tules had grown up for generations. The heavy growth of each year shoots up through the dead stalks of the preceding season till it forms a fairly good floating foundation. On the top of this the pelicans had perched and trodden down the tules till they formed a surface often strong enough to support a man. But it was like walking on the crust of the snow, for you never knew just when it would break through. However, these treacherous islands were the only camping places we had during the two weeks we cruised the Lower Klamath. We rowed on among these islands and found the pelican colonies scattered along for about two miles. There were eight or ten big rookeries, each containing from four to six hundred birds. Besides, there were about fifteen others that had all the way from fifty to two hundred birds. The birds nested a few feet apart on these dry beds, laying from one to three eggs.

Eggs.—The white pelican raises only one brood in a season and normally lays two eggs, sometimes only one and occasionally three.

Some of the earlier writers say that this bird lays from three to four eggs, but I think such large sets are exceptional. I have found as many as six eggs in a nest, but I believe that these were laid by two or three birds. The eggs vary in shape from "ovate" to "elongate ovate," and some are nearly "elliptical oval." The shell is thin, soft, and brittle, lusterless and rough on the exterior, with generally more or less calcareous deposit, which cracks or flakes off irregularly. The original color is dull white, but the eggs are usually more or less blood stained and sometimes are heavily smeared or streaked with it; they soon become very much nest-stained and dirty, so that they are far from attractive in appearance. The measurements of 62 eggs in the United States National Museum collection average 90 by 56.5 millimeters; the eggs showing the four extremes measure 103 by 54, 81.5 by 62, 62.5 by 45, and 85.5 by 34 millimeters.

Young.—Both sexes share the duties of incubation, which lasts for about a month. Major Bendire (1882) recorded the period of incubation as 29 days for eggs hatched under a domestic hen. The young when first hatched are naked, blind, and helpless, of a livid flesh color, and most unattractive in appearance. They remain in the nests for two or three weeks and are fed by their parents on regurgitated food. Mr. Finley (1907) says of this process:

The parent regurgitated a fishy soup into the front end of its pouch and the baby pelican pitched right in and helped himself out of this family dish. As the young bird grew older and larger, at each meal time he kept reaching farther into the big pouch of his parent until finally, when he was half grown, it was a remarkable sight. The mother opened her mouth and the whole head and neck of her nestling disappeared down her capacious maw while he hunted for his dinner in the internal regions.

When one-third or half grown the young pelicans are strong enough to leave the nests and wander about their island home in droves. They also learn to swim while still in the downy stage and when less than half grown. The feeding process during this active stage is most interesting and strenuous. Mr. Finley (1907) has well described it as follows:

Just then another mother dropped into the nursery and she was besieged by several ravenous children. Each began pecking at her bill, trying to make her feed them. But she moved off in apparent unconcern, or perhaps she was making some selection as to which one to feed. She waddled about till one of the youngsters began a series of actions that were very interesting. He fell on the ground before the old bird, grunting and flapping his wings as if he were in the last stages of starvation. Still the mother did not heed his entreaties and the youngster suddenly got well and began pecking her bill again. The old bird backed up as if she were getting a good footing and slowly opened her mouth to admit the bill of the little pelican. She drew her neck up till the ends of the upper and lower mandibles were braced against the ground and her pouch was distended to the limit. Jonah-like, down the mother's throat went the head of the child till he seemed about to be swallowed had it not been for his fluttering wings. He remained buried in the depths for about two minutes, eating everything he could find. Nor did he withdraw from the family cupboard voluntarily, but when the supply was exhausted or the mother thought he had enough she began slowly to rise and struggle to regain her upright position. The youngster was loath to come out and, flapping his wings, he tried in every way to hold on as she began shaking back and forth. The mother shook around over 10 or 12 feet of ground till she literally swung the young bird off his feet and sent him sprawling over on the dry tules.

Rev. S. H. Goodwin (1904) has published the following interesting account of the behavior of young white pelicans:

Young pelicans must certainly be given a prominent place in the front rank of the ridiculous and grotesque in bird life. Their excessively fat, squabby bodies, the under parts of which are bare, while the upper parts are covered with a wool-like coating, hardly distinguishable from that on the back of a four weeks' old lamb; these bodies set on a pair of legs, of the use of which the youngsters seem to have no clear notion, so that when they undertake to move about they wobble and teeter and balance themselves with their short, unfledged wings, often tumbling over; many of them (on this occasion) with their mandibles parted, and panting like a dog after a long run on a hot day, the pouch hanging limp and flabby, like an empty sack, shaken by every breath—form, appearance, movement, all combined to make these birds absurdly ridiculous.

When we approached these birds, those nearest the water would not move an inch, while those nearest us in their frantic endeavor to get away would try to climb up and over the struggling, squirming mass in front of them, sometimes succeeding, but oftener rolling back to the ground where, not infrequently they alighted upon their backs, and lay helplessly beating their wings and kicking their feet in the air—after the fashion of some huge beetle—till they were helped to right themselves. When left to themselves, not a few of these birds would "sit down," just as a dog sits on his haunches, the wings sometimes hanging limp at the sides, at others folded back. The larger part of them, however, simply squatted in the usual manner. They made no sound, save when we attempted to drive them, when an occasional puppy-like grunt would be heard, as if some hapless youngster had fallen or been trodden upon.

As the young pelicans increase in size they are fed more and more on solid food which consists wholly of fish. Mr. John F. Ferry (1910) says of the food of the young " Sometimes they disgorged the contents of their pouches, usually a mass of salamanders (*Necturus maculatus*), though occasionally a 'jock-fish' (one of them was about a foot long), and some brook sticklebacks (*Eucolia inconstans*)." As is generally the case with the larger birds, pelicans are not at all solicitous for the welfare of their eggs or young; they seem to think only of their own safety. If pelicans and eagles were half as aggressive as humming birds or thrushes, collecting their eggs would be a hazardous undertaking; but fortunately for the collectors and for predatory gulls the white pelicans promptly depart and leave their nests to be despoiled.

Plumages.—From the naked stage of nativity the young pelican develops rapidly in size and soon begins to acquire its downy covering. A young bird in my collection, with a body about the size of a mallard and a head as large as a swan, has the head and neck practically naked, the down only just starting, and the body thickly covered with soft, dense fleece-like down which is pure white. This bird was probably two or three weeks old. The soft woolly down increases until the young bird is completely covered; the flight feathers develop rapidly and the bird attains its full size before the body plumage appears. The first winter plumage is acquired in the fall when the young birds closely resemble the adults. Young birds may be distinguished from adults in the spring by the absence of the special adornments of the nuptial season, the heads and breasts are pure white and the bills and feet are duller colored. At the first postnuptial molt old and young become practically indistinguishable, except that the highest development of maturity is not reached until the third or fourth year. In adults the prenuptial molt is incomplete, producing in highly plumaged birds, the pale yellow crest and breast plumes, the brilliant orange bill and feet and the horny protuberance on the bill, which is common to both sexes. The horn is shed soon after the eggs are laid and the occipital crest is soon replaced by a mottled gray cap. I believe that only a few of the oldest and most highly developed birds have well-marked yellow crests and plumes; the greater number of breeding birds have the gray caps, which are lost at the end of the breeding season, or at the following postnuptial molt.

Food.—The white pelican does not dive for its food like the brown pelican, but catches it on or near the surface by swimming or wading in shallow water. The process has been well described by several writers, but the following account by Mr. N. S. Goss (1888) seems to give the best idea of it:

I have often noticed the birds in flocks, in pairs, or alone, swimming on the water with partially opened wings, and head drawn down and back, the bill just clearing the water, ready to strike and gobble up the prey within their reach; when so fishing, if they ran into a shoal of minnows, they would stretch out their necks, drop their heads upon the water, and with open mouths and extended pouches scoop up the tiny fry. Their favorite time for fishing on the seashore is during the incoming tide, as with it come the small fishes to feed upon the insects caught in the rise, and upon the low forms of life in the drift as it washes shoreward, the larger fish following in their wake, each from the smallest to the largest eagerly engaged in taking life in order to sustain life. All sea birds know this and the time of its coming well, and the white pelicans that have been patiently waiting in line along the beach, quietly move into the water, and glide smoothly out, so as not to frighten the life beneath, and at a suitable distance from the shore, form into a line in accordance with the sinuosities of the beach, each facing shoreward and awaiting their leader's signal to start. When this is given, all is commotion; the birds rapidly striking the water with their wings, throwing it high above them, and plunging their heads in and out, fairly make the water foam, as they move on in an almost unbroken line, filling their pouches as they go. When satisfied with their catch, they wade and waddle into line again upon the beach, where they remain to rest, standing or sitting, as suits them best, then, if disturbed, they generally rise in a flock and circle for a long time high in the air.

While fishing in this way, the pelican must catch enormous numbers of small fish.

Audubon (1840) speaks of finding " several hundred fishes, of the size of what are usually called minnows in the stomach of one bird;" and he says:

Among the many which I have at different times examined, I have never found one containing fishes as large as those commonly swallowed by the brown species, which, in my opinion, is more likely to secure a large fish by plunging upon it from on wing, than a bird which must swim after its prey.

Dr. P. L. Hatch (1892) says:

Whether seizing a minnow, or a pickerel weighing three and a half pounds, as in one instance, the fish is grasped transversely, when it is tossed into the air and invariably received with its head foremost in its descent into the pouch.

The white pelican frequently feeds on large fish, such as trout, bass, chub, carp, catfish, suckers, pickerel, and pike, which it must catch by some other method than that described above; probably the larger fish are caught by swimming with the head partially or wholly submerged. In the breeding colonies on Lake Winnipegosis the ground around the nests was strewn with large numbers of the heads of pike and jackfish of great size; many of these must have belonged to fish weighing between twenty and thirty pounds; these large pike are very abundant in this lake, but I can not understand how the pelicans could have caught such large fish or have transported them to the islands, yet I can not see what else could have brought them there.

Mr. C. J. Maynard (1896) says of the food of a captive white pelican:

Johnny ate not only fish but meat, and the quantity which he devoured was surprising, for he often consumed six or eight pounds at a meal. Not that he was a glutton, for when he was satisfied no temptation would induce him to take another morsel. His favorite method of eating was to have his food thrown to him, when he would catch it in his beak, slip it into his pouch, then he would wait until I grasped him by the bill, when I would raise it and shake his head until the food passed downward into his stomach.

Behavior.—The white pelican is, all things considered, one of the largest birds in North America, and it maintains the dignity of its position in the grandeur of its flight. I know of no more magnificent sight, in American bird life than a large flock of white pelicans in flight. Its enormous expanse of wing is sufficient to lift its great weight easily and quickly from either land or water; its light hollow bones and the large air sac under its skin give it great displacement. The effort to rise seems labored at first, and is accomplished by rapid flappings, with a great swishing of powerful pinions beating the air; the great wings are thrown well forward at every stroke; the feet are dangling and the neck is only half extended. In a moment, as the bird gains headway, the feet are held out straight behind, the head is drawn back upon the shoulders, and the bird proceeds upon its way with slow majestic wing strokes. At intervals it sails for long distances on motionless, decurrent wings, a perfect picture of aerial grace and dignity. In the teeth of the strongest gale it soars aloft in majestic circles until almost out of sight, adjusting its aeroplanes to the wind and moving at will in any direction, without the slightest apparent effort. White pelicans are particularly fond of indulging in aerial exercise. Mr. Finley (1907) describes their daily performance as follows:

After returning from the fishing grounds and lounging about the nests for a while the pelicans began to circle over the colony in a large company, rising higher and higher till they were almost lost in blue. By watching we could occasionally see the faint flashes of white as the snowy breasts reflected a gleam of the sun. For hours the sky would glitter with these great birds as they soared about. Then it was thrilling to see some of them descend with rigid, half-closed wings. They used the sky as a big toboggan slide and dropped like meteors, leaving a trail of thunder. Several times when we first heard the sound we were deceived into thinking it was the advance messenger of a heavy storm and jumped up expecting to see black clouds rising from behind the mountains.

Doctor Chapman (1908) gives the following account of one of their aerial feats:

On the afternoon in question a thunderstorm developed rapidly, the sky became ominously black and threatening, and a strong wind whipped the tules into a rustling troubled sea of green. This atmospheric disturbance acted upon the soaring birds in a remarkable manner, stimulating them to perform aerial feats of which I had no idea they were capable. They dived from the heavens like winged meteors, the roar of the air through their stiff pinions sounding as though they had torn great rents in the sky. Approaching the earth they checked their descent by an upshoot, and then with amazing agility zigagged over the marsh, darting here and there like swallows after insects.

On land the white pelican is not graceful, but it walks well, with a stately and dignified air. On the water it floats lightly as a cork, on account of its great displacement, and it swims rapidly and easily, but it is not built for diving. It looms up large and white even at a great distance. Its color pattern is somewhat similar to that of three other large birds, the gannet, the whooping crane, and the wood ibis, but in size and shape the four are distinctly different.

White pelicans are particularly silent birds; the only notes that I have heard them utter are the low-toned grunts or subdued croaking notes heard on their breeding grounds and not audible at any great distance. Doctor Chapman (1908) refers to this note as "a deep voiced, not loud, murmuring groan," and Doctor Grinnell (1908) calls it "a grunting quack." Audubon (1840) likens it to a sound "produced by blowing through the bunghole of a cask."

Dr. P. L. Hatch (1892) says:

This immense bird usually signals his arrival in the early part of April by his characteristic notes from an elevation beyond the range of vision except under the most favorable circumstances. The sound of those notes is difficult to describe, but, unforgetable when once certainly heard from their aerial heights. I have sometimes scanned the heavens in vain to see them, but am generally rewarded for my vigilance and patience if the sky is clear, and if cloudy, also, when I watch the rifts closely with my field glass.

This seems to be a loud note, which I have never heard or seen described elsewhere. Doctor Chapman (1908) describes the note of the young bird as "a low, coughing whining grunt," a chorus of such cries from a large colony creates quite a volume of sound.

In spite of its great size and superior strength the white pelican is a gentle bird of mild disposition; like most giants it is good natured. It is easily tamed and makes an interesting and devoted pet in confinement; in fact no confinement is necessary if raised by hand in captivity. It never makes any trouble for its neighbors on its breeding grounds, where it is often intimately associated with cormorants and gulls. Aside from the damage done to eggs and young pelicans by gulls, it seems to have no enemies. Its habits of nesting on islands, probably developed by natural selection, saves it from certain extermination by predatory animals. It has not suffered materially from hunting for the millinery trade, although at one time a few skins were sold in the New York market; the demand did not seem to warrant the risk involved.

Winter.—From its breeding grounds in the fresh water lakes of the interior, the white pelican migrates southward in the fall through the interior valleys of our large rivers, lingering to feed or rest on the way and finally spreads out both east and west to spend the winter along our warmer sea coasts. Along the south Atlantic and Gulf coasts, it is fairly common all winter; many individuals remain until late in the spring and some stay all summer on the coasts of the Gulf of Mexico. It has been said to breed on the coast of South Carolina and Florida in the past and Capt. W. M. Sprinkle told me that it had bred recently on some islands near the mouth of the Mississippi River; it is undoubtedly common on the coast at times in summer, but birds seen there at that season are probably nonbreeding birds which have lingered in their winter resorts.[1] In its winter home it is associated with the brown pelican, frequent-

---

[1] A breeding colony has recently been discovered near Corpus Christi, Texas.

ing salt water bayous, estuaries, and shallow bays, where it is very conspicuous at a long distance standing in the shoals or on the sand flats, looming up large and white among its smaller companions. It finds abundant food in the warm and shallow waters of the Gulf coast and secure roosting places on the sand bars and small islands, where it often congregates in large numbers, pursuing its own peculiar methods of fishing and indulging in its favorite pastime of aerial evolutions.

In closing I must quote Doctor Chapman's (1908) tribute to the antiquity of pelicans:

We must also accord to pelicans that respectful attention which is the due of extreme age. Pelicans became pelicans long before man became man, a study of the distribution of the eleven existing species leading to the conclusion that at least as late as the latter part of the Tertiary period our white pelican, and doubtless also other species, presented much the same appearance as it does to-day.

Of the eight Old World species, the one inhabiting southern Europe so closely resembles our American white pelican that early ornithologists regarded them as identical. Nevertheless, the localities at which their ranges are nearest are separated by some 8,000 miles. Such close resemblance, however, is neither an accident of birth or breeding. Pelicans did not appear independently in the two hemispheres. Birds so like each other and so unlike other existing birds must have a common ancestry. Common ancestry implies, at some time, continuity of range, and with the European and American white pelican we may well believe this to have occurred in that later portion of the Tertiary period, when a warm-temperate or even subtropical circumpolar climate existed. At this time, the pelican, from which we assume that the European and American white pelicans have both descended, inhabited the shores of the Arctic Ocean.

Eventually, by those climatic changes, resulting from a continuously decreasing amount of heat and culminating in the Ice Age, the individuals of this hypothetical polar pelican were forced southward, some in Europe, some in America, but whether at the same time or not is unknown.

Should some swing of the temperature pendulum ever reestablish the preglacial polar climate, the European and American pelicans, following in the wake of an advancing favorable isotherm, may meet again on the shores of the Polar Sea (whether as two species or one, who can say?) ; but in the meantime we look on them with special interest as but slightly differentiated from the bird which fished in the Arctic Ocean before, so far as we know, man appeared upon the scene.

DISTRIBUTION.

Breeding range.—Lake regions of the western interior. East and south to central Manitoba (Lake Winnipegosis), central North Dakota (Chase Lake), northwestern Wyoming (Yellowstone Lake), northern Utah (Great Salt Lake), western Nevada (Pyramid Lake), and southern California (Salton Sea). Formerly south to north central Wisconsin (Lincoln County, 1884), central western Minnesota (Grant County, 1878), South Dakota, and Colorado. West to the interior of California (Buena Vista, Tulare, Eagle, and Tule

Lakes) and southern Oregon (Klamath Lakes). North to central British Columbia (Chilcotin) and Great Slave Lake. An outlying breeding colony exists in Laguna de la Madre, south of Corpus Christi, Texas. Breeding grounds protected in the following reservations: In Oregon, Lake Malheur and Klamath Lake; in North Dakota, Chase Lake; and in Nevada, Anaho Island, Pyramid Lake.

Winter range.—North to southern California (Ventura and Riverside Counties), southwestern Arizona (Yuma), the coasts of Texas and Louisiana, and northern Florida (mouth of the St. John River). South through the Greater and Lesser Antilles (Cuba, Isle of Pines, Antigua, Trinidad, etc.) and along both coasts of Mexico, as well as in the interior, as far south as Panama.

Spring migration.—Northward through the interior, beginning in March. Early dates of arrival: Kansas, Cimmaron, March 9; Iowa, Mount Pleasant, March 18; Nebraska, April 8; South Dakota, Fort Sisseton, April 20; North Dakota, Huron, April 3; Saskatchewan, Indian Head, April 28; Manitoba, April 29 to May 4; Mackenzie, Pelican River, May 9. Late dates of departure: Louisiana, April 2; Missouri, May 9; Kansas, May 22; Minnesota, Heron Lake, May 12. West of the Rocky Mountains the migration route is comparatively short. Migrants pass through southern California in April and May; Fresno County, April 6; Los Angeles County, April 27 to May 25.

Fall migration.—Early dates of arrival: Iowa, Grinnell, September 13; Missouri, St. Louis, September 14; Arkansas, Helena, September 3; Texas, Galveston, September. Late dates of departure: Manitoba, Waterhen River, October 3; South Dakota, Fort Sisseton, October 30; Iowa, Sioux County, October 4; Kansas, Emporia, October 13; Missouri, St. Louis, October 7; Arkansas, Turrell, November 15. On the Pacific slope migrants reach the coast of Washington, Bellingham Bay, as early as September 5 and linger in southern California through November; Pasadena, November 25; Fresno County, December 5.

Casual records.—Has wandered on migrations to practically every Province in Canada and nearly every State in the United States. Eastern records include: New Brunswick (Cape Spencer, April, 1881), Maine (Saponica Lake, May 28, 1892, and Eliot, June 8, 1897) and Massachusetts (North Scituate, October 5, 1876, and Sandwich, May 13, 1905). Recorded once on the Arctic coast of Mackenzie (Liverpool Bay, summer, 1900).

Egg dates.—Utah and Nevada: Thirty-four records, May 1 to June 25; seventeen records May 16 to June 3. Manitoba and Saskatchewan: Nine records, June 4 to July 18; five records, June 4 to 19. Oregon: Three records, April 16 to July 8.

PELECANUS OCCIDENTALIS OCCIDENTALIS Linnaeus.

BROWN PELICAN.

HABITS.

My first morning in Florida dawned clear, calm, and hot, a typical April morning. The rich, varied whistle of the cardinal and the striking song of the Florida wren attracted me outdoors to explore my surroundings and make new acquaintances. An attractive path led through a dense hammock of large, grotesque live oaks, festooned with hanging mosses and a forest of heavily booted palmettos toward the shore. I had hoped to enjoy the cool of the early morning hours, but I had not then learned that the morning is the hottest part of the day on the east coast, before the cool sea breeze of midday brings relief. The heat was intense as I crossed a broad tract of saw palmettos back of the beach, and I was glad to seek shelter under an old bathhouse. The sea was smooth as glass and the horizon hardly visible, but the ocean swell rose and fell on the white sand in a long line of rolling breakers. Way off to the southward, in the shimmering heat which obstructed the shore line, I made out a long waving line of black specks, a flock of large birds coming toward me; they were flying close to the water and just off the beach over the breakers; with slowly measured wing beats they came on in regular formation. They were pelicans, of course, for at regular intervals they all set their wings and scaled along, barely skimming the tops of the waves or sailing along the valleys between them. With grotesque and quiet dignity they passed, and with the military precision of well-drilled soldiers they alternately scaled or flapped their wings in perfect unison, as if controlled by a common impulse. Before they had disappeared to the northward another flock was in sight, and so they came and passed on as long as I cared to watch them, with one or more flocks constantly in sight.

Nesting.—Whence they came and whither they were going we learned a few days afterwards when we visited their breeding grounds at Pelican Island, from which pelicans were constantly departing for their fishing grounds up and down the east coast and returning with food for their young. At the time of our visit, April 16, 1902, the breeding season was at its height and the colony was in flourishing condition. Pelican Island, long famous in the annals of American ornithology, is a small triangular island of less than 3 acres in extent, conveniently located in the quiet waters of Indian River, the long narrow lagoon which separates the east coast of Florida from the main land. Although not essentially different from the many other small islands in the same region, it has been occupied practically continuously since the earliest records we have as the only breeding resort of brown pelicans on the east coast of Florida. "In 1858" Doctor Bryant (1859) wrote:

The most extensive breeding place was in a small island called Pelican Island, about twenty miles north of Fort Capron. The nests here were placed on the tops of mangrove trees, which were about the size and shape of large apple trees. Breeding in company with the pelicans were thousands of herons, Peale egret, the rufous egret, and little white egret, with a few pairs of the great blue heron and roseate spoonbills; and immense numbers of man-o-war birds and white ibises were congregated upon the island.

At the time of our visit all but a few scattered dead or dying black mangrove trees and one cabbage palmetto had disappeared and even those have since succumbed. All of the birds but the pelicans have long since gone, leaving the silent, dignified and stupid birds in sole possession of what is now a Government reservation for their protection. I know of no more favorable place for the intimate study of the home life of an interesting species than Pelican Island, where continual protection has made it possible to watch and photograph the birds at short range, even without concealment. When we landed in our small sailboat the nearest pelicans of course took wing, but they circled about the island and soon came scaling back to settle again upon their nests or stand in solemn rows upon the shore. Many settled upon the water near us, floating buoyantly upon it in their characteristic attitude, with head and neck erect and with bill pointing downward against the breast. The same pose is assumed when standing or walking, but when fully settled upon the nest or when sleeping the head is drawn down between the shoulders and the bill points forward.

The breeding season at Pelican Island is very much prolonged, sometimes covering the greater part of the year. Ordinarily the birds arrive in November or December, but sometimes as early as October, congregating about the island in large flocks. Nest building soon begins, and by December egg laying is well under way. This continues all through the winter and spring uninterruptedly and often well into the summer. We found plenty of fresh eggs in April, as well as young of all ages up to fully grown birds on the wing, showing at a glance the whole life history of the young bird. Whether their prolongation of the breeding season is due to protection or to the fact that this is the only breeding resort to which the pelicans of so many miles of coast have access, I am unable to say; but probably both causes have had their effect and certainly the vast number of pelicans which rear their young on this island could not do so in a breeding season as short as prevails elsewhere. It has been suggested that the later layings are second broods of the same birds that had bred earlier, but I doubt if this has been satisfactorily proven, and there seems to be no evidence of second broods elsewhere.

On the west coast of Florida the normal breeding season begins in April and on the Louisiana coast in February, only one brood being raised in these localities, so far as I know. The pelicans of the Louisiana reservation are well protected, but they are not overcrowded and can all breed at one season. On the South Carolina coast their nesting season begins in May, fresh eggs having been taken by Mr. C. S. Day, of Boston, on May 8, 1904, and, according to Mr. Arthur T. Wayne, the breeding season is extended into August. Here the nests are placed on the ground on small islands barely above high-water mark, so that the eggs are frequently washed away by spring tides. That the brown pelicans of Pelican Island formerly built their nests in trees is shown by Doctor Bryant's (1859) report of the conditions prevailing in 1858, but with the disappearance of the trees the birds gradually adopted the habit of nesting on the ground, though on two occasions they resorted to nearby islands and built their nests in the mangroves. On the west coast of Florida there are still several large colonies of brown pelicans nesting in trees. In the reservations at the mouth of the Mississippi there are several immense and many smaller colonies of brown pelicans breeding on the mud lumps where there are no trees.

The ground nests vary greatly in size and structure from practically nothing to large well-built nests of sticks, reeds, straws, palmetto leaves and grasses, this material being selected from what is most readily available; the remains of old nests are frequently used and often fresh material is stolen from newly constructed nests provided the owner is not on hand to defend its property. The average nests on Pelican Island measured from 18 to 24 inches in diameter and were built up usually 4 or 5 inches but sometimes as high as 10 inches. Arboreal nests are more firmly constructed of similar materials on substantial platforms of sticks securely interwoven with the branches of the mangroves which are well adapted for supporting them, even with the additional weight of the fully grown young.

Courtship.—Mr. Stanley Clisby Arthur has sent me the following notes on the courtship of the brown pelican, which I have never seen:

The courtship of the pelican is quite what one would expect from a bird of its other undemonstrative habits. I witnessed it once on *Isle Grandgosier* and it marks the only time I have seen a pair of brown pelicans together when I could unhesitatingly identify the male from its mate. The female squatted close to the bare ground while the male slowly circled her with ponderius, elephantine tread. While he circumnavigated the course he lifted his wings slightly and tilted his neck far back, but there was none of the pronounced strutting usually indulged in by other birds, particularly those of the gallinaceous order. Both wore most lugubrious expressions during the whole of the courtship and the occasion was more befitting the solemnity of a funeral than the joyous display attending most nuptials. Neither uttered an audible sound while the male pursued his dignified circuitous meandering. Suddenly she rose from her squatting position with a *gruff-gruff* of wing-strokes and flew to the ocean, but a short distance from the shore, and after stolidly watching her going, he followed, still wearing his mask-like expression of weighty solemnity, to the consummation of the courtship on the surface of the quiet swelling waters of the gulf.

Eggs.—The brown pelican normally lays three eggs, though two eggs often constitute a full set; I have found four and on one occasion five eggs in a nest, though in the latter case the eggs were apparently laid by two different birds. The eggs are dull, lusterless, dirty white, usually more or less nest stained, and with a rough granular surface. The measurements of 46 eggs in the United States National Museum average 73 by 46.5 millimeters; the eggs showing the four extremes measure **83** by 49, 81.5 by **54, 68** by 47, and 70.5 by **45** millimeters.

Young.—The period of incubation is about four weeks. When first hatched the young are far from attractive, looking more like shapeless masses of half-dried meat than young birds, with swollen protuberances for heads which they are unable to hold up; the livid, dark reddish naked skin gradually turns to dull black; the eyes open during the first few days and by the end of a week the youngster is able to sit up and take notice. When about two weeks old the black goose-flesh produces little tufts of white down which rapidly covers the whole body. When about half grown the wing quills begin to sprout and are soon followed by the light brown first plumage of the back. The fully grown young are light brownish gray above, darker on the wings and white below. This first or juvenal plumage is probably worn for about a year. Subsequent molts and plumages are undoubtedly the same as in the California brown pelican, which I have been able to work out more satisfactorily and to which I refer the reader.

The feeding of young pelicans is a most remarkable performance and in a thickly populated colony where the struggle for existence is keen it is not lacking in excitement. The youngest birds are fed on regurgitated or semidigested food which is allowed to flow to the tip of the parent's bill, where it can be readily reached by the almost helpless little bird. As the young increase in size they are gradually weaned and soon learn to thrust their heads and necks, sometimes two at a time, deep down into the innermost recesses of the parental pouch, where with much struggling and squawking they find a hearty meal of fish in various stages of digestion. The old birds have evidently learned by experience just what kind of food is best suited to the age of the young, feeding larger fish as the young increase in size, but occasionally they make a mistake and give the little pelicans more than they can swallow, which means that the objectionable morsel must be removed by the parent or left to be gradually swallowed as the lower end is digested. The parents evidently know their own young and attempt to drive away others in the wild scramble which follows the arrival of a pelican with a well-filled pouch. Young pelicans reared in tree nests remain in the nests until nearly ready to fly, which simplifies the feeding problem for their parents, but where they nest on the ground the young leave the nests as soon as they are able to walk and wander about in great droves. This makes the work of the parents both difficult and strenuous and many an exciting struggle occurs in which the poor parent is besieged by a hoard of lusty young, fully her equal in size, and either overwhelmed by the excited mob or forced to retreat.

Dr. Frank M. Chapman (1908) describes in this connection an interesting performance which I have never witnessed, as follows:

The parent does not, of course, always have to fight its way through a mob to feed its offspring. Often only a bird or two is to be driven off and on such occasions the rightful young assist, the method of attack employed by both being thrusts of the bill from which no harm appears to follow. The actions of the rejected young bird are remarkable. With an only-son air he prances confidently up to the food-bearing adult and without so much as by your leave attempts to insert his bill. When, however, he receives a blow where he expected a fish, his demonstrations of disappointment are uncontrolled. He acts like a bird demented, swinging his head from side to side, biting one wing and whirling around to bite the other in the most ludicrous manner.

It is inexplicable that the same performance, in an exaggerated degree, is gone through with by the bird which has been permitted to feed, after it emerges from the parent's pouch. For a moment it seems dazed, perhaps because of lack of air as well as by the size of the meal it has secured. It lays its head on the ground as though it had received a violent blow, but soon this apparent semiconsciousness is followed by the most violent reaction as the bird arising to its feet grasps its wing, waves its head and behaves in the same crazy way as the bird which has been denied a meal. Possibly this surprising exercise may aid the bird in swallowing, when the same exhibition after the bird has attempted and failed to get a meal, should be considered the result of suggestion.

His account in the same chapter of the ceremony of nest relief, which I have never seen, is also worth quoting.

Brown pelicans do not differ in color sexually. It is impossible, therefore, to determine by external appearance the sex of the sitting bird. Observation from a blind, however, reveals the fact that both sexes incubate, the change of places being usually preceded by an interesting little performance which I have called the Ceremony of Nest Relief. As a rule the bird on the nest is not attended by its mate, who may be feeding, bathing, resting on the shore, or sailing high in the air. The returning bird alights near the nest and, with bill pointed to the zenith, advances slowly, waving its head from side to side. At the same time the sitting bird sticks its bill vertically into the nest, twitches its half-spread wings, and utters a low, husky, gasping chuck, the only note I have ever heard issue from the throat of an adult wild brown pelican. After five or six wand-like passes of its upraised head, the advancing bird pauses, when both birds, with apparent unconcern, begin to preen their feathers, and a moment later the bird that has been on duty steps off the nest, and the new comer at once takes its place. This was the "ceremony" in its full development; often it was not so complete. Doubtless it possesses some sexual significance, and observation points to the conclusion that the relieving bird is the male and that the ceremony is omitted when he gives place to his mate.

Food.—The food of the brown pelican consists entirely of fish, chiefly menhaden, mullets, and other fish unfit for human food. Complaints that it is very destructive to food fish, and therefore unworthy of protection, have been proven as not well founded by an exhaustive investigation conducted by the Department of Conservation in Louisiana, in cooperation with the Biological Survey.

Its methods of fishing is more effective than it is graceful; it appears to be quite awkward and clumsy, even ludicrous, but it is nearly always successful in accomplishing the desired result. It flies along over the water at heights varying from 10 feet to 50 feet above it. Mr. John T. Nichols (1918) has published the following interesting observations, made by Dr. Russell J. Coles:

When these birds are feeding, the distance of their flight above the surface of the water is carefully regulated by the depth at which the fish are swimming and one, who has not especially studied this point by many careful observations, does not realize how accurately this is gauged. I have often seen a brown pelican suddenly dart forward and upward ten to fifteen feet higher and circle back over his prey before making his plunge, indicating that the fish was swimming at a greater depth than expected.

The plunge is interesting in that it is always headed down wind. As it thrusts its neck down, its wing are three-quarters closed and extended backward as far as possible, thus throwing the center of gravity in front of any wing support, and the following wind instantly catches in the partly closed wing tips and completes the inversion, then by deft manipulation of its almost closed wings, it maintains its perpendicular position as it volplanes downward.

It is necessary for such a heavy bird to rise against the wind, therefore, it is only a case of instinctive preparedness that the brown pelican always rises to the surface headed up-wind, in order to be ready for instant flight.

Thus, by entering the water down wind and emerging from it up wind, the pelican makes a complete turnover or turnabout under water; many writers have referred to this, and almost every observer has noticed it. The buoyancy of the bird's body brings it quickly to the surface, where it shakes the water from its plumage, points its bill first downward to drain out the water, and then upward to swallow the fish. It is then ready to rise against the wind and look for more fish. As it emerges from the water with a well-filled pouch it is often preyed upon by its companions, the laughing gulls and mano'-war-birds. The former have even been seen to alight upon the pelican's head and steal the fish protruding from its bill.

Behavior.—Adult brown pelicans are practically voiceless, but the young are exceedingly noisy at all ages. They begin to make themselves heard during the hatching process with a grunting sound, as the young bird emerges from the shell; this develops into a barking note and finally into a shrill, piercing scream as the young birds struggle for their food, making feeding times on Pelican Island both boisterous and noisy.

The flight of brown pelicans when well under way is strong, graceful, and well sustained on their long and powerful wings, but when starting from either land or water the first few efforts to overcome the inertia of their heavy bodies seem awkward and labored. They fly long distances to their feeding grounds, relieving their slow sweeping wing strokes with frequent periods of soaring or scaling. At times they may be seen sailing about high in the air, apparently for sport or exercise, but they are by no means equal to the white pelicans in this respect.

Fall.—Brown pelicans are not strictly migratory, as they are generally resident in the near vicinity of their breeding grounds, but after the cares of the nesting season are over they become more or less nomadic and some few of them, generally young birds, often wander long distances.

Winter.—But the greater number spend the remainder of the summer, fall, and winter traveling about in large flocks, young and old usually in flocks by themselves along the coasts of Florida and the Gulf States, resorting to the inland lakes to fish and resting in long lines on the sand bars, mud flats, or beaches of the outer islands. They are particularly abundant among the shallow bays of southern Florida, among the Florida Keys, and in the great bird reservations of the Louisiana coast, where food fish are abundant and where they spend their leisure season in the congenial, if not always friendly, companionship of the royal terns, laughing gulls, man-o-war-birds, and Florida cormorants.

DISTRIBUTION.

Breeding range.—Mainly on south Atlantic and Gulf coasts of the United States, from South Carolina (Bull's Bay) to southern Texas (Padre Island). Probably breeds among the Greater Antilles (Cuba, Jamaica, and Porto Rico). Said to breed in the Bahamas and on the coasts of Central and South America, as far south as Brazil. Breeding grounds protected in the following reservations: In Florida, Pelican Island; and in Louisiana, Breton Island, and East Timbalier.

Winter range.—From the Bahamas, Florida, and the Gulf coast of the United States southward, including all the West Indies and the eastern coasts of Central and South America, as far south as Brazil.

Casual records.—Accidental in Bermuda (April, 1850). Has wandered as far east as Nova Scotia (Pictou, three records, and Cape Breton, Louisbourg, May 19, 1904), as far west as Michigan (St. Joseph, June 7, 1904), Wyoming (Cheyenne, July 12, 1899), and Colorado (Thomasville, June, 1908).

Egg dates.—Florida: Thirty-four records, February 1 to June 30, seventeen records, April 16 to May 15. Texas: Fifteen records, April 4 to May 28; eight records April 16 to May 28. South Carolina: Nine records, May 8 to June 23.

PELECANUS OCCIDENTALIS CALIFORNICUS Ridgway.

CALIFORNIA BROWN PELICAN.

HABITS.

Although long regarded as a distinct species, perhaps at no very distant epoch in the history of evolution, this large Pacific coast species was connected by intergrading forms with the common brown pelican of our tropical and subtropical coasts, for it is not difficult to imagine the former existence of a continuity of range across the isthmus of Panama. The California brown pelican differs from its eastern relative chiefly in its much larger size, the darker color of its hind neck, which is nearly black, and the color of its pouch, which is largely reddish at certain seasons.

On the coast of southern California and Lower California pelicans are almost as common and conspicuous as they are on the coasts of Florida, grotesque and striking features in the landscape. The habits of the two species are so much alike and their life histories are so nearly identical that it would involve much useless repetition to do more than to describe the nesting habits of this species and add a few points of interest.

Nesting.—The California brown pelican breeds from the Santa Barbara Islands southward. On these islands and on Los Coronados Islands it seems to prefer to nest on steep rocky slopes, building a bulky nest of sticks, grasses, and rubbish; such sites seem strange when compared with the low flat islands in which we are accustomed to find the eastern bird breeding; the California birds also seem to be much shyer than our birds and to nest in smaller or more scattered colonies.

Mr. A. W. Anthony (1889), writes:

The largest colony that I have found thus far was discovered on San Martin Island April 12, 1888. The island of San Martin lies about 5 miles offshore and nearly due west from San Quentin, Lower California, in about Lat. 30° 33' N. With the exception of a few acres of sand on the east and northeastern sides, it is composed entirely of lava, which has escaped from an extinct volcano on the southern end of the island; the greatest elevation is found at this point, which is perhaps 450 feet above the sea. The entire island comprises about 1,200 acres. Three days were spent here in investigating the bird life, most of which time was expended in making life a burden to a colony of about 500 pelicans, which were found nesting on the north end of the island. The nests were located in groups of 20 or 30 about a quarter of a mile from the beach and about 250 feet above the sea. They were largely composed of the accumulated filth of several generations of pelicans, and many of the older ones had obtained a height of 3 feet, evidently having been added to from year to year. Most of the nests were built on the tops of low bushes, but many were resting on the bare ground or placed upon blocks of lava. Sticks, twigs, kelp, sea grass, and in a few cases bones of defunct sea birds, were used as building material, and a little sea grass spread over the top as a lining, no attempt being made to form anything more than a mere platform 18 inches or 2 feet in diameter, and in nests of a single year's growth 4 or 5 inches in depth. At this date, April 12th, most of the nests contained young ranging from those just hatched to the full-fledged birds capable of flying. The birds at this colony did not appear to be very wild, only flying up when we had approached to within 50 or 60 yards and settling down again as soon as we had passed by. Hundreds of pounds of small fish were scattered all about the colony, in little bunches or singly, having been disgorged entirely undigested. I could not see that the young were making any use of these provisions, nor did any of the birds of the island except the gulls. They were probably designed, however, for the nearly fledged young that were still unable to fish for themselves.

To illustrate variations in the choice of nesting sites and irregularities in breeding dates, the following observations of Mr. Edward W. Gifford (1913) in the Galapagos Islands are interesting:

I saw a pair copulating on their nest at Tagus Cove, Albemarle Island, on April 1. They had no eggs in the nest. All of the other nests of the colony of ten or twelve had single birds on them. Some had eggs, others none. The nests were bulky affairs of sticks built in bushes on a steep hillside close to the water. The area occupied was about one hundred yards by twenty-five yards. The birds were somewhat wary, some flying upon the near approach of the boat.

At South Seymour Island, on November 22, three nests were seen in a low tree near the shore. Two had one youngster each, and the third two. On northern Indefatigable, November 25, nests with young were observed in the mangroves and also on the ground. On Jervis Island, December 18, a young bird in the down was found in a nest in a low bush at the top of the beach. At Academy Bay, Indefatigable Island, in early November, young were observed in nests built at least twenty feet above the ground in the mangroves. In the middle of the following January the same birds were observed fishing, apparently under the supervision of their parents, whose example they followed in diving into the water.

On March 12, a few miles west of Villamil, Albemarle Island, four occupied nests were found in the low mangroves fringing the rocky shore. They were built in the usual bulky style, and the two which were examined each contained three incubated eggs. At Banks Bay, Albemarle, April 11, three nests were found in some small mangroves about eight feet high. They were shallow, built of sticks, lined with grass, and placed very little above the high-water mark. One had naked youngsters in it; the second contained three eggs; and the third was new.

In the middle of July, at Academy Bay, the same nests which had young in them the previous November, again contained partly fledged, squawking youngsters, eight months only having elapsed since the previous brood. They were fed by running their bills well into the parent's pouch and gulping in the food.

Eggs.—The eggs are like those of the brown pelican, but decidedly larger. The measurements of 48 eggs, in various collections, average 78.5 by 50.6 millimeters; the eggs showing the four extremes measure **85** by 51.2, 78 by **54, 69** by 49, and 75 by **47** millimeters.

Young.—Mr. A. B. Howell has sent me the following notes on the behavior of the young:

They are noisy little fellows, clucking to themselves continuously, and with a flirt of the wings at each cluck. In spite of their tender age they are very pugnacious, and they need to be, even though it does not do them much good when the western gulls take a notion to peck out their brains. When two-thirds grown they remind one of partly plucked geese, especially as they are given to flocking before an intruder. They are only too ready with a vicious lunge of the bill and they disgorge at a suspicion of danger; which act the gulls accept as the act of a kind Providence. They are always willing to step off a ledge into a patch of cactus, where they flounder around in a most helpless way. If one is induced to take his maiden flight under slight excitement, he will launch out on slow unsteady wings with feet fully extended, teeter a moment and return, but he is unable to check his speed and brings up against the cliff with a shock that kills him instantly, much to the amusement of the audience of gulls, who troop down to investigate.

Plumages.—The sequence of plumages to maturity is apparently the same as in the eastern brown pelican. The juvenal, or first year, plumage is characterized by the dull, light-brown upper parts and the white under parts. It is worn for about a year, or until the first postnuptial molt, when the young bird is about 14 or 15 months old. A complete molt, prolonged through the summer and fall of that year, produces the second winter plumage. In this plumage the silver-gray feathers are, at least partially, acquired on the back, wings, and scapulars, but not in the perfection of the adult; the head and neck are similar to those of the adult, but are more or less mottled with dusky; the under parts are of a somewhat lighter shade of the same brown as in the adult, more or less mottled with white on the belly, and the brown feathers have each a central streak of white. A partial molt during the winter and spring produces the second nuptial plumage, in which the birds begin to breed. At this season the under parts become browner, but still with white median streaks, the head becomes whiter, and some dark brown appears in the hind neck. At the next complete molt, the second postnuptial, the adult winter plumage is assumed, when the young bird is 26 or 27 months old.

Adults have a partial molt in the late winter and early spring, involving mainly the head and neck, which produces the well-known nuptial plumage, and a complete postnuptial molt in the summer and fall, which produces the winter plumage, in which the hind neck becomes white instead of dark brown.   Probably the fullest development of plumage, with such nuptial adornments as the yellow crown and golden breast patch, is not acquired until the bird is three years old or older.

Food.—The food consists largely of fish, but not wholly so, as the following quotation from Mr. Gifford's (1913) notes will show:

In the Galapagos Islands brown pelicans serve as scavengers. On several occasions they were observed to pick up the bodies of large birds, after we had skinned them and thrown them overboard. In one case an immature pelican had got the bodies of two Galapagos hawks into its pouch, and was unable to swallow them. Likewise it was unable to fly on account of the weight. It was probably grateful when we rowed up to it, where it was sitting on the water, and removed the impedimenta, for it flew away joyfully enough afterwards.

We never saw a pelican make a graceful dive. Invariably they just tumbled into the water from a few feet above it. They often fished along the line of small breakers close to the shore, and after making such a dive, frequently had to get up hurriedly to avoid being overwhelmed by a wave.

Mr. H. R. Taylor (1893) describes the pelicans' fishing methods, as follows:

These curious " troopers of the raging main " are great fishers. A thoughtful looking pelican comes flapping along, perhaps about fifteen feet above the water, and when there is a good fish near the surface you see him pause uncertainly in the air and point his long, spear-like bill down to the almost perpendicular, and in a second his wings slant back, and down he goes with a rush, sending the spray in every direction and stunning his finny quarry before it has time to wink. The great splash hides the fisher entirely from view, and as he reappears he is observed gulping the big mouthful into his convenient pouch. All this occupies but a brief space of time, and with a lumberly struggle of wings, touching the waves with his feet for a short distance, he is off, carrying an important air, as though he had remarkably pressing business in hand. Occassionally the pelican rests on the water awhile after the capture, looking very sedate and pensive, with his great bill dropped down closely to his breast. Sometimes the fish is found to be so large that the bird is compelled to go through a ludicrous struggle before he can dispose of it, and trying to rise from the water he seems to exert himself painfully.

Behavior.—Referring to the daily flights of this species to and from its feeding grounds, Mr. Anthony (1889) writes:

Flocks of from five or six to twenty were constantly arriving from far out at sea, flying in one long line, each following directly in the track of the one next in front, and but just keeping above the water until within a few hundred yards of the island, when they rose gradually to the elevation of their nests. Toward night the flocks grew larger, as the birds that had been over to San Quentin Bay for the day's fishing began to arrive. These birds after fishing until sunset along the southern shore of the bay, gather in large flocks, and most of them fly directly up the bay, or almost at right angles with the course taken by those birds that fly directly toward the island. For some time I was at a loss to know where these flocks were going, as I knew that there was no resting place in that direction; but I found that after reaching the head of the bay, ten miles from the feeding grounds, they turned through a pass between the hills, and after flying five miles over land, reached the ocean at a point opposite the island, having flown eighteen or twenty miles to reach a point ten miles distant, rather than fly two miles over a range of hills one hundred feet high. Above ten per cent of the birds, however, were wise enough to take the shorter route.

Mr. A. B. Howell (1912) noted a very interesting flight performance of the California brown pelican, which he describes as follows:

At 4 o'clock I noted a very large flock of pelicans feeding, and shortly afterwards the school of fish which they were pursuing left. Some of the birds settled down upon the water while others began circling in the air on motionless wings. A moderate breeze was blowing. Singly the ones in the water took wing and joined the circling throng until there must have been a hundred and fifty birds in the air, forming an irregular but clearly defined column or rather cylinder, some hundred yards in diameter. Gradually some birds mounted higher until they were specks in the sky, while others were but fifty yards above the water. More than an hour elapsed between the start and finish of this flight. The flock remained over almost the same spot, and at no time did a bird show indications of diving or looking for fish. Their soaring was very even, and I noticed no flapping at all after a bird was fairly launched. Slowly, as darkness approached, the pelicans left toward the north, singly or in twos and threes.

Pelicans are not always allowed to fish for themselves in peace, as several observers have noted. Mr. William L. Finley (1907) says:

One day while standing on the wharf at Santa Monica I saw a brown pelican flapping along with a pair of gulls a few feet behind. A moment later the big bird spied a fish, for with a back stroke of his wing he turned to dive. He gathered speed as he went and with wings partly closed and rigid, he hit the water with a resounding splash. The lower mandible of his bill contracted and opened his pouch that held about as much water as the weight of his body. He came to the surface and was in a helpless condition till the water ran out, and at this moment he was pounced upon by the swift-moving gulls, who snatched the fish and were away before the slow pelican could retaliate.

At another time I saw a band of a dozen pelicans hovering over a school of fish. The birds rose from the surface, swung around till about twenty feet above, and two or three of them dropped into the water at a time. A bevy of twenty gulls were fluttering around to pounce on every pelican that dove. The instant one dropped and came up with fish he was surrounded by a bunch of gulls, each scrambling to get a nose in the pelican's big fish bag.

Mr. Gifford (1913) writes:

Brown pelicans bathe after the manner of most water birds, by beating the water with their wings. They were occasionally " decoyed " to wounded birds. One day two or three of this species and several man-o'-war birds flocked about when a blue-footed booby was shot. As a rule the pelicans did not associate with other species. Once or twice, however, they were observed fishing along with blue-footed boobies, and at times roosting with them.

It was not unusual to see several noddies fluttering excitedly about a pelican when it was fishing, and often sitting on its head while it swallowed the fish. Once I saw two on a pelican's head at one time. The pelicans never seemed to be annoyed, nor did the noddies ever get any fish so far as I could see. Dusky shearwaters would occasionally fly about a pelican, apparently to pester it, for one day I observed a pelican take refuge on the top of a cliff from a number of them.

The California brown pelican is practically nonmigratory, like its eastern relative, but it is much given to wandering both north and south of its breeding range between nesting seasons.

DISTRIBUTION.

Breeding range.—Islands off the Pacific coast from the Santa Barbara Islands (San Miguel, Anacapa, Santa Cruz, etc.) southward along the Mexican coast to the Tres Marias and Galapagos Islands.

Winter range.—Between breeding seasons it extends its range northward along the coast to southern British Columbia (Burrard Inlet) and in the interior to central British Columbia (Chilcotin District) and southward along the Pacific coast of South America to Chile (Atacama and Valdivia).

Migration.—Irregular and prolonged. Main northward movement seems to come in July.

Casual records.—Rarely wanders inland in California; Stanislaus County, September 19, 1913.

Egg dates.—Los Coronados Islands: Thirty-three records, March 29 to June 22; seventeen records, April 4 to May 6.

Family FREGATIDAE, Man-o'-war-birds.

FREGATA MAGNIFICENS ROTHSCHILDI Mathews.

MAN-O'-WAR-BIRD.

HABITS.

This well-known buccaneer is widely distributed over the warmer waters and tropical coasts of both hemispheres, where several species and subspecies have been recognized by recent investigators, all of which are closely related. Its popular names, man-o'-war-bird, frigate bird, or frigate pelican, reflect its well-known character as a pirate and a tyrannical freebooter. But, with all its faults, it is a picturesque character and one can not help admiring its wonderful aerial evolutions, for which it is so highly specialized, and which make it such a noticeable and an interesting feature in the bird life of tropical seas.

Courtship.—One of the most curious traits of this species is the inflation of the great red pouch of the male, which plays such a conspicuous part in his courtship. Dr. Walter K. Fisher (1906) gives a very good account of it as follows:

The man-o'-war-bird proved scarcely less entertaining than the albatrosses. The curious and excessively bizarre appearance of the male at this season of the year compels attention. His antics are as extraordinary as his looks, and when engrossed in the task of making himself attractive his self-absorption and apparent vanity are highly diverting. During the courting period the gular pouch of the male is enlarged, and before the brooding cares have begun he inflates it to a large size, and at the same time it becomes a bright red color. The bird looks as if there were a balloon, such as children dangle on a string, fastened to its throat.

The pouch is apparently a large air-sac, connected only indirectly with the lungs, which can not be emptied readily nor inflated instantly. It varies in the intensity of its carmine or crimson, and catching on its surface the sheen of the sky, shows at times bluish hues, or, becoming somewhat collapsed, turns a translucent orange about the sides. It is no uncommon occurrence to see a male bird sitting on the nest with the sac blown out, obscuring the whole front of the creature, only the bill and eyes appearing over the top. For hours he sits on a newly-made nest without once leaving, or scarcely altering this position. But if the female appears somewhere overhead, sailing to and fro, he suddenly arouses himself from the lethargy, and as she passes he rises partially from a sitting posture, throws back his head, spreads his wings, and protruding the brilliant pouch, shakes his head from side to side, uttering a hoarse cackle. Occasionally, when the female alights near, he waves his pouch from side to side, the head being thrown well back and the wings partially spread. At the same time the long, greenish, iridescent, scapular feathers are fluffed up and the creature presents a most unusual and absurd appearance. In this posture he chuckles again and again, and rubs his breast against his mate, who usually ignores him completely and flies away. These performances take place before the egg is laid; afterwards the male ceases to inflate his sac.

Nesting.—Prof. Homer R. Dill (1912) estimated that the number of man-o'-war-birds nesting on Laysan Island was about 12,500, and says: "They nest in colonies in the tops of low bushes which, if placed near together, would cover about 6 acres. As it is, however, they appear to cover many times that amount of space." This seems like a large colony, but it looks very small beside the immense colonies of other sea birds on this wonderful island.

Of their nesting habits on this island Doctor Fisher (1906) says:

At Laysan the birds live in colonies varying from a few pairs to many, and the nests are always built on the tops of low bushes, sometimes very close together. The species has congregated almost entirely on the eastern half of the island, and their villages are spread over the inner slope of the old atoll basin. The nests, which are sometimes so old that they have become mere masses of filth, are scarcely more than platforms of sticks, not entirely devoid of leaves, woven together loosely with morning-glory (*Ipomaea insularis*) vines.

Both parents take turns in covering the egg, which is a necessity, for if the nest were left without an occupant other frigate birds would quickly appropriate its material, especially if the nest were new. Consequently, even before the egg is laid, either bird holds down the property, as it were, against marauding neighbors. After the nestling is out this vigilance is all the more necessary, for if left unprotected a young bird would very likely serve as food for some watchful reprobate of the vicinity. Mr. Snyder saw an old frigate bird snatch up and fly away with a young of the same species, whose parent had

been frightened off the nest. According to Henry Palmer, who visited the
island a few weeks later in 1891, this is a very common occurrence, but the
young were so scarce we considered the accidental demonstration mentioned
above as sufficient evidence of the heartless trait.

On the west coast of Mexico, Mr. H. H. Bailey (1906) found them
nesting on Isabella Island, of which he writes:

The nests on the island were placed on the top of the bushes or on crotches of
limbs, the nests being a loosely made platform of sticks and twigs, with generally a few straws or grasses on the inner surface. In some cases the nests
were not more than from eighteen inches to two feet above the ground, as on
the west side of the island where the bushes are low and stunted, while on the
south and eastern sides they were sometimes placed as high as twelve and
fifteen feet above ground, the bushes and scrubby trees here permitting of it.
At the time of my visit the majority of these birds had eggs, one being a complete set. A few young birds were, however, found on the western side of the
island, and it did not take the hot sun long to kill any small young that the
parents left unsheltered for even a few moments. The majority of these birds
were very tame, allowing one to approach within a few feet of them.

Great numbers of dead birds, hanging from the bushes by wings, feet, or
heads, were scattered over the island, the cause of which I discovered when
flushing one from its nest. Their short legs and extremely long wings make
it a hard matter for the birds to rise from their nests, especially so when the
nest is placed on the top of the bushes, and their wings come in contact with
other branches in their effort to rise. A number of times as I watched them
in their attempts to alight on or depart from their nest I saw them become
entangled in the foliage, from which position they were unable to rise. The
odor from the dead birds, with that given out by the birds themselves, was far
from agreeable.

On the Galapagos Islands the man-o'-war birds nest in colonies
on the ground or on the rocks, as well as on low bushes. But on the
islands off the coast of British Honduras, Capt. D. P. Ingraham
writes, in his notes sent to Major Bendire, that he found them nesting in the high mangrove trees, 60 or 70 feet from the ground, several
nests in a tree.

Referring to some of the breeding colonies in the Bahamas, Dr.
Henry Bryant (1861) writes:

I found a few man-of-war birds breeding at the Biminis. Their nests were
placed upon the mangroves, amidst those of the brown pelican and Florida
cormorant. As these birds are much disturbed by the inhabitants, their breeding places will probably be given up in a few years. On the central and highest
part of Booby Key a colony of about 200 pairs was breeding. The nests here
were on the bare rock and closely grouped together, the whole not occupying
a space more than 40 feet square. There were no boobies amongst them,
though thousands were breeding on the key. The largest breeding place visited
by me is situated on Seal Island, one of the Ragged Island keys, and is 5 or 6
acres in extent. The nests, thickly crowded together, were placed on the tops
of prickly pear, which covered the ground with an almost impenetrable thicket.
On the 8th of April the young were hatched in half of the nests, the largest
about one-third grown; the other nests contained eggs more or less hatched.
Out of many hundreds, I procured only 7 that were freshly laid.

I have visited the breeding places of many sea birds before, and some well worth the trouble, but none so interesting to me as this. It was a most singular spectacle. Thousands and thousands of these great and ordinarily wild birds covered the whole surface of the prickly pears as they sat on their nests or darkened the air as they hovered over them, so tame that they would hardly move on being touched; indeed, the specimens that I procured were all taken alive with my own hands. When I had penetrated as far among them as possible, I fired my gun; the whole colony rose at once, and the noise made by their long and powerful wings striking against each other was almost deafening. In a moment they commenced settling upon their nests and were soon as quiet as before.

From Dr. Frank M. Chapman's (1908a) contribution to the life history of this species, in the Bahamas, I quote as follows:

The luxuriant growth of cactus among the sea grapes in which the man-o'-war birds nested added to the difficulty with which these thickly branched, shrubby trees were penetrated, and we did not attempt to make a census of the number of birds of this species which were breeding on Cay Verde. We estimated, however, that there were between 200 and 300 pairs.

The man-o'-war birds awoke at about the same time as the boobies and at 5.30 a. m. were sailing over their rookery. From this time until they retired, considerably before the boobies, and while it was yet light, a flock of birds was constantly over the sea grapes. The birds may be said to have perched in the air above their homes. Only one bird is in attendance on the young at the same time. Both sexes assumed this duty, as well as the task of incubation; but there appeared to be no regularity as to when male or female should be on guard.

The nests are frail, open-worked, slightly hollowed platforms, composed of small sticks and twigs placed in the tops of the sea grapes, at a height of 6 or 7 feet, or among the cactuses within 2 feet of the ground. Several nests are often placed in one bush within reaching distance of one another. They become matted with filth as the young increase in size. One adult was seen carrying nest-building material in its bill.

Eggs.—The man-o'-war bird lays but one egg, which is approximately "elliptical ovate" in shape and pure dead white in color. The shell is very thin for an egg of its size, smooth and lusterless. The measurements of 50 eggs, in several collections, average 68.4 by 46.5 millimeters; the eggs showing the four extremes measures **74** by 48.5, 72.5 by **50, 64.5** by 46, and 66.5 by **43.5** millimeters.

Young.—Doctor Chapman (1908a) says of the development of the young:

The man-o'-war bird lays but one egg, and in a number of nests fresh eggs were found. The young are born naked and are brooded by the parents. As they increase in size and become covered with white down, their wings seem to be much too large for them to hold close to the body, and relaxing are permitted to rest on the nest. Their whole attitude suggests extreme dejection; not only do the wings droop, but the head often hangs over the edge of the nest. When approached they utter a squealing, chippering call, and snap their bills with a rattling sound, both the note and action strongly suggesting similar habits of the young brown pelican.

The black feathers of the interscapular region appear immediately after the down on this portion has pushed through the skin, and "before there is any evidence of the remiges and rectrices they cover the back like a mantle * * *. Not only are the wing feathers late in appearing, but the secondaries precede the primaries, the former averaging 2 inches in length, with the greater and median coverts showing, when the latter are just observable." This seems remarkable and contrary to the rule with birds of great wing and tail development.

Plumages.—The sequence of molts and plumages in this species are puzzling and their study is complicated by the prolonged and variable breeding season, which makes it difficult to estimate the age even approximately. In the juvenal or first-year plumage, the head, neck and under parts are white, in both sexes, with dusky flanks and sometimes more or less brownish mottling on the head and neck; the lesser wing coverts are brownish and the upper parts are dull, dark brown, without any luster; the tail is comparatively short and the lateral rectrices are not much longer than the others. I have seen birds in this plumage in January, May, July, and October, from which I infer that it is worn for one year, but the date of the molt into the next plumage is very variable, depending, I suppose, on the date at which the young bird was hatched. An interesting phase of this first year plumage of the male which I have seen in nearly every Pacific specimen that I have examined and have *never* found in *any* Atlantic specimen, is the rich " cinnamon " suffusion which partially or largely covers the breast, neck, and head. Mr. Edward W. Gifford (1913) says of the birds collected for the California Academy of Sciences, in the Galapagos Islands: " Birds in juvenal plumage, have the entire head and neck a rich cinnamon-rufous. No exception to this is found in the academy series." I have also seen cinnamon-headed birds from Lower California, Necker Island, Madagascar, Laysan Island, and the Phillipines. That this character should hold constant in the large series of birds that I have examined from both oceans is confirming evidence that they are distinct species. This plumage is also probably worn throughout the first year, as I have seen it in January, March, May, September, and October birds.

After the first year the sexes become dissimilar in plumage. The male becomes much darker on the upper parts, almost black, but still lacks the glossy tints of the adult; the lateral rectrices become more elongated; and the head, neck, and under parts become mottled with dusky and white. The female acquires more dusky on the head and neck, as well as on the belly, but the breast and sides still remain white. During the third year, probably at the second postnuptial molt, when the birds are a little over two years old, the adult plumages of the male and female are assumed. The plumage of the male is then entirely black, with its beautiful metallic luster and lanceolate feathers on the upper parts; and the flight feathers have reached their fullest development; the bright red gular sac of the male is an adornment of the nuptial season only. The female in full plumage has the head and neck clear blackish brown and the breast and sides pure white; she is less glossy above than the male, there is more or less brownish in the wing-coverts, and the feathers of the upper parts are less lanceolate.

Food.—The food of the man-o'-war bird consists largely of fish, but it includes much of the varied bills of fare indulged in by the various species of boobies, pelicans, cormorants, gulls, and terns on which it makes its piratical raids. It is not wholly predatory in its feeding habits and obtains much of its food by its own efforts from the surface of the sea at which it is very skillful. Doctor Fisher (1904*b*) says:

Frigate birds glean a portion of their livelihood from the host of creatures which live at the surface of the ocean—flying fishes, ctenophores, jelly fishes, vellela, janthina, and in fact anything that may attract their fancy. I even observed one bird aimlessly carrying a splinter of wood, uncertain of its utility, yet unwilling to release it. As they never alight on the water they seize such bits of food by swooping down in a broad curve. They are able to measure distance so accurately that no disturbance is created when the object is grasped.

Prof. William A. Bryan (1903) has given us an excellent account of the frigate bird's attacks on the boobies of Marcus Island, as follows:

I have before referred to the large colonies of common brown boobies about the north point of the island. It was in the vicinity of this colony that the man-o'-war birds were most abundant. Here they would lie in ambush for the old boobies and tropic birds as they returned from the sea heavily laden with fresh food for their young. Sitting quietly on the tree tops, or more often wheeling high overhead industriously patrolling the island, out where the surf broke on the reef, these birds would keep a sharp lookout to sea for a sight of the returning fishing fleet of boobies. Sighting one (sometimes consisting of one, sometimes of several individuals), as many as half a dozen hawks would make for them under full sail, and without a moment's warning would engage a helpless bird in battle. Swooping down upon it from every side, buffeting it with their wings, snapping at it with their long hooked bills, flying now above, now before, now below it, the hawks would so confuse their victims that eventually, feeling that the only safety for its life lay in letting go part of its store of supplies as a sop for its assailants to quarrel over, the booby would on a sudden drop one of its fish, whereat a hawk would swoop down, more rapidly than the eye could follow, and catch the food before it had touched the wave, then taking it securely in its bill would fly majestically off to feed its own ever-expectant offspring. The unfortunate booby meanwhile was farther pursued by the less fortunate hawks until, reft of her quarry, she was allowed to return to her young.

Audubon (1840) gives the following graphic account of its fishing prowess:

Yonder, over the waves, leaps the brilliant dolphin, as he pursues the flying-fishes, which he expects to seize the moment they drop into the water. The frigate-bird, who has marked them, closes his wings, dives toward them, and now ascending, holds one of the tiny things across his bill. Already fifty yards above the sea, he spies a porpoise in full chase, launches toward the spot, and in passing seizes the mullet that had escaped from its dreaded foe; but now, having obtained a fish too large for his gullet, he rises, munching it all the while, as if bound for the skies. Three or four of his own tribe have watched him and observed his success. They shoot toward him on broadly extended pinions, rise in wide circles, smoothly, yet as swiftly as himself. They are now all at the same height, and each as it overtakes him, lashes him with its wings, and tugs at his prey. See! one has fairly robbed him, but before he can secure the contested fish it drops. One of the other birds has caught it, but he is pursued by all. From bill to bill, and through the air, rapidly falls the fish, until it drops quite dead on the waters, and sinks into the deep. Whatever disappointment the hungry birds feel, they seem to deserve it all.

Behavior.—The flight of the man-o'-war-bird is an inspiration; the admiring observer is spellbound with wonder as he beholds it and longs for the eloquence to describe it; but words are powerless to convey the impression that it creates. It is the most marvelous and most perfect flying machine that has ever been produced, with 7 or 8 feet of alar expanse, supporting a 4-pound body, steered by a long scissor-like tail. It is not to be wondered at that such an aeroplane can float indefinitely in the lightest breeze. I shall never forget an exhibition I once saw among the Florida keys. We had anchored for the night near a small mangrove key, a famous roosting place for this species, and saw that it was black with hundreds of the birds sitting on the low trees. As we rowed toward it they all arose into the air and hung over it in a dense cloud, as thick as a swarm of insects. Gradually they spread out, floating without the slightest effort on motionless wings, separating into three great flocks and then into five flocks. By counting and carefully estimating the flocks, we concluded that there were between 1,000 and 1,200 birds in all. For over an hour we watched them as they floated out over us in a leisurely, dignified manner and slowly drifted away. At times they seemed to be almost stationary and never once did we detect a flap of the long, half-flexed wings, though it was almost calm. Like painted birds upon a painted sky they faded into the shadows of the night.

The active flight of the frigate-bird and its control of its powers is fully as wonderful as its passive sailings. While floating high in the air, almost out of sight, its keen eye detects some morsel of food in the water below it; with wings half closed it shoots downward like a meteor, and so accurately does it gauge its speed and distance that, just as it seems as if it must plunge like a falling arrow into the water, it checks its momentum with a marvelous twist of its great wings and lightly picks up the morsel from the surface with its bill without wetting a feather. It indulges in some startling, playful antics in the air, performs much of its courtship on the wing, and caresses its mate as gracefully in mid-air as on the ground. It strikes terror into its victim by darting at him at such speed that it is useless for him to attempt to escape; over, under, and around him at will, as if playing with his powers of flight; it is mere sport for the man-o'-war, the swift frigate, to overtake the fastest flier, and when the poor victim drops its fish, the frigate bird quickly catches it and, perhaps, tosses it in the air, drops and catches it again as if it enjoyed the game.

While soaring, either in a calm or in the teeth of a howling gale, the long tail feathers are held parallel and close together, and are moved only slightly to steer or balance the bird, but when fighting in the air, as the males often do, or when courting or playing they are frequently opened and closed like a pair of scissors. The man-o'-war-birds' wings have been developed at the expense of its feet, which are very small and weak; it can hardly stand upon them, and can hardly walk; it never dives and is a very poor swimmer; it becomes wet and helpless in the water. But in the air it is a past master.

Harsh grating cries indulged in by fighting males, a clucking note heard during the mating season, and a rough croak are about the only sounds made by these birds as they are usually silent. The young birds are often quite noisy in the rookeries.

Enough has already been said above about the behavior of the man-o'-war-bird toward other species, by whom it is justly dreaded and cordially hated. But it is apparently sometimes moved by unselfish motives toward birds of its own species, as the following incident, related by Mr. A. W. Anthony (1898a) seems to illustrate:

At a considerable distance from the colony a bird was found that was unable to fly, and thinking that it had been recently injured, and must necessarily starve, where food was not easily obtained by even the best of flyers, I killed the cripple and made an examination of its injuries. One wing was withered and useless; evidently the bird had never enjoyed its use, though it was fat and its stomach was well filled with flying fish. Those who know the feeding habits of *Fregata* need not be told that all their food is obtained on the wing, and a bird deprived of the use of its wings would speedily starve if not fed by its fellows. The precipitous sides of San Benedicte also made it impossible for a man-o'-war-bird to gain the top of the island if deprived of its wings. So it was quite evident that the pensioner had never left the island, but had been dependent on the bounty of its fellows all of its life. From its excellent condition it was evident that even in that busy community of thousands some of them found time to feed the unfortunate.

This remarkable exhibition of altruistic unselfishness hardly seems to be in keeping with its well-known habit of eating its neighbors' young.

Winter.—The man-'o-war-bird is not a migratory species and is practically a resident throughout the year in the general vicinity of its breeding range. But between nesting seasons it is apt to wander far from home and has often been noted or taken in most unexpected places, even in the interior of the continent. During the summer, fall, and winter it is often as gregarious as during the breeding season, especially in its roosts at night, where it gathers in enormous rookeries, frequenting the same roost regularly. Large flocks of man-o'-war-birds may often be seen resting on the mangroves during the daytime, in company with pelicans, cormorants, and other water birds. It is also a common sight to see them perched in flocks on sand bars, coral reefs, old wrecks, or abandoned structures, lazily digesting their food or waiting for another meal.

Since the above life history was compiled and long since most of the above observations were made, the species then known as *Fregata aquila* has been split into various species and subspecies, some of which are undoubtedly worthy of recognition. But rather than attempt to discuss or separate them, the author prefers to let the life history stand as it is, for the habits of all of them must be practically the same.

DISTRIBUTION.

Breeding range.—The North American form breeds on some of the Bahama Islands (Cay Verde, Biminis, Seal Key, Atwood's Key, etc.), Cuba (Puerto Escondido), Isle of Pines, Porto Rico (Mona and Desecheo Islands), some of the Lesser Antilles (Guadeloupe, Battowia, Carriacou, etc.), on islands off the coast of Venezuela (Margarita, Los Hermanos, Los Testigos, etc.), and in the Caribbean Sea as far west as Honduras (Little Cayman and Swan Islands). The birds breeding on islands in the tropical Atlantic, and in the Pacific and Indian Oceans are now regarded by some authorities as distinct species or subspecies, but others regard the birds which breed on islands off the west coast of Mexico (as far north as Santa Margarita Island) as identical with the birds of the West Indies. Breeding grounds protected in Porto Rico, Desecheo Island Reservation.

Winter range.—Includes the breeding range and adjacent seas, extending northward, more or less regularly, to northern Florida and the coast of Louisiana. Birds which wander to the coast of California, as far north as Humboldt Bay, may be referable to one, or perhaps more, of the Pacific forms.

Casual records.—Accidental in Bermuda (four records). Has wandered as far east as Nova Scotia (Halifax, October 16, 1876), as far north as Quebec (Manicouagan, August 14, 1884) and Wisconsin (Humboldt, August, 1880), and as far west as Kansas (Osborne County, August 16, 1880).

Egg dates.—Bahama Islands: Twenty-one records, February 3 to May 11; eleven records, March 3 to April 16. Off west coast of Mexico: Eighteen records, January 15 to June 1.

REFERENCES TO BIBLIOGRAPHY.

ALEXANDER, BOYD.
  1898—An Ornithological Expedition to the Cape Verde Islands. The Ibis, 1898, p. 74.
ALLEN, GLOVER MORRILL.
  1913—An Essex County Ornithologist. The Auk, vol. 30, p. 19.
ALLEN, JOEL ASAPH.
  1904—Black-capped Petrel in New Hampshire. The Auk, vol. 21, p. 383.
  1905—Report on the Birds Collected in Northeastern Siberia by the Jesup North Pacific Expedition. Bulletin of the American Museum of Natural History, vol. 21, p. 219.
ANTHONY, ALFRED WEBSTER.
  1889—Nesting Habits of the California Brown Pelican (*Pelecanus californicus*). Proceedings of the California Academy of Sciences, Second Series, vol. 2, p. 83.
  1895—The Fulmars of Southern California. The Auk, vol. 12, p. 100.
  1896a—Eggs of the Black Socorro and Least Petrels. The Nidologist, vol. 4, p. 16.
  1896b—The Black-vented Shearwater (*Puffinus opisthomelas*). The Auk, vol. 13, p. 223.
  1898—Four Sea Birds New to the Fauna of North America. The Auk, vol. 15, p. 38.
  1898a—Avifauna of the Revillagigedo Islands. The Auk, vol. 15, p. 311.
  1898b—Petrels of Southern California. The Auk, vol. 15, p. 140.
  1898c—Two New Birds from the Pacific Coast of North America. The Auk, vol. 15, p. 36.
  1898d—Two New Birds from the Pacific Coast of America. The Auk, vol. 15, p. 36.
  1898e—The Boobys of the Revillagigedo Islands. The Osprey, vol. 3, p. 4.
  1900—Nesting Habits of the Pacific Coast Species of the Genus *Puffinus*. The Auk, vol. 17, p. 247.
  1900a—A Night on Land. The Condor, vol. 2, p. 28.
  1906—Random Notes of Pacific Coast Gulls. The Auk, vol. 23, p. 129.
AUDUBON, JOHN JAMES.
  1840—The Birds of America, 1840-44.
AUDUBON, MARIA REBECCA.
  1897—Audubon and His Journals.
BAILEY, FLORENCE MERRIAM.
  1902—Handbook of Birds of the Western United States.
BAILEY, HAROLD HARRIS.
  1906—Ornithological Notes from Western Mexico and the Tres Marias and Isabella Islands. The Auk, vol. 23, p. 369.
BAIRD, SPENCER FULLERTON, BREWER, THOMAS MAYO, and RIDGWAY, ROBERT.
  1884—The Water Birds of North America.
BANGS, OUTRAM.
  1902—The Occurrence of Boobies in Numbers on the East Coast of Florida. during a Storm. The Auk, vol. 19, p. 395.

BANNERMAN, DAVID ARMITAGE.
    1914—An Ornithological Expedition to the Eastern Canary Islands. The
        Ibis, 1914, p. 38.
BARLOW, CHESTER.
    1894a—Nesting of the Ashy Petrel. The Nidiologist, vol. 1, p. 171.
BARNES, R. MAGOON.
    1890—List of Birds Breeding in Marshall County, Ill. Ornithologist and
        Oologist, vol. 15, p. 113.
BECK, ROLLO HOWARD.
    1904—Bird Life among the Galapagos Islands. The Condor, vol. 6, p. 5.
    1910—Water Birds of the Vicinity of Point Pinos, California. Proceedings
        of the California Academy of Sciences, Fourth Series, vol. 3, p. 57.
BEEBE, C. WILLIAM.
    1905—Two Bird Lovers in Mexico.
BENDIRE, CHARLES EMIL.
    1882—Malheur Lake, Oregon. Ornithologist and Oologist, vol. 7, p. 137.
BENT, ARTHUR CLEVELAND.
    1918—*Pterodroma gularis* in North America. The Auk, vol. 35 p. 221.
BERLEPSCH, HANS, GRAF VON.
    1906—On a New Form of *Oceanodroma* Inhabiting San Benito Island, off
        the Coast of Lower California. The Auk, vol. 23, p. 185.
BEWICK, THOMAS.
    1847—A History of British Birds.
BONHOTE, JOHN LEWIS.
    1903—On a Collection of Birds from the Northern Islands of the Bahama
        Group. The Ibis, 1903, p. 272.
BOWDISH, BEECHER SCOVILLE.
    1909—Ornithological Miscellany from Audubon Wardens. The Auk, vol. 26,
        p. 116.
BRADLEE, THOMAS S.
    1906—Audubon's Shearwater and Peale's Petrel Breeding in Bermuda.
        The Auk, vol. 23, p. 217.
BREWSTER, WILLIAM.
    1881—Critical Notes on a Petrel New to North America. Bulletin of the
        Nuttall Ornithological Club, vol. 6, p. 91.
    1883—Notes on the Birds Observed during a Summer Cruise in the Gulf
        of St. Lawrence. Proceedings of the Boston Society of Natural
        History, vol. 22, p. 364.
    1886—Additional Notes on Peale's Petrel (*Aestrelata gularis*). The Auk,
        vol. 3, p. 389.
BROWN, FRANK A.
    1911—Machias Seal Islands. Bird-Lore, vol. 13, p. 239.
BRYAN, WILLIAM ALANSON.
    1903—A Monograph of Marcus Island. Occasional Papers of the Bernice
        Pauahi Bishop Museum, vol. 2, p. 77.
    1912—Report on Conditions on Laysan, with Recommendations for Pro-
        tecting the Hawaiian Islands Reservation. United States Depart-
        ment of Agriculture, Biological Survey, Bulletin No. 42.
BRYANT, HENRY.
    1859—(On some birds observed in East Florida.) Proceedings of the Bos-
        ton Society of Natural History, vol. 7, p. 5.
    1861—A List of Birds seen at the Bahamas, from January 20 to May 14,
        1859. Proceedings of the Boston Society of Natural History, vol. 7,
        p. 102.

BRYANT, HENRY—Continued.
1862—Remarks on some of the Birds that breed in the Gulf of St. Lawrence. Proceedings of the Boston Society of Natural History, vol. 8, p. 65.
BRYANT, WALTER E.
1888—Birds and Eggs from the Farallone Islands. Proceedings of the California Academy of Sciences, Second Series, vol. 1, p. 25.
BULLER, WALTER LAWRY.
1888—History of the Birds of New Zealand, Second Edition with Supplement, 1888–1905.
CAMPBELL, A. G. and MATTINGLEY, A. H. E.
1906—A Rookery of Storm-Petrels. The Emu, vol. 6, p. 185.
CAMPBELL, ARCHIBALD JAMES.
1901—Nests and Eggs of Australian Birds.
1904—At Phillip Island, Western Port. The Victorian Naturalist, vol. 20, p. 166.
CASSIN, JOHN.
1858—United States Exploring Expedition. Mammology and ornithology.
CHAMBERLAIN, CORYDON.
1895—An Inland Rookery of Phalacrocorax d. albociliatus. The Nidologist, vol. 3, p. 29.
CHAMBERLAIN, MONTAGUE.
1891—A Popular Handbook of the Ornithology of the United States and Canada, based on Nuttall's Manual.
CHAPMAN, FRANK MICHLER.
1902—List of Birds Collected in Alaska by the Andrew J. Stone Expedition of 1901. Bulletin American Museum of Natural History, vol. 16, p. 231.
1908—Camps and Cruises of an Ornithologist.
1908a—A Contribution to the Life Histories of the Booby (Sula leucogastra) and Man-o'-War Bird (Fregata aquila). Papers from the Tortugas Laboratory of Carnegie Institution of Washington, vol. 2, p. 141.
1912. Handbook of Birds of Eastern North America.
CLARK, AUSTIN HOBART.
1903—Notes on the Habits of certain Venezuelan Birds. The Auk, vol. 20, p. 285.
CLARKE, WILLIAM EAGLE.
1905—On the Birds of Gough Island, South Atlantic Ocean. Ornithological Results of the Scottish National Antarctic Expedition. The Ibis, 1905, p. 247.
1905a—Birds of the Flannan Islands. Annals of Scottish Natural History.
1906—On the Birds of the South Orkney Islands. Ornithological Results of the Scottish National Antarctic Expedition. The Ibis, 1906, p. 145.
1907—On the Birds of Weddell and adjacent Seas. Ornithological Results of the Scottish National Antarctic Expedition. The Ibis, 1907, p. 325.
1912—Plumage of the Fulmar. British Birds, vol. 6, p. 165.
CLAY, CHARLES IRVIN.
1911—Some Diving Notes on Cormorants. The Condor, vol. 13, p. 138.

COLLINS, JOSEPH WILLIAM.

1884—Notes on the habits and methods of Capture of Various Species of Sea-birds that occur on the fishing banks off the Eastern coast of North America, and which are used as bait for catching Codfish by New England fisherman. United States Commission of Fish and Fisheries. Report of the Commissioner for 1882, p. 311.

1899—The Shearwaters and Fulmar as Birds and Bait. The Osprey, vol. 4, p. 35.

CORY, CHARLES BARNEY.

1881—Description of a New Species of the Family Procellariidae. Bulletin of the Nuttall Ornithological Club, vol. 6, p. 84.

DARWIN, CHARLES.

1889—A Naturalist's Voyage.

DAVIES, R. H.

1843—Some Account of the Habits and Natural History of the Sooty Petrel (Mutton Bird). The Tasmanian Journal, vol. 2, p. 13.

DAWSON, WILLIAM LEON.

1908—The New Reserves on the Washington Coast. The Condor, vol 10, p. 45.

1909—The Birds of Washington.

1911—Another Fortnight on the Farallones. The Condor, vol. 13, p. 171.

DILL, HOMER R. and BRYAN, WILLIAM ALANSON.

1912—Report on Conditions on the Hawaiian Bird Reservation with List of the Birds found on Laysan. United States Department of Agriculture, Biological Survey, Bulletin No. 42.

DIXON, JOSEPH.

1907—Some experiences as a Collector in Alaska. The Condor, vol. 9, p. 128.

DUTCHER, BASIL HICKS.

1889—Bird Notes from Little Gull Island, Suffolk Co., N. Y. The Auk, vol. 6, p. 124.

ELLIOTT, HENRY WOOD.

1875—A Report upon the Condition of Affairs in the Territory of Alaska.

1880—Report on the Seal Islands of Alaska.

EMERSON, WILLIAM OTTO.

1886—Egg of the Yellow-nosed Albatross. Ornithologist and Oologist, vol. 11, p. 21.

1906—Oceanodroma leucorhoa and Its Relatives on the Pacific Coast. The Condor, vol. 8, p. 53.

FEILDEN, HENRY WEMYSS.

1889—On the Breeding of *Puffinus auduboni* in the Island of Barbados. The Ibis, 1889, p. 60.

FERRY, JOHN FARWELL.

1910—Birds observed in Saskatchewan during the Summer of 1909. The Auk, vol. 27, p. 185.

FINLEY, WILLIAM LOVELL.

1905—Among the Seabirds off the Oregon Coast. The Condor, vol. 7, pp. 119 and 161.

1907—Among the Pelicans. The Condor, vol. 9, p. 35.

FISHER, WALTER KENRICK.

1903—Notes on the Birds Peculiar to Laysan Island, Hawaiian Group. The Auk, vol. 20, p. 384.

1904—On the Habits of the Laysan Albatross. The Auk, vol. 21, p. 8.

FISHER, WALTER KENRICK—Continued.
  1904a—The Albatross Dance at Sea. The Condor, vol. 6, p. 78.
  1904b—The Home Life of a Buccaneer. The Condor, vol. 6, p. 57.
  1906—Birds of Laysan and the Leeward Islands, Hawaiian Group. Bulletin of the United States Fish Commission, vol. 23, Part 3, p. 769.

FORBES, HENRY OGG.
  1893—A List of the Birds inhabiting the Chatham Islands. The Ibis, 1893, p. 521.

FRAZAR, MARTIN ABBOTT.
  1887—An Ornithologist's Summer in Labrador. Ornithologist and Oologist, vol. 12, p. 1.

GIFFORD, EDWARD WINSLOW.
  1913—The Birds of the Galapagos Islands. Proceedings of the California Academy of Sciences, Fourth Series, vol. 2, p. 1.

GODMAN, FREDERICK DuCANE.
  1872—Notes on the Resident and Migratory Birds of Madeira and the Canaries. The Ibis, 1872, p. 209.
  1907—A Monograph of the Petrels, 1907–1910.

GOODWIN, S. H.
  1904—Pelicans Nesting at Utah Lake. The Condor, vol. 6, p. 126.

GOSS, NATHANIEL STICKNEY.
  1888—Feeding Habits of *Pelecanus erythrorhynchos*. The Auk, vol. 5, p. 25.
  1888a—New and Rare Birds Found Breeding on the San Pedro Martir Isle. The Auk, vol. 5, p. 240.

GOULD, JOHN.
  1841—The Zoology of the Voyage of H. M. S. Beagle.
  1865—Handbook to the Birds of Australia.

GRINNELL, JOSEPH.
  1897—Petrels of Sitka, Alaska. The Nidologist, vol.. 4, p. 76.
  1908—Birds of a Voyage on Salton Sea. The Condor, vol. 10, p. 185.
  1909—Birds and Mammals of the 1907 Alexander Expedition to Southeastern Alaska. University of California Publications in Zoology, vol. 5, p. 171.
  1918—The Status of the White-rumped Petrels of the California Coast. The Condor, vol. 20, p. 46.

GRINNELL, JOSEPH, and DAGGETT, FRANK SLATER.
  1903—An Ornithological Visit to Los Coronados Islands, Lower California. The Auk, vol. 20, p. 27.

GROSS, ALFRED O.
  1912—Observations on the Yellow-billed Tropic-bird (*Phaethon americanus* Grant) at the Bermuda Islands. The Auk, vol. 29, p. 49.

GURNEY, JOHN HENRY.
  1913—The Gannet.

HALL, ROBERT.
  1900—Field Notes on the Birds of Kerguelen Island. The Ibis, 1900, p. 1.
  1902—On a Collection of Birds from Western Australia. The Ibis, 1902, p. 180.

HATCH, PHILO LUOIS.
  1892—Notes on the Birds of Minnesota.

HEADLEY, FREDERICK WEBB.
  1907—Life and Evolution.

HEATH, HAROLD.
    1915—Birds Observed on Forrester Island, Alaska, during the Summer of
        1913. The Condor, vol. 17, p. 20.
HOWELL, ALFRED BRAZIER.
    1912—Notes from Todos Santos Islands. The Condor, vol. 14, p. 187.
HOWELL, ARTHUR H.
    1911—Birds of Arkansas. United States Department of Agriculture, Bio-
        logical Survey, Bulletin No. 38.
HURDIS, J. L.
    1850—Ornithology of the Bermudas. Jardine's Contributions to Ornithol-
        ogy, p. 37.
HUTTON, FREDERICK WOLLASTON.
    1865—Notes on some of the Birds inhabiting the Southern Ocean. The Ibis,
        1865, p. 276.
    1903—Remarks on the Flight of Albatrosses. The Ibis, 1903, p. 81.
JONES, LYNDS.
    1908—June with the Birds of the Washington Coast. The Wilson Bulletin,
        vol. 20, pp. 19, 57, and 189, and vol. 21, p. 3.
JOSSELYN, JOHN.
    1674—An Account of Two Voyages to New England.
KAEDING, HENRY B.
    1903—Bird Life on the Farallone Islands. The Condor, vol. 5, p. 121.
    1905—Birds from the West Coast of Lower California and Adjacent Islands.
        The Condor, vol. 7, p. 105.
KIDDER, JEROME HENRY.
    1875—Contributions to the Natural History of Kerguelen Island. Bulletin
        of the United States National Museum, No. 2.
KNIGHT, ORA WILLIS.
    1908—The Birds of Maine.
KOBBÉ, WILLIAM HOFFMAN.
    1900—The Birds of Cape Disappointment, Washington. The Auk, vol. 17,
        p. 349.
KUMLIEN, LUDWIG.
    1879—Contributions to the Natural History of Arctic America. Bulletin of
        the United States National Museum, No. 15.
LABAT, JEAN BAPTISTE.
    1722—Nouveau voyage aux isles de l'Amérique contenant l'histoire naturelle
        de ces pays, l'origine, les moeurs, la religion, et le gouvernement
        des habitans anciens et modernes, etc. Vol. 2, pp. 349–353.
LAWRENCE, GEORGE NEWBOLD.
    1853—Additions to North American Ornithology, No. 3. Annals of the
        Lyceum of Natural History, vol. 6, p. 4.
    1878—Catalogue of the Birds of Dominica from Collections made for the
        Smithsonian Institution by Frederick A. Ober, together with his
        Notes and Observations. Proceedings of the United States Na-
        tional Museum, vol. 1, p. 48.
    1889—An Account of the breeding habits of *Puffinus auduboni* in the
        island of Grenada, West Indies, with a note on *Zenaida rubripes*.
        The Auk, vol. 6, p. 19.
    1891—Description of a New Subspecies of Cypselidae of the Genus *Chae-
        tura*, with a Note on the Diablotin. The Auk, vol. 8, p. 59.
LINTON, CLARENCE BROCKMAN.
    1908a—Pacific Fulmars and Pacific Kittiwakes at Long Beach. The Con-
        dor, vol. 10, p. 238.

LOOMIS, LEVERETT MILLS.
1895—California Water Birds, No. 1. Proceedings of the California Academy of Sciences, Second Series, vol. 5, p. 177.
1896—California Water Birds, Nos. 2 and 3. Proceedings of the California Academy of Sciences, Second Series, vol. 6, pp. 1 and 353.
1900—California Water Birds, Nos. 4 and 5. Proceedings of the California Academy of Sciences, Third Series, Zoology, vol. 2, pp. 277 and 349.
1918—Expedition of the California Academy of Sciences to the Galapagos Islands, 1905-1906. A Review of the Albatrosses, Petrels, and Diving Petrels.
LOWE, PERCY R.
1911—A Naturalist on Desert Islands.
LUCAS, FREDERIC AUGUSTUS.
1897—The Nostrils in Young Cormorants. The Auk, vol. 14, p. 87.
MACGILLIVRAY, WILLIAM.
1852—A History of British Birds.
MACKAY, GEORGE HENRY.
1894—Habits of the Double-crested Cormorant in Rhode Island. The Auk, vol. 11, p. 18.
MACPHERSON, HENRY ALEXANDER.
1898—British Birds with their Nests and Eggs, Order Tubinares, vol. 6, .p. 206.
MAILLIARD, JOSEPH.
1898—Notes on the Nesting of the Forked-tailed Petrel (*Oceanodroma furcata*). The Auk, vol. 15, p. 230.
MAWSON, DOUGLAS.
1914—The Home of the Blizzard.
MAYNARD, CHARLES JOHNSON.
1889—Description of a Supposed New Species of Gannet. Ornithologist and Oologist, vol. 14, p. 40.
1896—The Birds of Eastern North America.
MCGREGOR, RICHARD CRITTENDEN.
1906—Birds Observed in the Krenitzin Islands, Alaska. The Condor, vol. 8, p. 114.
MONTGOMERY, HENRY HUTCHINSON.
1898—On the Habits of the Mutton-bird of Bass Strait, Australia (*Puffinus tenuirostris*). The Ibis, 1898, p. 209.
MORRIS, FRANCIS ORPEN.
1903—A History of British Birds. Fifth Edition.
MURPHY, ROBERT CUSHMAN.
1914—Observations on Birds of the South Atlantic. The Auk, vol. 31, p. 439.
1915—The Atlantic Range of Leach's Petrel (*Oceanodroma leucorhoa* [Vieillot]). The Auk, vol. 32, p. 170.
1922—Notes on Tubinares, Including Records which Affect the A. O. U. Check-list. The Auk, vol. 39, p. 58.
NELSON, EDWARD WILLIAM.
1883—The Birds of Bering Sea and the Arctic Ocean.
1887—Report upon Natural History Collections made in Alaska.
1899—Birds of the Tres Marias Islands. North American Fauna, No. 14, p. 21.
1903—Notes on the Mexican Cormorant. The Condor, vol. 5, p. 139.

NEWTON, EDWARD.
   1861—Ornithological Notes from Mauritius. The Ibis, 1861, p. 180.
NICHOLS, JOHN TREADWELL.
   1913—Notes on Offshore Birds. The Auk, vol. 30, p. 505.
   1918—Bird Notes from Florida. Abstract of Proceedings, Linnaean So-
         ciety of New York, No. 30, pp. 20–27.
NICHOLS, JOHN TREADWELL, and MOWBRAY, LOUIS L.
   1916—Two New Forms of Petrels from the Bermudas. The Auk, vol. 33,
         p. 194.
NICHOLS, JOHN TREADWELL, and MURPHY, ROBERT CUSHMAN.
   1914—A Review of the Genus Phoebetria. The Auk, vol. 31, p. 526.
NICOLL, MICHAEL JOHN.
   1906—On the Birds collected and observed during the Voyage of the
         Valhalla, R. Y. S., from November, 1905, to May, 1906. The Ibis,
         1906, p. 666.
NOBLE, GEORGE KINGSLEY.
   1916—The Resident Birds of Guadeloupe. Bulletin of the Museum of
         Comparative Zoology at Harvard College, vol. 60, No. 10.
NORTON, ARTHUR HERBERT.
   1881—Leach's Petrel. The Ornithologist and Botanist, vol. 1, p. 50.
NUTTALL, THOMAS.
   1834—A Manual of the Ornithology of the United States and Canada,
         Water Birds.
OBERHOLSER, HARRY CHURCH.
   1917—A Review of the Subspecies of the Leach Petrel, Oceanodroma leu-
         corhoa (Vieillot). Proceedings of the United States National
         Museum, vol. 54, p. 165.
OGILVIE-GRANT, WILLIAM ROBERT.
   1896—On the Birds observed at the Salvage Islands, near Madeira. The
         Ibis, 1896, p. 41.
   1905—On the Birds of the Azores. Novitates Zoologicae, vol. 12, p. 80.
PALMER, WILLIAM.
   1899—The Avifauna of the Pribilof Islands. The Fur-Seals and Fur-Seal
         Islands of the North Pacific Ocean, Part 3, p. 355.
PATTERSON, R. L.
   1880—The Birds of Belfast.
PEARSON, THOMAS GILBERT.
   1899—Notes on some of the Birds of Eastern North Carolina. The Auk,
         vol. 16, p. 246.
   1905—The Cormorants of Great Lakes. Bird-Lore, vol. 7, p. 121.
PEARSON, THOMAS GILBERT, BRIMLEY, CLEMENT SAMUEL, and BRIMLEY, HERBERT
   HUTCHINSON.
   1919—Birds of North Carolina. North Carolina Geological and Economic
         Survey, vol. 4.
PENNOCK, CHARLES JOHN.
   1889—Nesting of the Florida Cormorant. Ornithologist and Oologist, vol.
         14, p. 154.
PLATH, KARL.
   1913—The Tropic Birds of Bermuda. Bird-Lore, vol. 15, p. 345.
PUTNAM, FREDERIC WARD.
   1856—Catalogue of the Birds of Essex County, Massachusetts. Proceed-
         ings of the Essex Institute, vol. 1, p. 201.

RAY, MILTON SMITH.
1904—A Fortnight on the Farallones. The Auk, vol. 21, p. 425.
REID, SAVILE G.
1884—The Birds of Bermuda. Part 4 in contributions to the Natural History of the Bermudas. Bulletin of the United States National Museum, No. 25.
REINHARDT, J.
1824—Gronlands Fugle ester de nyeste Erfaringer. Tidskrift fur Naturvidenskaberne, vol. 3, p. 52.
RICHARDS, THEODORE WRIGHT.
1909—Nesting of *Diomedea nigripes* and *D. immutabilis* on Midway Islands. The Condor, vol. 11, p. 122.
RIDGWAY, ROBERT.
1885—A New Petrel for North America. The Auk, vol. 2, p. 386.
RILEY, JOSEPH HARVEY.
1905—List of the Birds Collected or Observed during the Bahama Expedition of the Geographic Society of Baltimore. The Auk, vol. 22, p. 349.
ROTHSCHILD, LIONEL WALTER.
1893—Avifauna of Laysan.
SAUNDERS, HOWARD.
An Illustrated Manual of British Birds.
SCOTT, ROBERT F.
1905—The Voyage of the Discovery.
SCOTT, WILLIAM EARL DODGE.
1891—Observations on the Birds of Jamaica, West Indies. The Auk, vol. 8, p. 249 and p. 253.
SEEBOHM, HENRY.
1890—On the Birds of the Bonin Islands. The Ibis, 1890, p. 95.
1891—On the Birds of the Volcano Islands. The Ibis, 1891, p. 189.
SELOUS, EDMUND.
1901—Bird Watching.
1905—The Bird Watcher in the Shetlands.
SHUFELDT, ROBERT WILSON.
1916—The Bird Caves of the Bermudas and their Former Inhabitants. The Ibis, 1916, p. 623.
SMITH, FRANK.
1911—Double-crested Cormorants Breeding in Central Illinois. The Auk, vol. 28, p. 16.
SMITH, JOHN.
1629—General History of Virginia.
SNODGRASS, ROBERT EVANS, and HELLER, EDMUND.
1902—The Birds of Clipperton and Cocos Islands. Proceedings of the Washington Academy of Sciences, vol. 4, p. 501.
SPINNEY, HERBERT L.
1903—The Stilt Sandpiper in Knox Co., Maine. The Auk, vol. 20, p. 65.
STEAD, E. F.
1906—The Wry-bill Plover of New Zealand. Bird-Lore, vol. 8, p. 185.
STEJNEGER, LEONHARD.
1885—Results of Ornithological Explorations in the Commander Islands and in Kamtschatka. Bulletin of the United States National Museum, No. 29.

STOCKARD, CHARLES R.
1905—Nesting Habits of Birds in Mississippi.   The Auk, vol. 22, p. 146.
STREETS, THOMAS HALE.
1877—Contributions to the Natural History of the Hawaiian and Fanning
Islands and Lower California.   Bulletin of the United States National Museum, No. 7.
TAIT, WILLIAM C.
1887—A List of the Birds of Portugal.   The Ibis, 1887, p. 372.
TAVERNER, PERCY ALGERNON.
1915—The Double-crested Cormorant (*Phalacrocorax auritus*) and its Relation to the Salmon Industries on the Gulf of St. Lawrence.
Museum Bulletin, No. 13, Geological Survey, Canada.
TAYLOR, HENRY REED.
1893—Observations on the California Brown Pelican.   The Nidiologist,
vol. 1, p. 37.
DU TERTRE, JEAN BAPTISTE.
1654—Historie générale des isles des Christophie, de la Guadeloupe, de la
Martinique, et autres dans l'Amérique.
THAYER, JOHN ELIOT, and BANGS, OUTRAM.
1908—The Present Status of the Ornis of Guadaloupe Island.   The Condor,
vol. 10, p. 101.
TOWNSEND, CHARLES HASKINS.
1890—Birds from the Coasts of Western North America and adjacent
Islands, collected in 1888–90, with Descriptions of New Species.
Proceedings of the United States National Musum, vol. 13, p. 131.
TOWNSEND, CHARLES WENDELL.
1905—The Birds of Essex County, Massachusetts.   Memoirs of the Nuttall
Club, No. 3.
TURLE, WILLIAM H.
1891—A Visit to the Blasket Islands and the Skelling Rocks.   The Ibis,
1891, p. 1.
TURNER, LUCIEN MCSHAN.
1886—Contributions to the Natural History of Alaska.
VAN KAMMEN, I. I.
1916—Whale Birds.   The Oologist, vol. 33, p. 172.
VERRILL, ADDISON EMORY.
1902—The Bermuda Islands.   Transactions of the Connecticut Academy of
Arts and Sciences.   Vol. 11, part 2.
VERRILL, ALPHEUS HYATT.
1901—Notes on the Birds of the Bermudas with Descriptions of two New
Subspecies and Several Additions to the Fauna.   The Osprey, vol.
5, p. 83.
VERRILL, GEORGE ELLIOT.
1895—Notes on Birds and Eggs from the Islands of Gough, Kerguelen and
South Georgia.   Transactions of the Connecticut Academy, vol.
9, part 2.
WALTER, WILLIAM.
1902—More about Mutton Birds.   The Emu, vol. 2, p. 219.
WAYNE, ARTHUR TREZEVANT.
1894—Effect of the Great Cyclone of August 26–27 upon certain Species
of Birds.   The Auk, vol. 11, p. 85.
1910—Birds of South Carolina.   Contributions from the Charlestown
Museum, I.

WELLS. JOHN GRANT.
    1902—Birds of the Island of Carriacou. The Auk, vol. 19, p. 239.
WILLETT, GEORGE.
    1912—Report of G. Willett, Agent and Warden, Stationed on St. Lazaria
        Bird Reservation, Alaska. Bird-Lore, vol. 14, p. 419.
WILSON, EDWARD A.
    1907—National Antarctic Expedition, 1901–1904. Natural History, vol. 2,
        Zoology, part 2, Aves.
WOOD, WILLIAM.
    1634—New England's Prospects.
WRIGHT, CHARLES A.
    1864—List of the Birds observed in the Islands of Malta and Gozo. The
        Ibis, 1864, p. 42.
WRIGHT, HOWARD W.
    1913—The Birds of San Martin Island, Lower California. The Condor,
        vol. 15, p. 207.
YARRELL, WILLIAM.
    1871—History of British Birds. Fourth Edition, 1871–85, Revised and
        enlarged by Alfred Newton and Howard Saunders.

INDEX

PLATES

PLATE 1. BLACK-FOOTED ALBATROSS. Black-footed albatross, adult and downy young, Laysan Island, photo presented by Mr. Alfred M. Bailey.

PLATE 2. BLACK-FOOTED ALBATROSS. A nesting colony of black-footed albatrosses, Laysan Island, Pacific Ocean, photo presented by Mr. Alfred M. Bailey.

PLATE 3. LAYSAN ALBATROSS. *Upper:* A nesting colony of Laysan albatrosses, mostly young birds, Laysan Island. *Lower:* Adults and young Laysan albatrosses, Laysan Island. Photos presented by **Dr. Walter K. Fisher,** referred to on page 12.

PLATE 4. LAYSAN ALBATROSS. *Upper:* Nuptial dance of Laysan albatross, first step. *Lower:* Nuptial dance of Laysan albatross, second step, Laysan Island. Photos presented by Dr. Walter K. Fisher, referred to on page 12.

PLATE 5. LAYSAN ALBATROSS. *Upper:* Nuptial dance of Laysan albatross, finale, Laysan Island. *Lower:* A more common method of ending the dance. Photos presented by Dr. Walter K. Fisher, referred to on page 12.

PLATE 6. LAYSAN ALBATROSS. *Upper:* Young Laysan albatross, Laysan Island. *Lower:* Adult Laysan albatross, feeding its young, Laysan Island. Photos presented by Dr. Walter K. Fisher, referred to on page 13.

PLATE 7. SOOTY ALBATROSS. *Upper:* Adult and young sooty albatrosses, South Georgia. *Lower:* Group of sooty albatrosses in the Brooklyn Museum. Photos presented by Dr. Robert Cushman Murphy, courtesy of the Brooklyn Museum and the American Museum of Natural History.

PLATE 8. GIANT FULMAR. Nesting colony of giant fulmars, Sea Lion Island, Falkland Islands, photo by Mr. Rollo H. Beck, presented by the American Museum of Natural History.

PLATE 9. GIANT FULMAR. *Upper:* Giant fulmar, in the white plumage, on its nest, South Georgia, photo by Dr. Robert Cushman Murphy. *Lower:* Giant fulmar, in the ordinary dark plumage, on its nest, Sea Lion Island, Falkland Islands, photo by Mr. Rollo H. Beck. Photos presented by the American Museum of Natural History.

PLATE 10. GIANT FULMAR. *Upper:* Young giant fulmar, one day old, Sea Lion Island, Falkland Islands, photo by Mr. Rollo H. Beck. *Lower:* Young giant fulmar, nearly full grown, South Georgia, photo by Dr. Robert Cushman Murphy. Photos presented by the American Museum of Natural History.

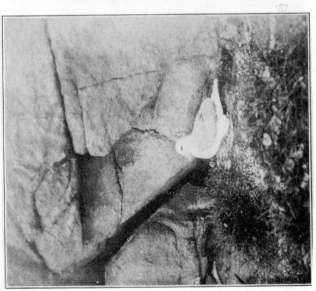

PLATE 11. FULMAR. *Left:* Fulmar on its nest, St. Kilda, Scotland, June, 1907. *Right:* Nest and egg of fulmar, some locality and date. Photos presented by Mr. C. H. Wells.

PLATE 12. RODGERS FULMAR. *Upper:* Rodgers fulmar on its nest,
St. Matthew Island, Bering Sea, July 9, 1911; referred to on page 43.
Lower: Nest and egg of Rodgers fulmar, Semidi Island, Alaska, July 1,
1911, photo by Mr. Johan Koren, presented by Col. John E. Thayer.

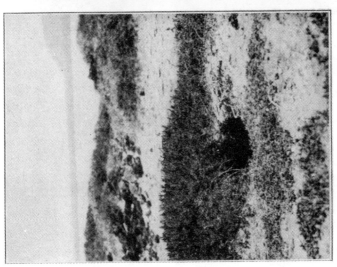

PLATE 13. CORY SHEARWATER. *Left:* Nesting burrow of Cory shearwater, in sandy soil, Montana Clara, Canary Islands. *Right:* Nesting site of Cory shearwater, in caves in outer wall of crater, 600 feet above sea level, Graciosa, Canary Islands. Photos presented by Mr. David A. Bannerman, referred to on page 56.

PLATE 14. PINK-FOOTED SHEARWATER. *Upper:* Nesting site of pink-footed shearwater Juan Fernandez Island. *Lower:* Pink-footed shearwater in its nest, Goat Island, off Santa Clara, Chile. Photos by Mr. Rollo H. Beck, presented by the American Museum of Natural History, referred to on page 62.

PLATE 15. *Upper:* AUDUBON SHEARWATER. Young Audubon shearwater, Washerwoman Key, Bahama Islands. *Lower:* SHEARWA-TER. Adult shearwater, leaving its nest, same locality. Photos by Dr. Frank M. Chapman, presented by the American Museum of Natural History.

PLATE 16. TOWNSEND SHEARWATER. Mr. Rollo H. Beck digging out burrows of Townsend shearwater on Clarion Island, Revillagigedo Islands, Mexico, photo presented by him, referred to on page 84.

PLATE 17. SOOTY SHEARWATER. *Upper:* Mr. Rollo H. Beck collecting a sooty shearwater and egg, on Wollaston Island, Chile, 15 miles north of Cape Horn. *Lower:* Sooty shearwater, its nest and its egg in above locality. Photos presented by the American Museum of Natural History.

PLATE 18. WEDGE-TAILED SHEARWATER. Nesting burrows of wedge-tailed shearwater, San Benedicto Island, Revillagigedo Islands, Mexico, photo presented by Mr. A. W. Anthony, referred to on page 97.

PLATE 19. WEDGE-TAILED SHEARWATER. *Upper:* Pair of wedge-tailed shearwaters, Laysan Island, Pacific Ocean, photo presented by Dr. Walter K. Fisher. *Lower:* Nesting colony of same in same locality, photo by Mr. C. T. Albrecht, presented by the Biological Survey.

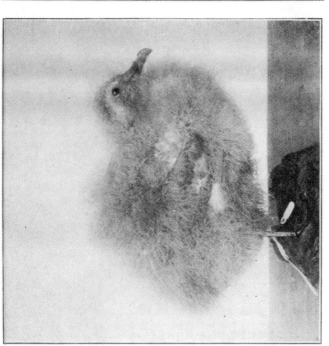

PLATE 20. *Left:* PEALE PETREL. Young Peale petrel, photo of a mounted specimen loaned to the author by the Park Museum, referred to on page 119. *Right:* BULWER PETREL. Nesting site of Bulwer petrel, under huge boulders just above high-water mark, Montana Clara, Canary Islands, photo presented by Mr. David A. Bannerman.

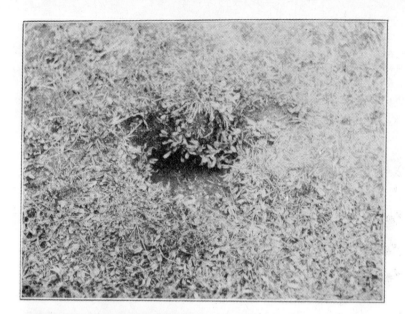

PLATE 21. LEACH PETREL. *Upper:* Nesting burrow of Leach petrel, Big Spoon Island, Jericho Bay, Maine, July 12, 1915. *Lower:* Same burrow, opened to show bird, nest and egg. Both referred to on page 138.

PLATE 22. LEACH PETREL. *Upper:* Burrows of Leach petrel, in the woods, Seal Island, Nova Scotia, July 4, 1904, referred to on page 139. *Lower:* Downy young and egg of Leach petrel, Matinicus Rock, Maine, July, 1906, photo presented by Mr. Herbert K. Job.

PLATE 23. BEAL PETREL. *Upper:* Nest and eggs of Beal petrel, Three Arch Rocks, Oregon. *Lower:* Beal petrel on its nest, same locality. Photos by Bohlman and Finley, presented by Mr. William L. Finley.

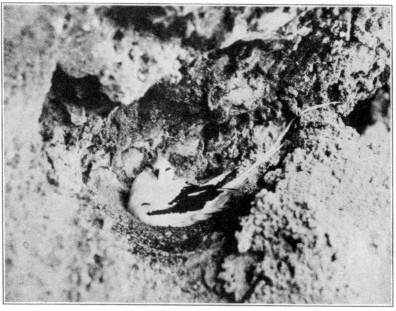

PLATE 24. YELLOW-BILLED TROPIC-BIRD. *Upper:* Nesting site of yellow-billed tropic-bird, Morgan's Island, Bermuda Islands. *Lower:* Yellow-billed tropic-bird on its nest, same locality. Photos presented by Dr. Alfred O. Gross, referred to on page 182.

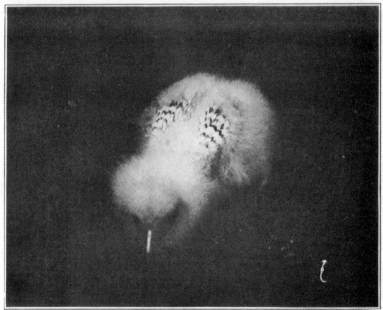

PLATE 25. YELLOW-BILLED TROPIC-BIRD. *Upper:* Young yellow-billed tropic-bird, four days old. *Lower:* Young of same, twenty days old. Photos presented by Dr. Alfred O. Gross, referred to on page 184.

PLATE 26. YELLOW-BILLED TROPIC-BIRD. *Upper:* Young yellow-billed tropic-bird, thirty-four days old. *Lower:* Young of same, sixty days old. Photos presented by Dr. Alfred O. Gross, referred to on page 184.

PLATE 27. RED-BILLED TROPIC-BIRD. *Upper:* Red-billed tropic-bird on its nest, Isabella Island, Mexico, April 9, 1905, photo presented by Mr. Harold H. Bailey. *Lower:* Red-billed tropic-bird on its nest, Galapagos Islands, photo presented by Mr. Rollo H. Beck.

PLATE 28. RED-TAILED TROPIC-BIRD. *Upper:* Red-tailed tropic-bird on its nest, Laysan Island, Pacific Ocean, photo presented by Dr. Walter K. Fisher. *Lower:* Red-tailed tropic-bird and young, Laysan Island, photo by Mr. C. T. Albrecht, presented by the Biological Survey.

PLATE 29. BLUE-FACED BOOBY. *Upper:* Blue-faced booby, guarding eggs. *Lower:* Blue-faced booby, brooding young. Photos taken on Laysan Island, Pacific Ocean, and presented by Dr. Walter K. Fisher.

PLATE 30. BLUE-FACED BOOBY. *Upper:* Pair of blue-faced boobies guarding young. *Lower:* Blue-faced booby feeding young. Photos taken on Laysan Island, Pacific Ocean, and presented by Dr. Walter K. Fisher.

PLATE 31. BLUE-FOOTED BOOBY. *Upper:* Blue-footed booby and egg, Galapagos Islands. *Lower:* Blue-footed booby and young, Galapagos Islands. Photos presented by Mr. Rollo H. Beck.

PLATE 32. BOOBY. *Upper:* Boobies on the wing. *Lower:* Booby colony, adults and young, Cay Verde, Bahama Islands. Photos by Dr. Frank M. Chapman, presented by the American Museum of Natural History.

PLATE 33. BOOBY. *Upper:* Booby, nest, and eggs. *Lower:* Pair of boobies and young. Photos taken by Dr. Frank M. Chapman, on Cay Verde, Bahama Islands, and presented by the American Museum of Natural History.

PLATE 34. RED-FOOTED BOOBY. *Upper:* Red-footed booby alighting on its nest, Laysan Island, Pacific Ocean, photo by Mr. C. T. Albrecht, presented by the Biological Survey. *Lower:* Another bird on its nest, same locality, photo presented by Dr. Walter K. Fisher.

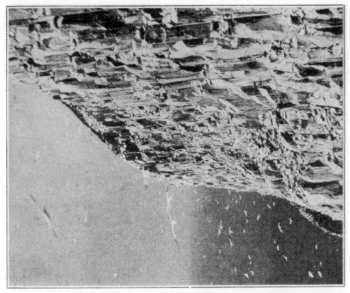

PLATE 35. GANNET. *Left*: Main gannet ledge, Bonaventure Island, Quebec, June 21, 1920, referred to on page 218. *Right*: Gannets on Ailsa Craig, Scotland, photo by Mr. B. Beetham, presented by Mr. J. H. Gurney.

PLATE 36. GANNET. *Upper:* Gannet ledges, Bonaventure Island, Quebec, June 24, 1920, referred to on page 218. *Lower:* Nesting gannets on one of the above ledges.

PLATE 37. GANNET. *Upper:* Gannets' nests, North Bird Rock, Quebec, June 25, 1904, referred to on page 219. *Lower:* Nesting gannets, Bird Rock, Quebec, June 25. 1904, photo presented by Mr. Herbert K. Job, and referred to on page 219.

PLATE 38. GANNET. *Upper:* Young gannet, recently hatched. *Lower:* Adult and young gannet, downy stage. Photos taken on North Bird Rock, Quebec, July 24, 1915, referred to on page 221.

PLATE 39. GANNET. *Upper:* Gannet feeding young, about half grown, photo by Mr. J. M. Campbell. *Lower:* Young gannet, fully grown and nearly fledged, photo by Mr. A. C. Adams. Photos presented by Mr. J. H. Gurney.

PLATE 40. WATER TURKEY. *Upper:* Nesting colony of water turkeys, St. Johns River, Florida, April 21, 1902, referred to on page 231. *Lower:* Nests in above colony.

PLATE 41. WATER TURKEY. *Upper:* Nests of water turkeys, showing eggs and young, St. Johns River, Florida, April 21, 1902. *Lower:* Young water turkeys in nest, Cuthbert Lake, Florida, photo presented by Mr. Herbert K. Job.

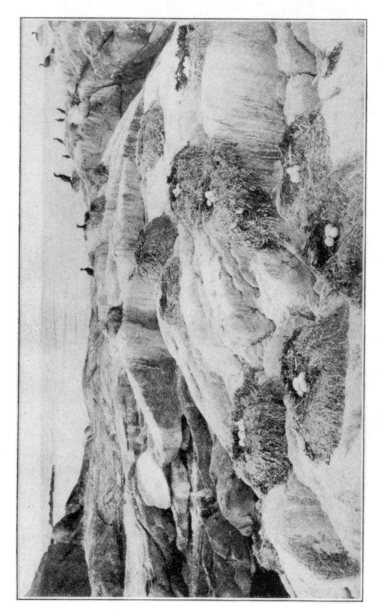

PLATE 42. COMMON CORMORANT. Nesting colony of common cormorants, Lofoten Islands, Norway, photo by Professor Robert Collett, loaned by Dr. R. W. Shufeldt.

PLATE 43. COMMON CORMORANT. *Left:* Nesting site of common cormorant, Isle of Man, England. *Right:* Common cormorant and young, same locality. Photos presented by Mr. C. H. Wells.

PLATE 44. DOUBLE-CRESTED CORMORANT. *Upper:* Nest and eggs of double-crested cormorant, Stump Lake, North Dakota, May 31, 1901. *Lower:* Group of nests in above colony.

PLATE 45. DOUBLE-CRESTED CORMORANT. *Upper:* Nesting colony of double-crested cormorants and murres, Gull Island, off Cape Whittle, Labrador, July 14, 1916, photo presented by Dr. Charles W. Townsend. *Lower:* Nests of double-crested cormorant in the largest colony in Lake Winnipegosis, Manitoba, June 18, 1913, referred to on page 245.

PLATE 46. DOUBLE-CRESTED CORMORANT. *Upper:* Young double-crested cormorants in the nest, Lake Winnipegosis, Manitoba, June 18, 1913. *Lower:* Young birds in same colony, later on, fully grown, but flightless, photo presented by Mr. Herbert K. Job.

PLATE 47. FLORIDA CORMORANT. *Upper:* Nesting colony of Florida cormorants, Ellis Lake, North Carolina. *Lower:* Adult feeding young in above colony. Photos presented by Mr. P. B. Philipp.

PLATE 48. WHITE-CRESTED CORMORANT. *Upper:* Nesting colony of white-crested cormorants, Carroll Islet, Washington, June, 1907, photo presented by Dr. Lynds Jones. *Lower:* Nest and eggs of white-crested cormorant, coast of Washington, photo presented by Mr. W. Leon Dawson.

PLATE 49. FARALLON CORMORANT. *Upper:* Nesting colony of
Farallon cormorants and white pelicans, Tule Lake, Oregon, photo by
Finley and Bohlman, presented by Mr. William L. Finley. *Lower:* Farallon cormorant on its nest, Los Coronados Islands, Mexico, photo presented by Mr. Donald R. Dickey.

PLATE 50. FARALLON CORMORANT. *Upper:* Nesting colony of Farallon cormorants, Salton Sink, California, photo presented by Mr. W. Leon Dawson. *Lower:* Nest and eggs of Farallon cormorant, Salton Sea, California, April 20, 1908, photo by Dr. Joseph Grinnell, presented by the Museum of Vertebrate Zoology.

PLATE 51. MEXICAN CORMORANT. *Left:* Nests of Mexican cormorant, Lake Chapala, Jalisco, Mexico, December 25, 1902. *Right:* Mexican cormorant on its nest in above colony. Photos by Mr. E. A. Goldman, presented by the Biological Survey, referred to on page 261.

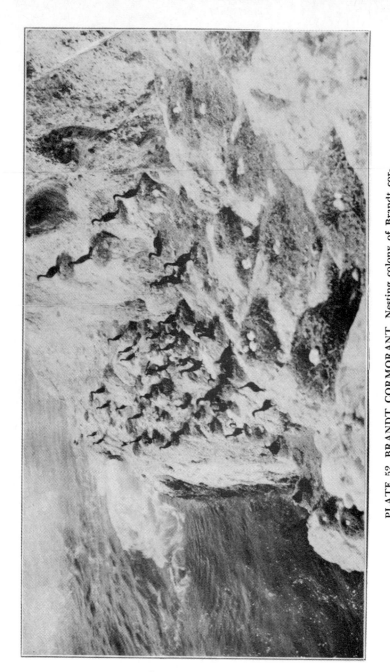

PLATE 52. BRANDT CORMORANT. Nesting colony of Brandt cormorant, Los Coronados Islands, Mexico, photo presented by Mr. Rollo H. Beck.

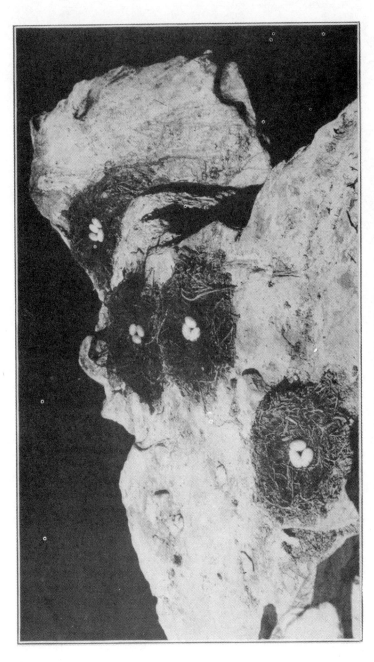

PLATE 53. BRANDT CORMORANT. Nests and eggs of Brandt cormorant, Los Coronados Islands, Mexico, photo presented by Mr. Donald R. Dickey.

PLATE 54. BRANDT CORMORANT. *Left:* Brandt cormorants, nest and young, one young bird asleep. *Right:* Young Brandt cormorants. Photos by Finley and Bohlman, Three Arch Rocks, Oregon, presented by Mr. William L. Finley.

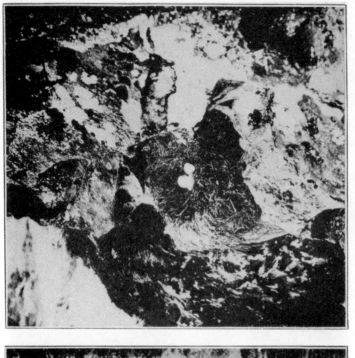

PLATE 55. BAIRD CORMORANT. *Left:* Nesting site of Baird cormorant, Carroll Islet, Washington. *Right:* Nest and eggs of same in above locality. Photos presented by Dr. Lynds Jones, referred to on page 276.

PLATE 56. RED-FACED CORMORANT. *Upper:* Red-faced cormorants at their nests, Walrus Island, Bering Sea, July 7, 1911. *Lower:* Nest and eggs of same in above locality, referred to on page 280.

PLATE 57. WHITE PELICAN. *Upper:* Nest and eggs of white pelican, Lake Winnipegosis, Manitoba, June 19, 1913, referred to on page 284. *Lower:* Another nest of same in above locality, containing four eggs of double-crested cormorant. Note also the heads of large pike.

PLATE 58. WHITE PELICAN. *Upper:* Nests and eggs of white pelican, Salton Sea, California, April 19, 1908. *Lower:* Nest and eggs of same in above colony. Photos by Dr. Joseph Grinnell, presented by the Museum of Vertebrate Zoology.

PLATE 59. WHITE PELICAN. *Upper:* Pair of white pelicans and small young, Malheur Lake, Oregon. *Lower:* Adult and young of same in above locality. Photos by Finley and Bohlman, presented by Mr. William L. Finley.

PLATE 60. BROWN PELICAN. *Upper:* Nesting colony of brown pelicans, Pelican Island, Indian River, Florida, April 15, 1902, referred to on page 295. *Lower:* Nest and eggs of brown pelican, Bull's Bay, South Carolina, May 23, 1915, referred to on page 296.

PLATE 61. BROWN PELICAN. *Upper:* Small naked young of brown pelican, Pelican Island, Indian River, Florida, April 15, 1902. *Lower:* Adult and large young of same, in tree nests, in above locality, referred to on page 297.

PLATE 62. BROWN PELICAN. *Upper:* Brown pelican feeding small young, two days old. *Lower:* Brown pelican feeding large young, fully grown. Photos taken on the coast of Louisiana, June 11, 1918, and presented by Mr. Stanley Clisby Arthur.

PLATE 63. BROWN PELICAN. *Upper:* Drove of young brown pelicans, Pelican Island, Indian River, Florida, photo presented by Mr. Herbert K. Job. *Lower:* Nesting colony of brown pelicans, Pass au Loutre mud lumps, Louisiana, June 11, 1918, photo presented by Mr. Stanley Clisby Arthur.

PLATE 64. CALIFORNIA BROWN PELICAN. Nesting colony of California brown pelicans and Farallon cormorants, Los Coronados Islands, Mexico, photo presented by Mr. Donald R. Dickey.

PLATE 65. CALIFORNIA BROWN PELICAN. *Upper:* Nests and eggs of California brown pelicans, Anacapa Island, California. *Lower:* Nest, eggs, and newly hatched young of same. Photos presented by Mr. Donald R. Dickey.

PLATE 66. CALIFORNIA BROWN PELICAN. *Upper:* California brown pelican flying, photo presented by Mr. Donald R. Dickey. *Lower:* California brown pelican on its nest, Galapagos Islands, photo presented by Mr. Rollo H. Beck.

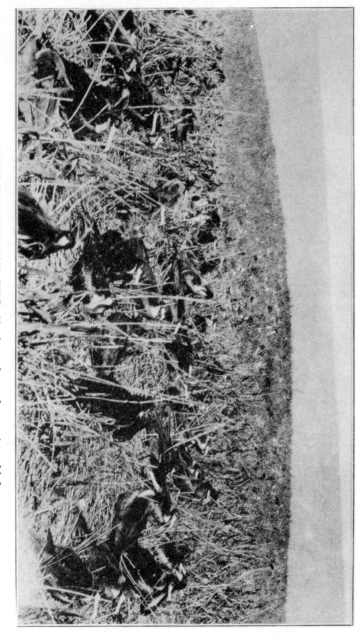

PLATE 67. MAN-O'-WAR-BIRD. Nesting colony of man-o'-war-birds, San Benedicto Island, Mexico, photo presented by Mr. Rollo H. Beck.

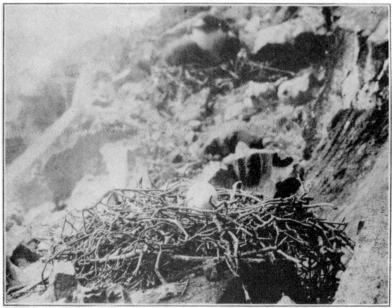

PLATE 68. MAN-O'-WAR-BIRD. *Upper:* Male man-o'-war-bird on its nest, Laysan Island, photo presented by Dr. Walter K. Fisher. *Lower:* Nest and egg of man-o'-war-bird, Galapagos Islands, photo presented by Mr. Rollo H. Beck.

PLATE 69. MAN-O'-WAR-BIRD. *Upper:* Male man-o'-war-bird and small young in nest, Galapagos Islands, photo presented by Mr. Rollo H. Beck. *Lower:* Young man-o'-war-birds in nests, Cay Verde, Bahama Islands, photo by Dr. Frank M. Chapman, presented by the American Museum of Natural History.

A CATALOG OF SELECTED
DOVER BOOKS
IN ALL FIELDS OF INTEREST

A CATALOG OF SELECTED DOVER
BOOKS IN ALL FIELDS OF INTEREST

DRAWINGS OF REMBRANDT, edited by Seymour Slive. Updated Lippmann, Hofstede de Groot edition, with definitive scholarly apparatus. All portraits, biblical sketches, landscapes, nudes. Oriental figures, classical studies, together with selection of work by followers. 550 illustrations. Total of 630pp. 9⅛ × 12¼.
21485-0, 21486-9 Pa., Two-vol. set $25.00

GHOST AND HORROR STORIES OF AMBROSE BIERCE, Ambrose Bierce. 24 tales vividly imagined, strangely prophetic, and decades ahead of their time in technical skill: "The Damned Thing," "An Inhabitant of Carcosa," "The Eyes of the Panther," "Moxon's Master," and 20 more. 199pp. 5⅜ × 8½. 20767-6 Pa. $3.95

ETHICAL WRITINGS OF MAIMONIDES, Maimonides. Most significant ethical works of great medieval sage, newly translated for utmost precision, readability. Laws Concerning Character Traits, Eight Chapters, more. 192pp. 5⅜ × 8½.
24522-5 Pa. $4.50

THE EXPLORATION OF THE COLORADO RIVER AND ITS CANYONS, J. W. Powell. Full text of Powell's 1,000-mile expedition down the fabled Colorado in 1869. Superb account of terrain, geology, vegetation, Indians, famine, mutiny, treacherous rapids, mighty canyons, during exploration of last unknown part of continental U.S. 400pp. 5⅜ × 8½. 20094-9 Pa. $6.95

HISTORY OF PHILOSOPHY, Julián Marías. Clearest one-volume history on the market. Every major philosopher and dozens of others, to Existentialism and later. 505pp. 5⅜ × 8½. 21739-6 Pa. $8.50

ALL ABOUT LIGHTNING, Martin A. Uman. Highly readable non-technical survey of nature and causes of lightning, thunderstorms, ball lightning, St. Elmo's Fire, much more. Illustrated. 192pp. 5⅜ × 8½. 25237-X Pa. $5.95

SAILING ALONE AROUND THE WORLD, Captain Joshua Slocum. First man to sail around the world, alone, in small boat. One of great feats of seamanship told in delightful manner. 67 illustrations. 294pp. 5⅜ × 8½. 20326-3 Pa. $4.50

LETTERS AND NOTES ON THE MANNERS, CUSTOMS AND CONDITIONS OF THE NORTH AMERICAN INDIANS, George Catlin. Classic account of life among Plains Indians: ceremonies, hunt, warfare, etc. 312 plates. 572pp. of text. 6⅛ × 9¼. 22118-0, 22119-9 Pa. Two-vol. set $15.90

ALASKA: The Harriman Expedition, 1899, John Burroughs, John Muir, et al. Informative, engrossing accounts of two-month, 9,000-mile expedition. Native peoples, wildlife, forests, geography, salmon industry, glaciers, more. Profusely illustrated. 240 black-and-white line drawings. 124 black-and-white photographs. 3 maps. Index. 576pp. 5⅜ × 8½. 25109-8 Pa. $11.95

THE BOOK OF BEASTS: Being a Translation from a Latin Bestiary of the Twelfth Century, T. H. White. Wonderful catalog real and fanciful beasts: manticore, griffin, phoenix, amphivius, jaculus, many more. White's witty erudite commentary on scientific, historical aspects. Fascinating glimpse of medieval mind. Illustrated. 296pp. 5⅜ × 8¼. (Available in U.S. only) 24609-4 Pa. $5.95

FRANK LLOYD WRIGHT: ARCHITECTURE AND NATURE With 160 Illustrations, Donald Hoffmann. Profusely illustrated study of influence of nature—especially prairie—on Wright's designs for Fallingwater, Robie House, Guggenheim Museum, other masterpieces. 96pp. 9¼ × 10¾. 25098-9 Pa. $7.95

FRANK LLOYD WRIGHT'S FALLINGWATER, Donald Hoffmann. Wright's famous waterfall house: planning and construction of organic idea. History of site, owners, Wright's personal involvement. Photographs of various stages of building. Preface by Edgar Kaufmann, Jr. 100 illustrations. 112pp. 9¼ × 10. 23671-4 Pa. $7.95

YEARS WITH FRANK LLOYD WRIGHT: Apprentice to Genius, Edgar Tafel. Insightful memoir by a former apprentice presents a revealing portrait of Wright the man, the inspired teacher, the greatest American architect. 372 black-and-white illustrations. Preface. Index. vi + 228pp. 8¼ × 11. 24801-1 Pa. $9.95

THE STORY OF KING ARTHUR AND HIS KNIGHTS, Howard Pyle. Enchanting version of King Arthur fable has delighted generations with imaginative narratives of exciting adventures and unforgettable illustrations by the author. 41 illustrations. xviii + 313pp. 6⅛ × 9¼. 21445-1 Pa. $5.95

THE GODS OF THE EGYPTIANS, E. A. Wallis Budge. Thorough coverage of numerous gods of ancient Egypt by foremost Egyptologist. Information on evolution of cults, rites and gods; the cult of Osiris; the Book of the Dead and its rites; the sacred animals and birds; Heaven and Hell; and more. 956pp. 6⅛ × 9¼. 22055-9, 22056-7 Pa., Two-vol. set $20.00

A THEOLOGICO-POLITICAL TREATISE, Benedict Spinoza. Also contains unfinished *Political Treatise*. Great classic on religious liberty, theory of government on common consent. R. Elwes translation. Total of 421pp. 5⅜ × 8½. 20249-6 Pa. $6.95

INCIDENTS OF TRAVEL IN CENTRAL AMERICA, CHIAPAS, AND YUCATAN, John L. Stephens. Almost single-handed discovery of Maya culture; exploration of ruined cities, monuments, temples; customs of Indians. 115 drawings. 892pp. 5⅜ × 8½. 22404-X, 22405-8 Pa., Two-vol. set $15.90

LOS CAPRICHOS, Francisco Goya. 80 plates of wild, grotesque monsters and caricatures. Prado manuscript included. 183pp. 6⅜ × 9⅜. 22384-1 Pa. $4.95

AUTOBIOGRAPHY: The Story of My Experiments with Truth, Mohandas K. Gandhi. Not hagiography, but Gandhi in his own words. Boyhood, legal studies, purification, the growth of the Satyagraha (nonviolent protest) movement. Critical, inspiring work of the man who freed India. 480pp. 5⅜ × 8½. (Available in U.S. only) 24593-4 Pa. $6.95

ILLUSTRATED DICTIONARY OF HISTORIC ARCHITECTURE, edited by Cyril M. Harris. Extraordinary compendium of clear, concise definitions for over 5,000 important architectural terms complemented by over 2,000 line drawings. Covers full spectrum of architecture from ancient ruins to 20th-century Modernism. Preface. 592pp. 7½ × 9⅝. 24444-X Pa. $14.95

THE NIGHT BEFORE CHRISTMAS, Clement Moore. Full text, and woodcuts from original 1848 book. Also critical, historical material. 19 illustrations. 40pp. 4⅝ × 6. 22797-9 Pa. $2.25

THE LESSON OF JAPANESE ARCHITECTURE: 165 Photographs, Jiro Harada. Memorable gallery of 165 photographs taken in the 1930's of exquisite Japanese homes of the well-to-do and historic buildings. 13 line diagrams. 192pp. 8⅜ × 11¼. 24778-3 Pa. $8.95

THE AUTOBIOGRAPHY OF CHARLES DARWIN AND SELECTED LETTERS, edited by Francis Darwin. The fascinating life of eccentric genius composed of an intimate memoir by Darwin (intended for his children); commentary by his son, Francis; hundreds of fragments from notebooks, journals, papers; and letters to and from Lyell, Hooker, Huxley, Wallace and Henslow. xi + 365pp. 5⅜ × 8. 20479-0 Pa. $5.95

WONDERS OF THE SKY: Observing Rainbows, Comets, Eclipses, the Stars and Other Phenomena, Fred Schaaf. Charming, easy-to-read poetic guide to all manner of celestial events visible to the naked eye. Mock suns, glories, Belt of Venus, more. Illustrated. 299pp. 5¼ × 8¼. 24402-4 Pa. $7.95

BURNHAM'S CELESTIAL HANDBOOK, Robert Burnham, Jr. Thorough guide to the stars beyond our solar system. Exhaustive treatment. Alphabetical by constellation: Andromeda to Cetus in Vol. 1; Chamaeleon to Orion in Vol. 2; and Pavo to Vulpecula in Vol. 3. Hundreds of illustrations. Index in Vol. 3. 2,000pp. 6⅛ × 9¼. 23567-X, 23568-8, 23673-0 Pa., Three-vol. set $36.85

STAR NAMES: Their Lore and Meaning, Richard Hinckley Allen. Fascinating history of names various cultures have given to constellations and literary and folkloristic uses that have been made of stars. Indexes to subjects. Arabic and Greek names. Biblical references. Bibliography. 563pp. 5⅜ × 8½. 21079-0 Pa. $7.95

THIRTY YEARS THAT SHOOK PHYSICS: The Story of Quantum Theory, George Gamow. Lucid, accessible introduction to influential theory of energy and matter. Careful explanations of Dirac's anti-particles, Bohr's model of the atom, much more. 12 plates. Numerous drawings. 240pp. 5⅜ × 8½. 24895-X Pa. $4.95

CHINESE DOMESTIC FURNITURE IN PHOTOGRAPHS AND MEASURED DRAWINGS, Gustav Ecke. A rare volume, now affordably priced for antique collectors, furniture buffs and art historians. Detailed review of styles ranging from early Shang to late Ming. Unabridged republication. 161 black-and-white drawings, photos. Total of 224pp. 8⅜ × 11¼. (Available in U.S. only) 25171-3 Pa. $12.95

VINCENT VAN GOGH: A Biography, Julius Meier-Graefe. Dynamic, penetrating study of artist's life, relationship with brother, Theo, painting techniques, travels, more. Readable, engrossing. 160pp. 5⅜ × 8½. (Available in U.S. only) 25253-1 Pa. $3.95

HOW TO WRITE, Gertrude Stein. Gertrude Stein claimed anyone could understand her unconventional writing—here are clues to help. Fascinating improvisations, language experiments, explanations illuminate Stein's craft and the art of writing. Total of 414pp. 4⅝ × 6⅜. 23144-5 Pa. $5.95

ADVENTURES AT SEA IN THE GREAT AGE OF SAIL: Five Firsthand Narratives, edited by Elliot Snow. Rare true accounts of exploration, whaling, shipwreck, fierce natives, trade, shipboard life, more. 33 illustrations. Introduction. 353pp. 5⅜ × 8½. 25177-2 Pa. $7.95

THE HERBAL OR GENERAL HISTORY OF PLANTS, John Gerard. Classic descriptions of about 2,850 plants—with over 2,700 illustrations—includes Latin and English names, physical descriptions, varieties, time and place of growth, more. 2,706 illustrations. xlv + 1,678pp. 8½ × 12¼. 23147-X Cloth. $75.00

DOROTHY AND THE WIZARD IN OZ, L. Frank Baum. Dorothy and the Wizard visit the center of the Earth, where people are vegetables, glass houses grow and Oz characters reappear. Classic sequel to *Wizard of Oz.* 256pp. 5⅜ × 8. 24714-7 Pa. $4.95

SONGS OF EXPERIENCE: Facsimile Reproduction with 26 Plates in Full Color, William Blake. This facsimile of Blake's original "Illuminated Book" reproduces 26 full-color plates from a rare 1826 edition. Includes "The Tyger," "London," "Holy Thursday," and other immortal poems. 26 color plates. Printed text of poems. 48pp. 5¼ × 7. 24636-1 Pa. $3.50

SONGS OF INNOCENCE, William Blake. The first and most popular of Blake's famous "Illuminated Books," in a facsimile edition reproducing all 31 brightly colored plates. Additional printed text of each poem. 64pp. 5¼ × 7. 22764-2 Pa. $3.50

PRECIOUS STONES, Max Bauer. Classic, thorough study of diamonds, rubies, emeralds, garnets, etc.: physical character, occurrence, properties, use, similar topics. 20 plates, 8 in color. 94 figures. 659pp. 6⅛ × 9¼. 21910-0, 21911-9 Pa., Two-vol. set $14.90

ENCYCLOPEDIA OF VICTORIAN NEEDLEWORK, S. F. A. Caulfeild and Blanche Saward. Full, precise descriptions of stitches, techniques for dozens of needlecrafts—most exhaustive reference of its kind. Over 800 figures. Total of 679pp. 8⅛ × 11. Two volumes. Vol. 1 22800-2 Pa. $10.95 Vol. 2 22801-0 Pa. $10.95

THE MARVELOUS LAND OF OZ, L. Frank Baum. Second Oz book, the Scarecrow and Tin Woodman are back with hero named Tip, Oz magic. 136 illustrations. 287pp. 5⅜ × 8½. 20692-0 Pa. $5.95

WILD FOWL DECOYS, Joel Barber. Basic book on the subject, by foremost authority and collector. Reveals history of decoy making and rigging, place in American culture, different kinds of decoys, how to make them, and how to use them. 140 plates. 156pp. 7⅞ × 10¾. 20011-6 Pa. $7.95

HISTORY OF LACE, Mrs. Bury Palliser. Definitive, profusely illustrated chronicle of lace from earliest times to late 19th century. Laces of Italy, Greece, England, France, Belgium, etc. Landmark of needlework scholarship. 266 illustrations. 672pp. 6⅛ × 9¼. 24742-2 Pa. $14.95

ILLUSTRATED GUIDE TO SHAKER FURNITURE, Robert Meader. All furniture and appurtenances, with much on unknown local styles. 235 photos. 146pp. 9 × 12. 22819-3 Pa. $7.95

WHALE SHIPS AND WHALING: A Pictorial Survey, George Francis Dow. Over 200 vintage engravings, drawings, photographs of barks, brigs, cutters, other vessels. Also harpoons, lances, whaling guns, many other artifacts. Comprehensive text by foremost authority. 207 black-and-white illustrations. 288pp. 6 × 9. 24808-9 Pa. $8.95

THE BERTRAMS, Anthony Trollope. Powerful portrayal of blind self-will and thwarted ambition includes one of Trollope's most heartrending love stories. 497pp. 5⅜ × 8½. 25119-5 Pa. $8.95

ADVENTURES WITH A HAND LENS, Richard Headstrom. Clearly written guide to observing and studying flowers and grasses, fish scales, moth and insect wings, egg cases, buds, feathers, seeds, leaf scars, moss, molds, ferns, common crystals, etc.—all with an ordinary, inexpensive magnifying glass. 209 exact line drawings aid in your discoveries. 220pp. 5⅜ × 8½. 23330-8 Pa. $3.95

RODIN ON ART AND ARTISTS, Auguste Rodin. Great sculptor's candid, wide-ranging comments on meaning of art; great artists; relation of sculpture to poetry, painting, music; philosophy of life, more. 76 superb black-and-white illustrations of Rodin's sculpture, drawings and prints. 119pp. 8⅜ × 11¼. 24487-3 Pa. $6.95

FIFTY CLASSIC FRENCH FILMS, 1912–1982: A Pictorial Record, Anthony Slide. Memorable stills from Grand Illusion, Beauty and the Beast, Hiroshima, Mon Amour, many more. Credits, plot synopses, reviews, etc. 160pp. 8¼ × 11. 25256-6 Pa. $11.95

THE PRINCIPLES OF PSYCHOLOGY, William James. Famous long course complete, unabridged. Stream of thought, time perception, memory, experimental methods; great work decades ahead of its time. 94 figures. 1,391pp. 5⅜ × 8½. 20381-6, 20382-4 Pa., Two-vol. set $19.90

BODIES IN A BOOKSHOP, R. T. Campbell. Challenging mystery of blackmail and murder with ingenious plot and superbly drawn characters. In the best tradition of British suspense fiction. 192pp. 5⅜ × 8½. 24720-1 Pa. $3.95

CALLAS: PORTRAIT OF A PRIMA DONNA, George Jellinek. Renowned commentator on the musical scene chronicles incredible career and life of the most controversial, fascinating, influential operatic personality of our time. 64 black-and-white photographs. 416pp. 5⅜ × 8¼. 25047-4 Pa. $7.95

GEOMETRY, RELATIVITY AND THE FOURTH DIMENSION, Rudolph Rucker. Exposition of fourth dimension, concepts of relativity as Flatland characters continue adventures. Popular, easily followed yet accurate, profound. 141 illustrations. 133pp. 5⅜ × 8½. 23400-2 Pa. $3.50

HOUSEHOLD STORIES BY THE BROTHERS GRIMM, with pictures by Walter Crane. 53 classic stories—Rumpelstiltskin, Rapunzel, Hansel and Gretel, the Fisherman and his Wife, Snow White, Tom Thumb, Sleeping Beauty, Cinderella, and so much more—lavishly illustrated with original 19th century drawings. 114 illustrations. x + 269pp. 5⅜ × 8½. 21080-4 Pa. $4.50

SUNDIALS, Albert Waugh. Far and away the best, most thorough coverage of ideas, mathematics concerned, types, construction, adjusting anywhere. Over 100 illustrations. 230pp. 5⅜ × 8½. 22947-5 Pa. $4.00

PICTURE HISTORY OF THE NORMANDIE: With 190 Illustrations, Frank O. Braynard. Full story of legendary French ocean liner: Art Deco interiors, design innovations, furnishings, celebrities, maiden voyage, tragic fire, much more. Extensive text. 144pp. 8⅜ × 11¾. 25257-4 Pa. $9.95

THE FIRST AMERICAN COOKBOOK: A Facsimile of "American Cookery," 1796, Amelia Simmons. Facsimile of the first American-written cookbook published in the United States contains authentic recipes for colonial favorites—pumpkin pudding, winter squash pudding, spruce beer, Indian slapjacks, and more. Introductory Essay and Glossary of colonial cooking terms. 80pp. 5⅜ × 8½. 24710-4 Pa. $3.50

101 PUZZLES IN THOUGHT AND LOGIC, C. R. Wylie, Jr. Solve murders and robberies, find out which fishermen are liars, how a blind man could possibly identify a color—purely by your own reasoning! 107pp. 5⅜ × 8½. 20367-0 Pa. $2.00

THE BOOK OF WORLD-FAMOUS MUSIC—CLASSICAL, POPULAR AND FOLK, James J. Fuld. Revised and enlarged republication of landmark work in musico-bibliography. Full information about nearly 1,000 songs and compositions including first lines of music and lyrics. New supplement. Index. 800pp. 5⅜ × 8¼. 24857-7 Pa. $14.95

ANTHROPOLOGY AND MODERN LIFE, Franz Boas. Great anthropologist's classic treatise on race and culture. Introduction by Ruth Bunzel. Only inexpensive paperback edition. 255pp. 5⅜ × 8½. 25245-0 Pa. $5.95

THE TALE OF PETER RABBIT, Beatrix Potter. The inimitable Peter's terrifying adventure in Mr. McGregor's garden, with all 27 wonderful, full-color Potter illustrations. 55pp. 4¼ × 5½. (Available in U.S. only) 22827-4 Pa. $1.75

THREE PROPHETIC SCIENCE FICTION NOVELS, H. G. Wells. *When the Sleeper Wakes, A Story of the Days to Come* and *The Time Machine* (full version). 335pp. 5⅜ × 8½. (Available in U.S. only) 20605-X Pa. $5.95

APICIUS COOKERY AND DINING IN IMPERIAL ROME, edited and translated by Joseph Dommers Vehling. Oldest known cookbook in existence offers readers a clear picture of what foods Romans ate, how they prepared them, etc. 49 illustrations. 301pp. 6⅛ × 9¼. 23563-7 Pa. $6.00

SHAKESPEARE LEXICON AND QUOTATION DICTIONARY, Alexander Schmidt. Full definitions, locations, shades of meaning of every word in plays and poems. More than 50,000 exact quotations. 1,485pp. 6½ × 9¼. 22726-X, 22727-8 Pa., Two-vol. set $27.90

THE WORLD'S GREAT SPEECHES, edited by Lewis Copeland and Lawrence W. Lamm. Vast collection of 278 speeches from Greeks to 1970. Powerful and effective models; unique look at history. 842pp. 5⅜ × 8½. 20468-5 Pa. $10.95

THE BLUE FAIRY BOOK, Andrew Lang. The first, most famous collection, with many familiar tales: Little Red Riding Hood, Aladdin and the Wonderful Lamp, Puss in Boots, Sleeping Beauty, Hansel and Gretel, Rumpelstiltskin; 37 in all. 138 illustrations. 390pp. 5⅜ × 8½. 21437-0 Pa. $5.95

THE STORY OF THE CHAMPIONS OF THE ROUND TABLE, Howard Pyle. Sir Launcelot, Sir Tristram and Sir Percival in spirited adventures of love and triumph retold in Pyle's inimitable style. 50 drawings, 31 full-page. xviii + 329pp. 6½ × 9¼. 21883-X Pa. $6.95

AUDUBON AND HIS JOURNALS, Maria Audubon. Unmatched two-volume portrait of the great artist, naturalist and author contains his journals, an excellent biography by his granddaughter, expert annotations by the noted ornithologist, Dr. Elliott Coues, and 37 superb illustrations. Total of 1,200pp. 5⅜ × 8.

Vol. I 25143-8 Pa. $8.95
Vol. II 25144-6 Pa. $8.95

GREAT DINOSAUR HUNTERS AND THEIR DISCOVERIES, Edwin H. Colbert. Fascinating, lavishly illustrated chronicle of dinosaur research, 1820's to 1960. Achievements of Cope, Marsh, Brown, Buckland, Mantell, Huxley, many others. 384pp. 5¼ × 8¼. 24701-5 Pa. $6.95

THE TASTEMAKERS, Russell Lynes. Informal, illustrated social history of American taste 1850's–1950's. First popularized categories Highbrow, Lowbrow, Middlebrow. 129 illustrations. New (1979) afterword. 384pp. 6 × 9.
23993-4 Pa. $6.95

DOUBLE CROSS PURPOSES, Ronald A. Knox. A treasure hunt in the Scottish Highlands, an old map, unidentified corpse, surprise discoveries keep reader guessing in this cleverly intricate tale of financial skullduggery. 2 black-and-white maps. 320pp. 5⅜ × 8½. (Available in U.S. only) 25032-6 Pa. $5.95

AUTHENTIC VICTORIAN DECORATION AND ORNAMENTATION IN FULL COLOR: 46 Plates from "Studies in Design," Christopher Dresser. Superb full-color lithographs reproduced from rare original portfolio of a major Victorian designer. 48pp. 9¼ × 12¼. 25083-0 Pa. $7.95

PRIMITIVE ART, Franz Boas. Remains the best text ever prepared on subject, thoroughly discussing Indian, African, Asian, Australian, and, especially, Northern American primitive art. Over 950 illustrations show ceramics, masks, totem poles, weapons, textiles, paintings, much more. 376pp. 5⅜ × 8. 20025-6 Pa. $6.95

SIDELIGHTS ON RELATIVITY, Albert Einstein. Unabridged republication of two lectures delivered by the great physicist in 1920–21. *Ether and Relativity* and *Geometry and Experience*. Elegant ideas in non-mathematical form, accessible to intelligent layman. vi + 56pp. 5⅜ × 8½. 24511-X Pa. $2.95

THE WIT AND HUMOR OF OSCAR WILDE, edited by Alvin Redman. More than 1,000 ripostes, paradoxes, wisecracks: Work is the curse of the drinking classes, I can resist everything except temptation, etc. 258pp. 5⅜ × 8½. 20602-5 Pa. $3.95

ADVENTURES WITH A MICROSCOPE, Richard Headstrom. 59 adventures with clothing fibers, protozoa, ferns and lichens, roots and leaves, much more. 142 illustrations. 232pp. 5⅜ × 8½. 23471-1 Pa. $3.95

PLANTS OF THE BIBLE, Harold N. Moldenke and Alma L. Moldenke. Standard reference to all 230 plants mentioned in Scriptures. Latin name, biblical reference, uses, modern identity, much more. Unsurpassed encyclopedic resource for scholars, botanists, nature lovers, students of Bible. Bibliography. Indexes. 123 black-and-white illustrations. 384pp. 6 × 9. 25069-5 Pa. $8.95

FAMOUS AMERICAN WOMEN: A Biographical Dictionary from Colonial Times to the Present, Robert McHenry, ed. From Pocahontas to Rosa Parks, 1,035 distinguished American women documented in separate biographical entries. Accurate, up-to-date data, numerous categories, spans 400 years. Indices. 493pp. 6½ × 9¼. 24523-3 Pa. $9.95

THE FABULOUS INTERIORS OF THE GREAT OCEAN LINERS IN HISTORIC PHOTOGRAPHS, William H. Miller, Jr. Some 200 superb photographs capture exquisite interiors of world's great "floating palaces"—1890's to 1980's: Titanic, Ile de France, Queen Elizabeth, United States, Europa, more. Approx. 200 black-and-white photographs. Captions. Text. Introduction. 160pp. 8⅜ × 11¼. 24756-2 Pa. $9.95

THE GREAT LUXURY LINERS, 1927–1954: A Photographic Record, William H. Miller, Jr. Nostalgic tribute to heyday of ocean liners. 186 photos of Ile de France, Normandie, Leviathan, Queen Elizabeth, United States, many others. Interior and exterior views. Introduction. Captions. 160pp. 9 × 12. 24056-8 Pa. $9.95

A NATURAL HISTORY OF THE DUCKS, John Charles Phillips. Great landmark of ornithology offers complete detailed coverage of nearly 200 species and subspecies of ducks: gadwall, sheldrake, merganser, pintail, many more. 74 full-color plates, 102 black-and-white. Bibliography. Total of 1,920pp. 8⅜ × 11¼. 25141-1, 25142-X Cloth. Two-vol. set $100.00

THE SEAWEED HANDBOOK: An Illustrated Guide to Seaweeds from North Carolina to Canada, Thomas F. Lee. Concise reference covers 78 species. Scientific and common names, habitat, distribution, more. Finding keys for easy identification. 224pp. 5⅜ × 8½. 25215-9 Pa. $5.95

THE TEN BOOKS OF ARCHITECTURE: The 1755 Leoni Edition, Leon Battista Alberti. Rare classic helped introduce the glories of ancient architecture to the Renaissance. 68 black-and-white plates. 336pp. 8⅜ × 11¼. 25239-6 Pa. $14.95

MISS MACKENZIE, Anthony Trollope. Minor masterpieces by Victorian master unmasks many truths about life in 19th-century England. First inexpensive edition in years. 392pp. 5⅜ × 8½. 25201-9 Pa. $7.95

THE RIME OF THE ANCIENT MARINER, Gustave Doré, Samuel Taylor Coleridge. Dramatic engravings considered by many to be his greatest work. The terrifying space of the open sea, the storms and whirlpools of an unknown ocean, the ice of Antarctica, more—all rendered in a powerful, chilling manner. Full text. 38 plates. 77pp. 9¼ × 12. 22305-1 Pa. $4.95

THE EXPEDITIONS OF ZEBULON MONTGOMERY PIKE, Zebulon Montgomery Pike. Fascinating first-hand accounts (1805-6) of exploration of Mississippi River, Indian wars, capture by Spanish dragoons, much more. 1,088pp. 5⅜ × 8½. 25254-X, 25255-8 Pa. Two-vol. set $23.90

A CONCISE HISTORY OF PHOTOGRAPHY: Third Revised Edition, Helmut Gernsheim. Best one-volume history—camera obscura, photochemistry, daguerreotypes, evolution of cameras, film, more. Also artistic aspects—landscape, portraits, fine art, etc. 281 black-and-white photographs. 26 in color. 176pp. 8⅜ × 11¼. 25128-4 Pa. $12.95

THE DORÉ BIBLE ILLUSTRATIONS, Gustave Doré. 241 detailed plates from the Bible: the Creation scenes, Adam and Eve, Flood, Babylon, battle sequences, life of Jesus, etc. Each plate is accompanied by the verses from the King James version of the Bible. 241pp. 9 × 12. 23004-X Pa. $8.95

HUGGER-MUGGER IN THE LOUVRE, Elliot Paul. Second Homer Evans mystery-comedy. Theft at the Louvre involves sleuth in hilarious, madcap caper. "A knockout."—Books. 336pp. 5⅜ × 8½. 25185-3 Pa. $5.95

FLATLAND, E. A. Abbott. Intriguing and enormously popular science-fiction classic explores the complexities of trying to survive as a two-dimensional being in a three-dimensional world. Amusingly illustrated by the author. 16 illustrations. 103pp. 5⅜ × 8½. 20001-9 Pa. $2.00

THE HISTORY OF THE LEWIS AND CLARK EXPEDITION, Meriwether Lewis and William Clark, edited by Elliott Coues. Classic edition of Lewis and Clark's day-by-day journals that later became the basis for U.S. claims to Oregon and the West. Accurate and invaluable geographical, botanical, biological, meteorological and anthropological material. Total of 1,508pp. 5⅜ × 8½. 21268-8, 21269-6, 21270-X Pa. Three-vol. set $25.50

LANGUAGE, TRUTH AND LOGIC, Alfred J. Ayer. Famous, clear introduction to Vienna, Cambridge schools of Logical Positivism. Role of philosophy, elimination of metaphysics, nature of analysis, etc. 160pp. 5⅜ × 8½. (Available in U.S. and Canada only) 20010-8 Pa. $2.95

MATHEMATICS FOR THE NONMATHEMATICIAN, Morris Kline. Detailed, college-level treatment of mathematics in cultural and historical context, with numerous exercises. For liberal arts students. Preface. Recommended Reading Lists. Tables. Index. Numerous black-and-white figures. xvi + 641pp. 5⅜ × 8½. 24823-2 Pa. $11.95

28 SCIENCE FICTION STORIES, H. G. Wells. Novels, *Star Begotten* and *Men Like Gods,* plus 26 short stories: "Empire of the Ants," "A Story of the Stone Age," "The Stolen Bacillus," "In the Abyss," etc. 915pp. 5⅜ × 8½. (Available in U.S. only) 20265-8 Cloth. $10.95

HANDBOOK OF PICTORIAL SYMBOLS, Rudolph Modley. 3,250 signs and symbols, many systems in full; official or heavy commercial use. Arranged by subject. Most in Pictorial Archive series. 143pp. 8⅛ × 11. 23357-X Pa. $5.95

INCIDENTS OF TRAVEL IN YUCATAN, John L. Stephens. Classic (1843) exploration of jungles of Yucatan, looking for evidences of Maya civilization. Travel adventures, Mexican and Indian culture, etc. Total of 669pp. 5⅜ × 8½. 20926-1, 20927-X Pa., Two-vol. set $9.90

DEGAS: An Intimate Portrait, Ambroise Vollard. Charming, anecdotal memoir by famous art dealer of one of the greatest 19th-century French painters. 14 black-and-white illustrations. Introduction by Harold L. Van Doren. 96pp. 5⅜ × 8½.
25131-4 Pa. $3.95

PERSONAL NARRATIVE OF A PILGRIMAGE TO ALMANDINAH AND MECCAH, Richard Burton. Great travel classic by remarkably colorful personality. Burton, disguised as a Moroccan, visited sacred shrines of Islam, narrowly escaping death. 47 illustrations. 959pp. 5⅜ × 8½. 21217-3, 21218-1 Pa., Two-vol. set $17.90

PHRASE AND WORD ORIGINS, A. H. Holt. Entertaining, reliable, modern study of more than 1,200 colorful words, phrases, origins and histories. Much unexpected information. 254pp. 5⅜ × 8½. 20758-7 Pa. $4.95

THE RED THUMB MARK, R. Austin Freeman. In this first Dr. Thorndyke case, the great scientific detective draws fascinating conclusions from the nature of a single fingerprint. Exciting story, authentic science. 320pp. 5⅜ × 8½. (Available in U.S. only) 25210-8 Pa. $5.95

AN EGYPTIAN HIEROGLYPHIC DICTIONARY, E. A. Wallis Budge. Monumental work containing about 25,000 words or terms that occur in texts ranging from 3000 B.C. to 600 A.D. Each entry consists of a transliteration of the word, the word in hieroglyphs, and the meaning in English. 1,314pp. 6⅝ × 10.
23615-3, 23616-1 Pa., Two-vol. set $27.90

THE COMPLEAT STRATEGYST: Being a Primer on the Theory of Games of Strategy, J. D. Williams. Highly entertaining classic describes, with many illustrated examples, how to select best strategies in conflict situations. Prefaces. Appendices. xvi + 268pp. 5⅜ × 8½. 25101-2 Pa. $5.95

THE ROAD TO OZ, L. Frank Baum. Dorothy meets the Shaggy Man, little Button-Bright and the Rainbow's beautiful daughter in this delightful trip to the magical Land of Oz. 272pp. 5⅜ × 8. 25208-6 Pa. $4.95

POINT AND LINE TO PLANE, Wassily Kandinsky. Seminal exposition of role of point, line, other elements in non-objective painting. Essential to understanding 20th-century art. 127 illustrations. 192pp. 6½ × 9¼. 23808-3 Pa. $4.50

LADY ANNA, Anthony Trollope. Moving chronicle of Countess Lovel's bitter struggle to win for herself and daughter Anna their rightful rank and fortune—perhaps at cost of sanity itself. 384pp. 5⅜ × 8½. 24669-8 Pa. $6.95

EGYPTIAN MAGIC, E. A. Wallis Budge. Sums up all that is known about magic in Ancient Egypt: the role of magic in controlling the gods, powerful amulets that warded off evil spirits, scarabs of immortality, use of wax images, formulas and spells, the secret name, much more. 253pp. 5⅜ × 8½. 22681-6 Pa. $4.00

THE DANCE OF SIVA, Ananda Coomaraswamy. Preeminent authority unfolds the vast metaphysic of India: the revelation of her art, conception of the universe, social organization, etc. 27 reproductions of art masterpieces. 192pp. 5⅜ × 8½.
24817-8 Pa. $5.95

CHRISTMAS CUSTOMS AND TRADITIONS, Clement A. Miles. Origin, evolution, significance of religious, secular practices. Caroling, gifts, yule logs, much more. Full, scholarly yet fascinating; non-sectarian. 400pp. 5⅜ × 8½.

23354-5 Pa. $6.50

THE HUMAN FIGURE IN MOTION, Eadweard Muybridge. More than 4,500 stopped-action photos, in action series, showing undraped men, women, children jumping, lying down, throwing, sitting, wrestling, carrying, etc. 390pp. 7⅞ × 10⅝.

20204-6 Cloth. $19.95

THE MAN WHO WAS THURSDAY, Gilbert Keith Chesterton. Witty, fast-paced novel about a club of anarchists in turn-of-the-century London. Brilliant social, religious, philosophical speculations. 128pp. 5⅜ × 8½.

25121-7 Pa. $3.95

A CEZANNE SKETCHBOOK: Figures, Portraits, Landscapes and Still Lifes, Paul Cezanne. Great artist experiments with tonal effects, light, mass, other qualities in over 100 drawings. A revealing view of developing master painter, precursor of Cubism. 102 black-and-white illustrations. 144pp. 8¾ × 6⅜.

24790-2 Pa. $5.95

AN ENCYCLOPEDIA OF BATTLES: Accounts of Over 1,560 Battles from 1479 B.C. to the Present, David Eggenberger. Presents essential details of every major battle in recorded history, from the first battle of Megiddo in 1479 B.C. to Grenada in 1984. List of Battle Maps. New Appendix covering the years 1967–1984. Index. 99 illustrations. 544pp. 6½ × 9¼.

24913-1 Pa. $14.95

AN ETYMOLOGICAL DICTIONARY OF MODERN ENGLISH, Ernest Weekley. Richest, fullest work, by foremost British lexicographer. Detailed word histories. Inexhaustible. Total of 856pp. 6½ × 9¼.

21873-2, 21874-0 Pa., Two-vol. set $17.00

WEBSTER'S AMERICAN MILITARY BIOGRAPHIES, edited by Robert McHenry. Over 1,000 figures who shaped 3 centuries of American military history. Detailed biographies of Nathan Hale, Douglas MacArthur, Mary Hallaren, others. Chronologies of engagements, more. Introduction. Addenda. 1,033 entries in alphabetical order. xi + 548pp. 6½ × 9¼. (Available in U.S. only)

24758-9 Pa. $11.95

LIFE IN ANCIENT EGYPT, Adolf Erman. Detailed older account, with much not in more recent books: domestic life, religion, magic, medicine, commerce, and whatever else needed for complete picture. Many illustrations. 597pp. 5⅜ × 8½.

22632-8 Pa. $8.50

HISTORIC COSTUME IN PICTURES, Braun & Schneider. Over 1,450 costumed figures shown, covering a wide variety of peoples: kings, emperors, nobles, priests, servants, soldiers, scholars, townsfolk, peasants, merchants, courtiers, cavaliers, and more. 256pp. 8⅜ × 11¼.

23150-X Pa. $7.95

THE NOTEBOOKS OF LEONARDO DA VINCI, edited by J. P. Richter. Extracts from manuscripts reveal great genius; on painting, sculpture, anatomy, sciences, geography, etc. Both Italian and English. 186 ms. pages reproduced, plus 500 additional drawings, including studies for *Last Supper*, *Sforza* monument, etc. 860pp. 7⅞ × 10¾. (Available in U.S. only) 22572-0, 22573-9 Pa., Two-vol. set $25.90

CATALOG OF DOVER BOOKS

THE ART NOUVEAU STYLE BOOK OF ALPHONSE MUCHA: All 72 Plates from "Documents Decoratifs" in Original Color, Alphonse Mucha. Rare copyright-free design portfolio by high priest of Art Nouveau. Jewelry, wallpaper, stained glass, furniture, figure studies, plant and animal motifs, etc. Only complete one-volume edition. 80pp. 9⅜ × 12¼. 24044-4 Pa. $8.95

ANIMALS: 1,419 COPYRIGHT-FREE ILLUSTRATIONS OF MAMMALS, BIRDS, FISH, INSECTS, ETC., edited by Jim Harter. Clear wood engravings present, in extremely lifelike poses, over 1,000 species of animals. One of the most extensive pictorial sourcebooks of its kind. Captions. Index. 284pp. 9 × 12. 23766-4 Pa. $9.95

OBELISTS FLY HIGH, C. Daly King. Masterpiece of American detective fiction, long out of print, involves murder on a 1935 transcontinental flight—"a very thrilling story"—NY Times. Unabridged and unaltered republication of the edition published by William Collins Sons & Co. Ltd., London, 1935. 288pp. 5⅜ × 8½. (Available in U.S. only) 25036-9 Pa. $4.95

VICTORIAN AND EDWARDIAN FASHION: A Photographic Survey, Alison Gernsheim. First fashion history completely illustrated by contemporary photographs. Full text plus 235 photos, 1840–1914, in which many celebrities appear. 240pp. 6½ × 9¼. 24205-6 Pa. $6.00

THE ART OF THE FRENCH ILLUSTRATED BOOK, 1700–1914, Gordon N. Ray. Over 630 superb book illustrations by Fragonard, Delacroix, Daumier, Doré, Grandville, Manet, Mucha, Steinlen, Toulouse-Lautrec and many others. Preface. Introduction. 633 halftones. Indices of artists, authors & titles, binders and provenances. Appendices. Bibliography. 608pp. 8⅜ × 11¼. 25086-5 Pa. $24.95

THE WONDERFUL WIZARD OF OZ, L. Frank Baum. Facsimile in full color of America's finest children's classic. 143 illustrations by W. W. Denslow. 267pp. 5⅜ × 8½. 20691-2 Pa. $5.95

FRONTIERS OF MODERN PHYSICS: New Perspectives on Cosmology, Relativity, Black Holes and Extraterrestrial Intelligence, Tony Rothman, et al. For the intelligent layman. Subjects include: cosmological models of the universe; black holes; the neutrino; the search for extraterrestrial intelligence. Introduction. 46 black-and-white illustrations. 192pp. 5⅜ × 8½. 24587-X Pa. $6.95

THE FRIENDLY STARS, Martha Evans Martin & Donald Howard Menzel. Classic text marshalls the stars together in an engaging, non-technical survey, presenting them as sources of beauty in night sky. 23 illustrations. Foreword. 2 star charts. Index. 147pp. 5⅜ × 8½. 21099-5 Pa. $3.50

FADS AND FALLACIES IN THE NAME OF SCIENCE, Martin Gardner. Fair, witty appraisal of cranks, quacks, and quackeries of science and pseudoscience: hollow earth, Velikovsky, orgone energy, Dianetics, flying saucers, Bridey Murphy, food and medical fads, etc. Revised, expanded In the Name of Science. "A very able and even-tempered presentation."—The New Yorker. 363pp. 5⅜ × 8. 20394-8 Pa. $5.95

ANCIENT EGYPT: ITS CULTURE AND HISTORY, J. E Manchip White. From pre-dynastics through Ptolemies: society, history, political structure, religion, daily life, literature, cultural heritage. 48 plates. 217pp. 5⅜ × 8½. 22548-8 Pa. $4.95

SIR HARRY HOTSPUR OF HUMBLETHWAITE, Anthony Trollope. Incisive, unconventional psychological study of a conflict between a wealthy baronet, his idealistic daughter, and their scapegrace cousin. The 1870 novel in its first inexpensive edition in years. 250pp. 5⅜ × 8½. 24953-0 Pa. $4.95

LASERS AND HOLOGRAPHY, Winston E. Kock. Sound introduction to burgeoning field, expanded (1981) for second edition. Wave patterns, coherence, lasers, diffraction, zone plates, properties of holograms, recent advances. 84 illustrations. 160pp. 5⅝ × 8¼. (Except in United Kingdom) 24041-X Pa. $3.50

INTRODUCTION TO ARTIFICIAL INTELLIGENCE: SECOND, EN-LARGED EDITION, Philip C. Jackson, Jr. Comprehensive survey of artificial intelligence—the study of how machines (computers) can be made to act intelligently. Includes introductory and advanced material. Extensive notes updating the main text. 132 black-and-white illustrations. 512pp. 5⅜ × 8½. 24864-X Pa. $8.95

HISTORY OF INDIAN AND INDONESIAN ART, Ananda K. Coomaraswamy. Over 400 illustrations illuminate classic study of Indian art from earliest Harappa finds to early 20th century. Provides philosophical, religious and social insights. 304pp. 6⅜ × 9⅜. 25005-9 Pa. $8.95

THE GOLEM, Gustav Meyrink. Most famous supernatural novel in modern European literature, set in Ghetto of Old Prague around 1890. Compelling story of mystical experiences, strange transformations, profound terror. 13 black-and-white illustrations. 224pp. 5⅜ × 8½. (Available in U.S. only) 25025-3 Pa. $5.95

ARMADALE, Wilkie Collins. Third great mystery novel by the author of *The Woman in White* and *The Moonstone*. Original magazine version with 40 illustrations. 597pp. 5⅜ × 8½. 23429-0 Pa. $7.95

PICTORIAL ENCYCLOPEDIA OF HISTORIC ARCHITECTURAL PLANS, DETAILS AND ELEMENTS: With 1,880 Line Drawings of Arches, Domes, Doorways, Facades, Gables, Windows, etc., John Theodore Haneman. Sourcebook of inspiration for architects, designers, others. Bibliography. Captions. 141pp. 9 × 12. 24605-1 Pa. $6.95

BENCHLEY LOST AND FOUND, Robert Benchley. Finest humor from early 30's, about pet peeves, child psychologists, post office and others. Mostly unavailable elsewhere. 73 illustrations by Peter Arno and others. 183pp. 5⅜ × 8½. 22410-4 Pa. $3.95

ERTÉ GRAPHICS, Erté. Collection of striking color graphics: *Seasons, Alphabet, Numerals, Aces* and *Precious Stones*. 50 plates, including 4 on covers. 48pp. 9⅜ × 12¼. 23580-7 Pa. $6.95

THE JOURNAL OF HENRY D. THOREAU, edited by Bradford Torrey, F. H. Allen. Complete reprinting of 14 volumes, 1837–61, over two million words; the sourcebooks for *Walden*, etc. Definitive. All original sketches, plus 75 photographs. 1,804pp. 8½ × 12¼. 20312-3, 20313-1 Cloth., Two-vol. set $80.00

CASTLES: THEIR CONSTRUCTION AND HISTORY, Sidney Toy. Traces castle development from ancient roots. Nearly 200 photographs and drawings illustrate moats, keeps, baileys, many other features. Caernarvon, Dover Castles, Hadrian's Wall, Tower of London, dozens more. 256pp. 5⅜ × 8¼. 24898-4 Pa. $5.95

AMERICAN CLIPPER SHIPS: 1833–1858, Octavius T. Howe & Frederick C. Matthews. Fully-illustrated, encyclopedic review of 352 clipper ships from the period of America's greatest maritime supremacy. Introduction. 109 halftones. 5 black-and-white line illustrations. Index. Total of 928pp. 5⅜ × 8½.
25115-2, 25116-0 Pa., Two-vol. set $17.90

TOWARDS A NEW ARCHITECTURE, Le Corbusier. Pioneering manifesto by great architect, near legendary founder of "International School." Technical and aesthetic theories, views on industry, economics, relation of form to function, "mass-production spirit," much more. Profusely illustrated. Unabridged translation of 13th French edition. Introduction by Frederick Etchells. 320pp. 6⅛ × 9¼. (Available in U.S. only)
25023-7 Pa. $8.95

THE BOOK OF KELLS, edited by Blanche Cirker. Inexpensive collection of 32 full-color, full-page plates from the greatest illuminated manuscript of the Middle Ages, painstakingly reproduced from rare facsimile edition. Publisher's Note. Captions. 32pp. 9⅜ × 12¼.
24345-1 Pa. $4.50

BEST SCIENCE FICTION STORIES OF H. G. WELLS, H. G. Wells. Full novel *The Invisible Man*, plus 17 short stories: "The Crystal Egg," "Aepyornis Island," "The Strange Orchid," etc. 303pp. 5⅜ × 8½. (Available in U.S. only)
21531-8 Pa. $4.95

AMERICAN SAILING SHIPS: Their Plans and History, Charles G. Davis. Photos, construction details of schooners, frigates, clippers, other sailcraft of 18th to early 20th centuries—plus entertaining discourse on design, rigging, nautical lore, much more. 137 black-and-white illustrations. 240pp. 6⅛ × 9¼.
24658-2 Pa. $5.95

ENTERTAINING MATHEMATICAL PUZZLES, Martin Gardner. Selection of author's favorite conundrums involving arithmetic, money, speed, etc., with lively commentary. Complete solutions. 112pp. 5⅜ × 8½.
25211-6 Pa. $2.95

THE WILL TO BELIEVE, HUMAN IMMORTALITY, William James. Two books bound together. Effect of irrational on logical, and arguments for human immortality. 402pp. 5⅜ × 8½.
20291-7 Pa. $7.50

THE HAUNTED MONASTERY and THE CHINESE MAZE MURDERS, Robert Van Gulik. 2 full novels by Van Gulik continue adventures of Judge Dee and his companions. An evil Taoist monastery, seemingly supernatural events; overgrown topiary maze that hides strange crimes. Set in 7th-century China. 27 illustrations. 328pp. 5⅜ × 8½.
23502-5 Pa. $5.00

CELEBRATED CASES OF JUDGE DEE (DEE GOONG AN), translated by Robert Van Gulik. Authentic 18th-century Chinese detective novel; Dee and associates solve three interlocked cases. Led to Van Gulik's own stories with same characters. Extensive introduction. 9 illustrations. 237pp. 5⅜ × 8½.
23337-5 Pa. $4.95

Prices subject to change without notice.
Available at your book dealer or write for free catalog to Dept. GI, Dover Publications, Inc., 31 East 2nd St., Mineola, N.Y. 11501. Dover publishes more than 175 books each year on science, elementary and advanced mathematics, biology, music, art, literary history, social sciences and other areas.